Human Sexuality

Human Sexuality

David A. Schulz

University of Delaware

Prentice-Hall, Inc., *Englewood Cliffs, New Jersey* 07632

Library of Congress Cataloging in Publication Data

SCHULZ, DAVID A (date)
   Human sexuality.

   Includes index.
   1.–Sex.   I.–Title.
HQ21.S325   301.41'7   78-27720
ISBN 0-13-447557-7

Printed in the United States of America

10   9   8   7   6   5   4   3   2   1

Editorial/production supervision: Alison D. Gnerre
Design and art direction: Ben Kann
Photo research: Helena Frost
Nontechnical illustration: Mulvey Ass./Jose Reyes
Manufacturing buyer: Nancy J. Myers

Prentice-Hall International, Inc., *London*

Prentice-Hall of Australia Pty. Limited, *Sydney*

Prentice-Hall of Canada, Ltd., *Toronto*

Prentice-Hall of India Private Limited,
New Delhi

Prentice-Hall of Japan, Inc., *Tokyo*

Prentice-Hall of Southeast Asia Pte. Ltd.,
Singapore

Whitehall Books Limited, *Wellington,
New Zealand*

Chapter Opening Illustrations

Chapter 1 © 1976 Joel Gordon
Chapter 2 Charles Harbutt, © Magnum
   Photos, Inc.
Chapter 3 Lolita Ehrlich
Chapter 4 Leonardo da Vinci
Chapter 5 © Thomas Hopker, Woodfin Camp
   & Assoc.
Chapter 6 © 1974 Clark/ Rhodes; © 1976, Tree
   Communications, Inc.
Chapter 7 Joanne Leonard, Woodfin Camp &
   Associates
Chapter 8 © Thomas Hopker, Woodfin Camp
   & Associates
Chapter 9 Paul Fusco, © Magnum
Chapter 10 William Accorsi, Photograph by
   Michal Heron

Chapter 11 Michal Heron
Chapter 12 M. & E. Bernheim, Woodfin Camp
   & Associates
Chapter 13 L. Reifenstahl, Woodfin Camp &
   Associates
Chapter 14 Paul Fusco, © Magnum Photos,
   Inc.
Chapter 15 © 1977 Jim Anderson, Woodfin
   Camp & Associates
Chapter 16 Ben Oyne/ Stern/ Black Star
Chapter 17 Reprinted with permission by V.D.
   Control Division, BSS, CDC, PHS, HEW
Chapter 18 Tim Eagan, Woodfin Camp &
   Associates

This book is dedicated to all of those who, out of the fullness of their life and work, have helped me grow in my understanding of human sexuality, and especially to Helena, Lisa, and Alison Schulz; Mark and Kathryn Harris; Stanley and Helen Rodgers; Robert and Lou Ribble; Gene and Margie Ehrhardt; Betty Dodson; Barbara Martin; James Ramey; Robert Rimmer; Charles Reich; and Robert and Anna Francoeur.

Chapter Opening Quotes

Chapter 1 Havelock Ellis, *Sex and Marriage:* Eros in Contemporary Life (Westport, Conn.: Greenwood Press, 1977).

Chapter 2 Mary S. Calderone, (ed.) *Sexuality and Human Values* (New York: Association Press, 1974), p. 10.

Chapter 3 Norman O. Brown, *Love's Body* (New York: Random House, Inc., 1966), p. 245.

Chapter 4 Francis Jacob, "Evolution and Tinkering," *Science,* 196 (June 10, 1977), 1165.

Chapter 5 Kingsley Davis and Judith Blake, "Social Structure and Fertility: An Analytic Approach," *The Family: Its Structure and Functions* (New York: St. Martin's Press, Inc., 1964).

Chapter 6 Mary Jane Sherfy, *The Nature and Evolution of Female Sexuality* (New York: Random House, 1972), p. 144.

Chapter 7 Gloria Steinem.

Chapter 8 Boston Women's Health Book Collective, *Our Bodies, Ourselves,* 2nd ed. (New York: Simon and Schuster, 1976), pp. 48–49. Copyright © 1971, 1973, 1976 by the Boston Women's Health Book Collective, Inc. Reprinted by permission of Simon & Schuster, a Division of Gulf & Western Corporation.

Chapter 9 Thomas Carlyle, quoted in Barnhardt J. Hurwood (ed.) *The Whole Sex Book* (New York: Pinnacle Books, 1975), p. 73.

Chapter 10 Sigmund Freud, "Letter to an American Mother," in Ernest Jones, *The Life and Work of Sigmund Freud* Vol. 3, © 1957 by Ernest Jones, Basic Books, Inc., Publishers, p. 195.

Chapter 11 Peter Wyden and Barbara Wyden, *Inside the Sex Clinic* (New York: New American Library, 1971), p. 7.

Chapter 12 Alan Watts, *Nature, Man and Woman* (New York: Pantheon Books, a Division of Random House, Inc., 1958), pp. 11–12.

Chapter 13 Bronislaw Malinowski, *The Sexual Life of Savages* (New York: Harcourt, Brace Jovanovich, 1929), p. 438.

Chapter 14 M. deSade.

Chapter 15 *My Secret Life,* Anonymous. Quoted in Steven Marcus, *The Other Victorians: A Study of Sexuality and Pornography in Mid-Nineteenth Century England,* © 1964, 1965, 1966 by Steven Marcus, Basic Books, Inc., Publishers, New York, p. 122.

Chapter 16 Robert Veit Sherwin, "The Law and Sexual Relationships," in Eleanor S. Morrison and Vera Borosage (eds.) *Human Sexuality: Contemporary Perspectives* (Palo Alto, CA: National Press Books, 1973), p. 283.

Chapter 17 Philippe Ricord, quoted in Louis Lasagna, *The VD Epidemic* (Philadelphia: Temple University Press, 1975), p. 18.

Chapter 18 Wardell Pomeroy, SIECUS NEWSLETTER.

Contents

ix

SECTION FIVE
VALUES, *471*

18

Sex and Love, 474

Cultural Relativity and Sexual Ethics   The Experience of Love

Preface

This book takes a generalist's approach to sex; it tries to make everyday sense out of the findings of specialists. The central question in the writing of each chapter has been, What does the reader need to know in order to more intelligently fashion a satisfying sexual life style? So, for example, the chapter on anatomy and sexual response is not concerned with providing a detailed account of the anatomy and physiology of sex, but rather, it provides the basic information that a man or woman might need in order to feel comfortable with their own bodies and to be more sensitive to their sexual response and the response of their partners. Likewise, the chapter on contraceptives and birth control could have been a detailed study of birth control technology, but I felt it was more important to present the practical issues of contraceptive use to the reader. The major findings of sex researchers have been covered in this text, but only in relation to issues of everyday life.

One of the most important contributions that sex researchers have made to our understanding of human sexuality is to have greatly increased our range of choice in sexual matters. The work of many specialists has broadened our knowledge about sex and given us choices that just a few years ago would have been thought impossible or imprudent. They have opened up little known areas of sexual behavior, explored the complex process by which we develop a sexual identity or become sexually aroused, perfected techniques of contraception, and improved our ability to eliminate infertility.

Today, we can reasonably choose to have sex without having children. It is now possible to choose to have sex without being married, or feeling the need to say "I love you." A much wider range of sexual behaviors is now acceptable. Some people have chosen to change their gender and follow through with the years of surgical and hormonal treatment that is necessary to make this change. The changes in our understanding of and control over sex that have taken place since my youth seem to me to be revolutionary.

One valuable aspect of a generalist approach is that it can provide a context within which these and other issues can be explored. Sex is not only of interest to scientists, it is also of great interest to philosophers, theologians, writers, and humanists. It is a very important element in the life of every human being. Daily experience can provide us with much insight about sex if we are aware of our experiences and are willing to reflect on them. These nonscientific elements are very important in our understanding of sex and should not be ignored, as they often are when specialists speak to specialists about sex.

Of all the things in life that are important to us, sex can certainly be one of the most enjoyable to learn about. It can be a source of intense pleasure and a great form of recreation, as well as a means of expressing love for ourselves and others, and a way of discovering more about who we are in this world. I firmly believe that only the reader can assume responsibility for his or her sex life, and that only the reader can say how important sex is in any of its forms. I also believe that society should give as much freedom as possible to individuals to develop a personally satisfying sexual life style. The sexual behavior of consenting adults in private should not be of concern to the law. Hopefully, this book will assist the responsible reader in intelligently and sensitively fashioning a fulfilling sexual life style.

I wish to acknowledge the contribution of many fine people to the generation of the manuscript and the completion of this text. The Institute for Sex Research at Indiana University permitted me to make use of its facilities and bibliographies during the early stages of the work. In November and December, 1977, a group of us met in St. Louis and San Francisco, reviewing the manuscript in detail from the point of view of those who might use such a text in their classes. André Cedras, Leah Clarke, Lee K. Frank, Carole Kirkpatrick, Judy F. Rosenblith, Barry Singer, J. Stanley White, Emily Davidson, and David A. Edwards provided many helpful suggestions for the revision of the manuscript. Many others have read the manuscript and provided valuable criticism. I especially want to thank Betty Dodson, Mark Harris, and Ron Mazur for their insights and suggestions. Helena Schulz helped in the library research and provided many occasions for reflection and insight on the value of sex in everyday life. Gloria Wilkins organized the efforts of several typists in the completion of the revision of the manuscript under the press of a tight production schedule. Ed Stanford and Alison Gnerre of Prentice-Hall have been most helpful and stimulating during the long months of manuscript preparation. Sandy Bloomfield has been an exceptionally talented editor, improving the style and organization of the manuscript, with careful consideration for the investment of the author in his own mistakes.

The result of the efforts of these people and many others has been a most readable, interesting, and enjoyable text. I hope that you, the reader, will agree with my assessment and I invite your evaluation. I alone accept the responsibilities of its shortcomings.

David A. Schulz

Human Sexuality

Introduction

1

I regard sex as the central problem of life. . . . Sex
lies at the root of life, and we can never learn to
reverence life until we know how to understand sex. So,
at least, it seems to me.

Havelock Ellis

One of the reasons we were able to put a man in space before we understood the orgasm is the fact that people are uncomfortable talking about sex. Even today, when sex is used to sell cars and shaving cream, some people insist that sex should be a private matter. According to these people, any public discussion of sex, including this book, is a disgrace and a sure sign that our society is falling apart. However, other people have come to see such discussions as healthy. These people see our society as being in need of relief from old-fashioned laws and outmoded notions about marriage and the family.

In addition to feelings about privacy and morality, our understanding of sex has been colored by its economic functions. In the past, property and social status were the primary basis for marriage. Virginity and chastity for women were therefore highly valued, as they still are in some cultures. Sex was a club that only men could join. Women were seen as a necessary part of the equipment needed to play the game.

This attitude has served as the basis for sex discrimination in employment and education, as women struggled to become economically and politically independent. Women were seen as particularly qualified for routine, undemanding work. When they were able to secure a "man's job," they were commonly paid much less for the same work. In addition, they were expected to be fully responsible for child rearing and all household chores. They were not supposed to be ambitious or to be very much interested in sex. As researchers began to prove that this was far from the case, many people saw sex as disruptive to society and wished to return to an earlier day when women knew their place, which was in the kitchen, barefoot, and pregnant.

In spite of these economic and social considerations, most of us are apt to equate sex with love. But which should come first? Do you have sex with someone because you love them, or do you love them because you have had sex with them? Does it matter? Of course, it does, but only you can decide what is right for you. One of the reasons our society is so confused about sex is that we have tried to make general rules about it. But sex is not, and should not be, the same experience for all of us. The material presented in this book is meant to provide you with the information you need to make intelligent decisions about what sex means to you.

There are many different ways of looking at sex. As a first step, let us consider some of the more common points of view and some of their implications. One of the most important implications is how these different points of view have affected scientific research on human sexuality.

Selected Perspectives on Sex

A number of different ways of looking at sex come readily to mind. Sex is very often thought of as the way to make a baby. It is also a way of making love, having fun, or of offending or hurting people. Sex is sometimes illegal. For some people in our society it is a way of earning a living or a means of worship. Therefore, we can talk about sex as baby making, lovemaking, as obscene, casual, sacred, or criminal. The clinical or medical approach to human sexuality is yet another way of looking at sex.

Most of us have probably thought about sex in most of these ways at one time or another. You may find that one of these points of view will sum up your attitude toward sexuality. It seems unlikely that all of these points of view will have equal importance at all stages of a person's life, but all should be carefully examined and considered. The way we choose to look at sex profoundly affects what we believe about it and often affects how we behave as well.

SEX AS BABY MAKING

There may be a few adults in our society who do not know where babies come from, but most of us take it for granted that the biological purpose of human sexuality is reproduction. Christian churches have widely declared that reproduction is the divine purpose of sexual intercourse. Only recently have some denominations come to recognize a second equally important purpose of sexuality: as play or pleasuring between sexual partners.

Baby making is a very visible, sometimes dramatic aspect of human sexual experience, and the only one we can be certain we share with other animals. How many children have gotten important lessons about sexuality while watching the birth of kittens or puppies? Seeing sex as primarily reproductive is also closely associated with the struggle for survival in agricultural societies. In such societies, large families are valued because they provide many hands with which to secure the necessities of life. Life in such societies is hard, and many children must be conceived in order to insure that some will survive.

The reproductive view of human sexuality is much more closely tied to the fields and forests than it is to cement and time clocks, and city children are economic liabilities rather than assets. In cities, the land is too valuable to use for farming, and children cannot legally work as laborers in factories and offices. They must therefore be supported through high school and perhaps on into college. Increasingly, both parents must work to support their children, and as a result, the size of the urban, middle-class family is decreasing.

Thinking about sexuality as primarily for the purpose of making babies has a number of implications. First, in order for a baby to be made, one of the partners in the sex act must be a man, while the other is a woman. In addition, the man must insert his penis into the woman's vagina. Thus, in this perspective, heterosexual intercourse is the only proper way to perform the sex act. Other forms of sexual expression are either ignored or considered perverted. Second, if sex is primarily for reproduction, then what possible use could it be to young children or to older men and women? In the past it was common to believe that there was something wrong with a young child or a person over sixty-five who expressed sexual desires or behaved in a sexually inviting way. Third, if sex is primarily for the purpose of making babies, then marriage is the only appropriate kind of relationship in which to have sex. It is irresponsible to have children outside of marriage, where their standing in society is uncertain and they are not as likely to receive good care. This way of looking at sex and marriage was more persuasive before there were adequate contraceptives, but the notion still persists.

Finally, looking at sex as primarily a means of making babies makes it possible to down play the importance of feminine sexual arousal. A man can impregnate a woman without getting her very excited—much less fully aroused or satisfied. He, on the other hand,

Figure 1–1
Ignoring the sensuality of motherhood is as much a mistake as seeing women simply as potential mothers rather than as sexual beings in their own right. (Wayne Miller, Magnum Photos, Inc.)

Figure 1–2
(© Leif Skoogfors, Woodfin Camp &
Associates)

7

INTRODUCTION

must achieve an erection in order to penetrate and impregnate, which makes his arousal seem right and proper, while a woman's can seem unnecessary or even disadvantageous.

Is it coincidence that the most popular style of intercourse in the west (the man on top, the woman beneath him in the "missionary position") is the position in which women are most likely to conceive a child? In this perspective, the woman is seen as an actual or potential mother, rather than as a sexual being in her own right. In our tradition, mothers are rarely thought of as sensuous and sexy. Sensuous and sexy women are more often found outside of marriage—at least so we have tended to think in the past.

Clearly, it is not necessary to hold all of these other convictions if you happen to think that sex is primarily for the purpose of reproduction, but it is very easy to do so. In fact, a large number of people have done so, and many do so today.

SEX AS LOVEMAKING

In our society, marriages have more recently come to be based on emotional rather than economic criteria. A young man and a young woman fall in love, get married, and have a baby. That's nature's way, or God's way, or simply the thing to do. Thus, sex as love making is tied by tradition to sex as baby making.

Sex should be an expression of love in this view, though it is readily recognized that it often expresses something else. Because of the emphasis on love, it has been necessary for young men in the past to express their physical passion in words like, "I love you." Of course, this is not always a deception, but sometimes it is. It is difficult to determine which is which in the heat of the moment. "Love" has therefore become a much used, much abused word in our language.

Some respect should be given to the emotions experienced in sexual play, but true love must be time-tested. Love is caring, and you can't care for someone unless you have lived with them "in sickness and in health." Such love is admirably suited for marriage and baby making, while "love at first sight" is viewed with suspicion. Because you haven't tested the relationship, it is foolish (as well as immoral) to go to bed too quickly. The institution of marriage was designed to provide a safe and secure contract to be entered into with due consideration after a period of engagement during which the love that is professed can be tested. Within marriage, sex can then proceed to intercourse, and in due time a baby will further bind the couple together in loving care. The pleasure of love thus derives more from the caring for others than from the sensations of lovemaking. Accordingly, many couples, even those who love each other deeply, have remained ignorant of the art of lovemaking.

Sex as love is captured for some people in the expression "making love." This expression suggests that sexual behaviors like kissing or intercourse can actually produce the feeling of love in the sexual partners. This emotion is seen as a legitimate experience of love. It need not be part of a long-term relationship. Is a flower any the less lovely because it wilts quickly? Giving oneself to a comparative stranger can be a loving, caring experience. Sensitive, experienced persons can risk self-disclosure in such fleeting encounters and can grow from the experience.

In the context of a long-term relationship, such a view of sex-as-love places greater importance on sexual satisfaction than on the obligations to care for others emphasized by the traditional view of marriage. Marriage must be a personally satisfying relationship in order to justify its continuance in this way of thinking.

OBSCENE SEX

When we think of obscene sexuality, we most often think of pornography. Pornography is a creature of the city streets. It arose in the seventeenth century with the emergence of a literate, urban middle class and flourished in the nineteenth century under Victorian censorship. It is alive and well today.

A common element in much of what is classified as obscene is that these sexual behaviors could not possibly produce a baby. Non-reproductive sexual behavior such as masturbation, intercourse with animals, oral-genital, and anal-genital sex between persons of the same or opposite sex are commonly considered "perverted" or obscene in part as a result of the long-established tradition that sex is essentially baby making. Any other kind of sex is unnatural—or obscene.

In spite of this, it is often very difficult to get widespread agreement on what makes a particular attitude or behavior obscene. The Supreme Court, for the moment, has given up on the attempt to legally define "obscenity" and decreed that it is up to local community sentiments to define it. Thus, obscenity is seen as a relative thing, not an absolute. What is obscene in rural Alabama may not be obscene in San Francisco.

Cities throughout the world are noted for their streetwalkers, peep shows, massage parlors, adult book stores, and "X" rated movies. Most pornography caters to people's fantasies rather than providing any actual physical release. These enterprises make money because

Figure 1–3
Human sexuality is to an unknown extent a creation of the human mind. (© George W. Gardner)

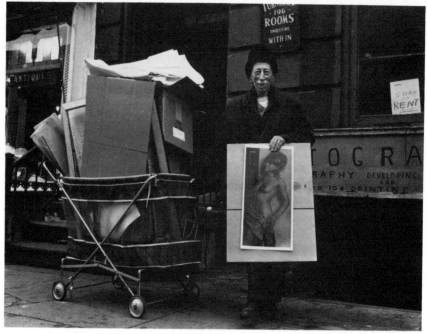

Figure 1–4
Matters of taste affect the notion of what is obscene. (© Jill Freedman, distributed by Magnum)

they parade what respectable society prohibits. "Prudery makes pornography."[1]

As the Supreme Court has realized, matters of taste affect the notion of what is obscene. For some people, *any* depiction of sexual attitudes or behavior is obscene. A common basis for this notion is the idea that sexual arousal is basically bad (it was so declared by reputable authorities of church and state in the past) and that anything that might produce arousal is, therefore, bad—regardless of its artistic merit.

Others consider depictions of human sexuality obscene for reasons of modesty—proper people do not allow such private matters to be made public. Closely related to this view are those who feel that obscenity is anything that is common or vulgar. For such people, a black and white photo of a naked woman is "obscene," while a well-done painting of the same subject is "art." We find the same sort of schizophrenia in language: "Cock" and "cunt" are obscene, while "penis" and "vagina" are not.

Obscenity can be humorous. Men have traditionally used sexual

[1]Wayland Young, *Eros Denied: Sex in Western Society* (New York: Grove Press, 1964), p. 65.

humor as a means of breaking down barriers between themselves as well as to demean women. For example, this well-known limerick exalts masculine sexuality at the expense of women.

There was a young man from Costairs
Who was screwing his girl on the stairs.
When the banister broke,
He doubled his stroke
And finished her off in mid-air.

In some instances, limericks and sexual jokes can lighten the discussion of human sexuality and permit more intimate self-disclosures to take place in sensitivity groups or other settings in which people are attempting to better understand their own sexuality.

There will always be aspects of sexuality that will be considered obscene by some people. Further, the specific aspects of what is commonly considered obscene change over time as respectable society refines its standards. New steps in research on human sexuality are sometimes considered obscene. For example, Masters and Johnson's

Figure 1–5
Graffiti—the men's room wall moved outdoors—is not a modern phenomenon. The Romans
doodled Latin versions of "Kilroy was here" and "Clodia for fun! Call Pompeii 4–3169"
long before the birth of Christ. (© Joel Gordon)

use of an artificial penis and their photographing of couples having intercourse are still considered obscene by some.

Sometimes obscene sex can serve social purposes in unexpected ways. For example, when medical schools first began to consider broadening their students' understanding of human sexuality beyond anatomy and physiology in the 1960s, there were no adequate teaching aids to depict lovemaking. Therefore, common, street-variety "blue movies" were used as teaching devices until more "tasteful and scientific" films could be produced.[2]

"Obscene" is a label readily tossed about these days. Whatever else it means, it is an indication that something, in someone's opinion, should be excluded from public conversation or awareness. Like Prohibition, much of what is thus excluded can be turned into profitable enterprises.

CASUAL SEX

Orgasm junkies, who contend that what really is important about sex is the pleasure it can generate, tend to take a very casual attitude toward sexual relationships. These emphasize the recreational aspects of sexuality, not the relational: play not people.

Casual sex either denounces commitment or says that the commitment is to the moment and not the future. In "swinging," for example, married couples enjoy sex with other single or married couples. Swinging does not involve any plans for the future with any of these people. They are not to "get involved." Some swingers insist that their preference for casual sexual encounters does not indicate a lack of commitment to their marriage but rather shows a commitment to be open to the present moment of sexual enjoyment with no contracts for the future.

The personal ads of many local newspapers express the desires many people have to meet others for "fun and games."

Young attractive couple seek same. Discreet and broadminded. Apt. and mountain hideaway. Will answer all, with photo, phone and frank letters. Singles OK. Believe in really enjoying the best things of life.

High flying couple: he's a pilot, she's a stewardess, would like to meet other interesting and stimulating couples. Please send complete resume and photo. All replies answered.

Swingers now have national magazines and clubs to further their getting together. Estimates of the numbers of people who participate in such adventures range from 1–8 million.

Swinging is not the only context for casual sexuality. Historically,

[2]Robert T. Francouer, "Sex Films," *Society/Transactions* (July/August 1977), p. 34.

the mistress, prostitute, or the "affair" also provided such contexts. Casual sex is a basic ingredient of the "Playboy philosophy." It is also part of the college scene for a very small percentage of students who are commonly called promiscuous. The dominant code on campus, however, is still probably abstinence from intercourse. The traditional double standard, which allows a young man to have intercourse with almost anyone he might choose, while a young woman must do so *only* within the context of a real or potentially long-term relationship, is still a popular code with most men. Petting within an affectionate relationship is the most common behavior among campus women. The norm that it is all right for both young men and young women to be sexually permissive within affectionate relationships is increasingly important—but not yet dominant—on campus.[3]

Casual sex can involve groups of people, while the other ways of looking at sex stress one-to-one relationships. Group sex, commonly called an "orgy," follows easily from the conviction that what is really important about sex is the pleasure it can provide. If one partner can provide pleasure, how much more pleasure can several provide? But not everyone can be pleased at an orgy. Some contend that successful orgies, in which everyone goes away smiling, have to be properly staged.[4] In order to enjoy orgies, the average person must learn new skills, and the tolerance of the group must be high. The presence of more experienced players no doubt helps to keep things moving smoothly.

Playful sex is a way of heightening the pleasure of sex within a long-term or at least committed relationship. Sex need not always be solemn and serious. Laughing in bed is a good thing. "Sex as work" would be pretty much of a turn-off, don't you think? But, in spite of its attractiveness in principle, playful sex seems to be much more of a future vision than a present reality. Alex Comfort's "cookbook approach" in the *Joy of Sex* and *More Joy* probably describes sexual encounters that few Americans experience as regular diet.[5] Shere Hite's study of American women contends that the "sexual revolution" for many women merely means the obligation to say "yes" rather than "no."[6] The frantic focus on intercourse and the notion that every sexual act should pave the way to orgasm that many associate with the

[3]Ira Reiss, *Family Systems in America*, 2nd ed. (Hinesdale, Ill.: Dryden Press, 1976), p. 153.

[4]Russel Ford, "My Wife and I Enjoy Orgies," in Robert Rimmer, ed., *Adventures in Loving* (New York: Signet, 1973), pp. 279–92. Different perspectives are provided in Tom Hatfield, *The Sandstone Experience* (New York: New American Library, 1976), and Alex Comfort, *More Joy* (New York: Crown, 1973).

[5]Alex Comfort, *The Joy of Sex* (New York: Crown, 1972); and Alex Comfort, *More Joy* (New York: Crown, 1973).

[6]Shere Hite, *The Hite Report* (New York: MacMillan, 1976), p. 311.

Figure 1–6
As all children know, play is healthy as well as fun. (© 1976 Joel Gordon)

sexual revolution can downgrade much that is warm and intimate in human lovemaking. It becomes more difficult to sexually play under such pressured conditions. Certainly Comfort's bold assertion that the biological function of human sexuality is play rather than reproduction is opposed to most of our heritage. Nevertheless, playful, joyful sexuality has much to offer.

SACRED SEXUALITY

Our Western heritage is not characterized by an acceptance of sexuality as sacred. Reproduction is sometimes regarded as sacred, but sexual arousal and pleasure have most often been condemned. Certain Eastern religions, however, take sexual arousal directly into the religious experience. Some forms of tantric yoga, for example, utilize intercourse as a means of worship and a form of meditation.[7] Much of yoga, however, is as puritanical as our Western religions have generally been. The body is something to be risen above, not enjoyed for what it is.

In the West, sexuality and sacredness have sometimes been brought together in folk religions. For example, a poem by Keats called "The

[7]See for example, Herbert V. Guenther, *The Tantric View of Life* (Boulder: Shambhala Publications, 1976); and Swami Janakananda Soraswati, *Yoga, Tantra and Meditation* (New York: Ballantine Books, 1975).

Eve of St. Agnes," is based on the legend that a virgin could receive a vision of her future husband by performing certain rituals on the night before St. Agnes's Day, St. Agnes being the patron saint of virgins.

Young virgins might have visions of delight,
And soft adorings from their loves receive
Upon the honeyed middle of the night,
If ceremonies due they did aright;
As supperless to bed they must retire,
And couch supine their beauties, lily white;
Nor look behind, nor sideways, but require
Of Heaven with upward eyes for all that they desire.

Baroque art of the late Rennaissance comes as close as any art in our heritage to enshrining sexuality in the churches, but this was a brief period in a generally antisensual trend. Various Christian sects (the Carpocratians, the Gnostics, the Blood Brothers, the seventeenth century Ranters, for example) have considered intercourse to be a means of worship. However, these all have been denounced as heretical by Orthodox Christians. In general, Western Christianity has seen sensuality—and particularly sexual passion—as sinful. Salvation in another world is achievable primarily by withdrawing from the sins of this world—particularly the "sins of the flesh."

CRIMINAL SEX

Sex is rarely seen as a matter of breaking the law. Nevertheless, the fact remains that much of human sexuality is considered illegal. Laws change more slowly than public opinion, and our laws on sexual behavior, though not strictly enforced, still reflect an outdated view of proper sexual conduct. The criminal codes of the fifty states vary enormously in what is considered a crime. But legal opinion throughout the country condemns those sex offenses that involve force or violence (rape), child molestation, and most offenses that could be considered a public nuisance. There is a trend toward general agreement that the law should not interfere with the sexual behavior of consenting adults in private, although at present most criminal codes do have such statutes. Finally, there is considerable controversy over how the law should respond to commercial sex such as prostitution and pornography. The difficulties of legally defining pornography and in regulating prostitution have led many law enforcement officials to support efforts to decriminalize both.

The problem with most current statutes regulating human sexuality is that they try to impose one particular sexual morality on a public that holds many other views. The law attempts to regulate the private behavior of consenting adults not because such behavior has been shown to be harmful or dangerous, but because in the past it has offended the lawmakers' sense of morality. Laws that describe sodomy and oral-genital sex as crimes against nature are examples of such thinking. Such laws are not taken off the books primarily because it is still difficult for public officials, regardless of their private beliefs and practices, to come out in favor of such behaviors as oral or anal intercourse. Large numbers of people who elect these officials still retain the old view of sex as baby making.

The way criminal codes are presently written sometimes makes it difficult to tell what a specific sex crime is, since the legal definitions do not ordinarily follow common usage or the classifications used by social scientists and physicians. For example, it is against the law to be a "sexual moron." What does that mean exactly? Does it refer to a clumsy lover, a person who has sex with retarded people, or someone who lacks carnal knowledge altogether? Actually, this category is on the books simply because some lawmakers awhile back believed that some people who had very low I.Q.s were apt to habitually commit sexual crimes. There is little evidence to support this reasoning, yet the crime does exist, and some unfortunates have undoubtedly been imprisoned as a result. The harm to society as well as to the individuals directly involved by such outmoded laws is incalculable.

In 1966 the American Law Institute issued its draft of a model penal code, which was designed to provide useful guidelines in reforming the various state criminal codes.[8] In general, the model penal code argues that the law should not interfere in the private sexual behavior of consenting adults. The creators of the code insist that religious or educational institutions, rather than the law, are the proper sources of influence in these intimate matters. The model penal code is not law. It is simply a guideline by which current laws can be reformed if the states so choose.

CLINICAL SEX

Clinicians, doctors, therapists, and other scientists strive to achieve a cool, detached view of human sexuality. Such an attitude is often found in marriage manuals and in textbooks on human sexuality. Much of the sex education provided by the public schools is intentionally clinical in tone. Typically, textbook illustrations strive to present a clinical approach to the body and its functions in order to avoid being condemned as obscene. The once-common illustrations of the sex organs being manipulated by forceps and probes are examples of this clinical orientation. The use of Latin words and the heavy use of professional jargon are other ways people try to distance them-

[8]American Law Institute, "Model Penal Code: Proposed Official Draft," Philadelphia, 1966.

selves from the subject. Objectivity is highly valued, and experts are expected to use a strange language, as though everyday language was lacking in precision and descriptive power. Masters and Johnson's ground-breaking study, *Human Sexual Response,* is a good example of the clinical approach to human sexuality.[9] Many people who read it hoping to be aroused by it were disappointed by its dry, objective, and scientific language.

Research and theory have given the modern clinician a distinctive view of human sexuality. In sex therapy this view focuses on the non-reproductive aspects of sex, especially pleasuring. Thus, the clinician sees sex as a good thing to be enjoyed in its own right. Clinicians see sexual variety, where others are more apt to see perversion or obscenity. Homosexuality, for example, is viewed as a fairly common form of normal sexual expression. Masturbation is now considered a major means of sexual pleasuring, not as a form of abuse or a sign of immaturity. Heterosexual intercourse has to share its place in the array of pleasurable sexual experiences with oral and anal intercourse, mutual masturbation, body rubbing, and massage. These are now seen as pleasurable in their own right whether or not they lead to intercourse. Scientists have shown that women have at least as much capacity for enjoying sex as men, and perhaps much more. Finally, we have learned that older people are sexual beings too. Old age gives sexual activities a different style and expression, but does not eliminate them entirely. The work of clinicians and scientists has led to a view of normal sexuality that contrasts rather dramatically with the "sex as baby making" tradition. This modern, clinical way of looking at human sexuality is supported by the work of such widely recognized authorities as Sigmund Freud, Havelock Ellis, Alfred Kinsey, and the team of William Masters and Virginia Johnson.[10]

The Limitations of Sex Research

People's attitudes toward sex are formed by their religion, the media, and their friends as well as by the work of scientists. However, the increasing emphasis on science and technology in this country has in-

[9]William Masters and Virginia Johnson, *Human Sexual Response* (Boston: Little, Brown, 1966).

[10]See, for example, Sigmund Freud, *The Standard Edition of the Complete Psychological Works of Sigmund Freud,* James Strachey, ed. and trans. (London: Hogarth Press, 1953), especially "Three Essays on the Theory of Sexuality," vol. 7, and "New Introductory Lectures on Psychoanalysis," vol. 22.; Havelock Ellis, *Studies in the Psychology of Sex* (New York: Random House, 1942); Alfred C. Kinsey et al., *Sexual Behavior in the Human Male* (Philadelphia: W. B. Saunders, 1953); William H. Masters and Virginia E. Johnson, *Human Sexual Response* (Boston, 1966); and William H. Masters and Virginia E. Johnson, *The Pleasure Bond* (Boston: Little, Brown, 1975).

creased the respect given to scientists, whether they deserve it or not. Because of this and because of our tendency to uncritically accept expert advice, it is appropriate to point out some of the limitations of this type of research.

SURVEY STUDIES

The first major study that had an impact on attitudes toward sex in America was done by Alfred Kinsey and his co-workers. Kinsey's findings were astonishing to the American public during the 1950s. Nearly half of all married women in his sample had experienced intercourse before marriage.[11] Women who experienced orgasm before marriage (by whatever means, including masturbation) were more likely to have satisfactory sexual relationships in marriage.[12] About a quarter of the women in his sample and about half of the men had experienced extramarital intercourse by the age of forty.[13] About half of his men and about a fifth of his women had had some homosexual experience by the age of 45.[14] These findings pulled the rug out from under conventional morality.

How did Kinsey find this out? He simply went and asked. Conducting interviews either in person as Kinsey did or by using printed questions is called a *survey study* and is a widely used technique in all the social sciences. It is an efficient way for social scientists to find out about real people and real life.

Now suppose you were Kinsey and you wanted to know what the American male's sex life was like. Obviously, it would cost too much in time and money for you to find every American male. Social scientists would solve this problem by selecting a *representative sample* of American men for their survey. To be truly representative, this sample would include men from all social classes, income brackets, geographical areas, educational levels, and so on, in correct proportion to those categories in the total population. Only then could the results of the survey be validly generalized to all American males, even though some men weren't questioned.

Thus, in a survey, who you ask is as important as what you ask. Kinsey's work, though highly influential, has been strongly criticized because he ignored that basic rule of good research. He did not select a sample that was truly representative of the total male population. For example, he studied only white males, and even these were not properly sampled. His male sample was too midwestern, too prison-

[11]Alfred C. Kinsey et al., *Sexual Behavior in the Human Female* (New York: Pocket Books, 1967).

[12]Ibid., p. 390.

[13]Ibid., p. 437.

[14]Ibid., p. 487.

oriented, too homosexual, too young, and too Jewish in comparison to census statistics for adult white American males as a whole. His sample of women was also not representative because there were too many upper middle-class, college-educated women to be representative of the entire population of white American women. Not even his enormous sample size (over 18,000 men and women) could correct for these distortions. This is not to say that Kinsey was wrong. He recorded his data accurately, but he would have been more correct to title his study *Sexual Behavior In Some Human Males (or Females)*. Knowing how his sample differs from a truly representative sample of white Americans and having smaller studies of different groups has helped us to make better use of his findings.

An even greater limitation of the Kinsey sample is the fact that all the people he interviewed were volunteers. A number of his critics have concluded that people who are willing to talk about sex, particularly in the 1950s, are apt to be more exhibitionistic about their sexual behavior than the average person. This might mean that Kinsey's portraits of sexuality are "oversexed"—his percentages of persons who engage in various kinds of sexual behaviors too high.

CLINICAL STUDIES

Clinical studies such as those conducted by Masters and Johnson are even more unlikely to be based on representative samples. For example, most of the people studied by Masters and Johnson came to them for help with sexual problems. This makes those people unusual because average Americans are not apt to admit they have sex, let alone sexual problems. In addition, these people could afford to pay the $2,500 and take two weeks away from home in order to undergo treatment in St. Louis, something only a small percentage of the total population could do. It is probable that social situations affect physiological responses and hormone levels—and perhaps even tissue structure. Do upper-class persons significantly differ from lower-class persons in terms of their physiology? We know that human anatomy and physiology is not the same in everybody, even in its more elemental components. But how does it vary by social characteristics? Masters and Johnson, themselves, appreciate the importance of social factors in alluding to their effect on the masculine fear of not getting an erection, and the feminine failure to perceive orgasm as pleasurable in our society. At present we know very little about the way in which the social environment affects the physiological aspects of human sexuality, but we know that it does. Because it does, there is greater need for a representative sample in such clinical studies. To date there are none.

Based on a strict view about the importance of sampling procedures, the best that can be said for *all* previous work in the study of human sexuality is that it is suggestive. Studies done with white college students can tell us much about the sexual attitudes and behaviors of white college students. But we cannot generalize the results to other segments of our population, such as black construction workers, or white secretaries. The fact that many people will not talk about their sexuality in any detail, and still more refuse to be observed, means that it will probably never be possible to obtain a truly representative sample. The understanding of sex researchers is enhanced by even limited studies and some reasonable assumptions about those who are not studied can be made on the basis of common sense. But, until those persons are studied, any statements about them must be considered merely as assumptions.

GENERAL METHODOLOGICAL ISSUES

Most current research on sex depends on what people say about their attitudes and behaviors. Often people are asked to recollect some aspect of their past sexual experience. If Freud is correct in his assumption that because sexual experiences arouse such strong emotions they are often repressed or distorted, then most survey data is very superficial if not downright misleading. Kinsey did not agree with Freud and, therefore, did not attempt to "go behind" what his respondents told him about their sexuality. We do not know how this affected his results.

Another major methodological limitation to sex research is that the

Figure 1–7
Kinsey took what people said about their sexuality at face value. Freud on the other hand, would probably want to have a long, private talk with the erector of this structure. (© George W. Gardner)

researcher affects what is studied simply by being present and by displaying the results. The effect of a researcher's presence can be partially controlled in some cases. Masters and Johnson, for example, feel that, after a period of getting adjusted to being observed their clients responded normally. Almost any instrument or mechanical device can, in time, fade out of a person's awareness and cease to have an effect. But care must be taken to insure that this occurs.

The effect of past findings on current behavior is more difficult to cope with. It is probably true that Kinsey's studies established a crude baseline for data on American sexual behavior, as well as set standards for some people to try to meet or beat. Kinsey's finding that the average married couple had intercourse about two or three times a week during the first year of their marriage has probably encouraged some people to be better than average.[15] Indeed, Morton Hunt found that the frequency of marital intercourse has increased slightly since Kinsey.[16] How much of this increase was because of Kinsey's studies? It is undoubtedly true that Kinsey made sex a household word in America in a way that was unknown in our past. What effect has this had on our sexual behavior? To some degree, scientific findings can influence the future by making us more aware of the present. If we assume, as some do, that Kinsey presented an oversexed view of sex in the United States, then it may be fair to say that Kinsey went a long way toward creating the sexual revolution that other researchers have been studying.

SCIENCE AND TECHNOLOGY

A final problem with scientific research on sexuality applies most directly to the utilization of scientific findings. How important are these findings in relationship to other aspects of human sexuality that are highly valued in our tradition? For example, Kinsey did not think very much about human loving. He was trained as a zoologist and treated human sexuality as another form of mammalian sexuality. One doesn't consider love in an analysis of the mating habits of lions and lemurs. But what if our mammalian inheritance is not something we should strive to follow but to overcome?

Scientists who study human sexuality can observe all the viewpoints we have discussed and develop many others. They might even be able to determine how prevalent each point of view is in the population at a given time. What they cannot tell us is how important any one of these should be in relationship to the others. This is fundamentally a philosophical question, but it is not without very practical con-

---

[15]Ibid., p. 348.

[16]Morton Hunt, *Sexual Behavior in the 1970s* (New York: Dell, 1974) pp. 190–91.

sequences. Each one of us must determine (with more or less aware-ness), what importance we will give to our sexuality in our lives. Is it the central question of our lives? Should it not be mentioned at all because any mention of it gives it more importance in the scheme of things than it deserves? Or do we come down somewhere in between? Is sexuality really basically baby making, or lovemaking, or fun and games, or some form of obscenity? If it is not any one of these things all of the time, when is it best to see it as one or another?

These very general questions have some more specific correlaries that science can help us to answer by providing useful information

Figure 1–8
Modern observers have come to understand that "mothering" is a human quality, not a masculine or feminine one. (Magnum)

Figure 1–9
People are becoming increasingly aware of the range of choices available in regard to their sexuality. (© Joel Gordon)

about sexual behavior (though it should not be the only perspective allowed). How important should sensual experience—including intercourse—be in your life? Should you devote a great deal of time and energy toward cultivating techniques of lovemaking and in "making out" with as many people as you can? Or should you place more importance on the character of your relationships with others? If you believe that your sexual life is not totally determined by a sexual drive or instinct, if you do not believe that anatomy is destiny and that masculinity and femininity are equally aspects of character as well as physiology, if you believe that individuals should be free to define their sexual life styles with minimum interference from external authorities, then these kinds of value issues confront you directly.

Perhaps the most important effect of scientific research thus far has been to increase our awareness of our range of choices in regard to our sexuality. Our traditional ways of understanding sex as baby making or lovemaking are only partial perspectives at best in the modern world. But having pointed out the range of possibilities, sex research does not in itself determine the range of desirable choices, nor should it dictate to us what the nature of our sexuality should be. Understanding what can help or harm ourselves and others is only partially a scientific undertaking. Philosophy, religion, the arts, and everyday experience all have their contributions to make. It is up to us to take the tools they offer us to build a better understanding of human sexuality.

24

Section One

Personal Sexuality

Although it is fairly evident that all aspects of human sexuality are intimately interrelated, it is useful to discuss the subject in terms of personal, interpersonal, and societal levels. A fourth section will carry the discussion of societal aspects to specific social issues.

This section on personal sexuality focuses upon the individual. The anatomical and physiological characteristics of the human organism that define its gender were once thought to determine all other aspects of its sexuality and to decisively influence the rest of the personality as well. Being born with a vagina or a penis not only established the gender of an individual, but prescribed social status and established basic modes of sexual and social interaction as well. Freud declared as much when he ventured, "anatomy is destiny." Sexuality, furthermore, has been commonly thought of as an expression of an innate biological instinct or drive. It was thought to be more powerful in men than women. Given the fact that most men were born with at least the potential for a powerful sex drive, the concern in the past has been not to explain sexual arousal, but rather to discover how it could be creatively used and socially controlled.

More recent research, however, points to the importance of social and cultural influences in shaping an individual's sexuality. Very recent work in gender clinics demonstrates how the biological factors can be overcome in many ways. Some individuals can change their genders. Anatomy is no longer destiny. Indeed, some researchers, such as William Simon and John Gagnon, strongly question the evidence for the existence of a powerful sex drive at all. They suggest that sexual arousal can adequately be accounted for in terms of social cues or "scripts." Most researchers, however, retain the notion of sexuality as a biological drive that is modified in various ways by social and cultural factors.

This section begins with chapter 2, "Fantasy and Sexual Arousal." The mind is a sexual organ whose complex role in sexual arousal is just beginning to be understood. In the mind internalized social cues and cultural symbols fashion a personally distinctive sexuality that is often expressed in fantasy. Apparently not everyone fantasizes. Of those who do fantasize, the fantasy may assist or detract from their sexual arousal. Some can readily control their sexual fantasies, others are controlled by them. Nevertheless, in fantasy the human organism and its socio-cultural environment interact. The individual is clearly a part of a social world. Human sexuality is more than an innate drive or instinct. Already some therapists are stressing the importance of fantasy in healthy sexual arousal. It seems reasonable to assume that greater importance will be attached to the role of fantasy in sexual arousal in the future.

Chapter 3 considers human anatomy and sexual response. Here, too, socio-cultural elements are present, although the focus is upon the human organism. Culture prescribes what is considered beautiful or attractive. Ideal models of beautiful bodies sometimes inhibit our own lovemaking because we fear that our own bodies will not favorably compare. But the human body comes in an enormous variety of shapes and sizes. Cultural prohibitions prevent us from seeing more than a very small portion of this variation. In the past, the notion that men and women were widely different in their sexual responses prevailed. They were different in part because their genitals were so different. Today the similarities in their genitals and sexual responses are being stressed. In part, this change in emphasis reflects the struggle of contemporary women to realize full equality.

Chapter 4 examines the process of conception, followed by chapter 5, which concentrates on the more common means to prevent it. Our understanding of sexual reproduction has greatly increased as a result of modern effort to control it. In a world concerned about pollution, population explosion, energy and food shortages, contraceptive techniques are extremely important. Furthermore, baby making can become much less associated with love-making in the future if we so desire it. The biological revolution suggests the possibility of developing the human embryo in a number of environments: For example, in suspension inside of a mechanical womb, in the uterus of an animal such as a cow, in the intestine of a man. These possibilities have far-reaching social implications. As a result, human reproduction in the future will be far less of a simple biological process than it has been in the past and probably far less identified with sexuality as well.

Finally, chapter 6 discusses pregnancy and childbirth. Giving birth to a child and caring for it were once thought to be essential to a woman's maturity and fulfillment. Today, however, more and more couples are remaining voluntarily childless or are adopting rather than conceiving their child. Others are planning to have the number of children they want, when they want to have them. Planned parenthood can increase the pleasure of having children by helping to insure that every child is wanted. Something of the wonder of pregnancy and childbirth is being recaptured in the effort to bring childbirth out of the hospital and into the home. It is possible to do so today with less risk than would be incurred in some hospitals. So also, the father is being brought back in his supportive role through natural childbirth and home deliveries. But such procedures are not standard. They must be sought after and prepared for if they are to be enjoyed.

Fantasy and Sexual Arousal

2

... we should be seeking to make it possible
for human beings to realize their erotic
potential in full and responsible conscience.
The energy now required to maintain the wasteful
blockage by fear and guilt of the erotic
could then be freed for creative purposes
in the life of humankind.

Mary S. Calderone

One way that human sexuality can be distinguished from the sexuality of animals is the extent to which it is influenced by fantasy. This influence is not felt to the same degree by all of us. Some people never seem to fantasize about sex. A few people seem to be obsessed by their fantasies. But the largest number of human beings seem to experience sexual fantasies as a normal part of their sexual lives. Not

Figure 2–1
Both males and females fantasize, and in a fantasy, as in any other daydream, everything is possible. (© Arthur Tress, distributed by Magnum Photos, Inc.)

Figure 2–2
(© Arthur Tress, distributed by Magnum Photos, Inc.)

everyone can use fantasy to stimulate arousal or enrich their sexual lives to the same extent. Currently, however, many modern clinicians are encouraging people who want a richer sexual life to learn to play with their fantasies.

Although most people fantasize about sex, they do not readily share their fantasies with others. Sexual fantasies are very personal. Sometimes fantasies suggest things about ourselves that we are ashamed or afraid of. They may make us feel foolish or simply very different from everyone else. "What kind of a person am I to get turned on by such thoughts?" is not an uncommon thought. But people are coming to realize the positive role that fantasy can play in our sexual lives. Understanding the role of fantasy in sexual behavior has been difficult partly because most fantasies were obtained from troubled people who were seeking clinical help. Modern anthologies, however, collect fantasies from everyday people. Such collections help us see how common many of our fantasies are. In addition, many men have been surprised to discover that perfectly normal women also enjoy sexual fantasies.

A sexual fantasy can be thought of as a daydream that is sexually exciting. Sexual fantasies can serve a number of purposes. For example, they can excite and arouse. For some people, fantasies can provide a trigger for orgasmic release. For others, fantasies simply enrich the experience of lovemaking. Fantasies can also inhibit sexual response by bringing to mind threatening experiences of the past and become a means of escape from the tasks of the present. On balance, fantasies should be seen as belonging to the fullness of human sexuality.

Fantasy is only one factor that may stimulate sexual arousal. The first portion of this chapter, therefore, provides a brief overview of the mechanisms of human sexual arousal and suggests the role that fantasy can play in it. Then it describes some of the more common types of sexual fantasies and suggests some of the roles they can play in an individual's sex life. The controversy over the meaning of the so-called rape fantasy that is commonly reported by women indicates that care must be taken in interpreting fantasy. It is sometimes difficult to determine whose fantasy is being dealt with, the teller's or the listener's. The chapter closes with the observation that some of us are afraid of the erotic, whether it is expressed in our own fantasy or in images that others present.

Human Sexual Arousal

The human mind is a sexual organ. We do not commonly think of the mind in this way because of our traditional association between sex and reproduction. The feeling that sex was a bodily function, and that the mind was "above all that," has led to a preoccupation with the genitals and to a neglect of the imagination. But the more sexuality is considered as a source of pleasure, the more important the mind becomes. For example, in his novel, *Sleeping Beauty,* Yasunari Kawabata writes of an elderly man named Eguchi who visits a house of pleasure designed to serve men in their old age. In this establishment, Eguchi is permitted to sleep six nights beside six different girls. Each young beauty is drugged so that she cannot be awakened, and Eguchi is instructed not to touch them. Yet each night he experiences great pleasure as each naked virgin releases thoughts that take in all his life and especially his attraction to the young loveliness of women.[1] Such passive appreciation of the sexual experience is rare in the West where satisfaction depends on action. Prostitutes are often used to act out their client's fantasies—perhaps he desires to be whipped, to dress in their clothes, or to have them urinate on him before he climaxes.

Eguchi's capacity to experience sexual pleasure in his thoughts without acting on them is undoubtedly culturally conditioned, as is the inclination of the prostitute's client to act out his fantasy. Both Eastern and Western men are aroused by the nakedness of women.

[1]Donald Keene, "Speaking of Books — Yasunari Kawabata," *New York Times Book Review,* December 8, 1965.

Both, in addition, are affected by their personal experience with sex that makes specific events sexually stimulating for them. Human sexual arousal is thus stimulated by a complex set of both external and internal factors.

A GENERAL READINESS

Internally, human beings can be considered to be in a general state of readiness for sexual experience throughout most of their lives.[2] It is possible that this general condition of readiness is maintained by the amount of sex hormones in the body and by the net balance of the incoming and outgoing signals from the "sexual control center" in the hypothalamus in the brain.

Human sexual arousal and response are controlled by the nervous system and by the hormones in the bloodstream. These interact in a

[2]This interpretation of the internal process of sexual arousal is based in part on the discussion given in Harold D. Swanson, *Human Reproduction: Biology and Social Change* (New York: Oxford University Press, 1974), pp. 82–102.

Figure 2–3
Men are aroused by the nakedness of women, but their personal experience with sex determines which specific activities will be sexually satisfying to them. (Photos by Erich Lessing/Magnum)

very complex way. A clear example of the interaction can be seen in the relationship between the hypothalamus and the pituitary gland. The pituitary gland in both sexes secretes androgens (male sex hormones) and estrogens (female sex hormones), as well as other hormones. The hypothalamus is a part of the brain that controls hunger, thirst, and emotional responses. It also secretes its own hormones that stimulate the pituitary gland to activity. Because of this dual role of the hypothalamus, it is possible for an emotional crisis to alter the hormonal rhythms of the body. For example, the menstrual cycle may be lengthened or shortened as a result of stress.

The basic level of activity of the sexual control center in the hypothalamus determines how interested one is in sexual activity. In lower animals, the hormonal patterns of the estrus cycle permit the female to be sexually receptive only at a particular time in her cycle—when she is "in heat" and thus most likely to become pregnant. Her readiness triggers the male's interest. In humans, on the other hand, our hypothalamus allows us to be interested in sex all the time. This general state of readiness makes the specific stimuli involved more of a factor in determining whether or not arousal will take place.

SPECIFIC STIMULI

Different people are turned on by different things. Watching an attractive person, seeing suggestive pictures or films, hearing a sexy joke, finding oneself in a stimulating setting such as Eguchi's, or simply fantasizing about sex can turn us on. Arousal continues to increase in intensity when the body is touched, especially on the mouth and genitals.

The internal mechanism of arousal is partially presented in terms of the role of the nervous system. The sexual control center in the hypothalamus basically acts as an amplifier, as it relays the signals it receives. It can amplify both arousing and inhibiting signals.

In general, the sexual control center receives two types of impulses. First, information about the environment is received by the eyes, ears, nose, genitals, and other sensitive parts of the body and is relayed to the sexual control center. The cerebral cortex also receives this sensory information, but refines it in a number of ways before it is sent to the sexual control center. This refinement is, in essence, an interpretation based on the person's learning experience and particular cultural context. The sexual control center has no standards. Without the mediation of the cortex, which determines whether the object of our desire is attractive (by personal and cultural standards) or repugnant, we might find ourselves leaping on everyone in sight. In addition to selecting the object of our arousal, the cerebral cortex also helps define which sounds, odors, tastes, sights, and so on will be perceived as stimulating or arousing.

Our sensory receptors may sometimes act directly on the sexual control center without interference from the cortex. For example, a male who has not had sex for a long time may experience a buildup of secretions in his prostate gland. These sensations of fullness could then be transmitted as stimulating messages to the sexual control center. In the female, the retention of water in the cells of the genitals before menstruation may similarly stimulate the sexual control center.

The cerebral cortex can also inhibit the sexual control center in a number of ways. For example, if the mind is preoccupied with nonsexual tasks such as paying bills or is caught up in feelings of fear and anxiety, the cortex sends fewer impulses to the sexual control center, and inhibits the signals coming from it. Thus, a person encountered in the context of a threatening situation—say, when one has to speak in front of an audience—will be perceived as less attractive than if one met that person at an informal party. Memories of unpleasant experiences may also be associated with a particular sexual opportunity, making it difficult to express sexuality in one's parents' house, for example. Our involvement in sexual activity may be interrupted by distracting sounds, such as those made by children. In such cases, the sexual control center receives mixed messages and, as a result, arousal may be inhibited.

As we have seen, the cerebral cortex can affect the signals sent out by the sexual control center. This process also works in reverse. When your thoughts and perceptions are peppered with sexual themes, it is the result of signals from the sexual control center to the cerebral cortex. Thus, it is an overactive hypothalamus, not spring, that lightly turns a young man's thoughts to love.

As a result of such signals, the cerebral cortex becomes more sensitive to signals from the genitals and other parts of the body such as the earlobes, nipples, and face. It becomes somewhat less sensitive to pain as a result of stimulation from the sexual control center. The respiratory and circulatory centers (also in the hypothalamus) increase the rate of breathing and blood circulation. In the genitals, the signals from the control centers expand the arteries carrying blood to the sexual organs and slightly decrease the size of the veins carrying it away. The result is an accumulation of blood in these tissues, creating what is called the orgasmic platform in the female and assisting an erection in the male.

In the male the process of erection is initiated by the stimulation of an erection center located in the lower sacral portion of the spine. This erection center can be stimulated by impulses from the brain (either the sexual control center or the cerebral cortex or both), or from impulses from the penis. Thus, if a man thinks sexually exciting thoughts, or the sexual control center picks up sexually exciting impulses from other parts of the body, the brain stimulates the erection center and an erection occurs. Similarly, if the penis is manipulated, the sensations can directly initiate an erection. Young male babies commonly erect to touch before there is any reason to believe that they are thinking sexy thoughts.

In the female the clitoris does not have the cavernous tissue analogous to the corpus spongiosum of the penis. The clitoris may become swollen and muscles may elevate it, but it rarely extends beyond the body. Indeed, the clitoris commonly retracts beneath its hood in the advanced stages of excitation. In Masters and Johnson's study an increase in the length of the stimulated clitoris occurred in only 10 percent of the cases. An increase in diameter occurred in every case, but most increases in size of the clitoris were hardly noticeable without special equipment.

Sexual arousal in both males and females involves the same nerves, but the erect penis provides a much more visible indicator in the male than the clitoris can provide for the female. The most noticeable indicator of arousal in the female is the lubrication of the vagina caused by the sweating of the vaginal walls. It is clear that fantasy does not always initiate arousal in either sex. It is probable, however, that human beings can learn how to use fantasy more effectively as a stimulant. Much of our cultural heritage has tried to control these dangerous images in the mind and most people are not altogether comfortable with their fantasies as a result. Some relearning must take place if this very human side of sexuality is to be better utilized.

Fantasy And Sexual Arousal

Fantasies, like dreams, primarily involve visual events. But sounds, odors, tastes, and textures can also appear in sexually arousing fantasies. Remembering the smell of a certain person can arouse as effectively as a complex scenario involving conversations and other fantasized activities. But, in general, the simpler a fantasy is, the less likely it is to be remembered. It may be that everyone makes use of sexual fantasies in arousal, but, because the fantasies are not particularly elaborate, people aren't aware of them. Because of this, longer, more detailed fantasies are most apt to be reported and studied.

The scientific study of fantasy is a tricky business. Researchers cannot deal with another person's fantasies directly. They must accept what people tell them about their fantasies. We all know that a story is apt to change when it is retold. Some people may leave out certain details of their fantasies, while others build a baroque skyscraper out of a pup tent. And some people may simply refuse to talk at all.

Researchers have not let the difficulty of the task interfere with satisfying their curiosity. In the process, they have been able to tell us a few things about this very private and interesting process.

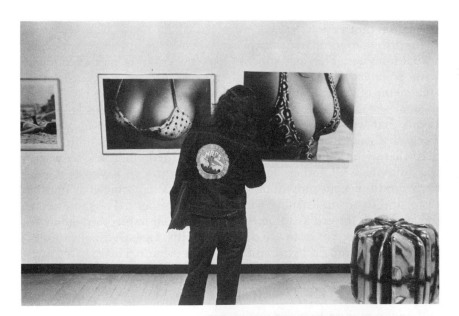

Figure 2–4
Some fantasies are simple and commonplace, while others require a lot of imagination. Because the simpler ones are apt to be forgotten, researchers have had trouble developing an accurate picture of the use of fantasy in our sexual lives. (© Charles Gatewood; Erich Lessing/Magnum)

People fantasize before, during, and after arousal. Some research suggests that men are more likely to fantasize as a means of becoming aroused, while women are more likely to fantasize after becoming aroused.[3] In some cases, women have reported using fantasy to trigger orgasm.[4] Often fantasies are simply more elaborate versions of the sexual pleasure actually being experienced. Sexual fantasies may simply provide a sense of warmth or pleasure without inducing erection or vaginal lubrication.

According to some researchers, sexual fantasies indicate our deepest sexual longings. They are not simple recollections of past experiences with possible allowances for elaboration, nor are they necessarily statements of concrete experiences desired in the future.

Some sexual fantasies are arousing because they are associated with events that were sexually stimulating in the past.[5] Sexuality was not freely discussed in the past, particularly around young children. Sex was where you found it. Some children learned about sex by watching animals, while others hid and peeped through keyholes. Under such conditions, an individual can easily develop somewhat unusual tastes and habits in learning how to achieve orgasm. The fantasies associated with these may reinforce these unusual habits throughout an individual's life. For example, Havelock Ellis, an early English sex researcher, was aroused by watching women urinate. He was able to reconstruct the events that led to his association of arousal with urinating women. As a child he occasionally stood guard as his mother urinated while they were on outings in the park (public restrooms are still uncommon in England). Why such events produce strong sexual tastes in one person and not in another is not well understood. Most of us at some time have found ourselves aroused by some odd thing or another, such as underwear or hairbrushes. But some people can only be aroused or achieve orgasm by means of a particular object. Such people are called fetishists. The object that causes sexual arousal, such as urine or a shoe, is called a fetish.

Most often, however, researchers have found sexual fantasies to be surprisingly ordinary. The sexual images that are most arousing for most people are those that could very likely occur within their actual

[3]Peter Daley, *The Fantasy Game: How Male and Female Sexual Fantasies Affect Our Lives* (New York: Stein and Day, 1975), p. 71.

[4]Daniel Goleman and Shirida Bush, "The Liberation of Sexual Fantasy," *Psychology Today* (October 1977), p. 51; Marc H. Hollender, "Women's Coital Fantasies," *Medical Aspects of Human Sexuality* (February 1970), p. 63.

[5]E. Barbara Hariton, "The Sexual Fantasies of Women," *Psychology Today* (March 1973), p. 41, reprinted from *Psychology Today* magazine, copyright © 1973 Ziff-Davis Publishing Company; Philip R. Sullivan, "Masturbation Fantasies as Indicators of Deepest Sexual Longings," *Medical Aspects of Human Sexuality* (January 1976), p. 155.

experiences. For example, Julia Heiman has found that the scene that most aroused her sample of college men and women depicted a couple on a secluded beach on a beautiful sunny day. The young woman initiates the lovemaking. They touch, kiss, begin to pet, and finally retire to a beach bungalow and make love.[6]

For most people, there is no single sexual fantasy that will guarantee sexual arousal, though many have their favorite themes that will increase the likelihood of their being aroused or enhance the pleasure of their arousal. In some studies, erection of the penis and lubrication of the vagina have been voluntarily enhanced through the use of such images. For other people, however, fantasizing was too much effort. Their attempts to enhance arousal through the use of visual images produced a reduction rather than an increase in arousal.[7]

Some of the strongest evidence that mental images affect sexual arousal comes from studies of people whose spinal cords have been damaged. One such person, Steven, had been impotent with his wife for ten years, but was potent with other women. Then, he became paralyzed below the waist after an accident that fractured his spine. Although the neural pathways from his brain to his penis were blocked, Steven could become erect when stimulated near his genitals. He was then able to have intercourse with his wife because the blockage of neural impulses prevented those images that had formerly inhibited him from affecting his arousal.[8]

[6]Goleman and Bush, "The Liberation of Sexual Fantasy," p. 51.

[7]Donald E. Hensen and H. B. Rubin, "Voluntary Control of Eroticism," *Journal of Applied Behavior Analysis,* 4 (Spring 1971), 37–44.

[8]Daley, *The Fantasy Game,* p. 77.

Figure 2–5
For a long time, clinicians saw fantasy
as a sign of neurosis or sexual
maladjustment. (© Arthur Tress,
distributed by Magnum Photos, Inc.)

THE STATUS AND FUNCTION OF FANTASY
IN CLINICAL OPINION

Fantasies are clearly voluntary creations, consciously and purposely fabricated. Freud felt that fantasies represented wishes or unfulfilled needs and declared, "happy people never make fantasies, only unsatisfied ones do."[9] Wilhelm Reich, an ex-disciple of Freud's, believed that sexual fantasies were tactics people used to resist full orgasmic surrender.[10] Both Freud and Reich felt that fantasies were signs of neurosis or sexual maladjustment.

Contemporary therapists take the same attitude in working with their women patients. Their clinical reports describe sexual fantasies or daydreams as tortuous efforts to satisfy other needs through sex, expressions of penis fears, as devices employed by women to put some psychoanalytical distance between themselves and their partners, and as mechanisms to deny responsibility for performing sex acts that otherwise would lead to intolerable guilt.[11]

A typical psychiatric interpretation is provided by Hollender, who concludes that

to an appreciable extent, the use of fantasies converts sexual intercourse into masturbation (or perhaps mutual masturbation), and an interpersonal relationship into an intrapersonal one.[12]

More recently, fantasies have been given somewhat higher status by clinicians, but they are still valued mainly because they are seen to reflect sexual pathology. For example, Sullivan is willing to concede that fantasies during masturbation are indicators of the person's deepest sexual longings. But he goes on to say that "certain masturbatory fantasies deviate so far from the norm (at least in our culture) that they strongly suggest psychopathology in themselves."[13] Clinicians are trained to deal with problems, and this orientation may prevent them from giving equal attention to the positive elements of fantasy.

This is now being remedied. Hariton, for example, found that how well women liked their husbands was unrelated to their fantasizing.[14]

[9]Hariton, "The Sexual Fantasies of Women," p. 40.

[10]Wilheim Reich, *The Function of the Orgasm* (New York: Pocket Books, 1975) p. 96. First English translation appeared in 1942.

[11]Hariton, "Sexual Fantasies of Women," p. 40.

[12]Hollender, "Women's Coital Fantasies," p. 68–70.

[13]Sullivan, "Masturbation Fantasies," p. 159.

[14]Hariton, "Sexual Fantasies of Women," p. 42.

Women who liked their husbands and women who didn't were equally likely to have sexual fantasies. Such fantasies did not necessarily reflect marital dissatisfaction. For example,

> *Sue considers herself happily married. She enjoys sexual intercourse with her husband and usually reaches orgasm. However, just as she approaches the peak she imagines that she's tied to a table while several men caress her, touch her genitals, and have intercourse with her. It is a fleeting image; as she passes into orgasm, it disappears.*[15]

When and what one fantasizes appear to be less of a problem than how rigid or flexible one's fantasy life is. There are some people who cannot achieve orgasm without visualizing a particular fantasy. There are people who get carried away into their fantasy so that a relatively few images dominate their imaginative world. These people are similar to fetishists even though they do not act out their fantasy as a fetishist does. Such rigidity is always unhealthy. It is also somewhat sad, as is any extreme self-limitation of thought, feeling, or experience.

More and more clinicians believe that people should be encouraged to enjoy and to explore their sexual fantasies. One team of therapists concluded that fantasy can have several positive effects. First, it can enhance your feelings of arousal and generally make you feel sexier. This helps you focus your attention on sex, and thus limits distractions that can interfere with arousal and enjoyment. Also, by means of fantasy you can take responsibility for turning yourself on, rather than relying on your partner to do it for you.[16]

If you want to make use of fantasy in such positive ways you must be able to control your fantasies sufficiently so that you are not frightened by what you dream up, or have the courage to face the fright if you can't control your daydreams. For most people, this will not be a problem. But for those whose fantasies derive from past frightening experiences, or whose fantasies are rigidly fixed upon a single theme, there may be some difficulty. In order to use fantasies as a means of enriching your sexual life, it is necessary to be able to understand and respect the boundary between the real world and fantasyland. Apparently fantasies are most effective when they are not lived out. Fantasists who do not live out their fantasies do not feel guilty about entertaining such thoughts in their minds. This is not to say that there are no fantasies that may safely be acted out in everyday life. But knowing that they are all right for their own sake may make you feel less uneasy about having them.

[15]Hariton, "Sexual Fantasies of Women," p. 42.

[16]Julia Heiman, Leslie LoPiccolo, and Joseph LoPiccolo, *Becoming Orgasmic: A Sexual Growth Program for Women* (Englewood Cliffs, N.J.: Prentice-Hall, 1974), p. 154.

Fantasy In Today's World

Almost all American men and women consciously fantasize about sexual behavior. Sometimes this accompanies sexual intercourse or masturbation, but often it is idle daydreaming with no other behavioral component save probable arousal. The fact that some people don't have sexual fantasies while masturbating or engaging in sexual play and yet manage to achieve adequate arousal suggests that fantasy is not absolutely necessary for this purpose. Fantasy seems to be a part of the richness of human sexuality, not a part of its essential characteristics.

OCCURRENCE

Kinsey found that 84 percent of the males in his sample were sometimes aroused by thinking about making love with women. Sixty-nine percent of the women in his sample were able to be aroused by thoughts of men. However, 31 percent of the women insisted that they had never been aroused by simply thinking about sex.[17] Kinsey used these findings to help account for sexual incompatibilities in heterosexual relationships. The male, commonly aroused through fantasy, found it difficult to understand why his partner was not aroused by suggestive pictures or by his own magnificent endowment when displayed before her. A higher percentage of males (89 percent) used fantasies as one source of stimulation during masturbation, 72 percent having done so more or less always. A lower percentage of women reported having masturbated (62 percent versus 92 percent), and, of these, only 64 percent reported the use of fantasy as a stimulant.[18] Hunt, however, concluded from his set of data that Kinsey's findings were strongly culturally conditioned and not determined by physiological differences, as Kinsey believed. In Hunt's opinion, "women today are far more likely to be aroused by erotic materials and fantasies, and to utilize fantasies while masturbating, than was true only a generation ago."[19]

The extent to which social and cultural factors influence sexual fantasy in men and women is unknown, but it seems as though reported rates of such activity are increasing for both sexes. This suggests that modern attitudes toward human sexuality are having a liberating effect on sexual fantasy as well as behavior.

[17]Alfred C. Kinsey et al., *Sexual Behavior in the Human Female* (New York: Pocket Books, 1967), p. 665.

[18]Ibid., p. 667.

[19]Morton Hunt, *Sexual Behavior in the 1970s* (New York: Dell Publishing Company, 1974), p. 92.

TYPES OF FANTASY

What is fantasized? Hunt provides us with a breakdown of the most common types of masturbation fantasies he encountered. One of the most common fantasies was having intercourse with a stranger. Forty-seven percent of the males and 21 percent of the females said that they had had such fantasies.[20] Barbara Hariton found that the most commonly mentioned sexual fantasy in her sample of women was, "thoughts of an imaginary lover."

Dotty was typical of the group of women who had varied erotic fantasies during intercourse. At times she imagined herself overpowered on a beach or carried away to the desert. The passivity expressed in these fantasies did not reflect her actual role in the sex act, however, since she often was aggressive with her husband. The imaginary men in her daydreams started out as someone else, but after undressing they resembled her husband (whom Dotty claimed was beautifully built). Sometimes she imagined two or more men making love to her, each touching a different part of her body. She found this kind of fantasy especially arousing and soothing. In some fantasies she pretended to be a $100.00 a day call girl. In others a

[20]Ibid., p. 92.

Figure 2–6
Sex with more than one person is a common fantasy among both men and women. (Erich Lessing/Magnum)

fabulous courtesan like Salome. Her fantasy partners were dominant men, intellectuals like William F. Buckley, or physically forceful movie stars like Steve McQueen.[21]

Movie stars and fictional heros and heroines are often selected to embody these imaginary lovers.

Sex with more than one person of the opposite sex is another common fantasy. Hunt found that 33 percent of his male subjects and 18 percent of his female subjects had such fantasies while masturbating.[22] In the National Sex Forum's (NSF) study of 329 people who attended its programs, 92 percent of the men and 65 percent of the women had thought of such activity.[23] It was also a common feature of the fantasy life of Hariton's subjects.[24] Here is a typical example of a woman's fantasy about sex with more than one partner:

> *Two men are undressing me. One slowly unbuttons my blouse, while the other unzips my skirt and lowers it to the ground. They caress my body as they work, one above the waist and one below. The one man removes my brassiere, while the other takes down my waist-slip and pants. Then they join forces to undo my suspenders (garterbelt) and, when I am naked, they lift me onto a big bed and lie, one on either side of me. I give myself up completely to them. My pleasure is doubled, for every part of my body gets twice the amount of attention it would normally receive. First one, then the other climbs between my legs and makes love to me.*[25]

A male fantasizes:

> *I am in a luxurious brothel where the girls are lined up for my inspection. I sit in a big chair before them and beckon them, one by one, to come to me. In turn, each girl stands in front of me and lifts her skirts. Underneath they are naked and I gaze at each one before making a selection. It is a very difficult choice but finally I settle on one girl and we go into a bedroom. I throw up her skirt and take her quickly, then send her off with instructions to send another girl to me. In this way, I manage to work through them all, one by one, until I am finally satisfied.*[26]

[21]Hariton, "Sexual Fantasies of Women," p. 43.

[22]Hunt, *Sexual Behavior in the 1970s,* p. 92.

[23]Glide Foundation, "Effects of Erotic Stimuli Used in National Sex Forum Training Courses in Human Sexuality," in *The Report of the Commission on Obscenity and Pornography,* 5 (Washington, U.S. G.P.O., 1970), 365. Because the people in the Glide Foundation sample were participating in programs about erotica, they represent a highly self-selected sample. They are more likely to be erotophiles.

[24]Hariton, "Sexual Fantasies of Women," p. 43.

[25]Ricardo Barros, *Sexual Fantasy* (London: Luxor Press, 1970).

[26]Ibid.

Another common element of sexual fantasy is forcing someone else to have sex. Thirteen percent of the males in Hunt's study and 3 percent of the females had such fantasies, as did 52 percent of the males and 22 percent of the females in the NSF study.[27] This male agressiveness is in keeping with sex stereotypes. Following are examples of the type of fantasy:

> *She is an Oriental queen, all powerful. She is surrounded by huge male slaves, almost naked. She selects one for a sexual partner and commands him to serve her. He does this in the way she prefers, she on her back and he above. She likes the feeling of being crushed by his weight. He is very potent and with a huge penis performs to her complete satisfaction. She lets herself go entirely in an orgiastic way. . . . But after it is over, because he has committed lese-majeste, she commands that he be decapitated, which is done. He does not protest but recognizes that this is inevitable, proper and suitable. She then commands another slave to do the same.[28]*

> *I get an enormous kick out of imagining that a young innocent girl is forced to fellate me. It is even better if I imagine that two women, sort of wardresses, are holding her. They twist her arms behind her back and lift her skirt to show her to me. Then one of them takes out my erect organ and forces the girl to please me with her mouth. I can imagine the look of fear and disgust on her face, but she has to do it. There is no pleasure in it for her, and that really excites me.[29]*

Being forced to have sex oneself was somewhat more common in Hunt's study. Nineteen percent of the men and 10 percent of the women so fantasized.[30] In the NSF Study, 58 percent of the men and 75 percent of the women did likewise.[31] According to one man,

> *I like to pretend that I am with a very tough, dominant woman, preferably dressed in leather. She forces me to kneel to her and to perform all sorts of indignities like kissing her shoes and her vagina. I am dressed as a little boy, school cap, blazer, shorts, but I am really a grown man. When she tells me to take off my shorts, she is surprised by the size of my penis and puts me over her knee to spank my bottom for being so excited. I love to imagine this and it makes me very excited.[32]*

[27]Hunt, *Sexual Behavior in the 1970s*, p. 93.

[28]Abraham Maslow et al., "Some Parallels Between Sexual and Dominance Behavior of Infra Human Primates and the Fantasies of Patients in Psychotherapy," *Journal of Nervous and Mental Diseases*, 131 (September 1960), 203.

[29]Barros, *Sexual Fantasy*.

[30]Hunt, *Sexual Behavior in the 1970s*, p. 92.

[31]Glide Foundation, "Effects of Erotic Stimuli," p. 365.

[32]Barros, *Sexual Fantasy*.

Seven percent of the males in Hunt's sample and 11 percent of the females admitted that they had fantasies about having sex with people of their own gender.[33] In the NSF study, 77 percent of the men and 78 percent of the women had thoughts of such activity.[34] Homosexual acts often take place in the safer context of heterosexual activity.

I've got this naked young girl on the bed with her legs thrown back. I'm kneeling between her legs and squeezing her breasts and generally having a great time. She's loving every minute of it, riding under me and pushing her belly up against me. But there is a good looking bloke there as well, standing by the side of the bed, stripping down and watching us. I don't mind. I'm getting mine and I feel a bit cocky that he's not enjoying what I'm enjoying. When he's naked, I can see that he's dying for it. He can't leave his erection alone and I know he's envying me. So I decide to give him a little treat. He sort of kneels down by us to watch more closely and it excites the hell out of him. At the last minute, I withdraw from the girl and shove it into his mouth.[35]

Schimel notes that homosexual fantasies occur in sexually mature males and are usually not of any consequence, although this can

[33]Hunt, *Sexual Behavior in the 1970s,* p. 93.

[34]Glide Foundation, "Effects of Erotic Stimuli," p. 368.

[35]Barros, *Sexual Fantasy.*

Figure 2–7
Some people do try to act out their fantasies, and many are disappointed with the reality. Most people simply value their fantasies for their own sake. (© Arthur Tress, distributed by Magnum Photos, Inc.)

cause great consternation to the fantasist.[36] Hunt developed a catchall category to cover most of what was left of the fantasies not covered by these themes. He called it "Doing Sexual Things You Would Never Do In Reality." Nineteen percent of the males and 38 percent of the females claimed to have such fantasies. One could conclude from this that women are kinkier than men. But it is more likely that there are simply fewer things that men feel uncomfortable about actually doing.

One of the firm conclusions drawn from the evaluation of reactions to erotic material by the Glide Foundation was that exposure to such material would not increase the likelihood of performing the particular behavior.[37] Friday contends that the few people who attempt to act out their fantasies are usually disappointed in the results.[38]

Living Out a Fantasy

Just as fantasies may or may not reflect actual events in a person's past, they may or may not be lived out in the future. Sometimes the fantasized opportunity presents itself (finding oneself alone with a delivery man or a friend of the same sex who becomes sexually interested) and the fantasist follows through. Most reports suggest, however, that the real life situation is not as exciting as the fantasy. But some people report being quite satisfied with the real life reenactment. Most people seem to feel that they will never act out their fantasies. This need not be because they realize that they do not really want what they are fantasizing (for example, being brutally beaten while making love) or that the behavior would be too shocking in real life. It may simply be a recognition that a fantasy is a fragile thing. Even sharing it with someone else can ruin its power to excite and arouse. The fantasy is simply valuable for its own sake.

SOME ACTING OUT BY MEN

One primary role of fantasy is to make us aware of the possibilities in life. These possibilities can give pleasure simply as mental statements or fantasies. They can also be lived out. Sometimes the prostitute is called upon to fulfill a male's fantasy. Indeed this has been the historic role of the brothel. A typical example is provided by Georgina

[36]John L. Schimel, "Homosexual Fantasies in Heterosexual Males," *Medical Aspects of Human Sexuality* (February 1972), pp. 138–51.

[37]Glide Foundation, "Effects of Erotic Stimuli," p. 365.

[38]Nancy Friday, *My Secret Garden: Women's Sexual Fantasies* (New York: Simon & Schuster, 1976), p. 285. Copyright © 1973 by Nancy Friday. Reprinted by permission of Simon & Schuster, a Division of Gulf & Western Corporation.

who has about eight regular gentlemen now for whom she provides special services. On Sunday afternoon she dresses like a little girl to await the visit of her uncle, Mr. X. She serves tea, they look at the album of pornographic pictures Uncle always brings with him. Georgina feigns shock, Uncle displays himself, and persuades Georgina to drop her drawers and let him caress her buttocks and thighs. As he does so, he ejaculates, aided by his own verbal debauch of the naughty little girl.

Georgina plays nurse to Mr. Z. She is a masterful nanny, and he is a naughty child. Under her gaze he undresses and is sent to bed. He thinks of ways of pestering his nurse, is reprimanded, and is eventually given an enema, which produces his orgasm. Georgina and her clients rarely derole. The show must go on. The fantasy makes its own demands.[39] Self-disclosure is clearly not the issue.

Another prostitute confided that she and her friend had been engaged by a gentleman to kidnap him for a weekend. He arranged the whole thing in advance, renting the house, buying enough food, scheduling the abduction, and so forth. He apparently had always wanted to be kidnapped and abused by two women and had saved for many years in order to enjoy his fantasy in real life. They did as they were told. They overpowered him and drove to a secluded cottage, where they bound him to a chair and gagged him. He remained bound in various positions all weekend. He was locked in a cupboard, forced to make oral love to the women, was fellated several times, and whipped before breakfast. He experienced several orgasms. He later declared to the women that it was the best weekend in his life—a truly devoted fantasist.[40]

A WOMAN'S APPROACH

Unlike men, women do not have as ready recourse to prostitutes who will fulfill their sexual fantasies. Yet they too can live out their fantasies in varying degrees. Martha, age thirty-four and married eleven years, has a favorite sexual fantasy. Part of it is an elaboration of an affair that did happen, but most of the fantasy is purely a daydream. Her affair took place with a married man before she was married.

Although I made it regularly with my boyfriend, this man really excited me. We were lucky that we had a room to go to and didn't have to make it in the back of a car. First, we would undress completely. He would always have the most incredible erection. He would fondle, kiss, and suck my breasts. He would caress my bottom and smack it. He would play with my clitoris and insert his fingers up me. Then he would suck my clitoris and

[39]Barros, *Sexual Fantasy.*

[40]Ibid.

insert his tongue in me. During all this I never used to touch his penis. He would concentrate wholly on me, making me cry with excitement, and he would talk to me, the language of lust: "Oh you beauty, you lovely little cunt, those lovely soft hairs I'm going to bury my cock against them, right up your cunt. I'm going to fuck, fuck, fuck, fuck you and I'm going to wet all those hairs with my come, and after that you are going to suck it for me, all of it."

Then he would insert his fingers up my bottom and suck me to orgasm. While I was still crying with pleasure he would put his huge penis in me and with my legs around his waist would fuck me to at least two orgasms. He would still not have come yet, and would have an erection like an iron bar. He would push it against my lips until I opened my mouth and took it in and I would suck it. He was capable of withholding his ejaculation for as long as he wanted. Still not having come, he would take it out of my mouth and I would caress it with my hand, wrapping my fingers around it. Suddenly he would roughly grab my legs, put them onto his shoulders and force his cock into me again and work hard and fast. Then he would come, and I would feel his warm semen spurting.[41]

This elaborated recollection of the past never occurred as she describes it, and Martha has no intention of seeking such a lover in the present. It serves its own purpose as a delightful fantasy.

SEX AND AGGRESSION

Martha's fantasy suggests that she enjoys being handled roughly on occasion. Many women enjoy the idea of being forced to have sex against their will, as long as it remains a fantasy. Julietta, for example, fantasizes while making love to her lover by putting a pillow or something over her head to shut out the light and allow her to feel everything he does while being in the dark with her own thoughts.

I imagine that I've been brought to some warehouse or place like that, against my will. I'm stripped naked and the only thing I'm allowed to wear is a black silk mask. This is because whatever powerful person that has brought me there does not want the men—yes, always more than one in this fantasy—for whom he has procured me, to know who I am. In this way, though he's brought me there against my will, he somehow wants to protect me too. I never know who he is, and he himself never fucks me. I just know that he's somewhere in the background, enjoying this feeling of power he has, not only over me, but over the men, too. That's because they're so hot with desire for me that they can barely control themselves. But he can take me away from them whenever he wants to. In my mind I can imagine the men, all big and powerfully built. They're naked too,

[41]Friday, *My Secret Garden,* p. 284.

while they wait their turn with me. I think of them watching each other as each of them performs, talking about various techniques, and what they're going to do when their turn comes with me.

Meanwhile the guy who is really with me, every time he tries a different position, or a different idea, I pretend to myself that it's the next man in line. So it's always exciting this way, because I seemingly have an endless supply of men fucking me.[42]

In real life, Jullietta refuses to marry because she does not want any man to have such a privileged position over her. Her fantasy of being forced to have sex against her will is clearly mixed with elements of protectiveness and her fascination with the intense desire that the naked men have for her. This fantasy does not focus on the pain of being gang raped. The key element is that the men assume the responsibility for the action, not she herself.

Why do women have fantasies about rape—something that they would never wish to experience in real life? In an expansion of psychoanalytic thought, Helen Deutsch, a disciple of Freud, contended that women are naturally masochistic, that they enjoy pain and punishment.[43] However, as a basis for this theory, Deutsch allowed the fantasies of women seeking help for their borderline psychotic problem to stand for those created by normal women. Another analyst has suggested that rape fantasies allow women to deal with their worst fears and thus helps them to cope with the problems of overcoming male domination in a sexist society.[44] Whatever the underlying processes are, the major difference between a rape fantasy and the real thing is simply the fact that the woman has control over the fantasy.

However, newspaper accounts help perpetuate the myth of women as wanting to be raped. These stories cater to male fantasies and do not include detailed descriptions of the brutality of the act. The rapist is often fantasized by the male as a super sex stud, with an enormous, erect penis. But rape is more reasonably seen as a crime of violence, as a violation of someone else, rather than as a crime of passion or desire. The rapist is apt to rely on his fist or other weapon, as his penis may fail him. Even personal accounts of being raped often omit the sordid details. All accounts are likely to be interpreted by the listener. "The odor, the ugliness, the hostility of the experience, disappear in the retelling; the episode is filtered through the imagination of my listener and turned into a sexual fantasy."[45] Finally, the ac-

[42]Ibid., p. 111.

[43]Helen Deutsch, *The Psychology of Women,* vol. 1 (New York: Grune and Stratton, 1944).

[44]Molly Haskell, "The 2000-year-old Misunderstanding: Rape Fantasy," *MS* (November 1976), p. 96. © Molly Haskell 1977.

[45]Ibid., p. 86.

counts that are retained are of dramatic events that have occurred. We are not told of the number of times women have successfully resisted the advance of a would-be rapist. Everything thus tends to perpetuate the myth of the woman as masochistic victim who probably unwittingly "asked for it," and the assertive male "who gave it to her."

It is also possible that other factors affect such fantasies. Abraham Maslow, for example, suggests that, in monkeys and apes, striving for dominance is intimately related to sexual behavior, though it is not the same thing.

When a pair of Old World monkeys are introduced to each other for the first time, they immediately go about establishing a dominance hierarchy. One will become the boss, the other the subordinate. In the wild, the male is almost always dominant because he is bigger, not because he is male. In the laboratory, too, size, not gender, proves a more likely basis for dominance. When monkeys of the same size are compared, more subtle factors establish dominance. "Sureness, lack of hesitation, a confident posture, cockiness—in short, what the observer is irresistibly impelled to call self-confidence, determines the issue." [46]

The establishment of dominance is often manifested in a pseudosexual act. The subordinate animal acts like a sexually receptive female, and the dominant one mounts, regardless of the gender of either animal. In rare cases, reluctant subordination is manifested in a face-to-face sexual position rather than the customary one in which the "female" is mounted from behind. This pseudosexual act most often occurs at the beginning of a relationship, rather than after the relationship has been stabilized.

Human beings compete for dominance in similar ways. Among males, boy's gangs, competitive sports, and other forms of combat provide opportunities to dominate. Sexual behavior is a prime area in which men and women strive to establish dominance. For example, in our society, the normal male traditionally expects to be dominant in his sexual relations with females. But, as with monkeys, there is no natural relationship between gender and dominance among humans.

Dominance striving mingles with sexual elements in complex ways. For example, Maslow discovered that women with strong needs to dominate were apt to transform the sexual act in a number of ways to express their feelings of domination.

These women insisted on being in the above position where they could control the lovemaking while their partner remained motionless. They could fantasize that they had a penis and not their partner. This fantasy of possessing a penis was also mentioned by dominant

[46]Maslow et al., "Some Parallels," p. 203.

women who assumed the more common position under their partner. Dominant women imagined that their partners were really working hard to please them, while they themselves were taking their ease. When masturbating, these women sometimes stretched their clitorises and treated them as though they were penises. Finally, they commonly denied any enjoyment of the sexual activity and commonly made fun of the efforts of their partners by yawning, laughing contemptuously, or smoking casually.[47]

According to Maslow, these feelings only become problems when a woman becomes concerned about "masculine dominance" or a male about "feminine submission." Males do fantasize about being submissive. Traditionally, in our society, men have few outlets for their submissive urges. Women have even fewer outlets for their dominance urges. As a result, both men and women are diminished. The issue, for Maslow, is not the elimination of either feeling, but their modification. Maslow advises both sexes to open up more, to be more flexible about who leads and who follows. Dominance is determined by circumstance and ability, not by gender. He assumes that this is the direction toward growth and health. This shift toward health can come about because we can intentionally redefine our sex roles and our sexual behavior.

Finally, sex and aggression are thought to be linked hormonally and this fact may have some bearing on rape fantasies. There is some evidence to suggest that sexual arousal and aggression are both partially triggered by the same hormone, testosterone. This hormone is commonly found in higher levels in men than in women, but the levels in women are sometimes high. Testosterone does not automatically release aggressive behavior. This kind of response has already begun to disappear in the primates. In humans it is even less automatic, but it probably has some effect. In addition to redefining the social institutions that reward male dominance and female submission, we can also redefine our fantasies. The healthy modification of sexual behavior will be enhanced to the extent that we can live with and enjoy our sexual fantasies as fantasies. Unfortunately, some of us cannot work with our sexual fantasies because of a culturally induced fear of the erotic. Some recent research suggests that such a fear of the erotic has some other very interesting, if unexpected, consequences as well.

EROTOPHOBIA

Erotophobia means "a fear of the erotic." It can be measured in a number of ways, by an analysis of dreams and fantasies, by direct

[47]Ibid., p. 205.

questioning, and in various indirect methods. Donn Byrne and his colleagues measured erotophobia by recording how people responded to an explicit erotic film. In the film, a couple undressed, aroused each other with mutual foreplay, and finally performed fellatio and cunnilingus until they reached orgasm. Those who rated the film "pornographic, shocking, and more explicit than expected" were called erotophobes. Those who reacted in the opposite way were considered erotophiles, or lovers of the erotic.[48]

Byrne found clear distinctions between erotophobes and erotophiles. Erotophobes were not well-informed about sex, didn't like to talk about it, and had sex infrequently. They felt guilty about sex and assigned it a peripheral place in their lives. They were regular churchgoers and described themselves as conservative. Erotophiles, on the other hand, did not go to church often, considered themselves sexually liberated, and discussed sex at home. Erotophobes disapproved of premarital sex, felt sex was unimportant, believed it should always be linked to love, felt that erotica is potentially harmful, disliked oral-genital sex, and disapproved of birth control clinics and abortion.

The erotophobe's negative images and feelings about sex are rarely strong enough to completely inhibit sexual behavior, but they are strong enough to inhibit the use of contraceptives. Byrne contends this attitude is not as paradoxical as it might first seem. The person who has negative ideas about sex avoids the idea that he or she is going to engage in intercourse and, therefore, prefers to be surprised and unprepared. In addition, such individuals are much more fearful of purchasing contraceptives because they are afraid that people will think they are immoral. Thus, erotophobic couples are less likely to discuss their mutual preparation for sex (or lack thereof) and are less likely to use contraceptives even if they have purchased them. Byrne found that erotophobes justified their irrational behavior by "convincing themselves that contraception is sinful, unnatural, dangerous, etc., and that it is immoral for contraceptives to be made easily available to the unmarried."[49] This attitude does not disappear after marriage. Byrne found that unhappily married erotophobic couples were often planning to have the largest families.

Byrne concludes,

It's not surprising that most people don't use contraceptives when they first engage in sexual intercourse. They have no role models and no imaginative cues to make them think of contraception as a part of sexuality.

We need to bring conception and its prevention into our fantasy lives.

[48]Donn Byrne, "A Pregnant Pause in the Sexual Revolution," *Psychology Today* (July 1977) p. 67, reprinted from *Psychology Today* magazine; copyright © 1977 Ziff-Davis Publishing Company.

[49]Ibid., p. 68.

(The condom manufacturers have tried to do this, for their own purposes, with ads promoting "sensuous contraceptives.") At any rate, people who want to enjoy sexual intercourse without fear of parenthood need more than simple facts. Since rationality does not always guide our actions, we need the appropriate cues intermeshed in the fabric of our erotic thoughts.[50]

If Byrne is correct, fantasies have a very important role to play not only in triggering arousal, but also in preventing the estimated one million unwanted pregnancies each year. We need adequate images, feelings, and attitudes, as well as information. The acceptance of the erotic image as a valuable part of one's fantasy life can help us to feel more comfortable about our sexuality and its consequences.

Summary

Human sexuality is to an unknown extent a creation of the human mind. I have in the previous chapter briefly suggested how sexuality has been shaped by different traditions and cultures. Our pluralist society contains a complex set of beliefs, attitudes, images, and emotions that help define what human sexuality is for a particular person. This complex gestalt is said to be held in the mind. Western societies have generally encouraged a particularly negative mind-set toward human sexuality. This is being undermined by a whole host of experiences in the process of industrialization and urbanization and is being directly challenged by sex research. In this chapter such a negative mind-set has been called erotophobia.

Our collective definition of human sexuality, therefore, is highly ambivalent. This makes it easier, on the one hand, to experiment with new life styles, but more difficult, on the other to find support for one's experimentation. At the moment, however, sexuality is probably more of a function of a particular person's experience that has been true in our past.

There is nothing that will automatically arouse us. However much the pain of adolescence may be experienced in the genitals, human sexual arousal is not a reflex response for either man or woman. The typical male is frequently aware of the effect of mental images in stimulating an erection and more women are reporting comparable effects upon vaginal lubrication. Nevertheless, not all persons are aware of these images, and not all report sexual fantasies even though they are fully aroused. Sometimes both men and women are so lost in the bodily sensations of making love that they do not fantasize. This

[50]Ibid., p. 68.

is not a better way of making love, nor a worse way. It is simply a different way. Sexual fantasies are not at present thought of as being essential to sexual arousal, but are widely becoming recognized as means of enhancing it.

The greatest domination of our sexually repressive past has probably been over the mental images of our fantasies. Although we have all been sired by an ejaculating penis, grown in a womb, passed through the vaginal vault and out into the world between the labia, it was not a totally natural passage. The body that emerged soon took up a cultural garb and the images of the genitals, and the natural odors and tastes of the body and its secretions took on fanciful significance in the mind. These natural stimuli no longer automatically arouse. But upon this uncertainty hangs all of the elaboration of human sexuality.

Anatomy and Sexual Response

3

This is my body. Mistake, or magic, or madness;
or child's play. This is a house and
this is a steeple.

Norman O. Brown

What do we need to know about our bodies in order to improve our understanding of human sexuality? No doubt we need to know some basic facts about how they are equipped sexually and how they respond to sexual stimuli in order to feel at ease with our bodies and be more artful in our loving. Arousal, as we have seen, can be triggered by a great many things. Artful stimulation will increase sexual response or maintain it on a plateau of delight, while clumsy efforts may well inhibit further response. A general description of sexual anatomy and response can help us empathize with our partner and understand our own reactions more fully.

There is something else that is important for us to know about our bodies that is usually overlooked. We need to know what our bodies look like. In spite of the explicitness found in the mass media, most of us really have a very limited knowledge of how men and women look in the nude. Not only do we not know the details of our own anatomy (we are usually too shy to look, or the camera hides more than it discloses), but we also lack a sense of how richly varied the human body contours are. From birth to old age our bodies differ. Bodies of the same age and sex differ, often dramatically. When we recognize something of the range of this variation, we can feel more at home with our own peculiar and distinctively beautiful body.

In this chapter, the genitals will be described from the perspective of human anatomy. The bulk of the chapter goes on to describe the processes involved in human sexual response.

The Body

Artists and scientists see things differently. Artists are interested in individual variation, in the unique expression of a personality that is found in all human form. Scientists are much more interested in making general statements about all bodies, or rather *the* human body. We need both perspectives, particularly when we consider human lovemaking. Human beings are much richer in body form, tone, and texture than the media would have us believe.

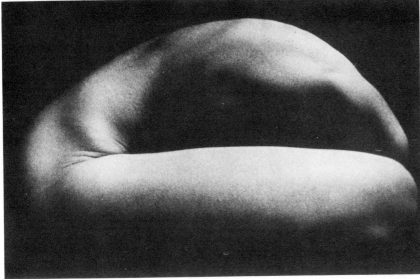

Figure 3–1
Through shyness and modesty, our own bodies may be as unfamiliar to us as a stranger's would be. By opening up to our own bodies, we become more open to others. (Magnum)

General Statements About Genitals

The male and female genitals are homologous, that is they develop from the same tissues in the process of psychosexual differentiation. The penis is the homologue of the clitoris. The scrotum develops from the same tissue as does the major lips, or labia majora. The testes and ovaries were initially undifferentiated gonads and both retain tissues more fully developed in their opposite sexed homologue. While looking at the apparent differences, it is well to remember the less apparent similarities.

MALE GENITALS

The penis and the scrotum are the external primary sexual organs of the male. (The testes, the male gonad that produces the sperm, are not technically considered external organs. They are carried in the scrotum.)

The average penis is about 7.5 to 10 centimeters long when relaxed and about 15.25 centimeters long when erect. The penis is not fully erect at the time of penetration. Full erection occurs only in the few brief seconds before orgasm. Measurements of the fully erect state,

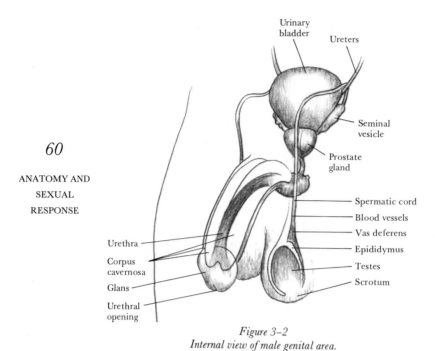

Figure 3–2
Internal view of male genital area.

therefore, are rarely attempted and lack the accuracy of the measurements of the relaxed state. The diameter of the average penis expands about one-half centimeter in erection from a flaccid diameter of about three centimeters. Physiologically the length of the penis bears little relationship to its capacity to stimulate the female in sexual arousal. A wider penis, however, does seem to be more stimulating than a narrower one. The size of the penis is not significantly related to body size.[1]

The root of the penis is attached to the pelvis. After puberty the root of the penis is hidden by the man's pubic hair. The body of the penis, the part that hangs down, is made up of three tubes. The smallest of these is called the corpus spongiosum. It is located on the underside of the penis and surrounds the urethra, the tube through which the urine and the ejaculata passes. Above the corpus spongiosum are two larger tubes, the corpus cavernosa. These are made up of sponge-like tissue served by a network of blood vessels and nerves. During erection they become engorged with blood. The tiny blood vessels (arterioles) connecting the arteries with this sponge-like tissue contain ridges that normally restrict the flow of blood into the corpus

[1]William H. Masters and Virginia E. Johnson, *Human Sexual Response* (Boston: Little, Brown & Co., 1966), p. 193.

cavernosum. When relaxed, they permit more blood to flow into the cavernosa, thus causing the erection. It is now possible to provide impotent men with a usable erection by the surgical insertion of plastic prostheses into the corpus cavernosum. In such a procedure the shaft of the penis remains permanently extended but a flexible portion of the prostheses permits the erect penis to be bent back against the body. Another hydrolic device permits the wearer to pump up an erection by means of a small pump carried near the waist.

The *glans penis* is the smooth round head of the penis. It is the most sensitive part of the penis and contributes greatly to the pleasure of sexual arousal when stimulated. The neck of the penis is also rich with nerve endings, but the shaft itself is relatively insensitive save for a narrow band of skin, the frenulum, which is particularly sensitive. The frenulum is on the underside of the penis between the shaft and the glans. Behind and beneath the penis is a small ridge of skin running back to the anus called the *perineum*. It is often quite sensitive to soft stimulation.

The foreskin of the penis, or prepuce, has been the object of ritual mutilation ever since the earliest times in recorded history. Removal of this skin, or circumcision, is often performed early in a boy's life for both religious and hygenic reasons. Uncircumcised males must pull back the prepuce and wash away the smegma, a cheesy substance secreted by the glands of the penis, or irritation and infection may occur. Authorities differ as to the sensuous value of the prepuce. Alex Comfort, author of the *Joy of Sex,* contends that it provides more erotic pleasure because of the greater variety of manipulations of the penis that are possible when it is present. Others contend that its removal increases erotic enjoyment because of the exposure of the sensi-

Figure 3–3
Examples of the varieties of male genitalia.

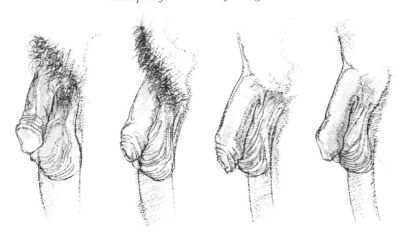

tive head of the penis. Indeed, for a long time it was believed that uncircumcised males had greater difficulty achieving ejaculatory control because of this sensitivity of the head. There is no evidence for this today.[2]

The scrotum is simply a sac of skin that contains the testes. Its skin is darker in color than the penis, and, in contrast to the smoothness of marble male nudes in museums, the scrotum is lightly covered with hair and bumps that are actually sweat glands. These glands help control the temperature of the testes, which are suspended in the scrotum in the first place because sperm will not be produced at normal body temperature. Sperm are continuously produced in the testes after puberty. Hundreds of millions of them are made in the testes and mature in the epididymis. If ejaculation does not occur within thirty to sixty days, the sperm die and are replaced by new ones. The dead sperm are broken down and reabsorbed by the body.

A change in temperature of even two to three degrees centigrade will adversely affect sperm production. The scrotum regulates the temperature of the testes by drawing them closer to the body on cold days and allowing them to hang away on hot days. The fact that sperm production is inhibited by increases in temperature has led to the widely held belief that taking a hot bath before sexual intercourse can serve as a contraceptive technique. A hot bath may reduce the chances of impregnating a woman by some small fraction of a percent, but it should not be relied upon as a means of contraception.

FEMALE GENITALS

The female's genitals are much more varied than the male's. Most of this variation, however, is hidden behind the *labia majora,* or major lips. The little used proper term for the entire external genital area is *vulva.* The *mons pubus,* the elevation of fatty tissue over the pubic bone, is the most visible portion of the female genitals. In a woman who has passed puberty, the mons is normally covered with hair.

The minor lips *(labia minora)* lie directly inside of the major lips and often lie over the entrance to the vagina. They are normally pinker and more moist than the outer lips. Because they are connected to the clitoris in front and the perineum behind, they are able to indirectly stimulate both of these sensitive areas as well as becoming quite stimulated themselves. Sexual arousal causes both sets of lips to become engorged with blood, forming a cushion to protect the clitoris and vagina. As Figure 3–5 suggests, both sets of lips are quite varied in appearance and do not perfectly overlap.

The clitoris is analogous to the penis. It does not hang free from the

[2]Ibid., p. 190.

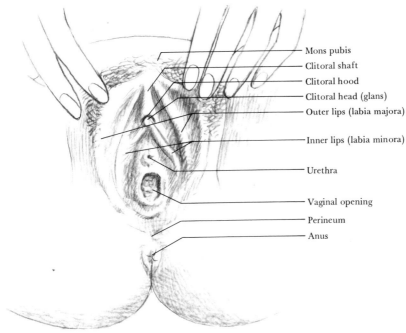

Mons pubis
Clitoral shaft
Clitoral hood
Clitoral head (glans)
Outer lips (labia majora)
Inner lips (labia minora)
Urethra
Vaginal opening
Perineum
Anus

Figure 3–4
External female genitalia.

body, however, and only its upper protion, or *glans clitoris,* is visible. It is one of the few organs of the body—if not the only one—whose sole purpose is to provide pleasure. Being essentially a bundle of nerve endings, it seems to have no other function. The discovery of the pleasure-providing role of the clitoris and the techniques by which it may be stimulated are essential components of the sexual revolution. Like the penis, the clitoris has been subjected to ritual mutilation in various societies.

The clitoris is located near the upper joining of the major lips. Its shaft may be located by tracing the finger upward between these lips until their juncture is reached. The glans—the most sensitive part of the clitoris—is about one inch below this juncture at the joining of the lower portion of the inner lips. The upper portion of the inner lips is sealed and covers the shaft of the clitoris. This is called the prepuce of the clitoris. Most women find direct stimulation of the glans irritating if not painful. It is, therefore, preferable in most instances to stimulate the glans indirectly by applying light pressure on either side or upon its shaft. Typically, the clitoris is a little over two centimeters in length, including its buried portion, and in diameter it measures about four to five millimeters.

Figure 3–5
Examples of the varieties of female genitalia.

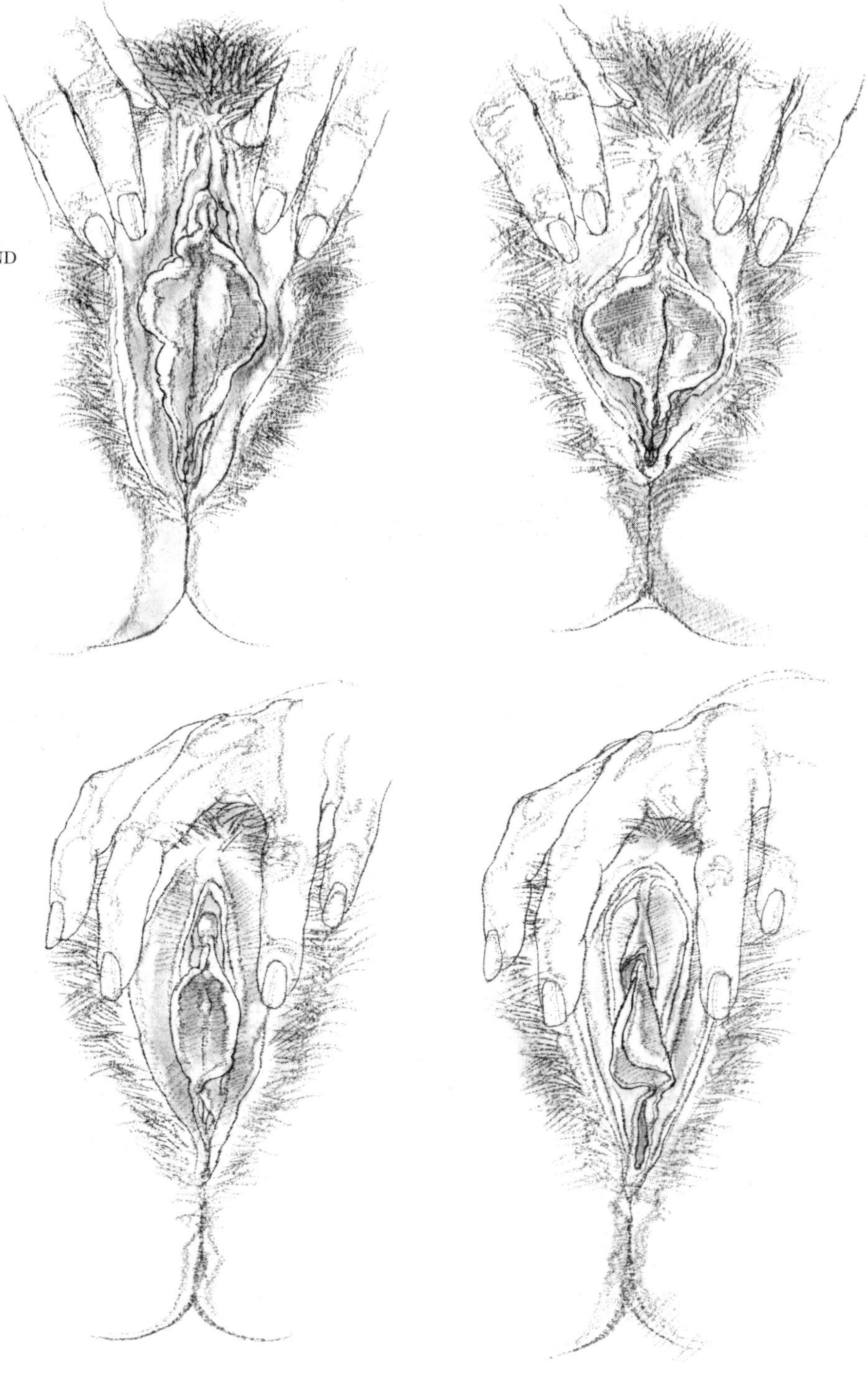

64

ANATOMY AND
SEXUAL
RESPONSE

The vaginal opening varies in appearance, depending upon the condition of the hymen, or maidenhead, a membrane located inside the vaginal opening. Much folk custom has been associated with the hymen. It has traditionally been regarded as the seal of the virgin under the mistaken assumption that the presence of an unbroken hymen was proof of virginity, while its absence was proof of prior sexual intercourse. In fact, some women do not have such a membrane at birth; in other instances, hymens have been ruptured without the woman being aware of it. It is also possible to engage in sexual intercourse without damaging the hymen. In most cases the hymen can be ruptured by finger pressure alone without undue discomfort, but there are females whose hymens may be so inelastic that surgery is required. It is a very unreliable seal. The rupture of the hymen is often accompanied by bleeding. This led to the folk custom in some countries of displaying the sheets of the wedding night with their blood stains testifying to the purity of the bride. No comparable test was applied to the groom.

The perineum extends backward from the lower joining of the minor or inner lips to the anus. In most women it is also quite sensitive to the touch, and some enjoy its stimulation. During childbirth this area may be torn or surgically cut. Doctors often add an extra little stitch—called the husband's knot—when they sew up this area to tighten the vaginal opening. Such a procedure is not necessarily a delight to the wife.

Strictly speaking, the female breasts are not a part of the reproductive system inasmuch as they do not play a role in the process of conception. But they are, of course, closely linked to the reproductive system. They undergo changes in size, color, and sensitivity in response to hormonal signals that are part of the menstrual and reproductive cycles. Male breasts also have nerve endings and in some men are quite sensitive to the touch. Lactation (the production of milk in the breast), which occurs during pregnancy, is also a hormonally triggered response. The breasts play an important part in sexual arousal for both men and women. The nipples are normally the most sensitive portion of the breast. This sensitivity is totally unrelated to the size or shape of the breasts.

The internal sex organs in women are two *ovaries,* two *fallopian tubes,* a *uterus,* and a *vagina.* The ovaries are the female version of the testes and are located along the side walls of the abdominal cavity below the fallopian tubes and a few inches from the uterus. If you drew a line between the navel and the clitoris, the ovaries could be found about halfway down and about fifteen centimeters apart. During the reproductive life of the woman, these flattened oval organs are about the size of a walnut (average three to six centimeters), but they shrink with loss of function upon aging.

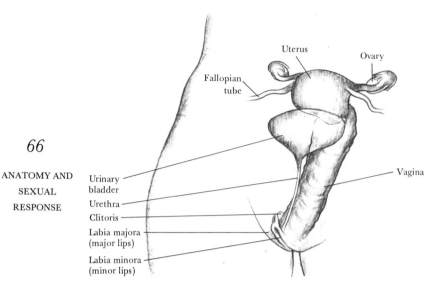

Figure 3–6
Internal view of female genital area.

The fallopian tubes are about ten to twenty centimeters in length, and are located between the ovaries and the uterus. At the ovarian end, the fallopian tube flares in trumpet fashion to about one centimeter. At the entrance to the uterus they are about one millimeter in diameter. The ovarian end of the fallopian tube is not attached to the ovaries but opens out into the abdominal cavity. One of the great unsolved mysteries is how the egg migrates from the ovary to the end of the tube. In some instances conception can occur outside of the fallopian tubes with the embryo developing partially in the abdominal cavity.

The uterus is a powerfully muscular, pearshaped organ that is about three inches long in women who are not pregnant. It lies behind the urinary bladder and above the anus and is held in place by strong ligaments. The lower neck of the uterus is called the cervix. Normally it partially extends into the vagina. The lower cervix is ordinarily blocked with mucus to prevent infection of the uterus and the interior of the abdomen.

The tube of the vagina joins the uterus to the outside world. The vagina varies in length in the unstimulated state between seven to eight centimeters in length and about two centimeters in width. Upon stimulation it normally lengthens to about 9.5 to 10.5 centimeters and the interior end flares to about 5.75 to 6.25 centimeters.[3]

[3]Ibid., p. 73.

Women who have given birth to babies have somewhat larger vaginas. Vaginas can accommodate babies during childbirth. As no penis has been found to be bigger than a baby's head, few women need to worry about pain during intercourse, provided that there is adequate lubrication of the vagina. Should there be some anatomical mismatching between penis and vagina in a particular instance, the remedy is usually no more complicated than adjusting the posture in lovemaking or timing the penetration so that it occurs when the vagina is fully lubricated.

At the entrance to the vagina behind the *labia minora* there is a ring of muscles, called the vaginal sphincter, that can be strengthened through exercise to more accurately control the size of the vagina for purposes of more efficient placement of tampons, birth control devices, or for increasing the friction between the vagina and the penis for more pleasurable intercourse.

Human Sexual Response

In talking about sexual arousal we focused on one phenomenon, fantasy, and its possible role as a sexual stimulant. Fantasy can serve as a sexual stimulant because human sexual response is much more under the control of the cerebral cortex than is the sexual response of lower animals. Some women have reported being able to reach orgasm solely through the use of fantasy. Men commonly experience wet dreams—ejaculation in their sleep as a result of sexually stimulating dreams. The studies of human sexual response conducted by William Masters and Virginia Johnson, upon which much of this chapter is based, describe sexual response largely in terms of responding to touch, either in the context of masturbation, or in the context of making love with a partner.[4] They were unable to find a woman who could fantasize to orgasm, and did not study wet dreams. And so we do not know how (if at all) these response patterns might differ.

It is important to bear in mind that sexual response is an area in which psychological passions run deep—deep enough, in fact, to have profound effects on the physiological processes we will be describing. For example, a noisy debate has been raging for a number of years about whether women experience orgasm in the vagina or in the clitoris. The simpliest way to settle this debate—by asking women—has not proved satisfactory. Some women report experiencing vaginal orgasm, and some report clitoral orgasms. This may indicate that both

[4]Ibid. and William H. Masters and Virginia E. Johnson, *Human Sexual Inadequacy* (Boston: Little, Brown & Co., 1970).

types of orgasm are physiologically possible, but it also may indicate that women who feel a strong psychological need to experience vaginal orgasms will experience orgasm as though it occurred in the vagina regardless of the fact that it was in actuality a clitoral orgasm. And vice versa. In short, our expectations may lead us to believe we are having experiences that are in fact physiologically impossible. Conversely, they may make it impossible for us to experience sensations that our physiological equipment can provide.

Thus, any account of the physiology of sexual response must be read with an awareness of the fact that people differ not only physiologically but also psychologically in the extent to which they conform to the response pattern outlined here.

SEXUAL RESPONSE IN THE MALE

The female's external genitals and breasts have been objects of sexual arousal for the male from time immemorial. In some cultures, the exposure of the vulva by the female constitutes an invitation to sexual intercourse. In our own tradition, there seems to be a preference for covering the sexually stimulating body parts and letting the suggestion of their presence produce the desired erotic effect.

Although there is considerable debate over the matter, it seems that men respond to visual stimuli differently than women do. Men commonly experience erection in response to visual stimulation. But it is often maintained that women are not commonly aware of such

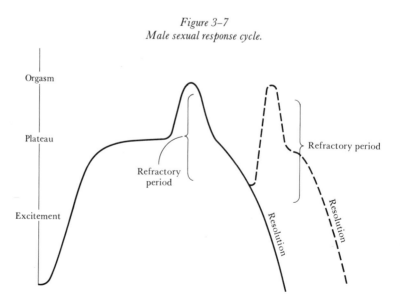

Figure 3–7
Male sexual response cycle.

signs of sexual arousal as lubrication of the vagina in response to purely visual phenomena. This difference—if in fact it exists—may well be a result of cultural conditioning rather than of physiological differences in the response mechanisms of the two sexes.

Masters and Johnson, who have conducted the most thorough study of human sexual response, describe both the male and the female response cycles in terms of four phases. Consider first the four phases of male sexual response.

Excitement Phase. Different men are "turned on" in different ways. As we noted, visual stimuli are frequently effective. The first response to effective stimulation is the erection of the penis. This occurs involuntarily, whether the man wants to respond or not. The penis becomes engorged with blood and achieves varying degrees of stiffness, depending on the style of arousal. A man cannot will an erection. He can only relax and remove the distractions that may interfere with its occurrence. Wishing will not make an erection go away, although by deliberately distracting oneself, one can effectively eliminate the source of stimulation from one's perceptual field, after which the erection will subside spontaneously.

Men are capable of maintaining an erection in the excitement phase for a long time. Various kinds of diversions, such as loud noises, obvious changes in lighting, or conversation on an extraneous subject, may cause partial or total loss of the erection.

During the excitement phase the scrotum contracts and the testes are pulled toward the body cavity. The folds in the scrotum disappear. During prolonged intercourse, the scrotum may relax without loss of erection.

Plateau Phase. The plateau phase is reached when the fully erect penis undergoes a slight involuntary enlargement of the cap and a small amount of fluid is secreted from the *Cowper's gland,* located on the urethra and just below the prostate gland. This secretion generally is clear or slightly clouded in color. Researchers are not certain of its function. It may serve to lubricate the urethra for the easier passage of the forthcoming semen, or it may serve to reduce the acidity of the urethra, which is essential if conception is to occur because sperm cannot survive in an acidic environment. In any case, this secretion may contain a small amount of semen, thus making it possible for conception to occur without ejaculation. For this reason the practice of coitus interruptus—withdrawing the penis from the vagina before ejaculation—may prove ineffective as a contraceptive technique.

There are no further changes in the scrotum in either the plateau or the orgasmic phase of sexual response. A reddening of the skin (sex flush) occurs infrequently in the plateau stage.

Internally, the testes enlarge up to about one and a half times their normal size and are pressed against the body. This pressing of the testes against the body is necessary for orgasm and anticipates its occurrence.

Orgasmic Phase. Orgasm is a highly pleasurable, involuntary response to sexual stimulation. In the male it normally lasts from two to ten seconds, after which the male must undergo a period of relaxation (refractory period), lasting a few minutes to several hours, before erection can occur again.

Orgasm in the male is experienced as an involuntary contraction of the urethra and the muscles around the base of the penis and the anus. These contractions involve the entire length of the urethra and are responsible for the ejaculation of the seminal fluid, which occurs at about 0.8 second intervals for the first three or four contractions. These initial contractions are followed by others at gradually lengthening intervals and with weakening intensity.

Orgasm is normally a very intense physiological response, as evidenced in the changes in heartbeat, blood pressure, and breathing. Heartbeat increases from a normal rate of about 70 to 80 beats per minute to a high of 110 to 180 beats per minute. Blood pressure may double. Respiratory rates increase from the normal eighteen per minute to as high as forty per minute, although if the orgasm is mild or of short duration there may be no increase in the rate of breathing at all. Many people experience a sense of loss of oxygen and respond by gasping for air, or breathing heavily.

The more effective the sexual stimulation, the more completely the entire body is involved in the release of tensions in orgasm. About 25 percent of the male population in Masters and Johnson's study experienced a well-developed sex flush or reddening of the skin during orgasm.[5]

Orgasm is almost always marked in the male by the ejaculation of semen. Semen is characteristically white or yellowish. Its substance varies from a thick, almost gelatin-like, fluid to a thin, watery substance. The amount of semen ejaculated is normally about three to four cubic centimeters, weighing about four grams. The amount of semen in the ejaculation is positively correlated to the pleasure experienced by the male in orgasm, particularly after long periods of abstinence. There is no evidence that ejaculation can weaken a man any more than any other strenuous physical activity. The folk notion that a man must conserve his semen in order to conserve his strength has no basis in fact.

The sperm, which have been maturing in the epididymis, are

[5]Masters and Johnson, *Human Sexual Response,* p. 290.

forced upward through the *vas deferens* by the contraction of its walls. Before entering the urethra, they are enveloped in milky liquid produced in the seminal vesicle and the prostate gland to form the semen. The passage of the semen through the urethra is encouraged by the contraction of the urethral walls. The contractions of these internal organs as they pour their secretions into the urethra are responsible for the feeling of the "inevitability of orgasm."

The ejaculate emerges from the erect penis in a series of spurts. Semen may be ejected from the penis with a force capable of propelling it a distance of three or four feet, or it may simply ooze from the urethra. Once ejected, the sperm will die unless they reach the fallopian tubes of the female, where they typically survive for two or three days. In rare instances they can survive in the fallopian tubes for five days or longer.[6]

Resolution Phase. Masters and Johnson observed that immediately after ejaculation, men found further sexual stimulation psychologically and physically unpleasant.[7] This period of time during which males are unresponsive to sexual stimuli is called the refractory period. Its length varies greatly. Masters and Johnson cite an example of one man who was able to "ejaculate three times within ten minutes of the onset of stimulative activity," but, for most men, stimulation within a few minutes after ejaculation will fail to produce a second erection and ejaculation, let alone a third.[8]

After the refractory period, the resolution phase begins. During this period, the body can either return to normal or become ready to respond to further sexual stimulation. The resolution phase may be prolonged or shortened, depending upon the effectiveness of sexual stimulation experienced. It is likely to be prolonged if the penis is kept in the vagina and the couple continue to hold each other close and to caress. The penis will rapidly lose its erection in both stages if the couple disengage and the male's attention is directed to non-stimulating activities such as urinating or smoking. During the first stage of the resolution phase, the penis typically shrinks to about twice its flaccid size. During the second stage of the resolution phase, the penis returns to its normal, prestimulated size. The testes return to normal size during resolution. This may occur rapidly or slowly, depending upon the length of the plateau phase. The scrotum loses its tenseness and returns to its prestimulated state.

[6]Lloyd Saxton, *The Individual Marriage and The Family,* 2nd ed. (Belmont, Calif.: Wadsworth Publishing Co., Inc., 1972), p. 56.

[7]Masters and Johnson, *Human Sexual Response,* p. 214.

[8]Ibid.

The female, of course, may receive semen from the male without being sexually aroused. She may be penetrated with the assistance of artificial lubricants—or by sheer force, as generally happens in cases of rape—and thus may conceive a child without ever experiencing sexual pleasure. Indeed, in puritanical cultures the female is not expected to enjoy sexual intercourse, and many women, in fact, do not. Masters and Johnson, however, have clearly demonstrated that the female's capacity to enjoy sexual stimulation is far greater than that of the male.[9] Women, in fact, are physiologically capable of experiencing a fairly large numer of orgasms in rapid succession, while men, as we have seen, generally cannot experience a second orgasm until a considerable period of time has elapsed after the first. Conclusions reached by Kinsey and Freud to the effect that women are not as excitable by sexual stimuli as men and do not have an adequate body image because of their supposed penis envy have reinforced common folk notions about the sexual inferiority of women. These notions, it is now becoming clear, have absolutely no basis in fact. Indeed, Dr. Seymour Fischer contends:

> *The woman can more easily integrate her body meaningfully into the pattern of her life than can the man. It is the man, rather than the woman, who is more likely to feel insecure from his body and alien from it.*

> *The material presented (in Fischer's study,* The Female Orgasm) *indicates with clarity that there is no factual basis for regarding women as psychologically less sexually secure or able than men. To continue to promulgate ideas about such alleged inferiority would seem to be an expression of antifeminine prejudice.*[10]

The female's sexual response cycle is divided into the same four phases as the man's.

Excitement Phase. During the excitement phase, the clitoral shaft increases in diameter and length. The major lips of women who have not had children flatten and separate, exposing the vaginal opening. In women who have had children there is a thickening of the major lips and a slight opening. The minor lips thicken and expand toward the vaginal vault. Within ten to thirty seconds after effective sexual stimulation, lubrication appears in the vagina, and the vaginal vault lengthens and expands.

[9]Ibid., p. 65.

[10]Seymour Fischer, *The Female Orgasm: Psychology, Physiology, Fantasy* (New York: Basic Books, Inc., 1973), p. 393. © 1973 by Basic Books, Inc., Publishers, New York.

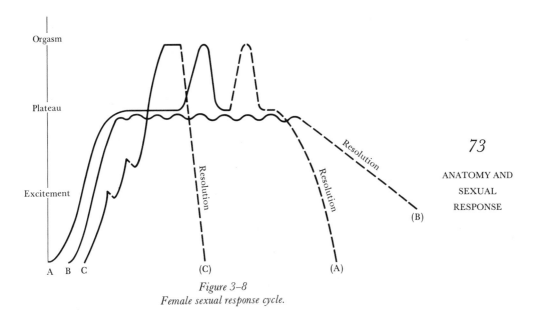

Figure 3–8
Female sexual response cycle.

In both sexes, the nipples of the breast become erect and increase in size when the person becomes sexually excited. The breasts of the female enlarge and develop a pronounced veinous engorgement. A reddening of the skin, called sex flush, typically appears first on the abdomen and then spreads to the breasts during the late stage of excitement. The entire uterus elevates at the onset of sexual stimulation. The cervix slowly retracts upward from the vaginal vault.

Plateau Phase. In the plateau phase, the clitoris draws back and is positioned directly above the pelvic bone. The major lips of women who have never given birth to children may become enlarged. In women who have borne children, the major lips continue to become engorged with blood at this phase of arousal. The outer third of the vagina further increases in length and depth, swelling into what Masters and Johnson have called an *orgasmic platform*. The *Bartholin gland* excretes a liquid which some say aids in the lubrication of the vaginal outlet. The major source of lubrication, however, is the simple perspiration of the vaginal walls.

The nipples become further enlarged and distended, breast size increases, and the engorgement of the *areola*—the pigmented area surrounding the nipple—increases. There is further voluntary and involuntary tension in the face and abdominal muscles.

The uterus becomes fully elevated as the cervix's continued retraction further increases the sensitivity of the vaginal vault.

Orgasmic Phase. During orgasm the clitoris and the major and minor lips do not change in position or appearance. Contractions in the vagina occur at about 0.8 second intervals (as in the male pattern) and recur from five to twelve times. After the first three to six contractions, the intervals lengthen and the intensity diminishes. The breasts do not undergo any noticable change. The sex flush coincides with orgasm in about 75 percent of females. There is a momentary loss of voluntary control of muscle groups, and involuntary muscle contractions are experienced in the face, arms, and legs.

As the involuntary contractions of the orgasmic platform take place in the vagina, there are also involuntary contractions of the anal sphincter. The experience of heavy breathing and increase in blood pressure and heartbeat generally are similar to the pattern experienced by the male. Because the female has a greater variation of orgasmic intensity than the male, she may experience heartbeat rates above 180 per minute.

Just as a male's anxiety over his sexual prowess focuses on his ability to achieve and maintain an erection, so the female's fear centers on her ability to experience orgasm. All women in the Masters and Johnson study were able to achieve orgasm with effective sexual stimulation. The failure of some women to experience it may result from an inability to accept sexuality rather than from a physiological impairment.[11] These fears and inhibitions that men and women bring to their sexual behavior in our society are to a large extent the products of cultural conditioning.

Resolution Phase. Unlike the male, the female does not have a physiologically determined refractory period. She is often capable of experiencing another orgasm immediately if stimulation is resumed. If unstimulated, the clitoris returns to normal size and position within five to ten seconds. The major and minor lips return to normal thickness and position within ten to fifteen seconds. The relaxation of the vaginal wall may take as long as ten to fifteen minutes. The cervical orifice remains open for twenty to thirty minutes.

The areolae rapidly decrease in size, and the nipples return to normal. The sex flush disappears. Muscle tensions rarely are carried more than five to ten minutes into the resolution phase.

In the resolution phase of the female's sexual response, the appearance of a widespread film of perspiration not related to the degree of physical activity is noticeable. In the male, this sweating reaction, when it occurs, is usually confined to the soles of the feet, the palms of the hands, and the genitals, but in females it is often more pervasive.

As Figure 3–8 indicates, there is considerable similarity in the sex-

[11]Masters and Johnson, *Human Sexual Response,* p. 139.

ual response cycle of the male and the female, especially through the plateau stage. The typical female pattern A closely approximates the typical male pattern except that there is no refractory period so that a second orgasm can occur within seconds of the first. (Some men also are capable of experiencing a second orgasm within a few seconds if their refractory period is short.) Figures 3–8 B and 3–8 C represent less typical feminine response patterns. In 3–8 B, the excitement mounts rapidly and immediately bursts into a series of orgasms that are experienced as one sustained climax. In such cases, the resolution phase lasts longer. Pattern C shows more abrupt moments of excitement followed by an intense climax and a rapid resolution.

THE REACTIONS OF OLDER PEOPLE

We are sexual beings all of our lives. Some of us, indeed, may not come to experience the full pleasures of sexual intercourse until we have reached what is commonly regarded as old age.[12] This is an unusual pattern but one that should cause us to think twice before we assume that older people are uninterested in or incapable of sex. The more common course is to bring the pattern of sexual behavior experienced in the middle age into old age, perhaps at a somewhat reduced level.

As with other parts of the body, the process of aging causes changes in the sexual organs. These changes modify, but need not radically alter, sexual performance. Most men and women over sixty-five are capable of experiencing orgasm, although our cultural conditioning often makes them embarrassed about this sexual capacity.

The older male requires a longer period of time to achieve an erection regardless of how exciting the sexual stimulation may be. In many instances, manual stimulation of the penis is necessary, where formerly visual stimulation was sufficient to achieve an erection. In the elderly male, the penis typically does not achieve its full erection until just before orgasm. If he should lose his erection in lovemaking, it is more difficult for him to recover it. However, he is also typically capable of maintaining an erection for longer periods than in his youth. Ejaculation declines in vigor, and in very old age the semen simply flows from the penis rather than being forcefully ejected.

The internal organs may be affected by the aging process. Typically, the scrotum does not change in appearance or structure, but the testes may cease to expand in size during sexual intercourse. The resolution stage is much more abrupt, and the refractory period is likely to last longer. Thus older men generally do not seek multiple orgasms, although some are quite capable of doing so.

[12]Isadore Rubin, *Sexual Life After Sixty* (New York: Basic Books, 1965).

The aging female has more obvious physiological changes to undergo. After *menopause,* the cessation of the menses, the vaginal walls decrease in thickness and lose their color, their texture, and much of their elasticity. Lubrication of the vagina is slower to occur and less complete. The swelling of the first third of the vagina, associated with the plateau stage, becomes less noticeable, but this change is partially compensated for by the increased tightness in the front of the vagina. As with the aging male, orgasmic responses are fewer in number, less intense, and of shorter duration.

The external genitals also undergo a reduction in size. The minor lips, however, continue to swell upon excitation, and the clitoris remains largely unchanged in its sexual sensitivity even into old age. The nongenital physiological response to orgasm in old age is generally less intense.

The uterus undergoes dramatic changes after menopause. When the reproductive period has passed, the uterus diminishes in size until it is no larger than the cervix. Although neither the elevation nor the contraction of the uterus occurs in the typical aging female, some women report unpleasant spasms of the uterus, which disincline them to engage in sexual intercourse. This phenomenon, however, is far from universal. Less than 10 percent of all women have problems during menopause that require the attention of a physician. The majority of women, like the majority of men, can continue to enjoy sexual intercourse into old age.

Thus, despite the stereotyped belief that sexual pleasure is reserved for the young, elderly people are in fact quite capable of leading full and rich sex lives.

Summary

While generalized statements about genitals are helpful in our understanding of human sexuality, particular individual differences may make us feel personally strange or cause difficulty in our adventures in loving. Therefore, we need to look at as well as think about our bodies.

Human sexual response, being much more under the control of the cerebral cortex, is prone to all of the problems that can be encountered in our experience and retained in our memories. Fantasies are occasions for both growth and the development of fear responses that may interfere with our lovemaking should they come to mind. Because so much of human lovemaking is learned behavior, it can be changed or elaborated upon to suit personal preferences and express nuances of meanings in continuing partnerships. Both hormones and social scripts undoubtedly place constraints upon our personal fashioning of our sexual life styles.

Masters and Johnson were much impressed with the similarity of the sexual response patterns they registered in both men and women. Each sex experienced an excitement, plateau, orgasm, and resolution stage. However, women did not experience a refractory period during which they were insensitive to sexual stimuli and could go on to additional orgasms. Men, on the other hand, experienced a refractory period varying in length from a few minutes to over an hour, during which time they could not be restimulated.

While age undoubtedly takes its toll in changing the pace and characteristics of human sexual response, it need not eliminate orgasmic capacity nor inhibit adequate sexual performance. The most common pattern is that older people carry with them the sexual patterns established in middle age, though they rarely have the occasion to feel good about such feelings in the golden years.

Conception

4

In various human populations, fifty percent
of all conceptions are estimated to result
in spontaneous abortion. A large fraction
of these abortions occur during the first
three weeks of pregnancy and generally pass
unnoticed. Thus, in half of the
total conceptions, something is wrong
to begin with.

Francis Jacob

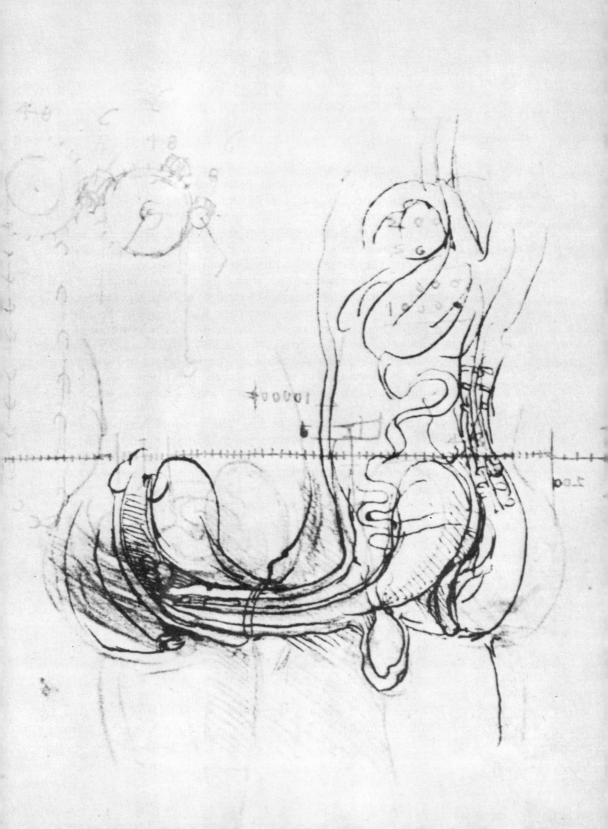

For a long time, one of the inevitable by-products of an active sex life was babies. As we have seen, baby making is one of the primary, and for some the only, purposes of sex.

The scientific name for baby making is *conception.* Conception occurs when a mature sperm meets and enters a mature egg in the female's fallopian tubes. This union of egg and sperm leads to the development of a new person within the mother's body.

Conception does not happen each time the penis is inserted in the vagina and ejaculation occurs. We cannot willfully generate an egg or a sperm, nor can we willfully unite them in conception. We can, however, intentionally increase the likelihood that conception will occur by timing intercourse so that it occurs near ovulation. We can also intentionally prevent conception by various means of birth control. Indeed, the development of contraceptives has depended on an increasingly precise understanding of the processes involved in conception.

The conception of a child by two healthy adults is a function of the timing of intercourse in relationship to ovulation and the lifespan of the egg and the sperm. Men continuously generate new sperm, but women release a mature egg only once a month. These processes are regulated by the sexual control center, whose commands are carried out by hormonal messengers.

Hormones and the Menstrual Cycle

The hypothalamus regulates the menstrual cycle in the human female. The sexual control center in the hypothalamus is sensitive to the amount of hormones in the body. When the level of a particular hormone drops too low, the sexual control center uses its special hormone to stimulate the pituitary gland. The pituitary, in turn, sends out its own hormones that regulate the activities of the other endocrine glands.

Two pituitary hormones that control the ovaries in the female are the follicle stimulating hormone (FSH) and the lutenizing hormone (LH). In response to these two pituitary hormones, the ovaries pro-

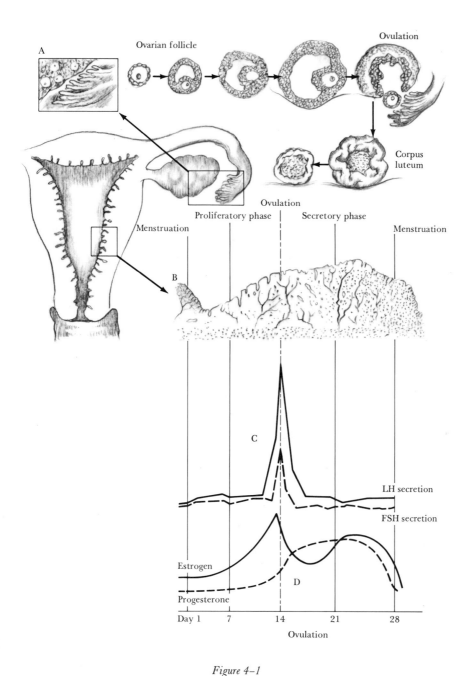

A

Ovarian follicle

Ovulation

Corpus
luteum

Ovulation

Proliferatory phase   Secretory phase

Menstruation   Menstruation

B

C

LH secretion

FSH secretion

Estrogen

D

Progesterone

Day 1   7   14   21   28

Ovulation

Figure 4–1

*A. Ovulation. B. Growth of the uterine lining: Menstrual bleeding (day 1–5); new lining
begins to grow, proliferatory phase (day 6–14); new lining is ready to accept a fertilized
egg, secretory phase (day 15–23); if fertilization does not take place, the lining breaks
down, and menstruation occurs. C. Pituitary hormone levels. D. Sex hormone levels.*
(Birth Control Handbook, *Montreal: Montreal Health Press, Inc., 1975.*)

duce the eggs and the female sex hormones, estrogen and progesterone. The ovaries also produce testosterone, the male sex hormone, in small amounts. (Both men and women have all of the sex hormones in their bodies, but normally in different amounts.)

The regulation of the levels of estrogen and progesterone by the sexual control center in the hypothalamus is a good example of a positive feedback system. The hypothalamus stimulates the pituitary to release FSH and LH. These, in turn, stimulate the ovaries to release estrogen and progesterone. FSH and LH, perhaps together, or perhaps LH alone, cause ovulation—the breaking away of the egg from the ovarian wall. When the levels of estrogen and progesterone are high enough, the sexual control center and the pituitary cease to secrete their hormones. This regular pattern of hormonal release from the hypothalamus, pituitary, and ovaries determines the characteristics of the menstrual cycle (see Figure 4–1).

The menstrual cycle is thought of as beginning on the first day of bleeding. The whole cycle is thought of as the time between the first day of one period and the first day of the next period of bleeding. The average length of this cycle is twenty-eight days, which gives thirteen cycles per year. However, there is considerable variation in this pattern between women and over a single woman's lifetime. Because the hypothalamus is a part of the brain and the nervous system as well as the endocrine system, it is affected by emotional stress. Strenuous or unusual physical exercise, and sometimes lovemaking, can alter the pattern as well.

The cycle is affected by the woman's age and general state of health. Bleeding, commonly referred to as "the period," lasts about five days (three to seven days is the common range). This bleeding is actually the shedding of the inner lining of the uterus, called the endometrium. The total blood loss is about two fluid ounces (about fifty milliliters). The flow is usually heavy at first and tapers off at the end. Most women experience some pain and cramping of the abdomen as the uterus contracts to force the flow out through the cervix into the vagina. In some women, especially those who have never been pregnant, the pain may require medication. Also, although the actual loss of blood is small, some women may feel weaker and more irritable during this time. Iron supplements, available in drugstores, can help if taken daily.

During the period of bleeding the amount of estrogen and progesterone in the blood is low. Therefore, the sexual control center in the hypothalamus signals the pituitary to secrete FSH and LH. These hormones stimulate the growth of several egg-containing follicles in the ovary. These follicles, in turn, secrete estrogen as they begin to develop.

The part of the cycle from day 6 to day 13 is called the *proliferation stage*. During this stage, the body prepares to receive a potential baby. The estrogen released by the ovarian follicles causes the endometrium to grow thicker and changes the composition of the plug at the opening of the cervix to permit easier entry of sperm. At about day 12, the amount of FSH and LH begins to increase rapidly, and one follicle develops more rapidly than the others. It sticks out like a pimple on the wall of the ovary.

Ovulation occurs on about the fourteenth day. The follicle is ruptured as a result of a surge of LH in the blood, and its egg is released into the abdominal cavity. The high level of LH also changes the ruptured follicle on the surface of the ovary into a hormone secreting gland called the corpus luteum. It is probable that this rupture will not occur unless there is a minimum amount of FSH also present in the blood.[1] The flared end of the fallopian tube draws the egg into the tube. In rare instances, the egg does not enter the fallopian tube. If conception occurs, the baby develops in the abdominal cavity outside the uterus. This is called an ectopic pregnancy and must be terminated surgically.

The fifteenth day to the twenty-fifth day of the cycle is called the *secretory phase*. During this phase, the corpus luteum secretes progesterone and estrogen, which causes further growth in the endometrium in preparation for the implantation of the egg that has begun its journey down the fallopian tube. This implantation will occur only if the egg becomes fertilized. Fertilization, or conception, must take place within about one day of ovulation.

If conception has occurred, the egg implants itself in the lining of the endometrium, which has become a bed of sugar-rich tissue and blood vessels. There the fertilized egg develops into two parts. One part becomes the *embryo* and the other the *placenta* ("afterbirth"), the membraneous tissue that lies on the surface of the endometrium and serves to connect the embryo with the mother's blood supply. The placenta also secretes estrogen, progesterone, and other hormones that prevent the pituitary from releasing more FSH and LH. If these pituitary hormones were not suppressed, ovulation could occur again. Thus, the complication of a second pregnancy while the first is underway is prevented.

If the egg is unfertilized (if conception has not occurred), the corpus luteum begins to be absorbed by the ovary along with the other follicles that did not rupture. This takes place about the twenty-fifth day.

[1]Seymour Lieberman et al., "Steroid Hormone Secretions," in *Frontiers in Reproduction and Fertility Control*, eds. Roy Greep and Marjorie Koblinsky (Boston: M.I.T. Press, 1977), p. 35 ff.

During the last three days of the cycle, day 26 to 28—the *premenstrual phase*—the breakdown of the corpus luteum reduces the level of estrogen and progesterone in the blood. Since the egg has not been fertilized, these hormones are not being secreted by the developing placenta either. The low level of estrogen and progesterone in the blood stimulates the sexual control center in the hypothalamus to release the hormone, which stiumulates the pituitary to release FSH and LH, and the cycle is begun again.

MIGRATION OF THE OVUM

In contrast to the male of the species who, after puberty, must continuously produce sperm, the female is born with almost 500,000 eggs already present in her ovaries. Less than 500 of these will be released in ovulation from puberty to menopause. The rest disintegrate.

As we have seen, the egg matures in a follicle on the surface of the ovary. When it ruptures, the egg is released into the abdominal cavity and, by means of a guidance mechanism that is not well understood, passes into the fallopian tube. Along with a small amount of fluid, the egg is propelled by the cilia (tiny hairs) of the fallopian tube toward the uterus. The passage takes about three days. Fertilization must take place within about one day of ovulation.

Fertilization is accomplished when a sperm enters the egg cell. Fertilization normally initiates the cell division of the egg and the development of an embryo. However, it has been possible to induce cell division in the eggs of lower animals such as frogs without the introduction of sperm. Embryos that develop under such circumstances contain the genetic information of the mother only. In the human species it is possible that such a phenomenon—called *parthanogenesis,* or virgin birth—occurs, but none has been unequivocally documented.[2]

As the fertilized egg moves down the fallopian tube, it begins the process of cell division that eventually will produce a full-term baby. There is little change in the overall mass of the fertilized egg as it moves down the fallopian tube, but it continues to divide into cells that form a shell around a liquid core. Between five to seven days after conception, the fertilized egg makes its way to the uterine wall and, with the assistance of enzymes that dissolve the lining of the uterus, it links itself up with the blood supply beneath the tissue. By the tenth to twelfth day, it becomes firmly attached to the uterine wall and has established a continuing supply of nutrient. There is no overt sign of pregnancy at this time, however, because menstruation is not due to occur for several days.

[2]Harold D. Swanson, *Human Reproduction: Biology and Social Change* (New York: Oxford University Press, 1974), p. 23.

Hormonal Control of Sperm Production

The hormonal regulation of sperm production was thought to be parallel to those processes that govern ovulation. That is, the sexual control center in the hypothalamus was thought to stimulate the pituitary to secrete LH and FSH in men as well as women. In the traditional view, LH and FSH regulate the production of testosterone and the production of sperm in the testicles, and male sex hormones, in turn, inhibit the secretion of LH and FSH.

However, recent improvements in the techniques for measuring small amounts of hormones have revealed that the secretion of hormones by the pituitary and the testes seems to come in spurts. Furthermore, the correlation between testosterone levels and the LH peaks in the blood stream of men is poor, in contrast to the reasonably good correlation between estrogen and LH peaks in the blood stream of women. This suggests that the moment-to-moment secretion of such hormones as testosterone is independent of the pituitary-testes feedback system. There is also accumulating evidence that a factor produced in the seminiferous tubules of the testes called *inhibin* may play an important role in the regulation of FSH.[3] Further research will be necessary to determine the precise nature of the hormonal control over sperm production, but the classic model probably adequately describes a part of the process.

Testosterone has been shown to play a decisive role in the generation of sperm. In the testes, testosterone is secreted by specialized cells called *Leydig cells.* These cells may be involved in an independent feedback control over sperm production by means of the regulation of testosterone levels within the tubules of the testes (Figure 4–2). The concentration of testosterone in the testes is many times greater than its concentration in the blood. The increased concentration of testosterone within the tubules seems to provide the right climate for sperm maturation. It also makes storage easier since it reduces their ability to move about once they are mature. Sperm would die if they were exposed to the environment of the normal man's blood stream.

It is now thought that this concentration of testosterone in the testes is maintained by a blood-testes barrier formed by adjacent Sertoli cells (the specialized cells within which the sperm mature; see Figure 4–2) within the testes. The proper maintenance of the barrier may be important in minimizing the production of mutations in human infants due to the effects of drugs. The reduction in the effective-

---

[3] Emil Steinberger et al., "The Control of Testicular Function," in Greep and Koblinsky, eds., *Frontiers in Reproduction and Fertility Control,* p. 279.

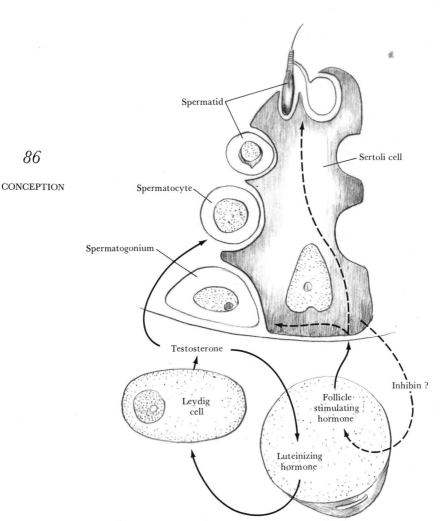

Figure 4–2

*LH action on the Leydig cells of the interstitial tissue and FSH action on
the seminiferous tubules. (Source: William B. Weaves "Leydig Cells," in
Greep and Koblinsky, op. cit, p. 328).*

ness of this barrier, perhaps by chemical means, might provide an effective means of controlling fertility in men (a male "pill").[4]

Eggs are present in the female ovaries at birth. As we have seen, their maturation to ovulation takes place over about a fourteen-day

[4]Emil Steinberger et al., "Sertoli Cells—Primary Site of FSH Activity in the Testes," Seventh Annual Meeting of the Society for the Study of Reproduction, Abstract 21, Ottawa, Canada, 1974.

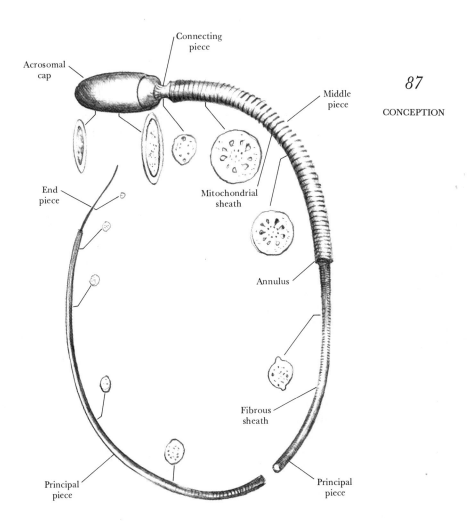

Connecting
piece

Acrosomal
cap

Middle
piece

End
piece

Mitochondrial
sheath

Annulus

Fibrous
sheath

Principal
piece

Principal
piece

Figure 4–3
*A schematic diagram of a typical mammalian spermatozoon. The acrosomal covers the anterior two-thirds of the
nucleus. The connecting piece is implanted in a cavity at the end of the nucleus. The internal structure of the
sperm flagellum is most clear when cross sections at various points are seen. The sperm tail is comprised of three
main pieces: the middle piece, the principal piece, and the end piece. Each piece can be differentiated by its
surrounding sheath. Plasma membrane envelops all of the structures. (In Greep and Koblinsky, op. cit.)*

period. In contrast, sperm production ordinarily begins at puberty in the male and is continuous thereafter. Since intercourse is not necessarily timed to coincide with ovulation, and since a great many sperm are required to insure conception, an enormous number of sperm must be produced to render the human species sufficiently fertile for reproduction. In fact, millions of sperm reach maturity each day. Their production takes about eight weeks. Human sperm are incredibly complex organisms (Figure 4–3). Unlike the much larger egg that must be propelled by the tiny hairs that line the fallopian tube, sperm are able to move around by themselves.

The development of sperm, which is called *Spermatogenesis,* can be divided into three phases. The first phase involves the generation of relatively simple cells called *spermatogonia* (Figure 4–2). Most of these cells proliferate to give rise to cells of the second stage called *spermatocytes,* but the remainder retain their number by renewing themselves. Spermatocytes undergo cell division (meiosis) to produce cells called *spermatids.* These contain half of the chromosome information of the spermatocytes. (The mature egg also contains half the chromosome information of the normal female cell. At conception, the two halves join to make a new whole.) The spermatids of the third phase of spermatogenesis undergo an extremely complex metamorphosis and emerge as the highly differentiated, mobile *spermatazoon* (Figure 4–3). The process by which this extremely complex cell is generated from the relatively simple spermatocytes is imperfectly understood.

MIGRATION OF THE SPERM

The sperm produced in the testes are stored for a period of time in the *epididymis,* a coiled tube lying alongside of the testes in the scrotum. During storage the sperm are immobile. Apparently some maturation occurs during storage in the epididymis, but the precise amount of time required for full maturity is not known. If sperm are stored for three or four weeks, they are less likely to be capable of fertilizing the egg. After a time, if the sperm are not ejected, they are absorbed into the cells lining the walls of the epididymis.

Most of the material that is ejaculated, however, is not sperm from the epididymis, but secretions from the accessory glands, particularly the seminal vesicles and the prostrate gland. These secretions are thought to spur the sperms' activity and to provide nourishment for them as they travel to meet the egg. The secretions may also serve to neutralize the acid environment of the vagina, which would otherwise exterminate the sperm. The vaginal fluids probably stimulate the sperm to swim faster. It is also probable, however, that muscular contractions of the various organs during orgasm greatly facilitate the sperm's journey to the egg. The sperm are immobilized if they remain in the vagina for more than a few hours. But, if they reach the fallopian tubes, they can remain capable of fertilizing the egg for a period of one to three days.

While 400 to 600 million sperm may be ejaculated into the vagina, fewer than 100 make it into the fallopian tubes. Only one sperm actually penetrates the egg and contributes its genetic material to the developing embryo, but many sperm are needed in order to soften the cellular layer surrounding the egg sufficiently so that one can penetrate. While there may seem to be an enormous wastage of sperm in this process, it is insignificant in comparison to the 100 billion cells replaced in the intestine or the billions of skin cells that are discarded each day. Certainly, there is no evidence to support the notion that the ejaculate represents a significant loss of energy to the male, thus causing him to feel "spent." The exercise required to deliver the sperm may produce such feelings, however.

Infertility

About 10 to 15 percent of all couples in the United States are involuntarily childless. Sometimes their childlessness can be overcome by minor adjustments in their lovemaking techniques or by hormonal treatment. For others surgery or extended treatment may be necessary. For some it is a permanent condition called *sterility*. About 40 percent of infertile marriages are a result of a sterile male partner.[5] When a couple wishes to have a child, a year of unsuccessful results should alert them to the need of seeing a physician.

The physician normally will take complete medical histories. Each partner will have a complete physical examination with particular attention given to the reproductive organs. A series of laboratory tests will be made to rule out infections, anemia, and hormonal deficiencies. The husband will be tested more thoroughly in the early stages because his infertility is more easily determined. He will be instructed to bring a complete ejaculation for a sperm count. Such a count should contain between 60 million and 100 million sperm per cubic centimeter, 60 percent of which should be active.[6] In this con-

[5]William Masters and Virginia Johnson, *Human Sexual Response* (Boston: Little, Brown, 1969), p. 107.

[6]Lawrence Crawley, Ames L. Malfetti, Ernest I. Stewart, Jr., and Nini Vas Dass, *Reproduction, Sex, and Preparation for Marriage,* 2nd ed. (Englewood Cliffs, N.J.: Prentice-Hall, Inc., 1973), p. 218.

nection, it is important for us to be clear about the distinction between infertility (or sterility) and low fertility. As the figures just cited indicate, a normal ejaculate contains an immense number of sperm, but only one sperm is needed to fertilize an egg. If a man's ejaculate contains a significantly smaller number of sperm, or if the sperm are significantly less active than normal, the chances of his impregnating a woman are reduced. Because fertilization is still possible, such a man is not sterile. But, unless steps are taken to increase the odds in his favor, he may not succeed in impregnating his mate. Various techniques are available for increasing the sperm count. Artificial insemination with the husband's sperm is also a possibility when the problem is one of low mobility of the sperm.

If tests of the husband indicate that the failure to conceive cannot be traced to a low sperm count or low sperm activity, the wife will be instructed to keep a temperature chart during her menstrual cycles in order to help determine when and if she ovulates. If it is determined that the female is ovulating and that the male is producing adequate sperm, further tests will be necessary. These tests will focus on the female.

For example, to see if the fallopian tubes are obstructed, "Rubin's test" will be performed. This test consists of forcing carbon dioxide into the uterus. If the pressure diminishes, the tubes are clear. If the tubes prove to be open, the cervix is examined. Normally, the mucus of the cervix impedes the progress of the sperm to a considerable degree, except during ovulation, when it becomes thinner and more penetrable. Thus abnormality in the composition and viscosity of this mucus is a possible cause of infertility.[7]

There are many more tests that can be performed to help diagnose the causes of infertility. About half of the infertile couples who come to clinics can be helped to have children. Many can be helped to conceive with a minimum of tests. In a few cases, a woman has conceived after she and her husband sought help from a clinic but before anything had been done for them—an indication that the couple's infertility may well have had a psychological cause.

Artificial Insemination

In those instances in which the wife has been shown to be fertile while her husband has been diagnosed sterile, the couple may wish to conceive through artificial insemination. This is not a totally successful

[7]Ibid., p. 219.

procedure, but many women have become pregnant by this means and it is now widely available. In artificial insemination, the sperm from a fertile male is mechanically inserted into the vagina by a physician at a time when the woman is ovulating. Conception and impregnation then take place in the normal way. Because the decision to use artificial insemination can involve religious, legal, moral, psychological, and physiological questions, it is important that any couple considering this approach learn all the facts about this procedure.

Many people, especially men, react to the idea of artificial insemination with a spontaneous feeling of aversion. The initial reaction of many husbands is one of repugnance, and they often express the feeling that a child produced by the sperm of an anonymous donor would not really be their child. In a sense, of course, this is true, but often husbands who feel this way are quite willing to adopt a child once they are convinced they are sterile—a clear indication that such husbands are not in fact unwilling to accept responsibility for the rearing of children who are not their biological offspring. Perhaps

Figure 4–4
A man can store his sperm in a sperm bank before having a vasectomy to be used if he should later decide to have children. A sterile man and his wife could obtain sperm from an anonymous donor through the sperm bank. In both cases, the woman would be impregnated by artificial insemination. (© John Marmaras, Woodfin Camp & Associates)

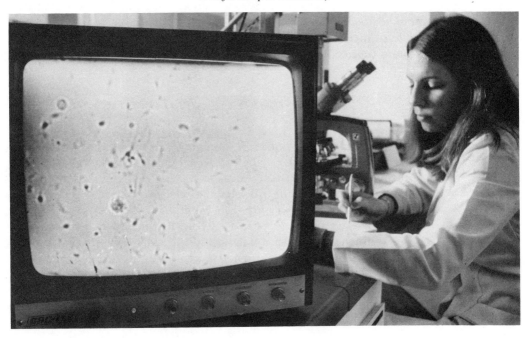

one way to look at artificial insemination is as a sort of semiadoption in which the husband agrees to raise what is in effect for him an adopted child, while the wife, who is capable of conception, can enjoy the personal satisfaction that comes from carrying and giving birth to a baby.

In some cases, women have been artificially inseminated with their husband's sperm. As mentioned previously, this procedure is recommended when either a low sperm count or low sperm mobility makes it extremely unlikely that the woman will conceive by her husband's sperm unless it is enriched—that is, concentrated—artificially and assisted in its journey to meet the egg. The enriched sperm can be inserted directly into the uterus, thus reducing the length of its journey and the likelihood that it will be exterminated by the acid fluids of the vagina.

Concubinage

An ancient custom recorded in the Old Testament permitted an infertile wife to appoint another woman, usually a slave, to bear a child for her. Thus Sarah had children for Abraham by means of the concubine, Hagar. Recent television coverage was given to a couple who asked a friend to fulfill this ancient role. The husband's sperm was artificially injected into the friend's womb and she conceived. Our social conventions are strongly opposed to concubinage, but given the marked decline in the number of babies available for adoption because of increasingly effective birth control techniques, we may come around to accepting this practice once again.

Summary

While human sexual behavior that might lead to conception is not determined by hormones, the internal production of egg and sperm and the preparation of the uterus to receive the fertilized egg is hormonally controlled. The menstrual cycle, ordinarily described as a twenty-eight day cycle, is affected by many influences such as stress, physical exercise, and general bodily health. In practice there is thus considerable variation in the length of this cycle. Ovulation normally occurs on the fourteenth day and conception must occur within about one day of ovulation. Because sperm can survive for three days or so after they have reached the fallopian tube, and because ovulation may occur within a few days of its expected time (or be induced by intercourse, perhaps), conception may occur when it is not expected. It requires careful analysis to precisely determine the day of ovulation in order to increase the likelihood that infertile couples will conceive. A year of trying unsuccessfully to have a baby should alert the couple to possible difficulties that might require medical attention. About half of all couples who seek such help can be helped.

93

CONCEPTION

Birth Control

5

Underdeveloped societies . . . practice little contraception and virtually no sterilization.
Consequently, the tendency is to postpone the issue
of controlling pregnancy until a later point in the reproduction process,
which means that when a couple wishes to avoid children, those
methods nearest the point of parturition—abortion and infanticide—are employed.
Industrial societies, on the other hand . . . [use] readily available
institutional mechanisms with respect to marriage and [employ] the possibilities
of their advanced technology for conception control.
Gradually, in the late stages of industrial development,
contraception has gained such predominance
that it has made [other approaches] unnecessary.

Kingsley Davis and Judith Blake

The average healthy couple has an estimated 60 percent chance of conceiving a child during the first year of lovemaking if they do not take any measures to prevent conception. By the choice of a suitable means of birth control and its intelligent use any couple can insure that they will have the number of children they want and no more. This permits both greater freedom to enjoy sex and greater responsibility to make sure that every child that is born is wanted and every wanted child is born.

Birth control is not limited to contraception, although it is frequently assumed that the two terms are synonymous. *Birth control* is a general term that applies to any method used to prevent the birth of children. *Contraception,* on the other hand, refers only to those methods that prevent conception from occurring in the first place. There are four basic techniques of birth control: abstinence, contraception, sterilization, and abortion. Each technique has its own costs as well as benefits. The decision to control conception by means of a particular technique must take these factors into consideration. Controlling conception by any artificial means is at odds with the official position of the Roman Catholic church, and some individuals, non-Catholics as well as Catholics, may also be opposed to birth control in any form. However, many other people have come to see the various birth control techniques as sensible solutions to the problem of unwanted pregnancy.

Abstinence

One method of birth control that is socially approved, especially for unmarried people, is abstinence, the self-imposed denial of sexual intercourse. The extent to which abstinence has actually been used in practice varies considerably from culture to culture and from time to time. As Martin Goldstein and Erwin Haeberle have written, "One can safely assume that, on the whole, this moral demand cannot be, has never been, and is not now being met because sexuality is an integral part of human life which cannot permanently be suppressed by public opinion or individual effort."[1] Nevertheless, some people—usu-

[1] Martin Goldstein and Erwin Haeberle, *The Sex Book* © 1971 by Herder and Herder, Inc. Used by permission of The Seabury Press, Inc.

ally those who are very religious—are able to practice abstinence as a form of self-discipline. Commonly, they are intent on transforming carnal love into a spiritual love that considers all people as worthy of love.

Within marriage temporary abstinence from sexual intercourse may be necessary during illness, in the later stages of pregnancy, or in the early postpartum period. But abstinence as a regularly practiced means of birth control runs contrary to the sexual urges of most people. Unless it is to have troublesome side effects, the practice of abstention must be a mutual decision on the part of both partners. For one partner to make such a decision unilaterally is to disregard the needs of the other. However, abstinence from one form of sexual behavior need not mean abstinence from all sexual behavior. Even in those cases where abstinence from intercourse is desirable, an imaginative couple still may enjoy sexual outlets such as mutual oral or manual stimulation.

Contraception

Techniques to prevent conception are part of the folk wisdom of most peoples. Early attempts to control fertility frequently involved magic, superstition, and religious beliefs. The practice of *coitus interruptus* (withdrawal of the penis before ejaculation) is thought to be forbidden in the Bible.[2] The oldest records on the subject come from Egypt and date from between 1900 to 1100 B.C. The methods employed were related to the understanding of the reproductive process at the time and to the traditional beliefs of the culture in question. The ancient Chinese, for example, believed that a woman would not become pregnant if she remained completely passive during intercourse. The Egyptians are responsible for the oldest known medical prescription for a contraceptive—a vaginal suppository concocted of crocodile dung and honey. Various other unbelievable substances have been advised at one time or another, including mouse dung, amulets, and induced sneezing. The Greeks believed that oil impeded the movement of the sperm and advised inserting oil-permeated material such as paper into the vagina to cover the cervix.

Ancient peoples are not alone in having folk methods for preventing conception. Even today various folk ideas persist, many of which are unsupported by evidence of their effectiveness. For ex-

[2]The Sin of Onan ("spilling one's seed on the ground"), which has been interpreted to mean masturbation, as well as withdrawal is probably an injunction against Onan's refusal to have children by his brother's widow, thus violating a custom of the time called the levirate (Gen. 38:8–9). See Paul Blanchard, "Christianity and Sex," *The Humanist* (March/April 1974), pp. 27–32.

ample, some people believe that having intercourse while standing will prevent pregnancy, or that if the woman urinates immediately after intercourse she will avoid becoming pregnant. We also tend to cloud the issue when we assert that certain periods of the month are "safe" periods. Masters and Johnson have shown this to be largely wishful thinking.

Recent studies of contraceptive use in the United States, however, indicate that we are rapidly becoming a nation of effective contraceptive users. According to a study conducted by Princeton University, by 1970 over half (52 percent) of the couples likely to conceive were protected by effective contraceptive techniques.[3] The most commonly used method over all ages is the oral contraceptive (the Pill), but among wives between the ages of thirty and forty-four, sterilization has become the most commonly used method. Most significantly, perhaps, is the fact that if all of the unwanted pregnancies were eliminated through totally effective contraceptive use, the United States fertility rate would be below replacement.[4] As late as 1965, it appeared that a family-planning approach would not be enough to insure zero population growth, as couples were continuing to want more children.[5]

In spite of the Roman Catholic church's official position on birth control, more and more Catholic women are using effective contraceptives (Table 5-1). Westcoff and Ryder predict that by 1980 there will be no significant difference in contraceptive practices between Catholics and non-Catholics. Differences between races and classes are also rapidly diminishing.[6] If these trends continue it seems reasonable to assume that the United States will reach the goal of zero population growth within a relatively short period of time, something that was hardly thought probable a decade ago.

CONTRACEPTIVE TECHNIQUES

Modern interest in contraceptive technology has produced a host of contraceptives that vary greatly in terms of effectiveness, cost, and convenience. Some have no side effects; some have considerable side effects. The choice of which contraceptive to use depends on many factors in a person's life, not the least of which is his or her motivation for using contraceptives. If a couple already has the number of

[3]Charles F. Westcoff and Norman B. Ryder, *The Contraceptive Revolution* (Princeton, N.J.: Princeton University Press, 1977), p. 333.

[4]Ibid., p. 336.

[5]Judith Blake, "Population Policy for Americans: Is the Government Being Misled?" *Science* (May 2, 1968), p. 524.

[6]Westcoff and Ryder, *The Contraceptive Revolution*, p. 335.

children they desire, for example, sterilization might be the best option for them. Age, marital status, frequency of sexual intercourse, and the pattern of a person's sexual life style all need to be taken into consideration.

The following is a survey of some common contraceptive alternatives. We begin with those available without a doctor's prescription, in order of effectiveness.

The Condom. Perhaps the most widely used contraceptive in the

Table 5-1

CONTRACEPTIVE PRACTICE. Method of contraception used most recently by white non-Catholic (NC) and Catholic (C) women, by age.

AGE OF WOMEN

Most recent method	Under 45				Under 30				30 to 44			
	1965		1970		1965		1970		1965		1970	
	NC	C	NC	C	NC	C	NC	C	NC	C	NC	C
Sterilized[a]	10	4	12	5	5	2	5	2	12	5	19	8
Pill[b]	21	12	33	28	37	24	49	38	11	6	19	19
IUD[c]	1	*	5	6	1	*	6	7	1	*	4	4
Diaphragm[d]	12	4	7	4	8	1	3	3	15	5	10	5
Condom[e]	20	14	12	10	17	11	10	10	22	15	15	11
Withdrawal	4	6	2	2	3	2	1	1	5	9	2	3
Foam	3	1	6	5	5	2	8	8	2	1	3	3
Rhythm	4	28	3	14	3	25	2	10	5	29	4	19
Douche	5	3	4	3	4	3	2	3	6	3	5	3
Other[f]	6	5	4	3	6	5	3	4	6	4	4	2
None	13	23	12	19	12	23	9	14	15	23	15	24
Percent total	100	100	100	100	100	100	100	100	100	100	100	100
Number of women	2,666	1,090	3,708	1,255	1,038	403	1,723	602	1,628	687	1,985	653

* Less than 1 percent.

[a] Surgical procedures undertaken at least partly for contraceptive reasons.

[b] Includes combinations with any other method.

[c] Includes combinations with any method other than the pill.

[d] Includes combinations with any method other than the pill or the IUD.

[e] Includes combinations with any method other than the pill, IUD, or diaphragm.

[f] Includes other multiple, as well as single, methods and a small percentage of unreported methods.

Source: From Charles F. Westcoff and Norman B. Ryder, *The Contraceptive Revolution* (Copyright © 1977 by Princeton University Press), published for the Office of Population Research, Princeton University, Table 11–9, p. 29. Reprinted by permission of Princeton University Press.

United States is the *condom*. It is the only mechanical device used by males. It is cheap, easy to use, easy to obtain, easy to dispose of, and effective.

The condom is a thin, flexible sheath that fits over the erect penis. It measures about seven and a half inches in length (eighteen centimeters). In common language, condoms are known as "rubbers," "prophylactics," "French letters," and "skins." The rubber type is the most widely used; an estimated 700 million are sold annually in the United States. They come packaged, rolled, and ready for use, sometimes with a small amount of lubricant. There are two major types of condom in use today—plain end and reservoir tip. Choice between them is wholly a matter of personal preference, as both are equally effective.

The cap type, which fits only over the glans of the erect penis, offers poor protection and is more likely to slip off.

Condoms without reservoir tips should be unrolled about a half an inch before being placed on the erect penis. This half inch should be firmly squeezed to prevent an air pocket from forming when the rest of the condom is unrolled. If the condom is not lubricated, some lubricant may be applied to increase the ease of insertion into the vagina. Petroleum jellies should not be used as lubricants with a condom. They tend to erode the rubber and can cause mild irritation.

Figure 5–1
Contraceptives that once had to be requested from behind the counter are now openly displayed on drugstore shelves. (© Jim Anderson, Woodfin Camp & Associates)

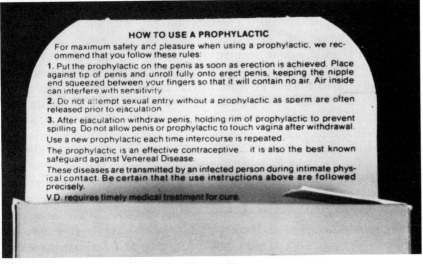

HOW TO USE A PROPHYLACTIC

For maximum safety and pleasure when using a prophylactic, we recommend that you follow these rules:

1. Put the prophylactic on the penis as soon as erection is achieved. Place against tip of penis and unroll fully onto erect penis, keeping the nipple end squeezed between your fingers so that it will contain no air. Air inside can interfere with sensitivity.

2. Do not attempt sexual entry without a prophylactic as sperm are often released prior to ejaculation.

3. After ejaculation withdraw penis, holding rim of prophylactic to prevent spilling. Do not allow penis or prophylactic to touch vagina after withdrawal.

Use a new prophylactic each time intercourse is repeated.

The prophylactic is an effective contraceptive... it is also the best known safeguard against Venereal Disease.

These diseases are transmitted by an infected person during intimate physical contact. Be certain that the use instructions above are followed precisely.

V.D. requires timely medical treatment for cure.

Figure 5–2
(Michal Heron)

Good lubricants are contraceptive foam or jelly. Once intercourse is completed, the ring end of the condom should be held tightly around the shaft of the penis as it is withdrawn. The condom should be checked for any obvious leakage. Any indication of condom failure should be followed up by a "morning-after pill" within seventy-two hours. Such a pill cannot be obtained without a prescription.

A condom can fail if it has a hole in it, breaks during intercourse, slips off, or loses sperm because the man does not retain his erection long enough after ejaculation to allow safe withdrawal of both penis and condom.

The use of condoms in combination with spermicidal foam or cream increases their effectiveness. Even when used alone, the condom produces an effectiveness rate of only 10 to 15 pregnancies per 100 women per year.[7] The condom is also the only contraceptive method presently available that reduces the chance of contracting gonorrhea and syphilis.

Spermicidal Substances. These are substances that kill sperm before they can enter the cervix. They are readily available in drugstores and are easy to use. They come in various forms, including foams, jellies, creams, and suppositories. Plastic applicators enable women to inject the substance into the vagina before intercourse. This must be done at least ten to fifteen minutes before ejaculation and must be re-

[7]Donna Cherniak and Allan Feingold, *Birth Control Handbook* (Montreal: Montreal Health Press, Inc., 1975) p. 22.

done if intercourse is to be repeated. The foam type of spermicide (actually a cream packaged in an aerosol can) provides the best distribution within the vagina.

Another chemical contraceptive is the vaginal suppository, a small solid cone that melts at ninety-five degrees Fahrenheit. These suppositories must be inserted at least fifteen minutes before ejaculation. Vaginal tablets that are supposed to dissolve in the vagina are also available. These tablets may present problems because they are very unstable in damp climates and may need more moisture than is present in the vagina in order to dissolve. Both tablets and suppositories are less effective than foam. They depend a great deal upon mixing with the natural lubricants and are difficult to disperse properly. The pregnancy rate with the suppositories is 5 to 27 pregnancies per 100 women per year; that of the tablets is 8 to 27.[8] Part of the reason for these high failure rates is the fact that if ejaculation occurs before the suppositories melt sufficiently to lubricate the vagina, mixing and dispersion of these agents does not occur to an adequate extent. Foam has a failure rate of about 3 to 10 pregnancies per 100 women per year when properly used—a somewhat better rate than that reported for creams and jellies.

Douches. The term "douching" refers to washing out the vagina. It is one of the most ineffective methods of contraception in common use, even if done immediately after intercourse. Indeed, many physicians feel that douching is less effective than doing nothing because the washing fluid, which is not a spermicide, may serve to increase the distribution of the sperm and thus may actually increase the likelihood of conception. About the best thing that can be said of the technique is that it is very simple. It requires only a douche bag and tap water, sometimes with the addition of some substance believed to make douche more effective. Some of the common products used for douching include vinegar, lemon juice, soap, and salt. In actuality, these additions add little to the spermicidal qualities of tap water and may, in fact, irritate the vaginal tissues. Since it is possible for sperm to make their way into the cervical canal (beyond the reach of the douche) within one or two minutes after ejaculation, douching as a contraceptive method is quite limited. The failure rate is about 20 to 62 pregnancies per 100 women per year.[9]

Withdrawal. Probably the oldest known method of birth control is withdrawal, technically known as coitus interruptus. This method,

[8]McCary, James L., *Human Sexuality: A Brief Edition* (New York: Van Nostrand Reinhold Company, 1973), p. 94.

[9]Westcoff and Ryder, *The Contraceptive Revolution*, Table 11-9.

which is still common throughout the world, requires that the male withdraw his penis from the vagina before he ejaculates. Although many people find this practice satisfactory, others find it very frustrating because the man must withdraw at the crucial moment—or sooner—and must wait a considerable time before engaging in intercourse again. Since a man may ejaculate without knowing it, this is a very unreliable technique. What is more, the secretion of the Cowper's gland, which is given off prior to ejaculation, may contain enough sperm to impregnate the woman. The withdrawal method has a failure rate of from 20 to 30 pregnancies per 100 women per year.[10] Cultural variations in style of lovemaking may make this method more effective in some societies.

The Rhythm Method. The rhythm method is the only contraceptive technique endorsed by the Roman Catholic church. It requires that a couple abstain from sexual intercourse during what is presumed to be the woman's fertile period. This method is unreliable, particularly in women whose menstrual cycles are irregular. Only about 30 percent

Table 5-2
The calendar rhythm method

Length of shortest period	First unsafe day after start of any period	Length of longest period	Last unsafe day after start of any period
21 days	3rd day	21 days	10th day
22 days	4th day	22 days	11th day
23 days	5th day	23 days	12th day
24 days	6th day	24 days	13th day
25 days	7th day	25 days	14th day
26 days	8th day	26 days	15th day
27 days	9th day	27 days	16th day
28 days	10th day	28 days	17th day
29 days	11th day	29 days	18th day
30 days	12th day	30 days	19th day
31 days	13th day	31 days	20th day
32 days	14th day	32 days	21st day
33 days	15th day	33 days	22nd day
34 days	16th day	34 days	23rd day
35 days	17th day	35 days	24th day
36 days	18th day	36 days	25th day
37 days	19th day	37 days	26th day
38 days	20th day	38 days	27th day

Source: Donna Cherniak and Allan Feingold, *Birth Control Handbook* (Montreal: Montreal Health Press, Inc., 1975), p. 36.

[10]Cherniak and Feingold, *Birth Control Handbook*, p. 22.

of all women have sufficiently regular menstrual cycles to enable a reasonable pinpointing of the so-called safe period.[11] When you consider that some women ovulate in response to sexual stimulation, the whole procedure becomes even more unreliable.

The calendar method of determining the safe period is based on the length of the woman's shortest and longest menstrual cycle over an eight cycle sequence. The fertile period is determined by subtracting eighteen days from the length of the shortest cycle to determine the first unsafe day, and subtracting eleven days from the longest cycle to determine the last unsafe day. A women using this method must continue to record the length of her cycles and base her calculations on the most recent eight cycles. Table 5-2 suggests how an essentially seven day unsafe period relates to cycles of varying length.

A more sophisticated variation of the rhythm method is based on the fact that a woman's temperature changes slightly during her menstrual cycle. To use this method, the woman must take her temperature every morning immediately after she wakes up, and before eating, drinking, smoking, or getting out of bed. One of the major problems with this method is that many women have no marked or consistent temperature changes. What is more, colds or sore throats may throw off the temperature chart. Both rhythm and temperature methods have a median pregnancy rate of 15 to 31 per 100 women per year.[12]

Hope. Hope is not a method. The consequences of sex should be treated seriously, not as a game of Russian roulette.

The most effective contraceptives are those that are obtainable only with a doctor's prescription. These are discussed in order from least to most effective. As we will see, increased risk goes along with increased effectiveness.

The Diaphragm. The diaphragm is a thin, rubber dome-shaped cup attached to a flexible rubber-covered metal ring about three inches (7.5 centimeters) in diameter. The diaphragm is meant to cover the cervix, thus preventing sperm from entering the uterus. The diaphragm must be fitted by a physician. If it is not the correct size and shape for a particular woman, it will be highly ineffective. A woman can be fitted for a diaphragm before she has experienced sexual intercourse, but, since sexual intercourse tends to enlarge the vagina, she should be checked again a few weeks after she has begun to experience intercourse. After childbirth a woman should not resume use of the diaphragm she was using before she decided to become pregnant.

[11]Ibid., p. 22.

[12]Garrett Hardin, *Birth Control* (New York: Pegasus, 1970), p. 129

Changes in the size or shape of her cervix may well cause it to be ineffective, so she should be fitted with a new one. She should be tested for possible refitting after any miscarriage, surgical operation on the lower abdomen, or after a loss or gain of weight of more than ten pounds. If properly inserted, the diaphragm should not interfere with the conduct or pleasure of sexual intercourse.

The diaphragm is properly in place when the front rim fits snugly against the pubic bone and the back rim fits tightly over the cervix (see Figure 5–4). Before insertion, about one tablespoon of spermicidal cream should be smeared over both surfaces of the diaphragm and some additional cream spread around the edges. The diaphragm is ordinarily inserted more or less like a tampon. The woman squats or stands with one foot raised. The diaphragm is squeezed into a long narrow shape between the thumb and first finger, with the dome pointing downward. The vaginal lips are spread apart with the other hand and the device is inserted into the vagina. It is pushed along the lower vaginal wall until the far rim passes the cervix. Then the front rim is tucked up behind the pubic bone. Once it is in place, the finger should check to be sure that the cervix is completely covered. After being fitted for a diaphragm, the woman will normally be allowed enough time to practice this procedure under the doctor's direction until she feels she does not need any further assistance.

The diaphragm must be used with spermicidal cream or jelly. A

Figure 5–3
A planned parenthood clinic is a good place to get information
about contraception. (© Watriss-Baldwin, Woodfin Camp & Associates)

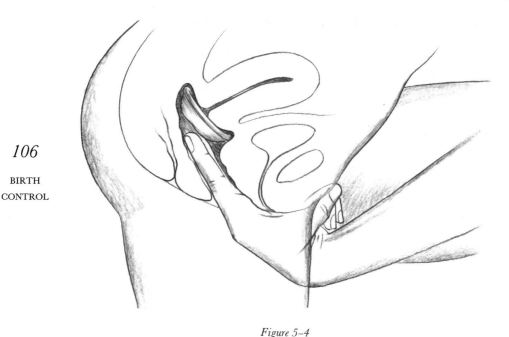

Figure 5–4
Diaphragm insertion.

common error is the mistaken assumption that a diaphragm itself is an adequate means of contraception. Another common misconception is that any form of jelly will work. Grape jelly belongs with peanut butter, not on a diaphragm. In order to insure the effectiveness of the jelly, the diaphragm should be inserted no more than four to six hours before intercourse. If a woman does not know in advance that she is going to have intercourse, she will either have to use a diaphragm habitually or stop during lovemaking to insert the diaphragm. An unwillingness to interrupt sex play in order to insert a diaphragm is one common reason for the failure of the diaphragm method. (Such an insertion could be made a part of the lovemaking, which might make it less annoying for some women.) If the device is habitually left in place, a spermicidal foam must be applied no more than an hour before intercourse. Insertion of a spermicidal could also become a part of love play. After intercourse, the diaphragm should remain in place for at least six hours, although it may be left in for as long as twenty-four hours.[13] The diaphragm should be removed and washed, and additional jelly should be applied, before reinsertion.

[13]Ruth Brecher and Edward Brecher, eds., *An Analysis of Human Sexual Response* (New York: Signet Books, 1966), p. 102.

The diaphragm fails because it is not used when it should be, because it is incorrectly inserted, because it cannot be perfectly fitted to accommodate all changes that occur in the vagina during love-making, and because vigorous lovemaking involving multiple insertions of the penis sometimes dislodges it.[14] It is more likely to fail when the woman is on top of the man than when the man is on top of the woman.

The diaphragm-plus-spermicide method fails for any one of a number of reasons between 4 and 10 percent of the time; the failure rate of diaphragms used without spermicidal substance increases to 5 to 20 percent.

The Cervical Cap. Another mechanical device similar to the diaphragm is the cervical cap. It is smaller than the diaphragm, shaped like a large thimble, and is made of rubber, plastic or metal. It is also known as a pessary (as is the diaphragm). This device is much more popular in Europe than in America. In contrast to the diaphragm, which covers the cervix and a portion of the end of the vagina, the cervical cap fits only over the end of the cervix. Because of the differing sizes and shapes of cervixes, not all women can use these caps. It takes more skill to insert a cervical cap properly than to insert a diaphragm, but once inserted it can be left in place for days or weeks. As with the diaphragm, it may become dislodged during intercourse, but this is less common. The failure rate for cervical caps is about 8 percent.

The IUD. There are a large number of intrauterine devices (IUDs) on the market. An intrauterine device is small, made of metal or plastic, and is implanted in the uterus to prevent pregnancy. IUDs come in a wide variety of sizes and shapes. They do not all have the same level of effectiveness, and different types have different side effects.

The use of intrauterine devices goes back to the ancient Greeks, and a version of the device that is centuries-old is still used on animals in the Sudan and Tunisia. Arab camel drivers insert a round stone in the uterus of the female camel before a long journey across the desert. During the nineteenth century a variety of intrauterine devices were used for gynecological disorders and for contraception, but in the early twentieth century these devices fell into disrepute. Many early models suffered from high rates of expulsion and often required surgical removal because they damaged the uterine wall, often causing hemorrhaging.

In the 1930s a German physician, E. Grafenberg, developed a

---

[14]Mary S. Calderone, ed., *Manual of Family Planning and Contraceptive Practice,* 2nd ed. (Baltimore: The William and Wilkin Company, 1970), p. 234.

coiled silver ring that produced a failure rate of 1.6 pregnancies per 100 women per year. Nevertheless, there was strong opposition to his device, and IUDs remained unpopular until 1959. In that year two reports, one by an Israeli who had worked with Grafenberg and one by a Japanese physician, triggered new enthusiasm for the IUD. Failure rates were 2.4 and 2.3 per 100 per hundred women per year, and no serious complications were reported. These studies involved a total of 21,500 women.[15]

In spite of the fact that physicians still do not know why the IUD works, its demonstrated effectiveness and ease of use has made it popular in the United States since 1959. The total number of IUD users is unknown, but informed estimates suggest that about 5 million women in the world were using the IUD in 1968—about 1 to 2 million of them in the United States.

For those women who can use the IUD successfully, it is probably the best device available. But, unfortunately, about 10 to 12 percent of all women users expel their IUDs within one year of insertion. About 8 to 10 percent must have it removed because of complications, and about 2 to 3 percent become pregnant even with it in place. Only about 75 percent, therefore, find it an effective method after one year of use. By the end of 2 to 3 years, only about half of these will continue to use the device.[16]

The IUD is most effective for women over thirty who have given birth. It should not be inserted if a woman has an infection of the uterus or has a uterus that is severely tipped back. Pregnant women and women who have had an abortion or delivery within eight weeks are also advised against having an IUD inserted.

While the insertion of the IUD is a simple procedure when done by a physician, women can experience great pain during and after insertion. This is normally due to the cramping of the uterine wall. This cramping is similar to what occurs during menstruation, but more constant. In most cases, the cramps become quite mild after the first few hours, but for other women medication may be required even after a number of days.

There are four basic kinds of IUDs.

1. Closed rings, such as the original Richter-Grafenberg ring, which are no longer used because they are not as effective as the modern devices.

2. Plastic IUDs, which can be used up to five years before they become too brittle and must be removed. Of the plastic IUDs now in use, the Lippes Loop is the most widely used and the

[15]C. Tietze, "Oral and Intrauterine Contraception: Effectiveness and Safety," *International Journal of Fertility,* 13 (October–December, 1968), pp. 337–84.

[16]Cherniak and Feingold, *Birth Control Handbook,* p. 22.

most effective. The Dalkon shield at first promised great effectiveness, but recent research has indicated that it is not as effective and has serious complications. This shield should not be used.

3. *Stainless steel IUDs* such as the Majzlin spring. This device should no longer be used because it tends to become buried in the uterine wall.

4. *Copper IUDs* such as the Copper T, which can be used up to two years before the copper coating becomes absorbed in the blood stream. More research is needed before the advantages and disadvantages of this device can be accurately determined.

A physician inserts the device by dilating the cervix and inserting a tube through which the IUD may be pushed through into the uterus. All IUDs have tiny nylon threads attached to them that hang down through the cervical opening into the vagina. The wearer or a doctor can tell if the IUD is in place by checking for the presence of these threads. This should be done after every menstrual period. Some of the new models are treated with barium so that they can be easily seen on x-rays. The IUD in no way affects the fertility of the woman or the health of the children she might bear after it has been removed. If a woman wishes to become pregnant, the IUD must be removed by a physician. After birth it may be repositioned in the uterus until another pregnancy is desired.

The current failure rate for the IUD is on the order of 1.5 to 8 pregnancies per 100 women during the first year of use, with slightly lower rates thereafter.[17] Because the IUD can be expelled without the user's notice, frequent checks to make sure it is in position are important.

The Pill. There are two basic types of pills: sequential and combination. Combination pills, which are the most common types of oral contraceptives, are composed of a mixture of synthetic progesterone and estrogen. Sequential pills provide these hormones in sequence rather than in combination. The first fifteen pills contain estrogen, while the last five contain a mixture of estrogen and progesterone. Enovid, Ortho-Novum, and Norinyl are examples of the progesterone-estrogen "combination" type pill. Ortho-Novum SQ and Norquen are examples of the "sequential" type. Both types prevent ovulation by creating the hormonal balance found in pregnancy. The sequential pills are less effective than the combination pills. While about 0.1 pregnancies per 100 women per year occur when combination oral contraceptives are used, this figure increases to 0.5 pregnancies per 100 women per year with sequential types.[18]

[17]Calderone, *Manual of Family Planning,* p. 288.

[18]Tietze, "Oral and Intrauterine Contraception," p. 378.

Research has established that high dosages of estrogen are mainly responsible for the pill's side effects. The pills on the market today contain less estrogen than the first birth control pills did. Recently, combination pills with still lower doses of estrogen have become available, for example, Demulen, Norestrol, and Lo/Orval. Each of these types—combination, sequential, and low estrogen combination—has its own effectiveness and side effects. The proper matching between a particular woman and a particular pill requires a doctor's evaluation and careful follow-up study. Most commonly, women are advised to change their prescription from time to time in order to reduce the risk of adverse side effects.

Two additional variations have been introduced, primarily to help the woman remember when she is to take her pill. Both techniques are based on a 21:7 sequence. In the first instance, the woman takes twenty-one pills, stops for seven days, and then resumes her pills regardless of when her period began. In the second instance, she takes one pill every day, but seven out of twenty-eight in the sequence are placebos.

Regardless of its form, the pill is a powerful agent in the human body. It can have both physiological and psychological effects. Therefore, to give clear indicators of who should not use the pill is a very difficult task. A complete medical examination is necessary before a physician can prescribe the proper pill—if one is to be used. Apparently, women who have very irregular menstrual cycles are likely to experience more complications—particularly in regard to having more children after they have stopped taking the pill—than those with more regular cycles. Also, women who have histories of cardiovascular troubles may experience complications from the use of the pill. Women who have had difficulty with blood-clotting, sickle cell anemia, severe heart disease or defect, severe endocrine disorders, or any form of cancer should not take the pill. The adverse psychological effects of the pill are more difficult to detect and predict.

Among the side effects of the pill, the most serious seems to be an increased risk of death from thromboembolic (clotting) disorders. About 3 out of every 100,000 women on the pill can be expected to die as a result of clotting caused by the pill.[19] This is about three times the rate for nonpregnant women who don't take the pill. On the other hand, women using other means of birth control have about 3.5 times greater likelihood than pill users of dying from complications caused by pregnancy, childbirth, and post partum problems, and women who use no contraceptive at all are 7.5 times more likely to die as a result of complications in maternity than pill users.[20]

[19]Celso-Roman Garcia, "Clinical Aspects of Oral Hormonal Contraception," in Calderone, ed., *Manual of Family Planning*, pp. 302–18.

[20]Calderone, ed., *Manual of Family Planning*, p. 318.

Many of the discomforts associated with use of the pill, such as dizziness, headaches, bleeding, weight gain, and the like, have not yet been reliably researched, largely because these symptoms also occur frequently in women not taking the pill. It is difficult to determine what percentages of instances are caused by the pill. Most of the symptoms pill users experience tend to diminish or disappear after a few months, but many women have become discouraged because of such discomforts.

The advantages of the pill are obvious. It does not interfere with sexual intercourse, does not depend on knowing beforehand that one is going to have intercourse, and, when taken properly, has the highest rate of effectiveness of any of the contraceptives yet made available. In principle, the effectiveness of the pill is 100 percent by the second month of use. Missing one pill will not normally have serious consequences if two are taken the next day, but missing two or more pills invites a fair risk of failure.[21]

CHOOSING THE PROPER CONTRACEPTIVE

Although the choice of a particular contraceptive technique should depend on personal as well as technical considerations, one authority has suggested that if medical safety is the major concern, then the proper order of choice should be the diaphragm, the IUD, and then the pill. On the other hand, if prevention of pregnancy is the major consideration, then the ranking should be the IUD, the pill, and the diaphragm.[22] (Other professionals, however, rank the pill first in terms of efficiency.) If prevention of venereal disease is a major factor to be considered, then the condom offers the greatest protection and the lowest risk. Even those contraceptives that may be obtained without a doctor's prescription offer considerable protection and are preferable to using nothing at all.

EXPERIMENTAL CONTRACEPTIVES

As is the case with the existing range of contraceptives, most experimental contraceptives are aimed at women. However, scientists have begun to develop male contraceptives. There are a number of promising contraceptives still in the experimental stage.[23]

The continuous progesterone pill (mini-pill) may eliminate most of the side effects commonly experienced with oral contraceptives, but it

[21]Cherniak and Feingold, *Birth Control Handbook,* p. 18.

[22]Hugh J. David, *Intrauterine Devices for Contraception: The IUD* (Baltimore: The William and Wilkin Company, 1971), p. 53.

[23]See Lawrence Crawley et al., *Reproduction, Sex, and Preparation for Marriage,* 2nd ed. (Englewood Cliffs, N.J.: Prentice-Hall, Inc., 1973), pp. 209–13.

	STERILIZATION	PILL	INTRAUTERINE DEVICE (IUD)
		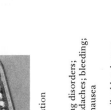	
How it works	Permanently blocks egg or sperm passages	Prevent ovulation	Uncertain; may stop implantation of egg
Possible side effects	Psychological only	Blood-clotting disorders; dizziness; headaches; bleeding; weight gain; nausea	Initial discomfort and irregular bleeding
Physician assistance required	Operation performed by physician	Must be prescribed by doctor; periodic checkups required	Must be inserted by physician; periodic checkups required
Average pregnancy rate/100 women/year	Hysterectomy: 0.0001 Tubal ligation: 0.04 Vasectomy: 0.15	Combination: 0.1 Sequential: 0.5	1.5–8

	DIAPHRAGM (WITH CHEMICAL)	CONDOM	SPERMICIDAL SUBSTANCES

How it works	Barrier to sperm	Prevents sperm from entering vagina	Barriers to sperm; kill sperm before entering cervix
Possible side effects	Chemical may cause irritation	Loss of sensation	May cause irritation
Physician assistance required	Fitting	None	None
Average pregnancy rate/100 women/year	4–10	10–15	Tablets: 8–27 Suppositories: 5–27 Foam: 3–10

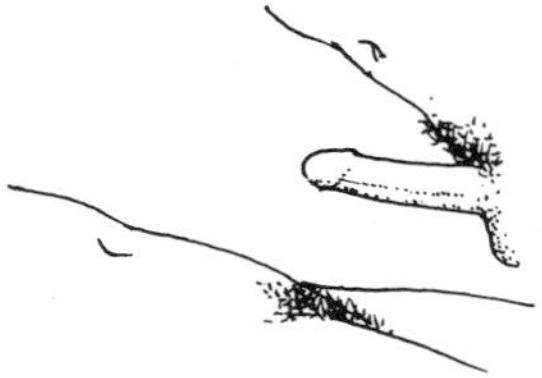

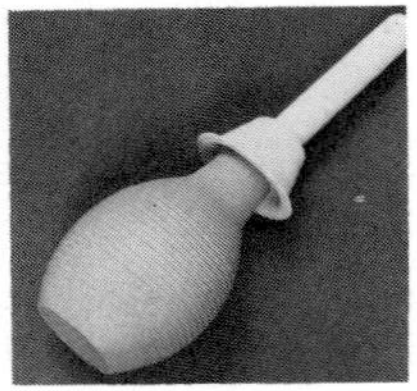

	WITHDRAWAL	RHYTHM	DOUCHE
How it works	Withdrawal of penis from vagina before ejaculation occurs	Abstinence during female's fertile period	Rinses sperm from vagina
Possible side effects	Psychological only	Psychological only	None
Physician assistance required	None	Consultation	None
Average pregnancy rate/100 women/year	20–30	15–31	20–62

Figure 5–5
Comparison chart of various methods of birth control.

must be taken at the same time every day without fail or the woman incurs a risk of pregnancy. The "morning after pill," an oral contraceptive that has been around for twenty years or more, prevents the implantation of the fertilized egg. But the massive dose of synthetic estrogen (called Stilbestrol) interferes with the normal endocrine balance, producing changes in the uterus that cause staining, bleeding, and disruption of the menstrual cycle. What is more, research findings indicate some dangers associated with it—particularly a higher rate of vaginal cancer in female offspring should the pill fail. In sum, it is erratic and unpredictable and leaves much to be desired at present, though it is better than nothing in emergencies such as rape. Continuous low-dose progestin injections promise to be more effective than the mini-pill, but at present the side effects seem much too costly. The implantation of a small capsule of progesterone under the skin will have lasting effects for a year, but has been found to have the same costly side effects as the low-dose progestin injections.

The vaginal ring is a chemical-mechanical device about the diameter of the diaphragm (7.5 centimeters). It is filled with synthetic progesterone that suppresses ovulation. Menstrual cycles are achieved by removing the ring for seven days every twenty-eight days. Preliminary reports have thus far indicated few side effects. The insertion of very small amounts of progesterone—about the same dosage as in a typical pill—directly into the uterus in a time capsule device that releases the hormone over the course of a year promises to be a vast improvement over the pill. By using an extremely low dosage of progesterone that affects only the uterus, researchers hope to eliminate the side effects associated with oral contraceptives. However, there is great variation from patient to patient in the effects produced by progesterone. This makes it very difficult to precisely determine the amount of the substance required to make the procedure effective at such low dosages.

Copper devices inserted into the uterus prevent the implantation of the egg in the uterine wall. This variation on the IUD has been tested with over six thousand women, with some complications beginning to suggest that this device is not an improvement over plastic IUDs.

There are only three points of control in developing male contraceptives: sperm production, sperm maturation, and sperm transportation. The production and maturation of the sperm is at present less well understood than the production and maturation of eggs. Under-the-skin capsules containing testosterone, a hormone which prevents sperm production, have been tested and evaluated, but the effective dosage has thus far escaped researchers. Similar capsules are being tested with compounds that interfere with sperm maturation. Stopping the transportation of sperm by inserting a removable plug into the vas deferens is currently being evaluated. A procedure that would reduce the testosterone level in the testes and thus inhibit sperm production seems theoretically feasible, but is not yet practical.

Sterilization

The prevention of conception through surgery is called *sterilization.* The sterilization of either the male or the female is a quite different kind of birth control from those we have been discussing because, for the most part, such operations are irreversible. Nevertheless, voluntary sterilization is becoming increasingly common in the United States.

Sterilization in either the male or the female can be eugenic, therapeutic, or a means of birth control. A eugenic sterilization is done to prevent the inheritance of genetic defects such as mongoloidism. A therapeutic sterilization is done when the husband or wife has certain chronic diseases or disabilities. As a means of birth control, sterilization is undertaken to insure that no unwanted children will be conceived. Some couples have themselves sterilized once they have had the number of children they desire. If the male stores some of his sperm in a sperm bank before he is sterilized, it then becomes possible for the couple to have children in case they should change their minds about family size. He can also use the sperm to impregnate another woman should he remarry.

VASECTOMY

There are two basic ways to surgically sterilize a man. One is castration, the surgical removal of the testicles. Few men would voluntarily submit to such a disfiguring and emotionally painful procedure. But, recently, a much more benign procedure called a vasectomy has been developed.

Vasectomy consists of cutting and tying the vas deferens (the tubes linking the testes with the urethra through which sperm travel during ejaculation). A local anesthetic is injected into each side of the scrotum, and an incision is then made on each side of the scrotum above the testicles. The vas is then tied in two places. The segment between the ties is then cut and usually removed. Vasectomy is a simple procedure that can be done in a doctor's office. The procedure takes about fifteen minutes. As a surgical procedure, it is not 100 percent effective because some men have more than one vas deferens, and one might be missed. But such cases are rare.

The vasectomy does not affect a man's sexual response. Some men have difficulty with the idea of voluntary sterilization because they

Intact male
reproductive
organs and
ducts

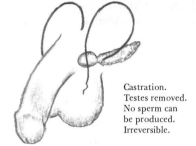

Castration.
Testes removed.
No sperm can
be produced.
Irreversible.

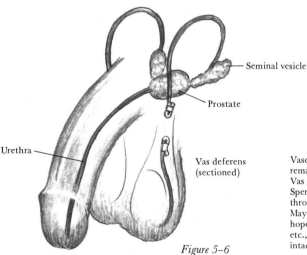

Seminal vesicle

Prostate

Urethra

Vas deferens
(sectioned)

Vasectomy operation. Testes
remain and produce sperm.
Vas deferens severed.
Sperm have no duct to pass
through and are reabsorbed.
May be reversed with some
hope of success. Blood vessels,
etc., to testes must remain
intact.

Figure 5–6

Vasectomy operation. (From Human Reproduction; Biology and Social Change *by
Harold D. Swanson. Copyright © 1974 by Oxford University Press, Inc.
Reprinted by permission.)*

equate masculinity with fertility and because they think of vasectomy
as castration. Such men may have some emotional problems to overcome should they finally decide on the operation. Procedures that can
reverse a vasectomy are being evaluated, but it is best to think of the
operation as final and permanent.

The major problem with vasectomy as a method of birth control
occurs when intercourse is resumed too soon after the surgery. Because many sperm remain in the vas after the vasectomy, it is necessary to verify sterilization by means of a sperm count. This should be
done after about twenty postoperative ejaculations. If there are no
sperm in the twenty-first ejaculate, the man can be considered sterile.
Until sterility has been determined, some other form of birth control

should be used. Because sperm constitute only a small portion of the semen, the amount of semen ejaculated by vasectomized males is not noticeably changed.

TUBAL LIGATION

Tubal ligation, commonly called "tying the tubes," is the most common operation for sterilizing women. In principle it is similar to the vasectomy. The cutting of the fallopian tubes prevents the egg from reaching the uterus and the sperm from reaching the egg. While this approach covers a number of techniques that are presently in use, they are all more complicated than the vasectomy because they require the surgeon to enter the abdominal cavity, thus increasing the risk of infection and surgical error. They also require the use of a general anesthesia that makes them major medical procedures even though some may be performed on an outpatient basis.

More recent techniques employ the use of a laparascope, a long tube-like instrument with light source, mirrors, and cauterizing equipment. This instrument is inserted through a surgical incision commonly made just below the naval or just above the pubic hair. The abdominal cavity is inflated with carbon dioxide in order to render the tubes accessible to view and to cauterization. The surgeon can see the tubes through the mirror system and seal them through the use of an electrical current. Cauterization, however, is sometimes not complete. In other cases the tubes heal sufficiently to restore fertility. In some cases the adjacent organs are damaged, thus requiring further surgery. In general, the procedure is effective, however.

Even if done on an outpatient basis, tubal ligation techniques are much more expensive than a vasectomy and, as we have said, place the patient at greater risk.

Figure 5–7
A man undergoing a vasectomy. The procedure takes about 15 minutes, requires only local anaesthesia, and can be done in the doctor's office. (Watriss-Baldwin, Woodfin Camp & Associates)

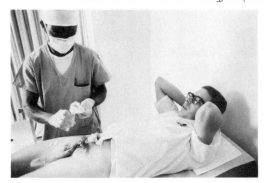
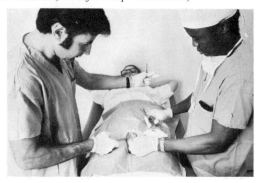

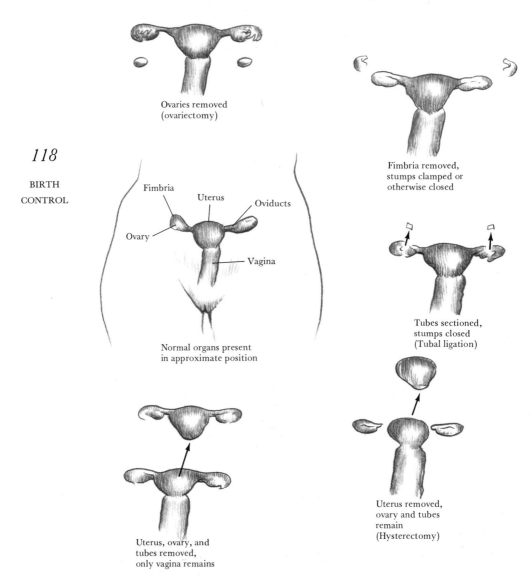

Ovaries removed
(ovariectomy)

Fimbria removed,
stumps clamped or
otherwise closed

Fimbria

Uterus

Oviducts

Ovary

Vagina

Normal organs present
in approximate position

Tubes sectioned,
stumps closed
(Tubal ligation)

Uterus removed,
ovary and tubes
remain
(Hysterectomy)

Uterus, ovary, and
tubes removed,
only vagina remains

Figure 5–8
Various methods of female sterilization. (From Human Reproduction
by Harold D. Swanson)

Three other procedures that result in sterilization for women are the panhysterectomy (removal of all internal reproductive organs) hysterectomy (removal of the uterus), the oophorectomy (removal of the ovaries), and the salpingectomy (removal of the fallopian tubes). These are normally performed for the purpose of correcting various abnormal conditions rather than for birth control purposes.

Research is being conducted on various procedures for clipping or tying the tubes in such a way as to permit reversibility, but none as yet are considered to be ready for widespread use.[24]

Female sterilization could be greatly simplified if surgery could be avoided altogether. This can be done by approaching the fallopian tubes through the body's natural passageway (vagina-cervix-uterus), and cauterizing the tubes by means of an electric current or caustic chemical that would cause scar tissue to form. Another possible use of this approach to the fallopian tubes would be to insert plugs or mesh into the tubes, thus blocking them without surgery. Neither of these techniques have been perfected as yet.[25]

Abortion

Abortion is considered to be a method of birth control, not contraception because conception has occurred. Abortion means the premature termination of a pregnancy. This may come about involuntarily as a result of some physical problem. Such *spontaneous abortions* or miscarriages occur in about one out of every ten pregnancies, usually within the first three months. Strictly speaking, although it may have the effect of controlling population growth, spontaneous abortion is not a form of birth control since it is not planned.

Induced abortion is a term used to describe the intentional termination of pregnancy through surgery. Menstrual extraction is a technique for removing the endometrium by means of a suction tube inserted into the uterus. Its purpose is to eliminate the nuisance of menstrual bleeding. It has been recommended by some as a procedure to be followed regularly or when a period is late—before the woman knows she is pregnant. If she is pregnant, it is a form of abortion.

HISTORICAL OVERVIEW OF ABORTION

Throughout history there have been a variety of attitudes toward abortion. A Chinese manuscript over four thousand years old is said to record the oldest method of abortion. Within the Jewish tradition there are no laws against abortion either in the Talmud or Judaic law because Judaism, like Japanese Shintoism, believes that the fetus becomes human only when it is born. Aristotle reflected Greek thinking on this matter when he said that abortion was an acceptable means of birth control when other means failed. In fact, the ruling classes prac-

[24]Roy O. Greep, Marjorie A. Koblinsky, and Frederick S. Jaffe, *Reproduction and Human Welfare: A Challenge to Research* (Cambridge, Mass.: The MIT Press, 1976), p. 288.

[25]Ibid., p. 289.

Figure 5–9
(above, © Joel Gordon;
right, © Leif Skoogfors, Woodfin Camp & Associates)

ticed abortion so extensively that the ratio of citizens to slaves declined alarmingly. Attempts to outlaw abortion to rectify this situation met with only partial success.

Today, the strongest and most vocal opponent of abortion is the Roman Catholic church. It is not widely known that the Church's position on abortion has changed over the centuries. In the twelfth century, abortions were allowed if the fetus was not over forty days old if it were a male, and eighty days old if female. (The Church in those days did not say how it was possible to make a determination of the sex of the fetus.) It was not until four centuries later, in 1588, that Pope Sixtus V declared that all abortions were a form of murder. But three years later Gregory XIV reverted to the earlier law. Gregory's pronouncement remained canon law until 1869 when Pius XI condemned all abortion. The present attitude of the Church is thus only a little more than one hundred years old. Until fairly recently, our laws reflected this attitude. Only therapeutic abortions in cases where the mother's health was in danger were allowed. However, public opinion has gradually come to favor liberalizing our laws on abortion. By 1972 eighteen states had greatly liberalized their abortion laws along the lines suggested by the American Law Institute's model penal code, and four (Alaska, Hawaii, New York, and Washington) had made abortion a matter of a woman's choice in consultation with her physician, provided the abortion was performed early in the pregnancy.[26] In 1973 the Supreme Court of the United States of America ruled that all existing state laws prohibiting abortion were unconstitutional. As a result of this ruling all states had to permit abortion in the early months of pregnancy at the discretion of the doctor and the patient. Abortion became a medical matter, not a legal one. But in 1976 the court modified its ruling and declared that the states should determine the conditions under which abortion was to be per-

[26]Ruth Roemer, "Legalization of Abortion in the United States," in *The Abortion Experience: Psychological and Medical Impact,* Howard J. Osofsky and Joy D. Osofsky, eds. (New York: Harper & Row, 1973), pp. 284–86.

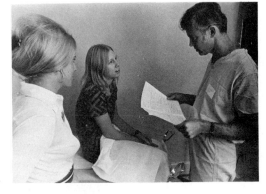

Figure 5–10
Abortions performed under medical supervision—
the procedure explained by the doctor and performed under
sterile conditions—are safer than childbirth.
(© Watriss-Baldwin, Woodfin Camp & Associates)

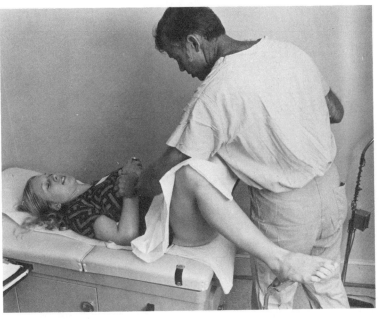

mitted. Thus there is considerable variation in the circumstances (age, consent, etc.) under which abortion is legal in this country.

HAZARDS OF ABORTION WITHOUT PROPER MEDICAL SUPERVISION

Because of the legal restrictions on abortion in the past, women had to resort to illegal means to obtain an abortion. As a result, many abortions were performed under nonsterile conditions by unskilled individuals. Understandably, the death rate under these conditions was very high. Where abortions are legal, they can be performed in sterile conditions under proper medical supervision with much greater safety for the woman. Indeed, abortion under such conditions is less dangerous than childbirth. For example, in Czechoslovakia, where abortion is legal, there was not a single death in 140,000 abortions during 1963–1964.[27] In New York City between July, 1970 and July, 1972, there were 4 deaths in 261,700 abortions. These figures translate into a death rate of 1.5 per 100,000 abortions. Childbirth, in contrast, causes death in about 83 per 100,000 pregnancies.[28]

[27]Lawrence Lader, *Abortion* (Boston: Beacon Press, 1966).

[28]Cherniak and Feingold, *Birth Control Handbook,* p. 46.

Figure 5–11
Vacuum curettage: A. the vacurette is inserted through the cervical canal; B. the suction is activated and material is processed through the tube; C. when the process is completed, the uterus pulls on the vacurette.

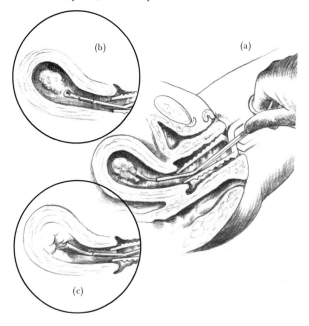

Figure 5–12
The misuse of abortion could best be avoided by educating
people about effective means of contraception.
Abortion should be a last resort, not one's first defense, against pregnancies.
(© Jim Anderson, Woodfin Camp & Associates)

Four medical procedures are available today to induce abortion.

1. vacuum extraction (Figure 5–11)
2. dilation and curettage
3. the saline method
4. hysterotomy

The first two methods can be used up to the twelfth or thirteenth week of pregnancy. A fifth method, which makes use of chemicals called prostaglandins, is in the experimental stage.

Abortion is not something that a woman can bring about herself without running serious risks. Many women believe that they can easily terminate a pregnancy by taking a pill or by some mechanical means such as falling downstairs, pounding the abdomen, or inserting some foreign substance into the uterus. Although amateur attempts at abortion often succeed in terminating the pregnancy, they commonly do so with grisly results for the woman, causing permanent and serious injury in many cases, and death in many others. There is no way short of clinical intervention that a pregnancy can be terminated without grave risks to the woman. The folk wisdom that says that pregnancy can be terminated by taking a "black pill" (ergot) neglects to mention that the dosage necessary to terminate the pregnancy may also terminate the mother's life. "Hot douches, strong purgatives, high diving, bouncing downstairs and parachute jumping are equally ineffective."[29]

Liberalized abortion laws were not designed to create a situation in which abortion becomes a major means of contraception. Abortion should be used only when all other contraceptive techniques have failed. Adequate understanding of contraceptives and other birth control techniques will help accomplish this objective. The most rational, humane, and healthy social approach is to prevent conception in the first place when children are not desired.

Summary

Contraception is increasingly common. During the past three quarters of a century, conception has come increasingly under the control of couples planning for a family. Over half of all couples in the United States who are likely to conceive an unwanted child are at

---

[29]Crawley, *Reproduction, Sex, and Preparation for Marriage,* p. 91.

present using an effective birth control technique such as the pill, the IUD, or sterilization. The number of wanted children has also dramatically declined during the past decade so that if all unwanted pregnancies were eliminated the fertility rate would drop below replacement. More and more persons are becoming effective contraceptive users. There will undoubtedly be more dramatic developments in the control of conception in the near future.

125

BIRTH
CONTROL

Pregnancy and Childbirth

6

The rise of modern civilization, while resulting
from many causes, was contingent
on the suppression of the inordinate cyclic
sexual drive of women. . . . Women's uncurtailed
continuous hypersexuality would drastically
interfere with maternal responsibilities . . . with
the rise of the settled agriculture
economies, man's territorialism became expressed
in property rights and kinship laws.
Large families of known parentage were
mandatory and could not evolve until the
inordinate sexual demands of women
were curbed.

Mary Jane Sherfy

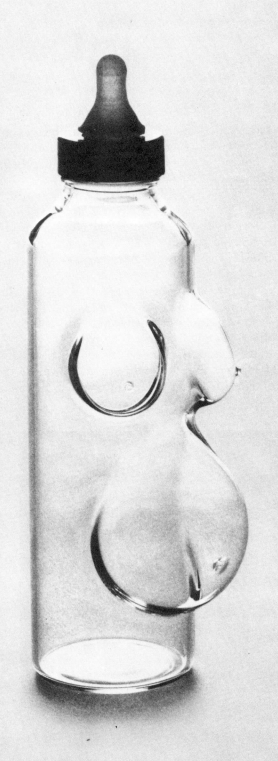

Having sex can produce a child. When this child is wanted by both partners, the time of pregnancy can be a time of preparation and expectation. But even wanted children require considerable alterations in the couple's routine. Pregnancy is just the first step in this series of changes.

Women who are expecting for the first time may feel considerable anxiety. Although it took two people to make the baby, only one gets to carry it. Because the baby develops within the woman's body, some women (and many men) feel that, until it is born, the baby is the woman's responsibility. Most women take this responsibility very seriously and worry a great deal about what is going on inside them. Pregnant women need to feel that people close to them understand what is happening to them and care about them. Given this support, pregnancy can be a time of great joy as the man and woman work together in preparation for the birth.

This chapter focuses on the events of pregnancy as experienced by the mother. Only brief attention is given to the progress of the developing fetus. The chapter closes with a discussion of childbirth.

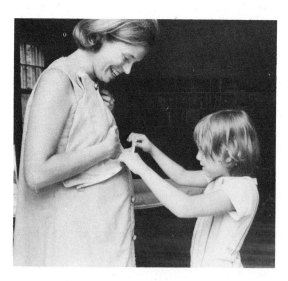

Figure 6–1
Feeling that people close to her are involved with what is happening to her and care about her is especially important to pregnant women.
(Michal Heron)

Pregnancy

The process of having a child can be looked at from two points of view: From the baby's viewpoint, the process is called *development* and involves changing from a one-celled organism to multicelled human being. The process of carrying a baby during its development is called *pregnancy*.

These two processes are even dated differently. Development begins when the egg is fertilized. But pregnancy is commonly timed from the date of the last menstrual period, which ordinarily occurs two weeks before fertilization. A normal pregnancy can vary in length from 240 to 300 days. During this time the mood of the expectant mother may change dramatically as her body adjusts to the different hormone levels and physical discomforts of pregnancy, and her relationship with her loved ones is stressed by this new circumstance in their lives.

EARLY SIGNS OF PREGNANCY

Some women become aware that they are pregnant very early in the process. Others may not notice anything until they are several months pregnant. One of the first signs of pregnancy is the failure to menstruate. Although not a reliable sign, it certainly is a sign that most women recognize. It is not considered a reliable sign because women may fail to menstruate for many reasons other than pregnancy. For example, emotional upsets, illnesses, age, and conditions associated with nursing a child, may also cause a woman to miss a period. To complicate the matter further, some women still emit a smaller menstrual flow even while they are pregnant. This diminished menstrual flow is called "spotting." Spotting can be an early

Figure 6–2
(Joel Gordon)

sign of miscarriage. However, it normally occurs in about 20 percent of all pregnancies and does not necessarily mean that something is wrong. Since missing a single period may not be a sign of pregnancy and, since some women continue to bleed for the first two or three months after conception—though usually at a much reduced rate—missing a period can not be considered a reliable sign.

Other more reliable signs include increased sensitivity and enlargement of the breasts, and tenderness of the vaginal opening. There may be a bloated feeling due to an increase in the amount of water retained by the body. Many women report feeling very tired. Bowel movements may become irregular and the woman may need to urinate more frequently. Constipation results from the higher levels of the hormone progesterone, which causes the smooth muscles of the intestine to relax, thus reducing their efficiency. The increased need to urinate also results from hormonal changes and from pressure on the bladder caused by the growing uterus.

Another common sign of pregnancy, nausea or "morning sickness," is not well understood. It varies in intensity from woman to woman and from pregnancy to pregnancy in the same woman. It usually occurs during the first six to eight weeks of pregnancy (two to four weeks after the missed period). According to one theory, morning sickness results from the accumulation of estrogen and acids in the stomach. Eating lightly throughout the day, munching crackers or dry toast slowly before getting up, avoiding greasy, spicy food, and drinking apricot nectar seem to help overcome the nausea.[1] Many women never experience morning sickness, and those who do usually feel better by the third or fourth month.

TESTS FOR PREGNANCY

A woman should see a doctor as soon as she suspects that she is pregnant. A doctor can tell for sure whether or not she is pregnant and can help the woman to take proper care of herself and her baby.

Two tests are commonly used to confirm pregnancy. These tests may be given by a doctor or nurse at a clinic, hospital, or pregnancy lab. Both involve the detection of a hormone called HCG (human chorionic gonadotropin), which is found in the bloodstream of pregnant women.

In the more old-fashioned biological tests, a urine sample is injected into a laboratory animal. If the hormone is present, the animal will ovulate. This process takes a few days and is less frequently done today. In the faster immunological procedure, a drop of urine is

[1]Boston Women's Health Book Collective, *Our Bodies, Ourselves,* 2nd ed. (New York: Simon and Schuster, 1976), p. 257. Copyright © 1971, 1973, 1976, by the Boston Women's Health Book Collective, Inc. Reprinted by permission of SIMON & SCHUSTER, a Division of Gulf & Western Corporation.

mixed on a slide with two other substances. If the hormone is present, the mixture will not form a clot. This process takes about two minutes. Either of these tests is 95 to 98 percent accurate if it is not performed too early (before sufficient HCG is present in the blood). HCG levels are high enough about three weeks after conception—about one week after missing a period. The tests are not perfect, however. Some women never have positive test results even when they are pregnant. The tests cost about five or ten dollars. Pregnancy labs can be found listed in the Yellow Pages, and local women's groups can help assess their services.

A do-it-yourself pregnancy test has recently been put on the market. It is available in drugstores without a doctor's prescription. The kit contains everything you need in premeasured amounts and costs about ten dollars. The advantages of using this at-home version are privacy and speed. The test is fairly accurate when done about nine days after a missed menstrual period. But, whether negative or positive, the results should be confirmed by a physician.

A newly developed test called the beta unit HCG radio immunoassay is not yet widely available. It is an extremely accurate test that measures the level of HCG in the blood and can detect pregnancy about eight days after ovulation or about five days *before* the first missed period.[2]

Another way to give a pregnancy test involves the injection of large amounts of progesterone into the blood stream. If the woman is not pregnant, such an injection will induce her delayed period. However, because the injection of large amounts of progesterone can accentuate the hormonal disturbances that are likely to have caused the delayed period in the first place, some authorities contend that this test should never be given.[3]

A pelvic examination is commonly used to confirm pregnancy. Pregnancy causes the tip of the cervix to soften and to change from a pale pink to a bluish color. The uterus changes its shape and softens. Such examinations are quite effective when done by trained clinicians. Sometimes a woman first realizes that she is pregnant when she is given such an examination during a physical checkup.

Once pregnancy has been established, the most likely date of delivery can be determined within five days in most instances by the use of the following formula: add one week to the first day of the last menstrual period, substract three months, then add one year. Sixty percent of all deliveries will be made within five days of the projected date.

A lot happens to the woman and the baby during the nine months

[2]Ibid., p. 258.

[3]Donna Cherniak and Allan Feingold, *Birth Control Handbook,* 12th ed. (Montreal: Montreal Health Press, Inc., 1974), p. 17.

of pregnancy. We can't see what's happening to the baby inside the uterus, but simple observation tells us that pregnant women go through a whole series of physical changes. For convenience, doctors divide pregnancy into three equal parts called *trimesters*.

THE FIRST TRIMESTER

Women respond to pregnancy, even one that is planned, in various ways. What is happening to her body and her changed status can combine to make a woman unsure of herself in her new role. She is now a pregnant woman. In some societies, pregnant women are considered beautiful. The Bible describes them as "great with child." However, in our society, with its emphasis on slim figures, the bulging lines of pregnancy are not as widely admired. Some of us have to cultivate our appreciation of those forms, while such appreciation comes more naturally for others.

Pregnancy brings about a change in social status that is difficult to define. Many women feel that it marks their maturity. Others feel

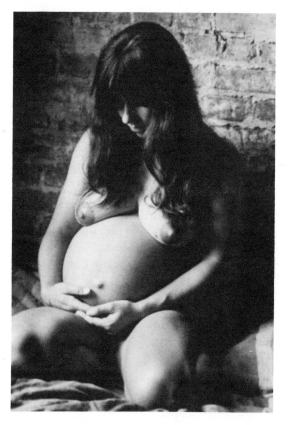

Figure 6–3
The physical changes associated with pregnancy can have a negative effect on a woman's self-image. An affectionate and considerate mate can do much to dispel such feelings.
(Joel Gordon)

that it marks their dependency. Still others insist that pregnancy cements their marriage because it is no longer an easy matter to get out of the contract. Some are excited about their new status and are pleased that they are noticed when they walk about in their maternity clothes.

Except for possible morning sickness and changes in urination and bowel movement patterns, the first trimester is not very physically demanding for the woman. If her doctor agrees, she can lead her life with a minimum of changes. Doctors do advise women to take especially good care of themselves as soon as they know they are pregnant. Extra rest, good diet, and elimination of drugs (including cigarettes and alcohol) help the woman as well as the baby to be healthy.

In the first trimester there is no reason why pregnancy or the suspicion of pregnancy should inhibit sexual activities. It is not likely to harm the developing fetus. There may be some practical considerations, however. Morning sickness may inhibit the desire for sexual activity in the early part of the day, just as fatigue and sleepiness may limit desire at night.

The first trimester is a critical time for the baby. All its organs and physical structures are forming and are thus especially vulnerable to illness or injury. Unfortunately, some women do not discover they are pregnant until this period is over and any damage has already been done. For example, poor diet has been found to be a major cause of birth defects. If a woman who does not eat well waits until she has missed two periods before going to see a doctor, her baby will already have suffered from malnutrition during its most critical stage of development. Eating right later in pregnancy cannot make up for damage done in the earlier stages. Thus, the sooner a woman finds out for sure, the better.

There are a number of feelings that pregnant women may have as they first become used to the idea of being pregnant. The positive ones include increased sexuality, a feeling of rediscovering the meaning of love, increased vitality, a feeling of being really special, creative, and potent. The negative ones may include feeling shock, rejection, of being a carrier, of being less important than the newly forming baby. The woman may be scared, tired, and sick, she may feel unready for parenthood, and caught up in a process beyond her control. She may have questions such as: What's happening to me? Can I cope with pregnancy? Can I manage childbirth? Will I miscarry? What will my baby be like? What does this do to my relationship with my man?

The father may also be concerned about the increased responsibilities of childcare. He may also be elated over his potency, or depressed over his feelings of irresponsibility. While he does not have to undergo the physiological changes, some men do experience sympathetic pains during pregnancy, and all are caught up in the social and psychological changes it brings about in their lives.

It is clear that, with all of the concern to plan for parenthood, there is a sense in which it cannot be fully anticipated. These negative feelings are quite common. It is better to face them than try to avoid them.

THE SECOND TRIMESTER

The second trimester begins with the fourth month of pregnancy. The fetus has begun to grow bulkier. It is possible to detect its heartbeat and movements. The fetus has been moving for some time, but the woman first begins to experience these movements by the fourth or fifth month of pregnancy. This is called the time of quickening. If there has been any uncertainty about the time of conception, the quickening of the fetus will provide a further cue since it is almost certain to occur between the eighteenth and twentieth week of pregnancy. The fetus may be felt to hiccup. Sometimes the movement of the arms and legs will cause a temporary protrusion to appear on the woman's abdomen.

The mother is also undergoing some dramatic changes as her abdomen begins to protrude and her clothes no longer fit. Because of hormonal changes, the area around her nipples (the areolas) becomes darker as does the line from the naval to the pubic region. Some women experience a darkening of the pigment in their faces during pregnancy. This will go away, but the darkening of the nipples and abdominal line will probably not.

By mid-pregnancy, the breasts are functionally ready for nursing, but no milk is present. A thin amber or yellow fluid called *colostrum* may be secreted from the nipples. This substance is believed to be very high in antibodies, which will help the newborn infant to fight off infection. Women who are planning to breastfeed their babies should probably begin to massage their breasts at this time. If the nipples are inverted, they can be gently pulled out several times a day.

Constipation and indigestion are common symptoms of middle pregnancy because of too much acid in the stomach; hormonal changes, which relax the intestinal muscles; and the continuing realignment of pelvic organs as the uterus grows larger. Blood circulation is strained because of the increased amount of blood in the system. The realignment of the pelvic organs may cause painful hemorrhoids. Varicose veins may act up as a result of the increased blood pressure. Pregnant women need more iron to produce more blood. Vaseline can help the hemorrhoids, and support stockings can help to prevent varicose veins in the legs. Many women experience nosebleeds because of the increased blood pressure. Vaseline will help stop this, too.

Edema, a swelling of the body because of the retention of water, is normal in pregnancy. Sometimes, however, it can become excessive, and often it is uncomfortable. Exercise will help squeeze out some of the water. Lying down with the feet elevated will sometimes help the woman feel better.

During the second trimester, the nausea and drowsiness experienced in the first trimester tend to disappear. Concern about miscarriage should diminish now, and the pregnant woman can continue her normal activities. With the decreases of nausea, drowsiness, and breast tenderness, sexual intercourse can be enjoyed more fully. Women often report an increase in interest in sexual activities and greater satisfaction from them during this period. Indeed, many women report that they find sexual intercourse to be more satisfying at this time than at any other time in their lives. This may be in part because of the increased congestion in the vagina. Since fear of pregnancy is not an issue, some women feel free for the first time. During sexual stimulation there is a significant increase in vaginal lubrication. Late in the second trimester, however, certain coital positions (the man on top, for example) become too tiring or painful for the woman. Intercourse should not take place if there is vaginal or abdominal pain; if there is any uterine bleeding; if the sac that keeps the fetus surrounded by amniotic fluid or "water" has broken; or if a miscarriage is likely. Other sexual activities may be tried out at this time, if both so desire.[4]

In the second trimester, the woman is obviously pregnant. She begins to receive instructions from everyone on how to take care of herself. Some women feel good about this. Others worry about having to give up their jobs or feel guilty about pampering themselves. For others, the baby becomes real to them for the first time during quickening, and they have to come to grips with their pregnancy in a new way.

Last night its kicking made me dizzy and gave me a terrible feeling of solitude. I wanted to tell it, stop, stop, stop, let me alone. I want to lie still and whole and all single, catch my breath. But I have no control over this new part of my being, and this lack of control scares me. I felt as if I were rushing downhill at such a great speed that I'd never be able to stop.[5]

The feelings toward this new being in the womb are often intertwined with feelings about the man who fathered it. What does he think of me now? How can he understand what is happening to me? There is

[4]Boston Women's Health Book Collective, *Our Bodies, Ourselves*, p. 264.

[5]Ibid., p. 263.

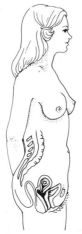

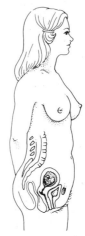

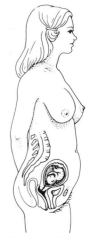

Woman in 6th week
of pregnancy

Woman in 12th week
of pregnancy

Woman in 16th week
of pregnancy

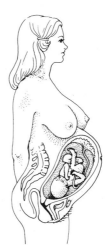

Woman in 24th week
of pregnancy

Woman in 36th week
of pregnancy

Woman in 40th week
of pregnancy

Figure 6–4
Development of fetus, by weeks. (David A. Schulz, Stanley F. Rodgers,
Marriage, the Family, and Personal Fulfillment, © *1975, p. 135.*
Reprinted by permission of Prentice-Hall, Inc.)

fear for the life of the baby and fear for the life of the mother. Though
the possibility of miscarriage is diminished in the second trimester,
the fear that it might occur is hard to remove, especially if a miscarriage has occurred in the woman's past. The mother might fear for
her own death. Facing death at the same time that one is facing a
new birth seems contradictory to many. "To deny that such unpleas-

ant things happen is to deny to ourselves and to our friends the reality and totality of our experience."[6]

Good communication between the partners is important at this stage. Both will have good as well as bad feelings. If these are not shared, they will fester and put additional stress on the relationship. Shared, they are drained of their power, and the fullness of the experience becomes more accessible.

THE THIRD TRIMESTER

During the third trimester the size of the uterus continues to increase. The abdomen protrudes and is hard to the touch. The developing fetus now may move about and kick to the point of keeping the mother awake at night. Sleeping becomes difficult for some women because of the increased weight. It sometimes helps to sleep on one side with a pillow under the upper knee.

How much weight should a woman gain during pregnancy? Not long ago it was assumed that a weight gain of about twenty pounds was ideal. Such an increase normally meant that the infant would be about 7.5 pounds at birth.[7] However, more recently it was discovered that a gain of about twenty-five to thirty-five pounds tended to produce somewhat healthier babies. Controlling weight is often difficult. Pregnant women tend to want to eat more because of the hormonal changes in their bodies that come with pregnancy. Women who gain too much weight have difficulty moving around and may suffer from high blood pressure and strain on the heart. Much of the increase in weight is water. The average woman retains from six and a half to thirteen pints of fluid, half of which accumulates in the last ten weeks of pregnancy. Good prenatal care can help determine the best weight for a particular woman.

Women in the third trimester tend to count the days until delivery. What will the baby be like? Will it be a healthy, normal child? How much longer will this go on?

The fetus's activity during this period is sometimes disturbing, and, by now, because of the baby's weight, women must adjust their walk to keep their balance. This adjustment in posture sometimes causes backaches.

Interest in sexual activity, particularly intercourse, tends to diminish. However, unless there is some medical reason against it, intercourse may continue, if the couple desires, until the last four to six weeks of pregnancy.

[6]Ibid., p. 263.

[7]Harold D. Swanson, *Human Reproduction: Biology and Social Changes* (New York: Oxford University Press, 1974), p. 238.

By the seventh month, the fetus may assume a head-down position. This is called *lightening* or dropping, because the mother now feels that she can breathe easier. The weight of the fetus has been taken off of her diaphragm, and its lower position tends to ease the strain on her back. However, it now rests more heavily against her intestines, and constipation is likely to occur.

Another name for this shift in position is *engagement*, because the baby is now engaged in the first step of the birth process. In most cases engagement occurs from two to four weeks before delivery. By full term only about 3 percent of all babies are still in the upright position. The head-down position makes delivery easier because the head is quite pliable at birth and may be elongated to permit an easier passage through the cervix and birth canal. The feet and arms are less flexible and tend to obstruct the passage when they come first.

Childbirth

Ninety-five percent of all full term births occur between the thirty-fifth and the forty-third week after the last menstrual period. The most likely time is forty weeks. About 7 percent of all live births in the United States are premature. Heavy smoking or drinking during pregnancy can increase the likelihood of premature birth and will reduce the weight of the baby even if it is full term. Mothers who have high blood pressure, heart disease, syphilis, or are experiencing multiple pregnancies are especially prone to giving birth prematurely. In about half of the cases, however, the causes of premature delivery are not known.

As the end of pregnancy approaches, some women, particularly those who have not previously given birth, may experience false labor—strong contractions of the uterus at irregular intervals. These irregular contractions, although they are as intense as the regular contractions of labor, do not in fact indicate that labor is about to begin. Throughout pregnancy the uterus has undergone contractions of various intensities. These *Braxton-Hicks contractions* are normally not painful, but may cause the mother to catch her breath. They are necessary exercises to prepare the uterus for labor.

Toward the end of pregnancy the cervix begins to soften and become thinner. This is called *effacement*. The cervix may also begin to dilate (open up) before labor begins. The precise mechanism that induces labor is not known. It probably is related to the aging of the placenta and to hormonal signals from the fetus indicating that it is ready. Just before labor begins, the woman may notice a small,

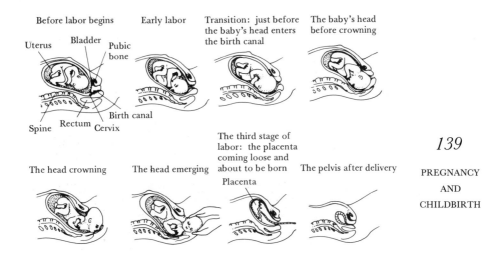

Before labor begins   Early labor   Transition: just before the baby's head enters the birth canal   The baby's head before crowning

Uterus   Bladder   Pubic bone

Spine   Rectum   Cervix   Birth canal

The head crowning   The head emerging   The third stage of labor: the placenta coming loose and about to be born   The pelvis after delivery

Placenta

Figure 6–5
Stages of childbirth. (David A. Schulz, Stanley F. Rodgers, Marriage, the
Family, and Personal Fulfillment, © *1975, p. 136.*
Reprinted by permission of Prentice-Hall, Inc.)

slightly bloody discharge. This is the plug of mucus that blocked the cervix to help prevent infection of the fetus.

LABOR

Labor is normally described as a three-stage process. The beginning of labor is somewhat imprecisely defined by the strong regular contractions of the uterus. The first stage lasts until the head of the baby has passed through the cervix into the vagina. The second stage is completed with the birth of the baby. In first pregnancies, this usually occurs between twelve and a half to fourteen hours after labor has begun. Second or later children usually come sooner. The third stage is completed with the emergence of the placenta, or afterbirth.

The First Stage of Labor. The first stage of labor is called *dilation* because it is associated with the dilation of the cervix. During this stage, the cervix expands from one or two centimeters in diameter to ten or eleven centimeters. Strong uterine contractions occur every ten to twenty minutes. Initially these contractions last for about thirty seconds. The average length of this stage is twelve hours, but the range is one to twenty hours. In general, the greater the number of previous pregnancies, the shorter the duration of this stage. This stage usually takes place in the labor room if it occurs in a hospital. It is usually handled without much difficulty by most women.

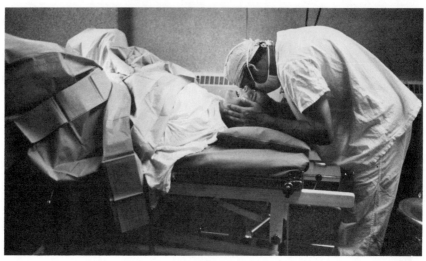

Figure 6–6
To fully appreciate the experience of childbirth, a woman
should be both awake and aware. (© Abigail Heyman, Magnum Photos, Inc.)

The amnion, the "bag of waters" that insures that the fetus is bathed in a protective liquid while in the womb, normally breaks some hours after the onset of labor (in the late first stage or early second stage). The doctor may deliberately puncture this bag since its rupture seems to speed up the process of labor. About 10 percent of all pregnant women approaching labor, however, will experience the breaking of the amnion before the onset of labor. In such an event the woman should be hospitalized within twenty-four hours for observation because of the increased risk of infection.

Late in the first stage of labor the cervix opens from about five to eight centimeters. This second dilation usually takes place over a shorter period of time than the first and is more intense. Women may rely on shallow breathing techniques to ease the discomfort. The last part of the first stage is called the *transition* and is the most difficult. The cervix expands from eight to about ten centimeters. This is the part of labor that most women feel is painful. It is usually brief.

The Second Stage of Labor. The second or *expulsion* stage begins when the head of the baby has passed through the cervix. Because the fetus may be variously positioned in the uterus, some other part of the body (buttocks or leg, for example) may be presented instead of the head. This is called a *breech birth.* Sometimes the fetus will be so positioned in the uterus that it is necessary to perform an operation and remove the baby through an incision in the abdominal wall. This is

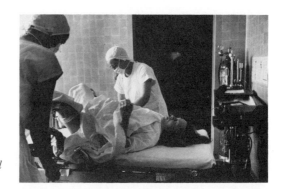

Figure 6–7
A hospital delivery. (Eve Arnold,
© Magnum Photos, Inc.; © Abigail
Heyman, Magnum Photos, Inc.)

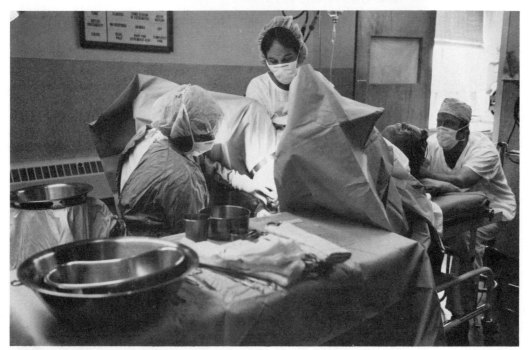

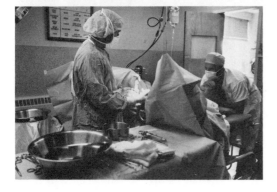

called a *Caesarean birth*. This is commonly done when the fetus is horizontal in the uterus or the placenta is closer to the cervix than the fetus is. Most often, however, the head of the baby passes through the cervix and then the shoulders, torso, and legs follow rapidly. Uterine contractions now occur at one to two minute intervals and are up to about two minutes in duration. The baby's passage through the vagina may create pressure intense enough to tear the vaginal wall. To prevent this the doctor usually performs an *episiotomy*—a cutting of the skin of the vaginal opening downward and toward the anus. This incision is cleaned and sewn up immediately after delivery of the afterbirth.

Figure 6–8
A newborn baby still attached to its mother by the umbilical cord. Holding the baby in this
position encourages the drainage of mucus from its nose, mouth, and throat, as well as
giving the doctor a chance to inspect it for defects.
(Wayne Miller, © Magnum Photos, Inc.)

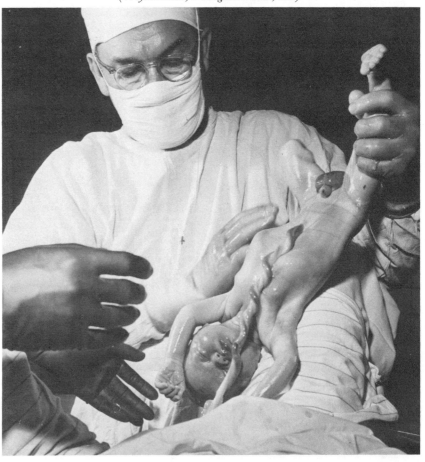

The second stage of labor normally occurs in the delivery room if it occurs in a hospital. Many doctors believe that women are experiencing great pain during this stage and, accordingly, want to anesthetize them. However, women often claim that the second stage is "the fun part."[8] That is, they feel that they can assist in the delivery of their baby by working with the contractions. Various techniques of "natural childbirth" are designed to teach the women how to do this. This second stage normally takes a half hour to two hours.

After birth, the baby is commonly held firmly by the ankles and inspected while the head is down so as to encourage the drainage of mucus from the throat, nose, and mouth. Sometimes a suction device will assist in this drainage. The arms and legs are checked, the fingers and toes counted, and the external genitals are examined. The baby is then placed on the mother's abdomen and its umbilical cord (the tube connecting the baby with the placenta) is cut after its blood has emptied into the baby's system. After the umbilical cord is cut, the doctor or midwife massages the baby's back or feet. This usually produces the first loud cry, and the baby breathes. If the mother has not been anesthetized, the baby may begin to cry before it is fully born. If she has been, the anesthesia will pass through the placenta into the baby. Sometimes this delays the baby's first breath and increases the problems of delivery. The less use of anesthesia, the better.

The Third Stage of Labor. The third stage of labor is the emergence of the placenta. This usually takes no more than a few minutes, but may take up to a half an hour. The placenta is examined to be sure that it has all emerged. Should any part of the placenta remain behind, the woman may experience hemorrhage from the torn blood vessels left by its partial removal.

NATURAL CHILDBIRTH

Natural childbirth is often used as a label for several techniques aimed at instructing the mother how to disassociate pain, fear, and tension from the experience of childbirth.[9] The English physician Grantly Dick-Read coined the term "natural childbirth" in 1932 for such procedures. The French physician Fernand Lamaze developed another approach based on Pavlovian conditioned reflex responses. Lamaze's technique trains the woman to mentally dissociate uterine contractions from pain by reinforcing the notion that such contractions are not painful. This mental training is accompanied with breathing exercises to relax the muscles of the abdomen. After proper

[8]Boston Women's Health Book Collective, *Our Bodies, Ourselves,* p. 272.

[9]The concerns expressed in this section are, for example, presented in Ibid., pp. 251–317.

training, it is possible for most women to experience a relaxed and relatively painless delivery.

Training for natural childbirth almost always involves the man as well as the woman. The man helps the woman by timing her contractions, coaching her on her breathing, helping her to be physically comfortable, and so on. The man's involvement during pregnancy gives the woman the emotional support she needs and gives the man a feeling of belonging to a process once thought to be solely the domain of women. Most men find that this involvement makes the whole experience more satisfying for them and gives them a greater stake in their relationship and in the child produced by it.

Some hospitals have been slow to follow this trend. They consider the father's presence during labor and delivery to be unnecessary. Some couples who have taken natural childbirth classes have been terribly disappointed when the father was barred from the delivery room door. Checking the hospital's policy in advance can prevent such disappointment.

Why do babies have to be born in hospitals anyway? Obviously, they don't. Women in primitive societies manage to have their babies without doctors in attendance. In our own society, women have had healthy babies in taxicabs, in stalled elevators, and in their own homes.

Home delivery used to be the common practice in this country. In the past, attitudes toward sex washed over onto pregnancy. Pregnant women had obviously had sex at least once in their lives, and, as people did not like to be reminded that sex was part of life, pregnant women generally stayed home once their condition became undisguisable. Delivery at home was another way of insuring the woman's privacy while protecting the sensibility of others.

Unfortunately, while the babies generally did all right, home delivery was very risky for the mothers. Childbed fever, an infection

Figure 6–9
Through classes in natural childbirth, couples can participate more actively in the birth of their child. (William Hubbell, Woodfin Camp Inc.)

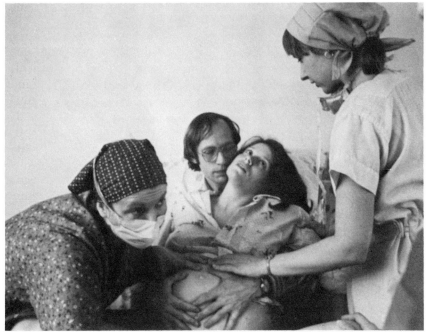

Figure 6–10
Childbirth at home is an increasingly popular alternative to hospital deliveries.
(Abigail Heyman, © Magnum Photos, Inc.)

caused by poor sanitation and lack of antiseptics in the home, often spread from woman to woman as the doctor made his rounds. Childbirth was truly something to be feared in those days and came to be thought of as a potential illness rather than as a natural event.

In the 1920s and 1930s, widespread use of antiseptic techniques, improved hospital facilities, and changes in people's attitudes toward sex and pregnancy resulted in a shift from home to hospital. Childbed fever has disappeared, but doctors continue to treat pregnancy as a "problem." Just as few of us would give up our cars and television in return for a simpler life, most people are still committed to the idea that a hospital is the only safe place to have a child in spite of the emotional appeal of natural methods and natural settings for childbirth.

Many people have come to realize, however, that much standard medical practice is designed for the physician's convenience and is not really beneficial for the woman or the baby. In delivery, for example, the woman lies flat on her back on a standard operating table. Doctors are used to doing it this way and find it comfortable. From the woman's point of view, however, this position makes it more difficult to exert the pressure needed to expel the baby. (Imagine moving

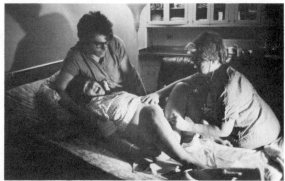
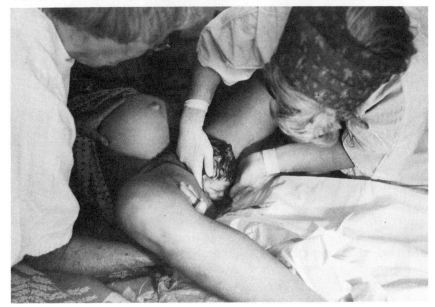

Figure 6–11
A delivery in a clinic. (© 1976, Joel Gordon)

your bowels while lying down.) In fact, in some primitive societies, women let gravity help them by assuming a squatting or leaning position during delivery. Perhaps, if there were more female doctors, delivery room design would be more efficient.

The major criticism of hospital delivery is that it has become routinized and tends to dehumanize the expectant mother. The routine, furthermore, tends to anticipate the worst and readily incorporates the latest device to assist doctors in their professional performance. Often this is done without adequate consideration of the effects on the mother and her body. Thus, for example, fetal monitors are routinely being used during the labor process. Some external monitors have ultrasonic equipment to measure fetal heart beat. There is some evidence from Japan that this procedure may cause brain damage to the fetus.[10] Internal monitors are attached directly to the baby (usually on its head) by means of clips or metal screws without thought for the possible pain this may inflict. The uterine contractions of the mother are measured by a special strap fastened around her abdomen or a catheter inserted into her uterus. These restrict the mother's movement and are sometimes uncomfortable.

Since the amnion must be broken in order to attach the electrodes to the presenting part of the baby, and, since there is a greater risk of bleeding because of this attachment, there is also a greater risk of infection. This is especially true when the catheter is used to monitor the uterine contractions. The most common results of the use of internal monitors, however, are a post-delivery rash on the baby where the electrodes were attached and possibly scalp abcesses. The point is clearly not that such devices should not be used. There are undoubtedly many babies whose lives are saved because of the use of the monitors. The argument is that there is enough evidence of risk and discomfort now to question their *routine* use.

[10]Ibid., p. 285.

Figure 6–12
A doctor performing an episiotomy as a routine part of the delivery procedure. As most women's vaginas can accommodate a baby without tearing, many people feel that routine episiotomies are unnecessary. (© Abigail Heyman, Magnum Photos, Inc.)

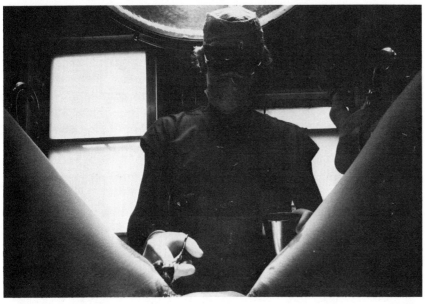

Since most physicians are men, medical practice has not benefited much from the direct experiences of people who have themselves given birth. For example, according to doctors, the episiotomy is routinely performed because it reduces the likelihood that the vaginal wall will be torn. The incision, however, is painful in healing, and some women are allergic to the stitches. This creates further discomfort. The vagina can normally expand to accommodate the baby without tearing. There are exercises that can increase the likelihood that it will do so. Thus, the routine episiotomy is not justifiable.

Another medical practice that has recently received much criticism is the routine use of anesthesia. Anesthesia represents a major risk in any surgical procedure. It is particularly dangerous in childbirth because it affects the baby as well as the mother. Many women have reported that childbirth was a wonderful experience. They were glad they could actively participate in the process and did not have to sleep through one of the high points in their lives. Though anesthesia may make the doctor's job easier, the psychological benefits of being conscious and the physical risks to the anesthetized mother and baby combine to make the routine use of anesthesia of questionable value. Childbirth is painful, but knowledge of what to expect, proper training, and strong desire can be effective painkillers for most women.

As more women become obstetricians and gynecologists, a different set of values will, no doubt, be considered. Among these will be an increase of cultivation of respect for the mother as a person and not simply as a patient, and an affirmation that giving birth should be a fulfilling experience for her and her man. For this to be, the woman must be awake and aware.

> *As women, we know that childbirth is an extremely important experience in our lives. If we are prepared and unanesthetized during childbirth, we are in touch with our entire self, mind and body, and we are working intelligently along with this inevitable biological process. We are in control. The experience of childbirth can have a positive effect on all the other aspects of our being. We can feel freer sexually, having experienced such a massive physical and sexual event. We can feel more in control of ourselves as whole people, having used both our mind and our body together, to see us through labor and delivery. We can be more confident mothers, having done our best from the start to give our children a safe and satisfying birth. And finally, we can be sure that as women we are strong, competent and beautiful.* [11]

As we said earlier, a doctor's care and advice are extremely important during pregnancy. Doctors can detect problems that might complicate delivery as early as possible. But doctors tend to keep things to

[11]Ibid., p. 296.

themselves. They are not apt, unless they are asked, to provide in-depth explanations of procedures and their implications. In order to ask the right questions and make the best choices, a woman should educate herself by reading and attending childbirth classes.

THE POSTPARTUM PERIOD

Postpartum means "after birth." The baby is born at last. The woman's body begins returning to normal, and mother and child begin to get to know each other.

If the birth has taken place in a hospital, most women remain there for two to four days after delivery. Women are encouraged to get up and exercise as soon as possible. A walk during the first day after delivery is common practice. During the first few hours, the mother's abdomen will begin to return to its normal shape. By the tenth day after delivery, the uterus has usually descended from the abdomen into the pelvic region. A postpartum discharge from the uterus called *lochia* is normal. During the first couple of weeks this discharge will change in color from red to pinkish brown to yellowish white. It should not smell bad. If it does, the doctor should be notified because it is a sign that infection is developing. During the first few days after delivery, the woman should be carefully watched for signs of infection, since the recuperating mother is more vulnerable than usual.

The breasts begin to fill with liquid shortly after delivery. The milk comes the second or third day after delivery in most cases. The breasts may become engorged with milk if the infant is not being fed on demand. In order to be able to feed on demand, the baby must be "rooming-in." Some hospitals permit this on a modified basis, allowing the mother to have the child as much as she wants, taking it to the nursery when she tires. Other hospitals insist that if the mother

Figure 6–13
(Wayne Miller, © 1967
Magnum Photos)

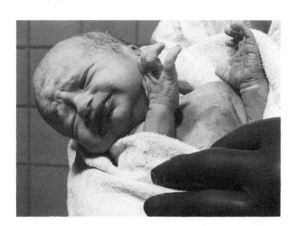

Figure 6–14
A mother who wishes to breastfeed her
baby should tell her doctor before
delivery, as certain hospital procedures
may interfere with the production of
milk or with her access to her baby.
(Joel Gordon)

wants to have the child in her room, she must care for it all the time. It is important to establish what the policy of the particular hospital is before hand, since continuous childcare is a heavy task for most women immediately after childbirth. Hospitals will sometimes routinely give an injection of estrogen or testosterone to reduce the development of milk in the breasts. If the mother intends to nurse her baby, she should so inform the staff. If she has been given the hormone injections, she can still nurse, but with greater difficulty.

Bringing the baby home from the hospital can be a challenging experience for the young couple. They must get used to the techniques and routines of feeding, changing diapers, and the countless other details of infant care. The process may be complicated by an anxious father who has had little to do with the whole matter until now and a host of curious, intrusive—but well-meaning—friends. The mother, who may want reassurance, comfort, and attention, may suddenly find herself upstaged by the new "star" of the family. A new mother experiencing these pressures may well feel fatigued and somewhat let down.

In addition, her body is undergoing further hormonal changes after delivery. It is quite likely that the phenomenon called *postpartum blues* or postpartum psychosis is triggered by these changes. At any rate, many women do feel very depressed after delivery. Such feelings are normal, but should not be ignored. There are postpartum groups organized in some communities to help mothers during this transition period. Most women get over these feelings after a few weeks, but some take longer.

The postpartum period is complicated further if there are other small children dependent on the mother. Feeding a baby and caring for other small children is draining. Much help is needed from father, family, and friends.

Common medical advice is to refrain from sexual intercourse from four to six weeks after delivery to allow the internal organs to return to more normal states and the stitches, if any, to heal. Intercourse increases the likelihood of infection. However, warm affectionate and sensual caressing of various sorts will not cause infection and is usually much needed. A lot depends on how the new mother feels. There is great variation in women's desire to return to sexual intercourse after delivery.

Summary

Women usually know that they are pregnant when they have missed a period. But this is not a totally reliable sign. Pregnancy tests based on the detection of HCG (human chlorionic gonadotropin) in the urine or bloodstream have been devised. These are about 95 to 98 percent accurate. A recent, but not widely available test, can accurately detect pregnancy as early as eight days after ovulation.

Figure 6–15
(Eve Arnold, Magnum Photos)

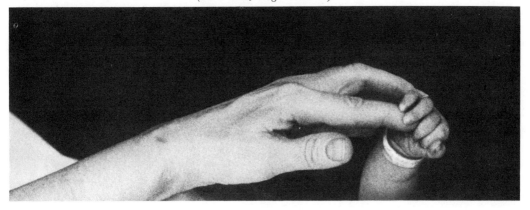

At one time medical practice insisted that the expectant mother be ferreted away to a hospital to deliver "in the delivery room" with the assistance of a qualified physician and his or her trained associates. Now, however, there is increasing demand that this event not be so cut off from the family and home. Couples work together in the preparation for delivery by learning various "natural childbirth" techniques and train for the care of the newborn in many "short courses" given in the evening by hospitals, the Red Cross, or other organizations. The father is sometimes encouraged to be present at delivery. Some people are working to replace the delivery room scene with the home and a trained midwife.

With proper prenatal care, the probability of a difficult birth can be reasonably well determined in advance and hospital care anticipated. But normal birth does not require the elaborate equipment of a hospital. In many instances the home may actually be a much safer environment because of the difficulties some hospitals are having with persistent staph infections. Clearly, the warmth of the home environment and the support of a loving circle of friends near at hand is very desirable. A midwife may actually be much better trained in the specialized skills necessary in a normal delivery than a physician who tends to be crisis-oriented. Giving birth at home can be an event of great love and beauty. It is so in our nostalgia. Proper preparation can make it even more so today.

Section Two

Interpersonal Sexuality

In this section, the discussion of human sexuality is organized around a set of concerns that can be called "interpersonal." In looking at sex at the interpersonal level, I will not ignore biological and social considerations. Rather, I will pursue them wherever necessary, but with the intention of relating them to sex as having something to do with free individuals who can, if they choose, relate to themselves and to one another. The interpersonal way of looking at sex is probably the way most of us look at sex most of the time. Much of the material in this section, therefore, will simply enrich what is common in our experience. At times, however, our common-sense, everyday understandings of sex will be challenged in dramatic ways.

The section begins with such a rebuttal of common sense. You and I are likely to assume that the most obvious thing about sex is the fact that there are two sexes, male and female. There are very apparent genetic, anatomical, and physiological differences between males and females. Along with this we have observed that women and men behave differently. "Boys will be boys" and "Isn't that just like a woman" are examples of how easily we accept these differences in behavior. Now, however, we are coming to understand that gender is much more flexible than we previously suspected. How much or how little we make of these biological and behavioral differences is more a matter of choice today.

At the interpersonal level, the social expectations called sex roles have shaped our personal understanding of sexuality from the moment of our birth. They influence how we relate to individuals of the same and opposite sex throughout our lives. They are present in our most intimate lovemaking. The extent to which these social expectations are based on biological differences between the sexes is a subject of continuing debate, as is the comparable concern about how much we can change them. Sex roles, therefore, are a critical issue in our exploration of human sexuality. They

stand between the biological and the personal, on the one hand, and the personal and the social, on the other. Chapter 7 examines sex roles in some detail.

In chapter 8, I concentrate on intimacy. Intimacy is not a necessary element of human sexual interaction, but it is widely recognized as a desirable one. What do we know about this feeling of being intimate? How can we improve our capacity to become intimate if we so desire? Becoming intimate seems to be very much dependent on our ability to be aware of our bodies and our feelings and our ability to accurately communicate how we feel to others. Getting in touch with ourselves can help us to get in touch with others, and vice versa. This progression toward increasing intimacy can be described in terms of a sequence of behaviors and guided by a set of understandings about what is happening between two people.

It is, perhaps, presumptuous to try and write a chapter on the art of lovemaking. Chapter 9 is not intended to be exhaustive, but only suggestive. The increasing acceptance of richness and variety in making love is, I think, a good thing. But technique is not the only important element in lovemaking. Accordingly, the chapter is organized around the possibilities for pleasure in intimate sexual relationships in which the partners are able to communicate some of their deepest feelings through their lovemaking. In writing the chapter in this way, I do not intend to imply that all sex should be this way. Rather I want to suggest that sex can be like this at times, and when it is, it is often very good.

Homosexuality is an increasingly accepted normal sexual variation. It is less and less thought of as an illness or pathological deviance. In spite of this, homosexual behaviors are illegal in most states, and gays continue to be persecuted. Clearly, the label "homosexual" makes it very difficult for some people to express their sexuality because they must constantly defend their sexual preference. Chapter 10 considers some aspects of the gay life. Of necessity it tends to emphasize how gays differ from straights. In reality this gay-straight dichotomy is a continuum. There are degrees of preference for sex with a person of the same sex in most of us that may or may not be expressed in overt behavior. Those people who are called gay are but the most public segment of this larger population. There are more similarities between gays and straights than we might at first suspect.

The concluding chapter in this section considers some of the most common sexual dysfunctions and their treatment. Since the publication of Masters and Johnson's *Human Sexual Inadequacy* in 1970, there has been a great deal of interest in sex therapy. The social has dramatically impinged upon the interpersonal by increasing the expectations that sex is a good thing everyone should be able to enjoy. Many married couples now expect their marriage to be sexually fulfilling, and they are less likely to resign themselves to it if it isn't. Young people also have greater pressures on them to perform and enjoy sex. Where society once placed great barriers in the way of its youth who wanted to become sexually active, now it seems to push them in that direction sometimes even before they are ready. In any case, sexual dysfunctions that once were thought to be untreatable (impotence, vaginismus) now can be easily cured in many cases. Sex therapy has as much of a role on helping people to enrich their sex lives as it has in helping them overcome their debilitating handicaps, and there are many ways by which this therapy can be made available.

Sex Roles and Sexual Behavior

7

The Woman's Movement is sometimes accused
of being "against love." I think the
opposite is true. . . . After all, real love
can only exist between equals. . . . The trouble
is that in our patriarchal system, a woman is
supposed to have a man's name, social identity
and to be dependent on his earnings, and his ability
to "give her children a name." That produces
anger and resentment—as men would understand if they
imagined themselves in the role of a wife. In fact, this
inequality probably kills love for men, too. They never
know whether they are being loved for themselves, or
for their bank account and their wall-to-wall
carpeting.

Gloria Steinem

"Men and women are different." Once we could simply take this simple statement for granted. But today things are not as clear-cut. Scientists of all sorts still study the differences between men and women. But now they have come to realize that, when you study the differences, you tend to accentuate them, sometimes to the extent of ignoring similarities that are also present.

Aside from their obvious physical differences, men and women have been distinguished by the roles they play and the work that they are expected to perform. However, "men's work" and "women's work" are not the same all over the world. Men are not expected to do the same things in all societies, nor are women. Some societies even permit men to assume the role of women if they do not want to accept the role assigned to men. In some societies men are socially credited with having given birth to the children. They "lie in" and express the pains of labor while their wife delivers in the field. In such societies, women are apt to respond to men with gnarled faces and say, "You should have seen him before he gave birth to all those children."

In our society, as well as in others, the socially acknowledged differences between men and women—their sex roles—have tended to suppress women. These sex roles were developed long ago and are not as relevant today as they once were. Emphasizing the differences between men and women and assigning separate tasks to each sex was functional in technologically primitive societies. Because women had to care for children, a sexual division of labor increased the likelihood that the family—and thus the species—would survive. In today's advanced technological societies, however, the male's strength is not as critical, nor is the woman's capacity to bear children. We have machines that can do our physical labor, and the decline in birth rates and smaller family size make the woman's child rearing tasks less demanding. Competitiveness and high fertility are liabilities rather than assets in today's world.

In this chapter we examine some of the differences between men and women that are documented in current research and the social roles and stereotypes that often support and sometimes exaggerate them. In this discussion, we make a distinction between *genetic sex,* which is determined by the presence or absence of the Y chromosome, and *anatomical sex,* the obvious physical differences between men and women. *Sex roles* are the attitudes and behaviors that are thought to be appropriate to people with a particular anatomy. Fi-

Figure 7–1
Scientists have come to realize that studies of the differences between men and women tend to obscure the many ways in which they are alike. (Joel Gordon)

nally, *sex identity* refers to an individual's inner responses to these physical and social factors, which result in the conviction that "I am a female" or "I am a male." The growing recognition that genetic sex, anatomical sex, sex roles, and sex identity do not always match as well as we once thought is dramatically changing our understanding of human sexuality. It is becoming clear that whatever we might wish to say about the differences between men and women and whatever theories we might wish to entertain regarding their origin, we are rapidly gaining the ability to make both women and men whatever we choose to make them, as far as their gender is concerned.

Sex Roles and Sex Stereotypes

The extent of our technical control over gender will be clear after we have examined the recent breakthroughs of the biological revolution. For now, let's begin our discussion of the differences between men and women with a look at sex roles and sex stereotypes. This has become a familiar topic as a result of the struggle of women to gain equality and the political controversy over the Equal Rights Amend-

Figure 7–2
Both men and women value the ability to display their bodies. (M. Durazzo, Magnum Photos)

ment. The social differences between men and women are not illusions, nor are they simply conveniences for the males of the species, nor are they naturally related to anatomical differences between the sexes. Their status is what we seek to more fully understand.

FUNCTIONS OF SEX ROLES

Sex roles are useful guides to behavior in public places. It is helpful to have a general idea of how to behave toward people you do not know. Sex roles can provide us with cues in unfamiliar social situations. Without some generally accepted expectations about behavior, for example, our courtship rituals would require even longer periods of time. But how much should these general guides to behavior in public places be based on differences between the sexes? How important is it that we have a sex identity? Would it be enough for us to identify ourselves primarily as people? The past can provide us with little guidance in these matters, because there has never been a society in which sex differences have not provided a significant base for behav-

Figure 7–3
(© Abigail Heyman, Magnum Photos, Inc.)

162

SEX ROLES AND
SEXUAL
BEHAVIOR

ior. At present, sex identity is virtually at the same level of importance as personal identity for most of us. And, of course, our sense of sex identity derives in part from what other people expect of us.

Even if we grant that sex roles have some positive social uses, stereotypes must be seen as destructive. Sex roles become stereotypes when they become rigid. When we use stereotypes, we refuse to acknowledge that each person is a unique expression of humanity with abilities that may or may not fit our expectations. John Money and Patricia Tucker offer the following description of the sex stereotypes of the 1970s. If you are a man:

> *You may fight but not cry.*
> *You must strive to outdo your fellow man, never admitting defeat.*
> *You may seduce girls to prove your masculiness, but you are entitled to a virgin bride.*
> *You may do any work, even the most menial, outside of your home, without damage to your pride, but you don't undertake cooking, cleaning, or laundering at home, or the day-to-day care of your children. (In a domestic emergency you cope, but perform even the simplest domestic chores sloppily to advertise that it is alien to you.)*

You take financial responsibility for supporting the women and children in your immediate family; your wife can perhaps go out to work if she wants to, but her real job is at home.

You may show affection for your wife and small children, but not for anyone else and most particularly not for another man; if you want to show a man that you love him, you make a mock attack—slap him on the back, shove, or lunge at him.

All your relations with women are strongly colored by sex, and the significant ones are those limited to sex. You brag about the fun and bawdy lustfulness of sex in any all-male group, and use a special prudish vocabulary with women, even your wife and any other sex partner.[1]

If you are a woman:

You're a failure unless you marry and have children. Until you marry, your job is to compete (not too openly) with other women for the attention of men and to hang on to your hymen, but it's unbecoming to show overt interest in a man until he has signified interest in you. After you marry, your job is to be a good wife and mother and to pay no attention to other men ("good" is defined not in terms of your own performance, but by the well-being of your husband and children or their regard for you).

Wile and guile are your weapons, manipulation is your tactic; you're not expected to have a strategy or to be consistent, but if your inconsistency—or your children—cause problems, it's your fault.

You read and write, but not too much of either, and even less of math.

If you earn a little money, that's great, as long as it doesn't interfere with your homework, but to surpass your husband or his colleagues in any kind of achievement outside of the domestic sphere puts everyone in grave psychological peril.

Your sexual feelings are not very important, it's not nice to think or talk about them.[2]

These stereotypes were seriously undermined during World War II, when women went to work in droves, but they still exert enormous power. While generations raised after the war are more inclined to dress alike and have somewhat different models of masculinity and femininity, students who live together while going to college—who may be considered to be fairly unconventional—still generally follow the traditional division of labor around their apartment. Some of the most rigid adherence to prewar stereotypes exists in otherwise "hip" communes.

[1]John Money and Patricia Tucker, *Sexual Signatures: On Being a Man and a Woman* (Boston: Little Brown & Company, 1975), pp. 11–12. Copyright © 1975 by John Money and Patricia Tucker.

[2]Ibid.

Some Differences between Males and Females

Sex roles and stereotypes are based on people's assumptions about the capabilities and qualities of men and women. Because of their rigidity, stereotypes should always be mistrusted. But what about sex roles? Do they have any basis in fact? After examining some 2,000 studies of the differences between males and females, Maccoby and Jacklin concluded that only the following generalizations are supported by the research.[3]

MALES ARE MORE AGGRESSIVE THAN FEMALES

From about the age of two to two and a half, boys are more verbally and physically assertive than girls. They fight more and play rougher. However, the primary victims of male aggression are other males, not females. Money and Tucker conclude that although competitiveness and assertiveness are more prevalent in boys than in girls, fighting and aggression are not. Since aggresssion is thought to be associated with the level of testosterone in the body, and since males have a generally higher level of testosterone than females, it is reasonable to conclude that they would be more likely to be aggressive. However, because there is great variation in testosterone levels in both sexes, it is not accurate to say that aggression is necessarily a function of maleness.

GIRLS HAVE MORE VERBAL ABILITY THAN BOYS

Girls generally develop ability to use language sooner than boys. The sexes become fairly equal in ability between the ages of six and eleven, but then girls generally take the lead again. Some researchers explain this by saying that girls are more sensitive to sound. But is this the result of nature or nurture? There are studies that show that mothers talk more to their girl babies than they do to their boy babies. But, if girls do like sounds better, they may be more responsive than boys, thus encouraging their mothers to talk to them more. In any case, girls do have a better command of language than boys do.

MALES EXCEL IN VISUAL-SPATIAL ABILITY
IN ADOLESCENCE AND ADULTHOOD

Tests that require the differentiation of a figure from a background are completed with greater ease by males than by females. But this

[3]Eleanor Emuons Maccoby and Carol Nagy Jacklin, *Psychology of Sex Differences* (California: Stanford University Press, 1974).

difference may be due to our culture rather than our genes. Little boys play differently than little girls. Boys play adventure games such as king of the hill and protect their territory against the Indians more than girls do. Girls play house, they color, and they play with dolls more than boys do. These play activities require different use of the eyes. In addition, researchers have found that overprotected boys perform similarly to girls on these tests. Parents are more apt to overprotect their daughters, and this overprotection, rather than innate differences, may also account for the difference in ability.

AFTER THE AGE OF ELEVEN BOYS EXCEL IN MATH

It seems very evident that this difference is not genetically determined, since younger girls are superior to boys in math. The increased skill of older boys may be a result of the difference in their play activities, but the probable cause is the fact that girls are socially discouraged from developing skill in math.

Maccoby and Jacklin also concluded that a number of other commonly believed differences were not supported by the evidence. For example, girls are not more social than boys. They are not more suggestible than boys. Boys and girls are about equal in self-esteem, even though during their college years males have a greater sense of control over their destiny than females. Girls do not lack motivation to achieve. They are not better rote learners. They are not less analytical when visual discrimination is not involved. In general, girls are not more auditory and boys more visual in their orientation to their world. Both sexes are equally sensitive to and interested in visual stimuli.

The evidence seems clear that most types of behavior don't belong to one sex or the other, but are in fact shared by both. A divorced father who has custody of his children can readily learn how to care for them if he does not already know how to do so. In another situation they might not be expressed, but nonexpression does not mean nonexistence.

Some critics have accused researchers who study male and female differences of perpetuating, rather than weakening, our social stereotypes. These critics insist that so-called masculine traits and feminine traits are outgrowths of these stereotypes, not vice versa, and that people should be studied as people rather than as a member of one sex or the other.[4]

The vocabulary of social science also encourages the stereotypical treatment of male and female differences. For example, "mothering"

[4]See, for example, Anne Constantinople, "Masculinity - Feminity," *Psychological Bulletin,* 80 (November 1973), 403–4; and Arlie Russell Hochchild, "A Review of Sex Role Research," *American Journal Of Sociology,* 78 (January 1975) 1015–29.

strongly implies that only women can manifest the trait and that "fathering" is a different sort of skill. Researchers speak of "father absence" and "mother deprivation," when, in fact, children need both parents equally. Ordinarily, this bias results from the importance attached to the reproductive role of the female. If it is thought of as very important by the researcher, it tends to color the interpretation of social data that could be used to describe sex role differences in another way.

In our society, sex role stereotypes are linked to our conceptions of what it means to be a good member of a family. This association gives the stereotypes added support because survival of the family is still seen as necessary to the survival of the species. Making good marriages and raising children are seen as needed to keep our society functioning well. These generalizations about the differences between women and men represent past wisdom regarding the nature of the sexes and their proper interrelationships. To the extent that these generalizations have served us well in the past, they persist as sex roles. They also persist as stereotypes because it is not easy to let go of old ways, especially in a rapidly changing world. But they offer us a false sense of security because without change, there can be no growth.

Becoming a Male or Female

The process by which an individual develops into a person with a sex identity that is congruent with sex roles, anatomy, and genetic sex is not a simple unfolding of natural tendencies. It is the result of a complex and more or less continuous interaction between a developing organism and its environment. It is no longer useful to distinguish between nature and nurture as though one did its work before birth and the other came into play afterward. The developing organism must adapt to environmental changes while still in the womb. These adaptations influence later social adaptations, but they do not determine them. The entire process that is involved in the achievement of an adult sex identity is called *psychosexual differentiation*. It will be described by looking first at the changes that take place in the womb; it will then turn to the social environment.

PRENATAL DEVELOPMENT

Elementary biology texts give the impression that gender is simply a function of chromosomal composition. For a long time this was common opinion. Females have XX chromosomes, and males have XY.

Now the process is seen as much more complex. In the prenatal stage, both hormones and chromosomes play a role.

Chromosomal Control. Since women have only X chromosomes, the man determines the gender of the fetus. His sperm carry either X or Y chromosomes and, by uniting with the X chromosome in the egg of the mother, provides the recognized XX or XY differentiation. This is clearly nature's most common pattern, but it is not perfect. In some cases sex chromosomes are added or deleted from this typical arrangement.

It first became possible to spell out some of the implications of a missing or an extra X or Y chromosome after 1956, when a new technique for counting chromosomes established that the true count in human beings was forty-six not forty-eight, as was previously thought.[5] Only recently has it been recognized that a large number of spontaneous abortions result from imperfect matching of sex chromosomes.[6] Those that lived were explained away as abnormalities or pathologies. Now we are taking them much more seriously because they suggest that humankind is more ambisexual (capable of being either masculine or feminine) than sex role stereotypes have suggested.

Although understanding of the role of the sex chromosomes in psychosexual development is just beginning, some things already seem apparent. The major function of the Y chromosomes in psychosexual differentiation appears to be to insure that the sex organs of the fetus will develop into testes rather than ovaries. The presence of at least one Y chromosome—regardless of the number of X chromosomes—will insure the development of testes. In the absence of a Y chromosome, the fetus will ordinarily develop ovaries. John Money has a useful guideline to psychosexual differentiation, which he calls the "Adam principle." Briefly put, it says, "If you want to develop a male, add something."[7] The first additive is the Y chromosome. There will be other additions later in the process.

One school of thought contends that the only thing that the chromosomes do is to determine the formation of the sex organs and insure their fertility. Others argue for something more. Corinne Hutt, for instance, contends that the Y chromosome not only determines masculinity, but confers a "male" flavor upon human development as well.[8] She notes that male fetuses are much more susceptible to

[5]Money and Tucker, *Sexual Signatures,* p. 29.

[6]Only about 1 percent of fetuses with sex chromosome abnormalities survive. Thus, only a very small percentage of the United States population is affected.

[7]John Money and Anke A. Erhardt, *Man and Woman, Boy and Girl* (Baltimore, Md.: The Johns Hopkins University Press, 1973), p. 3.

[8]Corinne Hutt, *Males and Females* (New York: Penguin, 1973) p. 23.

spontaneous abortion and more vulnerable to trauma of all sorts than females are.

Ounstead and Taylor have a theory to account for the "maleness" imparted by the Y chromosome. They contend that, although the Y chromosome carries no genetic information, it gets more from the other genes than the X chromosome does. This is made possible by the slower development of the male. If more genetic information is activated by the Y chromosome, both advantageous and disadvantageous traits will be more prevalent in males. So we note the greater prevalence of males at both extremes of the distribution of I.Q. scores, height, coming of age at puberty, and so forth. The slower rate of maturation means that males remain at risk to adverse experiences for longer periods of time before they fully develop. As a result, there is a greater number of male casualities at all stages of psychosexual development.[9]

Hormonal Influences. As soon as the sex organs differentiate into testes or ovaries (in about the sixth or seventh week for the male and about six weeks later for the female), two other additives affect male development. One is the Mullerian inhibiting substance, which prevents the development of a uterus. The other is the hormone testosterone. At first testosterone has a localized effect on the internal development of the testes, but gradually it expands its sphere of influence over the developing embryo as the testes produce both sperm and androgens. The androgens provide a hormonal environment for the con-

[9]Ibid., pp. 23–25 passim. Reference is to Ounstead and Taylor, eds., *Genetic Differences: Their Ontogeny and Significance* (London: Churchill, 1972).

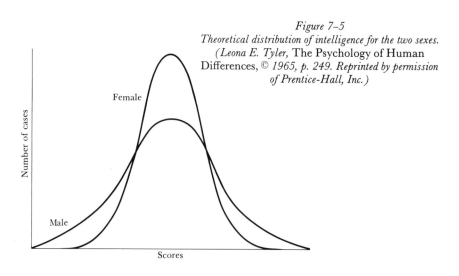

Figure 7–5
Theoretical distribution of intelligence for the two sexes.
(Leona E. Tyler, The Psychology of Human
Differences, *© 1965, p. 249. Reprinted by permission
of Prentice-Hall, Inc.)*

tinued development of the embryo. The ovary likewise has a dual function. It produces eggs and secretes female hormones (estrogen and progesterone).

The effects of these hormones are difficult to differentiate from the effects caused by the chromosomes. Money contends that, at this point, control of psychosexual development is passed to the sex hormones, and that genetic control is released. One basis for this conclusion is the fact that in some instances the hormones can have effects on the developing embryo that override the genes. For example, if androgen is not produced in adequate amounts, a female form will be produced in spite of the presence of a Y chromosome. This leads some observers to conclude that all mammals are initially female in their development—not male, as the psychoanalysts would have it, or neutral, as Money and others contend.

The hormonal environment of the developing embryo is complex because both male and female sex hormones are present. Embryonic ovaries have some tissue that produces androgens, and embryonic testes have some tissue that produces estrogens. Sex hormones are also produced by other glands in the endocrine system, such as the thyroid and adrenal glands, and are generated by chemical combination in the bloodstream. Thus, it is not the presence or absence of a specific sex hormone that makes people male or female, but rather the level of a particular hormone in their system. Females typically have higher levels of estrogen than androgen, while males have more androgens than estrogen.

Embryos are affected by their mother's hormones, as well as by those produced by their own bodies. Males need to maintain relatively high levels of androgens to counteract the effects of their mother's estrogen. Essentially, to develop normally, males must develop a resistance to estrogen. Females, on the other hand, are sensitive to the androgen produced by the mother. A very small amount of androgen will "masculinize" the female.

In most cases, the hormonal influence on the developing embryo matches its genetic sex. Genetic males develop testes that secrete higher levels of androgens, which continue the development of the male form and suppress the development of the uterus and the Mullerian Duct. Genetic females develop ovaries that secrete higher levels of estrogens, and the female form further develops.

INFANCY

At birth, the typical infant's sex is determined by the kind of genitals it possesses. The cry of "it's a girl" or "it's a boy" initiates a whole host of special cues that set the continuous process of sex role assignment in motion.

In most cases, it is easy to tell whether a baby is a boy or a girl. But about 1 percent of all babies are *primary hermaphrodites*—individuals who have the physical characteristics of both sexes and are not clearly one or the other. In spite of their rarity, hermaphrodites are interesting to study for the light they shed on the role played by society in the development of a person's sex identity. When the baby's external genitals are clearly male or female, its assignment as male or female seems to be a natural continuation of the process of development. Only in ambiguous cases, such as hermaphrodites, is gender assignment apt to be seen as a construct of society rather than nature.

On file at Johns Hopkins University are the case studies of thirty matched pairs of hermaphrodites who were sexually alike at birth. However, in each pair, one was assigned the masculine sex role and the other the feminine sex role. Their development has followed their assigned gender, and they differ from one another in the same fashion as normal women differ from normal men. This seems convincing evidence of the importance of social experience in establishing sex roles and sex identity. Whatever biological factors may operate in this process seem to have been clearly overridden. But perhaps this is simply because these biological factors were too weak in the first place. More evidence must be presented before the effects of social experience can be convincingly demonstrated.

A better understanding will be reached when one person, who was a normal male at birth, reaches full maturity. Because of a surgical accident during circumcision, which necessitated the removal of his penis, this person was assigned the gender of a female. Through further surgery and hormone treatments she became a female and appears to be developing normally in her assigned gender. Such cases are being carefully followed as scientists study the effects of social experience on the formation of sex identity.

In some cases, an imbalance of sex hormones before birth has been found to affect the structure of the brain. The prenatal brain of some females is masculinized by abnormally high levels of testosterone, producing certain kinds of "tomboys." These girls join in with the boys in rough-and-tumble play; prefer cowboy gear, toy cars, and guns to dolls; are less concerned about their appearance; and are less interested in weddings and babies and more interested in careers than a comparable group of normal girls. These girls are not totally distinct from the normal girls—they are not boys in girl's bodies. But, because they have been exposed to the masculinizing effect of testosterone in abnormally high concentrations during their prenatal development, they are more likely to behave like boys than females that have not been so exposed.

The masculine counterpart of the tomboy is not the over-estrogenized male. The amount of estrogen needed to cause a feminization of the male brain would also cause a miscarriage. Instead, the counterpart is the underandrogenized boy. Their profiles are pretty much like the mirror image of the overandrogenized girl: They are not girls, but are more apt to act like them.[10]

Some researchers have concluded that there is a period of about eighteen months after birth during which the infant can be considered psychosexually neutral. During this early period, infants are not consciously aware of their gender. Thus, up to about eighteen months, which is generally the time when infants are known to become aware of their own genital differences and also the time when language develops, infants can be assigned to either gender with relatively few complications. The parents must be in agreement with the assigned sex, must rear the child accordingly, and prepare the child for the proper hormonal treatment at puberty. Sex reassignment can take place after eighteen months of age, but with increasing difficulty for the child.

Although such young infants may not be aware of their own sex, they appear to make discriminations by gender at a very early age. By age twelve months, infants are somehow able to distinguish gender differences in other people. For instance, male babies move toward male babies more than they do toward female babies, and female babies more often select other female babies as playmates.[11] There are differences between the sexes that seem to be more related to physiological differences than to social influences, but the situation is not clear-cut. For example, female infants show a greater taste preference for sweets and have less range in elevating their heads than do male infants. It seems reasonable to assume that these behaviors reflect biology more than society, but the importance of these differences is still in doubt.

The parents have certain ideas about how men and women should behave, and they communicate these to their children from the time they are born. For example, in one study, parents were asked to describe their newborn babies. Those who had had girls were apt to describe their babies as sweet, beautiful, and delicate. Those who had had boys, on the other hand, were apt to use words like strong, robust, and active to describe their babies. The catch in this study was that all the babies selected were the same height and weight, so what the parents saw were their expectations rather than reality. These expectations will be passed on to the child in various ways.

The first year of life is also distinguished by the fact that the mother almost exclusively determines the rewards and punishments

[10]Ibid., p. 71.

[11]Michael Lewis, "Early Sex Differences in the Human Studies of Socioemotional Development," *Archives of Sexual Behavior* (July 1975), pp. 329–38.

received by the baby. Fathers are not uncaring, but they are typically uninvolved. This means that female babies have a strong model to imitate, but males must struggle more to develop their masculinity. Lewis determined that fathers of three-month old babies spent an average of thirty-seven seconds a day with their children—hardly enough time to have much effect on their socialization.[12] Even mothers who consciously try to avoid sex stereotyping have been observed to choose the appropriate sex-related color for their infants, even though they did not distinguish between the sexes of their infants in other behaviors. In the second year of life, the father enters the scene in a typically "masculine" fashion. He plays with the baby, rather than nourishing it.

CHILDHOOD

Conscious learning of sex roles begins at about age eighteen months. As soon as children begin to acquire language, they begin to internalize the expectations of others. "Little boys do not cry." "Little girls do not play so rough." The toys provided each sex differ significantly. There is evidence that the choice of toys for children as young as twenty months are in line with sex role stereotypes.[13] The thought of a boy playing with a doll or a girl playing with a gun is quite upsetting to some parents. Children are sensitive to their parents' subtle expressions of displeasure as well as the sometimes violent rebuffs they receive for gender-inappropriate behavior. Boys typically enjoy adventurous group play such as cops and robbers, war games, cowboys and Indians, and exploring. Girls tend to play house, jump rope, play hopscotch, color, and play with paper dolls, which are less adventuresome and more individualized activities. These play activities affect their neuromuscular development and may help to account for some of the differences between boys and girls, as noted earlier.

Children also pick up their parents' attitudes toward their own sex identity and society's preference for men over women. A little girl may not only learn that her brother is treated differently, but she may see him being treated better. Many preschool girls play at being boys by stuffing things into their pants to simulate a penis. Preschool boys almost never indicate a desire to be female, having already learned that being a male is more desirable. These attitudes are further reinforced when the child begins school.

The school exerts an enormous influence over sex role development from the age of about six and onward. Teachers pay a great deal of

[12]Ibid.

[13]Greta Fein, David Johnson, Nancy Kesson, Linda Stork, and Lisa Wasserman, "Sex Stereotypes and Preferences in the Toy Choices of 20 Month Old Boys and Girls," *Development Psychology* (July 1975), pp. 527–28.

Figure 7–6
Children learn and practice sex-role behavior through play. Traditional sex roles can be
weakened or reinforced by the kinds of toys given to children to play with and by parents'
attitudes toward the games children play. (© George W. Gardner)

attention to the stereotypes, and the segregation of activities on the basis of sex confirms the importance of the differences between boys and girls. The teacher's expectations that boys are likely to excel in math and girls in language turn out to be self-fulfilling prophecies in much the same way that such expectations foster racial stereotypes. If the sexes are segregated during the school year for the purpose of discussing health, hygiene, or sex, then it is more likely that they will continue to perpetuate the stereotypical differences, thereby rendering communication between the sexes even more difficult.

Textbooks and television also contribute to the definition of sex roles. A 1971 review of texts used in California in the second through sixth grades found that more than 80 percent of the story space presented male characters. Girls or women were found in only 15 percent of the illustrations, and then they were mainly in the background. Male coverage was found to far exceed female coverage in a Princeton study of 2,760 stories written for children.[14] A recent study of tele-

[14]John Gagnon, *Human Sexualities* (Glenview, Ill.: Scott Foresman, 1977), p. 74.

Figure 7–7
(Left, © George W. Gardner; right, Leonard Freed,
© Magnum Photos, Inc.)

vision commercials found that men were shown more frequently than women and that both were cast in roles that supported sexual stereotypes.[15] Clearly such an imbalance contributes to the notion of the greater importance of the male of the species.

Younger children often have friends of both sexes and, if left to themselves, would probably treat people as people, rather than as males and females. Many adults today also find traditional sex roles too limiting. But the memory of our early childhood training and the pressure of society as expressed in the media and in the schools combine to teach us our place and keep us there.

We train our children in sex roles before we tell them very much about sex itself. They do not learn about sexuality until their sex roles are already well established. "If we tell young girls that they really want to be mommies, then the social stereotype of 'mommy' begins to shape all the other things a girl does and wants."[16] The "mommy stereotype" includes much about sex role behavior, but nothing about how to be good in bed. Mommies are not supposed to express their sexuality in front of their children, so, from childhood on, women learn to downplay their sexuality.

Do children have sexual feelings, apart from the attitudes they acquire about being male or female? Until Freud, the Victorians were

[15]Leslie Zebrowitz, McArthur, and Beth Gabrielle Resko, "The Portrayal of Men and Women in American Television Commercials," *Journal Of Social Psychology* (December 1975), pp. 209–21.

[16]John Gagnon, *Human Sexualities,* p. 71. See also Janet Lever, "Sex Differences in the Games Children Play," *Social Problems* (April 1976), pp. 478–87.

so oriented toward reproductive sex that they thought that neither children nor old people (who could not reproduce) had any sexual feelings worth mentioning. When Freud first published his theory of childhood sexuality, people were outraged. The idea of connecting innocent children with such a dangerous and powerful feeling as sex! Much research since Freud has overreacted to such narrow-minded denials by tending to see adult sexual themes in children's play. Parents are inclined to violently suppress their children's sex play because they give it adult meanings. There is really little evidence for this position. It is more reasonable to assume that play, not sex, dominates the intersex activities of children, even when their behavior mimics adult sexuality.

Young boys have erections and experience orgasm from the age of five months. Young girls have also been observed to have orgasmic re-

Figure 7–8
In spite of Freud's theory of childhood sexuality, there is little evidence that children actually express adult sexual themes in their play.
(© George W. Gardner)

sponses. But this ability does not seem to lead to a desire for sex in young children. "If the orgasm were a natural phenomenon and the outcome of a strong drive, many more people should have it than there is any evidence for."[17] Kinsey commented on the distinctiveness of childhood sexuality.

> *The sexual life of the younger boy is more or less a part of his other play; it is usually sporadic, and . . . it may be without overt manifestations in a fair number of cases. The sexual life of the older male is, on the other hand, an end in itself, and . . . in nearly all boys its overt manifestations become frequent and regular, soon after the onset of adolescence.*[18]

PUBERTY

In our society, adolescence is a difficult period for most people because for the first time social expectations support the overt sexual ac-

[17]Ibid., p. 85.

[18]Alfred Kinsey et al., *Sexual Behavior in the Human Male* (Philadelphia: W. B. Saunders Publishing Company, 1948), p. 182.

Figure 7–9
At puberty, we must translate our
childhood sex roles into adult forms.
(Woodfin Camp & Associates)

Figure 7–10
Males in general are stronger than females, but females have lately begun to play traditionally male sports and games. (© Abigail Heyman, Magnum Photos, Inc.)

tivity of males (and to some lesser but increasing extent of females).[19] The double standard is still very much with us, though it may be declining in its influence. Peers provide the major information about sexuality to both young boys and girls. Most of this information is misleading and emotionally laden. It is no wonder that sexual awakening in the United States is not a smooth transition.

At puberty the level of sex hormones in the body increases. John Money believes that for the first time in the developing child's experience, these hormones exceed a certain threshold level, which permits visual stimuli to elicit sexual arousal in a new way. The child's fantasies become more sexual in nature and express what the child feels about being male or female or what he or she has learned about sexuality.

A part of the trauma of adolescence in our society is that these images may confront the young person with emotions and desires totally condemned by the society—though these are apparently the product of the person's experience in early childhood. The images cannot be controlled and, if inappropriate in terms of cultural norms, may cre-

[19]Adolescence is not a traumatic transition in all societies. See, for example, Margaret Mead, *Coming of Age in Samoa* (New York: Mentor Books, 1949).

ate havoc in a young person's life. Thus the young boy who experiences a wet dream while fantasizing a homosexual relationship may be confronted with a sense of perversion induced by the norms against homosexual behavior. At the same time he is gratified by the pleasure of his orgasm. An individual may experience a difficult transition to adult sex identity as a result of such experiences. The relationship of hormonal levels and the effect of fantasy on psychosexual development, however, are very imperfectly understood at present. For example, the hormonal clock for pubertal development is not perfectly synchronized with the experience of falling in love. Some children experience their first love affair before they become physically mature.

For the female, the most dramatic mark of puberty occurs with the onset of her menses. This physiological event is occurring at even earlier ages throughout the world (see Figure 7–11). The beginning of the menses and the development of the breasts give the female obvious confirmation of her physical maturity. The lowering of the voice and the development of a beard are less dramatic male counterparts. Most societies compensate for this fact by emphasizing the

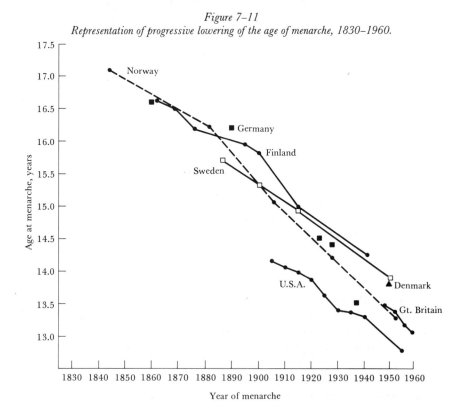

Figure 7–11
Representation of progressive lowering of the age of menarche, 1830–1960.

male rites of passage at puberty. Women in primitive societies, on the other hand, are typically secluded in their menstrual huts. They may be secluded because of their greater power, which is feared by the men, rather than ostracized because of their uncleanness, as has been commonly thought.

The development of the secondary sexual characteristics (breasts,

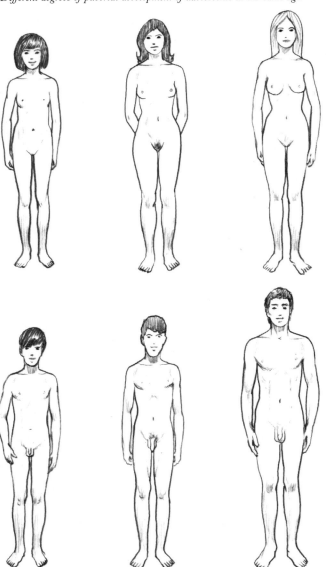

Figure 7–12
Different degrees of pubertal development of adolescents at the same age.

hair on the chest, and so on, of both sexes and the attainment of reproductive capability prepare the body for adult responsibilities long before our society considers individuals of either sex to be socially responsible. In contemporary Stone Age societies, the time span between the onset of puberty and marriage, which signifies full adult status, is usually quite short, rarely more than a few years. Industrial societies, however, have increased this time span. It is widening even more at present as a result of the trends toward later marriage and the earlier onset of menstruation. Since ovulation ordinarily follows about two years after the onset of menstruation, young women commonly wait about eight years in our society before they are socially permitted to do what they are biologically capable of doing—have a baby.[20]

The development of the secondary sex characteristics does not proceed uniformly or without complications. Figure 7–12 illustrates the variation in physical maturity of normal adolescents of the same age. The different rates of development among adolescents can affect their self-image, as well as their sense of sex identity in adolescence and adulthood. A boy who develops slowly may feel less manly than his friends who have developed at an earlier age. A girl who develops sooner than her friends may be exposed to sexual invitations before she is emotionally ready to accept herself as a sexual being. The extent to which the secondary sex characteristics confirm or deny an individual's sense of sex identity is thus another variant in psychosexual development.

However one may choose to view the process of acquiring a sex identity, it is by no means a simple, straightforward unfolding of natural propensities. Disjunctures may occur at every level of development. Even in the most typical cases, in which radical departures from the normal path do not occur, there is considerable trauma associated with becoming a man or woman that seems to be magnified in industrialized societies.

ADULT SEXUALITY

The end product of our learning to become sexual in the context of socially prescribed sex roles is the marked difference in masculine and feminine styles of lovemaking. The young man has learned about his sexual arousal and orgasmic capacity through the experience of masturbation. Sex fundamentally means pleasure to him regardless of the overlying layers of guilt that he may attach to the act. Sex is initially focused on the genitals as a result of his masturbatory practices. An

---

[20]This is probably just as well. There is evidence that babies born to mothers in their early teens are more prone to various disorders than babies born to older mothers.

old army cadence count goes, "This is my rifle and this is my gun. The first is for killing, the second for fun." Sex is something a boy does to a girl. He initiates. He penetrates. He satisfies himself, and her if he is so inclined. For the young man sexuality is something used to bolster his sense of masculinity and a means of providing pleasure. He can boast about his adventures and even his parents will probably approve while he sows his wild oats.

A young woman, typically, has a quite different experience. She is much less likely to have masturbated and, if she has had such an experience, is less likely to have shared it in any way with others. Her sexuality is linked not to the direct experience of pleasure, but to the anticipation of love, romance, and marriage. Her arousal is much less likely to be focused on her clitoris and is less expressed in fantasy. Having been trained to be passive, she expects to be swept off her feet, to be penetrated, to receive the semen, and to conceive the child.

In point of fact, both men and women are much more similar in their physiological response patterns than they are different. The similarities can be enhanced by a reduction in the genital focus or, as Albert Ellis would urge, in overcoming "the great coital myth." Men can learn to be more responsive to nongenital stimulation in lovemaking, and women can learn to take the initiative and express their fantasies in behavior more than they tend to do.

From the point of view of human lovemaking, sex roles are important because they shape our perception of sexual arousal and response. We learn about becoming sexually aroused in the context of well-established understandings about what it means to be a man or a woman, and these understandings affect the way in which we make love.

The Case of the Transsexual

Perhaps the most unusual problems in sex identity are of the transsexuals, those people who feel that their anatomy somehow conceals their true identity. Something of their dilemma can be caught in the following excerpts from *Conundrum,* written by Jan Morris. Jan is a transsexual who was formerly James Morris, a reporter for the *London Times,* a member of the Hilary expedition to Mount Everest, and formerly of the 9th Queens Royal Lancers. For forty-six years Jan lived as a splendid example of masculinity as far as outward appearances could indicate. But inwardly there was always a profound doubt.

I was three or perhaps four years old when I realized that I had been born into the wrong body, and should really be a girl. I remember the moment well, and it is the earliest memory of my life.

Figure 7–13
Transvestites and transsexuals
have sexual identity problems.
But while the transsexual
resolves these problems by
physically becoming the other
sex, the transvestite is content to
adopt the clothing and
superficial mannerisms of the
opposite sex. (Jason Lauré,
Woodfin Camp & Associates)

> *I was sitting beneath my mother's piano, and her music was falling*
> *around me like cataracts, enclosing me in a cave. . . .*
>   *What triggered so bizarre a thought I have long forgotten, but the con-*
> *viction was unfaltering from the start.*[21]

We do not presently know where such a discordant sense of sex identity originates. But some people have not been helped through any known treatment to bring their sense of being in the wrong body in line with their anatomy or their social roles, however unambiguously these have been laid down. Since Christine Jorgensen startled the world with her sex-change operation in 1952, more and more of these people are seeking relief through surgical, hormonal, and psychological treatment. While these transformed people may still have problems, the assessment they commonly give is that life is better for them after their change of sex. Because the surgery necessary to provide a functional vagina is simpler than that required to provide a functional penis, in most cases, the male-to-female transsexual has an easier adjustment to make than the female-to-male transsexual.

James Morris's transformation into Jan Morris, through surgery and hormonal treatment, took over eight years. She divorced her wife

[21]Jan Morris, *Conundrum* (New York: Harcourt Brace Jovanovich, 1974), p. 3.

Figure 7–14
Dr. Renee Richards (United
Press International Photo)

but remains very close to her wife and the children she sired as a man. Jan Morris shares some of her experience in *Conundrum.*

> *I invite my women readers to imagine how they would themselves have felt if, successfully disguised as a young man, they had been admitted to this . . . male society . . . like a spy in a courteous enemy camp . . . you would find yourself caught up in the fascination of observing how the other side worked. . . . But most of all you would have felt plain pleasure, at having handsome and high-spirited young men all around you.*[22]

Jan's hormone treatments had a direct affect on her feelings about her body.

> *The first result was not exactly a feminization of my body, but a stripping away of the rough hide in which the male person is clad. I do not mean merely the body hair, nor even the leatheriness of the skin, nor all the hard protrusion of muscle; all these indeed vanished over the next few years, but there went with them something less tangible too, which I now know to be specifically masculine—a kind of unseen layer of accumulated resilience, which provides a shield for the male of the species.*[23]

[22]Ibid., p. 31.

[23]Ibid., p. 106.

Have times really changed?

Would my conflict have been so bitter if I had been born now, when the gender line is so much less rigid? If society had allowed me to live in the gender I preferred, would I have bothered to change sex?

Is mine only a transient phenomenon, between the dogmatism of the last century, when men were men and women were ladies, and the eclecticism of the next, when citizens will be free to live in the gender role they prefer?[24]

Interestingly enough, Jan is opposed to the intolerant kind of militant feminism. She strongly defends the right of women to be treated as women traditionally have been, to be deferred to and romanced. Apparently there is a need for security in traditional values even in the case of the most adventuresome.

John Money recounts a part of Roberta Cowell's story—another transsexual.

During this training period (during which Roberta was learning the female gender role), while he was still appearing as a man, Cowell arranged to meet an author whose work he admired. The author turned out to be a full-bearded, pipe-smoking, very masculine type who expressed a low opinion of women. As Cowell rose to the defense of womankind, the author's attacks grew more vitriolic. Finally, after a prolonged pause, the author dropped this bombshell: "I don't really see why I shouldn't tell you—five years ago I was a woman."[25]

Such cases raise profound questions about our conception of gender. We are what nature has made us. We are what we have been taught. Most of us stop there. What would we be if we had the courage to make ourselves?

Summary

We can no longer assume that the differences we ascribe to men and women are important or based upon a natural biological base. The division of labor between the sexes beyond the primary roles in reproduction were perhaps once efficient means of insuring the survival of hunting and gathering families, but modern industrial societies have less need to stress the differences between the sexes.

The process of psychosexual differentiation can be variously described and the importance of genetic, hormonal, and psychosocial

[24]Ibid., p. 172.

[25]Money and Tucker, *Sexual Signatures,* p. 345.

factors valued differently, but the traditional distinction between nature and nurture seems less and less adequate. The growing organism develops in an environment over which we are gaining increased control. Anatomy is no longer destiny.

Getting in Touch

8

Sometimes I make love to get care and cuddling.
Sometimes I am so absorbed in the sensation
of touch and taste and smell and sight and sound
that I feel I've returned to that childhood
time when feeling good was all that mattered.
Sometimes I am the tom-girl as we tumble and tease.
Sometimes sex is spiritual—high mass
could not be more sacred. Sometimes I fuck to
get away from the tightness and seriousness in myself.
Sometimes I want to come and feel the
ripples of orgasm through my body. Sometimes tears
mix with come and sweat, and I am one
with another. Sometimes sex is more powerful than
getting high, and through it I unite with the
stream of love that flows among us all.
Sex can be most anything and everything for me.
How good that feels!

Our Bodies, Ourselves

Because human beings bring an inner life as well as an outward set of behaviors to their sexual encounters, sex can be almost anything and everything. For example, masturbation can be a solitary act performed for the sake of pleasurable sensation or a release from nervous tension. When the tension has been released in orgasm, the job is done. Masturbation can also involve others in fantasy or in mutual contact. Likewise, sexual intercourse can be a very lonely affair (neither partner getting much beyond their skin sensations) or it can be a fusion (a becoming one with another). The motivations for engaging in sex, the roles played, and the emotions felt vary from occasion to occasion. This diversity can be celebrated as a part of the richness of human sexuality, or denied by wishing that sex were less complicated or by attempting to make it just one thing (such as a deep expression of love). Sex can be experienced with awareness or simply endured. It is possible to be largely unaware of, or indifferent to, the sexual experience in any form.

This chapter is concerned with getting in touch with whatever feelings, sensations, or emotions that might be experienced in sex, whether sex is experienced alone or with others. Getting in touch with oneself also includes an examination of some of the beliefs and attitudes that one has about sex.

Getting in touch with others is related to how well we have gotten in touch with ourselves. If we are clear about how we feel about sex, and know what we want out of it on a particular occasion, it is easier to communicate our desires to others. Often being clear about one's own desires enables others to clarify theirs as well and a more enjoyable experience can be shared. Being able to ask for what one wants in sex may take time or it may seem to come naturally.

There is no obligation to always be aware in sexually relating. In fact, total awareness is rarely possible. To read this chapter as though it were a description of what ought to be done or experienced is to miss its intent, which is simply to point out that we all have the capacity to explore. Such an exploration of sexual awareness may not lead to problem-free sexual relationships. Indeed, problems may seem to increase because they are more likely to be noticed when lovers become more aware. Sexual technique may or may not improve with sexual awareness. More pleasure in sex may be a by-product. A major benefit of awareness in sexual experience is to be found in whatever increased capacity we experience for clearly defining what is happening so that no one is deceived. Another result is an increased capacity for using sex as a means of communication and confirmation, if we so desire.

Getting in Touch with Oneself

It has been said that the degree to which we are capable of knowing another person is directly related to the degree to which we know ourselves. The more I know about myself and my own feelings, the more receptive I can be when another person reveals something about himself or herself. For example, if in my own existence, I have known,

Figure 8–1
(Richard Kalvar, © Magnum Photos, Inc.)

Figure 8–2
Because none of us can count on finding someone to share our lives with, we must all learn
to be comfortable with ourselves. (Wayne Miller, Magnum Photos, Inc.)

tasted, and experienced loneliness, I can then recognize loneliness when another hints of it. With deepening awareness I can sort through the kinds of loneliness I experience and cope with each in more appropriate ways.

Sexual encounters promise a release from loneliness. But if I have sex simply in order to overcome the intense loneliness I feel, the promise is not likely to be fulfilled. This is not because sexual encounters cannot be mystical experiences of communion in which we are one with another. It is just that usually they are not. To expect to be transported into ecstasy on each occasion is to entertain expectations that are too unrealistic. When our expectations are too great, sex may increase our feelings of loneliness.

Getting in touch with loneliness in solitude, recognizing that as distinct individuals we cannot share all of our inner lives with one another, and accepting the creation of ourselves as a personal responsibility are marks of awareness. Such means of coping with the loneliness of limited human existence is found in the life stories of men and women throughout history. Some, like Ghandi, gave up sexual love in order to practice what to them was a higher form of love for all humankind. Because none of us can count on finding someone to share our lives with, we must all learn to be comfortable with ourselves.

Another kind of loneliness comes from being out of touch with our bodies and how they function. We live in them, but are not of them. So much of modern life is carried out in our heads that it takes some time for most of us to become aware of our bodies. It is an uncommon modern view to believe that we are our bodies. Most of us believe that we, in some way or another, live in our bodies. Some of us feel more comfortable about living there than others. A leisurely visual and tactile investigation of our own bodies can help us get in touch. For example, because a greater portion of the genitals of woman are inside their bodies, where they are difficult to examine, women commonly feel estranged from their genitals and sometimes from their sexuality as well. A personal examination of the clitoris, vagina, and cervix can help women to overcome this sense of being alien from their own bodies. Even though men have less of a problem in observing their genitals, they may be equally shy about touching themselves. The penis may be something that is only supposed to be touched when urinating and is never to be examined unless something is thought to be wrong with it. Techniques such as yoga and massage can increase our consciousness and thus increase our feeling of being at home and at ease with and within our bodies.

The pleasure of sex is greatly enhanced if we enjoy ourselves and our bodies. Given the marvelous versatility and sensitivity of the human body, one might think that we would naturally enjoy it. But this is not so. Most of us have been raised to have negative attitudes toward self-love and self-pleasuring, and we bring these negative attitudes to our sexual encounters with others. A childhood lacking warmth and affection, devoid of touching and tenderness, is not likely to produce an adult who enjoys touching, warmth, and intimacy. Our feelings about ourselves and our bodies, therefore, are clearly not simply the result of our personal efforts or shortcomings. If we have been warmly loved, we can warmly love ourselves and others. If our bodies have been accepted by others, it is likely that we will find them acceptable ourselves. If not, with care and patience we can learn to love ourselves.

Masturbation

While many factors have placed obstacles in the way of our getting in touch with our true feelings, our heritage has placed even greater barriers in the way of our getting physically in touch with our bodies.

Since our bodies offer such obvious and convenient delights, some people feel that our bodies must be intrinsically sinful. Bodily sensations are even more visceral—and thus less rational—than emotions. Yet Kinsey discovered that masturbation was practiced by almost all men and was the method of stimulation most likely to produce orgasm in women.[1] A greater number of men and women masturbate more often today than in Kinsey's time. But most are still worried about their masturbation.[2] Professional men and women, in particular, may give intellectual support to the idea that masturbation is all right and may even be beneficial. But when they themselves masturbate, their own enjoyment is often clouded over with second thoughts, reservations, and guilt.

You need not worry about how much or how little you masturbate. Most men and a growing number of women masturbate throughout their lives, and the frequency seems to be increasing among the young. Some consider masturbation to be a wholly adequate means of sexual release if no other outlets are available.

Masturbation is our primary sex life. It is our sexual base. Everything we do beyond that is simply how we choose to socialize our sex life. . . . Masturbation can help return sex to its proper place—to the individual.[3]

Many others think of masturbation as a way of discovering what turns them on and of learning how to better control their state of arousal in order to more fully enjoy lovemaking. Masturbation can be practiced alone or with a partner. Because we may find it hard to talk about sex, masturbation may be the best way of showing our partner what pleases us. In order for this to be true, however, both partners should feel free enough to enjoy such activity. Because many of us feel uncomfortable when we masturbate privately, it may take time for us to become open enough to share this activity with a partner.

There is no evidence that masturbation will necessarily make sex with a partner less desirable or less satisfying. A male's concentration on masturbation can focus his erotic attention on his genitals and make him less likely to value the nongenital sexuality of women, but this possibility can be offset by more adequate learning and varied technique.

The penis can be stimulated in a number of ways in masturbation.

[1]Alfred C. Kinsey et al., *Sexual Behavior in the Human Female* (New York: Pocket Books, 1967), pp. 148–56.

[2]Morton Hunt, *Sexual Behavior in the 1970s* (New York: Dell, 1974), pp. 75–87. Shere Hite, *The Hite Report* (New York: Macmillan, 1976), pp. 6–13.

[3]Betty Dodson, *Liberating Masturbation* (New York: Betty Dodson, Box 1933, 1974), pp. 1–55.

It can be rolled between the palms as the hands move back and forth. It can be rubbed against the body with one or both hands. It can be rubbed between the legs while in a squatting position, leaving the hands free to caress other parts of the body such as the nipples or anus. Lubricating the shaft of the penis with massage oil, soap suds, or other lubricants can vary the sensation and add to the pleasure.

Men typically masturbate by moving one hand rapidly up and down the shaft of the penis. When they feel the moment of inevitability—the point at which the prostate gland pushes the semen into the urethra—involuntary contractions take place in the abdomen and penis, and ejaculation shortly follows. Control over ejaculation can be obtained by consciously deferring this moment of inevitability. It can be approached many times by paying careful attention to the mounting sense of inevitability and delayed many times, thus prolonging the sense of pleasure. The initial task is to become aware of this sensation of inevitability and then learn to postpone it.

The practice of slow masturbation trains the man to postpone the moment of inevitability. Slow masturbation requires time and privacy. By whatever means that pleases him, the man brings himself to the point of inevitability and then stops any further stimulation until he feels that it is possible to begin again without ejaculation. With practice this can be continued without loss of erection for long periods of time. Such a form of masturbation helps prevent premature ejaculation in intercourse and is a very enjoyable form of self-pleasuring in its own right.

Since most men stop masturbating when ejaculation occurs, few are aware of the fact that their sexual response pattern is sometimes much like the woman's. With further stimulation—usually with the assistance of a vibrator—it is possible to ripple in and out of intense pleasure peaks for an extended period of time, with or without an erection. If lovemaking with a partner is based solely on vaginal penetration, this sort of training will not be very useful. If, however, lovemaking is defined more broadly—as giving pleasure, rather than only as intercourse—then such information may be useful in order to vary the sexual scenerio. The vibrator may be applied by the partner.

Since an ejaculation relieves the sense of urgency in most men, some find it desirable to masturbate before making love with a partner so that they can allow their arousal to build more slowly, whether or not it culminates in intercourse or orgasm.

Women may have to pay a bit more attention to themselves in order to learn how to masturbate. The clitoris is more difficult to discover and, in most cases, requires more careful stimulation than the penis. Since women are not traditionally supposed to enjoy sexual arousal, some may be more burdened than men with psychological hang-ups. The following seems to be common experience.

I'm about to have an orgasm in the middle of page 23. What to do? The page blurs and my body movements make the lines shift in all directions. My muscles tighten as the intensity rises. Finally, I put down the book and direct all my attention to the feelings my hands are creating. As my fingers move faster up and down, squeezing and massaging my clit, I direct all my energy into achieving climax. When it comes, I try to release myself in the feeling, to make it last longer. All this is a fairly regular occurrence for me. I often find myself masturbating as I read or as I lie in bed trying to fall asleep. I mentioned this to a friend one day and discovered that I'm not the only one reading blurry pages. . . .

So, here I am lying on the floor with my hand on my crotch, paranoid as hell. The result of culturally induced guilt. Is there anyone else in the house? I wouldn't want anyone to know what I'm doing. What would they think? What would *they think anyway? Livia's horney again. Too bad she doesn't have someone to fuck. It's disgusting. I wish she would stop! It's making me uncomfortable.*[4]

In spite of such emotional discomfort, a woman's ability to achieve orgasm with a partner seems to be related to her experience with masturbation. Those who have masturbated are much more likely to achieve and enjoy orgasm than those who have not.

Most women masturbate by lying on their backs and using their hands to indirectly stimulate the clitoris. They may try rubbing the fingers down either side of the clitoral shaft or massaging the mons pubis with circular movements of the hand or vibrator, or any of a number of other variations. The mons itself is very sensitive. Some women who have had their clitoris surgically removed are able to achieve orgasm through the stimulation of the mons area. When a vibrator is used, a towel may be wrapped around it to protect the clitoris. Direct stimulation of the clitoris is sometimes painful. Artificial or natural lubricants help reduce the sensitivity and generally create a more pleasing sensation.

Freud believed that masturbation, which concentrates on the clitoris, was an immature expression of sexuality. It was all right for young girls, but women were not considered fully mature until they had experienced a vaginal orgasm. Once the penis was present, the vagina was to be penetrated and the clitoris put aside. The result of this was a vast number of unorgasmic women who touched their clitorises secretly and bemoaned their immaturity.

Fortunately, the notion that the only mature orgasm is a vaginal orgasm is rapidly disappearing from the scene. While many women report being able to distinguish between vaginal sensations and clitoral sensations in orgasm, there is no evidence that one is superior to

[4]Livia Freeman, "Holding My Own," *New Time, New Space,* Wilmington, Delaware (September 1976), p. 1.

the other. Indeed, orgasm may be experienced as an all-pervasive flood of feeling seemingly coming from all parts of the body.

SELF-PLEASURING

Masturbation is only one form of self-pleasure. Some people feel very distant from their bodies and may feel very guilty about even thinking about masturbation. For such people, there are other ways of getting in touch with the body. Becoming aware of what is pleasant to the senses is one. It may take a bit of practice to tune into pleasant bodily sensations. But in a short time the practice usually pays off in increased pleasure, and the activities become self-rewarding.

For example, the taste of an orange can be a sensuous delight. Paying attention to the odor, texture, and taste can make an orange an instrument of pleasure, rather than simply something you eat because you are hungry. A shower can be much more than a means of getting clean if you let yourself experience the pleasurable sensations of suds and water. Cleaning oneself can also be an occasion for exploration and attentiveness to one's body. Listening to music, walking in the

Figure 8–3
How we feel about touching
ourselves forms the basis of our
attitudes toward touching others.
(Paul Fusco, © Magnum
Photos, Inc.)

woods, and lying in the sun are other ways we can tune into the feelings and sensations of things that seem good to our bodies and thus to ourselves.

Most of the time, in everyday life, we are bombarded with sensations. Our world has too many sights and sounds for us to deal with comfortably. The urban environment in which most of us live is a very noisy, smelly, diversified environment, which constantly exposes us to noxious and pleasant stimuli. The stresses and strains of everyday life lead to all sorts of internal sensations. In self-defense, we erect barriers to protect us from the experience of chaos; unfortunately, we screen out much that can please us in the process. We do this habitually, without noticing it. That is why we may have to train ourselves to be open when we can afford to drop our defenses. Focusing our awareness on things that please us and seeking to become more open to what they can give are necessary if we are to increase our pleasure. We can develop the habit of doing so regularly. We can cultivate new kinds of experiences that may surprise us in the pleasure that they provide. Simply sitting still in a relatively quiet spot and letting sensations and thoughts come and go as they will, without trying to identify them or think about them, can be an amazingly pleasurable experience. It usually takes some practice to be able to do this—most of us find it hard to relax completely enough the first time that we try it.

To most of us today, it seems unreasonable to reject and avoid the pleasures of the body. But it is possible that some of us will have a great deal of difficulty giving ourselves permission to experience pleasure without feeling guilty about it. Pleasure should not have to be justified. It is intrinsically meaningful and satisfying. Many of us may feel that we do not have enough of it. Some argue that the maximization of pleasure should be the goal of life. For some people, this philosophy, commonly called *hedonism,* seems to work. For others, its embrace leads to one catastrophe after another and provides little satisfaction.

There is also a middle way. Pleasure can be enjoyed whenever possible, but not sought after as the most important thing in life. Whatever way you choose will undoubtedly affect your capacity to experience pleasure and find enjoyment in your bodily sensations.

It is possible to test your beliefs to the extent that you are clear about them. It is possible to learn from another's experience. Becoming aware of our true convictions about pleasure can help us become more whole or enable us to effectively separate our beliefs from our behavior. If the sense of a whole life is desired, however, it is not possible to believe one way and live in a radically different way for any length of time. "Getting it all together" in this case seems to be a desirable objective. The sense of being whole and together is also a pleasure to be relished.

The Visceral Quality of Feelings

The feelings, thoughts, and emotions that fill our inner world are very important to us. We are these things and more, and not to share them is to isolate ourselves from others and from ourselves. To make believe that these feelings do not exist leads to disaster. When we no longer know how we truly feel about the world and ourselves we no longer know ourselves and we confuse others as to who we are. T. S. Eliot used the term "hollow men" in his poetry to describe people who cut themselves off from their own inner natures. When hollow men are angry, they do not know that they are angry and, of course, they do not know why they are angry.

Getting in touch with feelings is a tantalizing task. We know that emotions are real in a way that ideas are not, for they have a visceral origin that we can feel whenever we let ourselves. Although powerful forces in our culture tell us to control our emotions, we all have had moments of intense emotion when we could actually taste the reality of our feelings. Perhaps this is why we feel attracted to, and yet threatened by, our feelings. Getting in touch with our deepest feelings

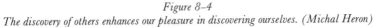

Figure 8–4
The discovery of others enhances our pleasure in discovering ourselves. (Michal Heron)

is in some ways a frightening thing, but should not blind us to the fact that savoring these feelings is also an exciting possibility.

Some of this excitement is reflected in the following passage from Carl Rogers.

Perhaps I can discover and come closer to more of what I really am deep inside—feeling sometimes angry or terrified, sometimes loving and caring, occasionally beautiful and strong or wild and awful—without hiding these feelings from myself. Perhaps I can come to prize myself as the richly varied person I am. Perhaps I can openly be more of this person. If so, I can live by my own experienced values, even though I am aware of all of society's codes. Then I can let myself be all this complexity of feelings and meanings and values with my partner—be free enough to give of love and anger and tenderness as they exist in me. Possibly then I can be a real member of a partnership, because I am on the road to being a real person. I am hopeful that I can encourage my partner to follow his or her own road to a unique personhood, which I would love to share.[5]

The ability to get in touch with who we are deep inside often eludes us. It is true that getting in touch with others depends on our getting in touch with ourselves, but it is no less true that, in important ways, getting in touch with ourselves depends on our getting in touch with others. We discover ourselves in interaction as well as in reflection. But, because interaction with others has so many variables, it seems at first glance to be a most difficult arena for self-discovery.

Congruence

Carl Rogers uses the term *congruence* to describe the ability to function successfully as private individuals and as members of partnerships with other human beings. According to him, a person is congruent when he or she is aware of the feelings that he or she has, and is able to communicate them accurately to another person. The sense of authenticity created by a congruent person tends to encourage other people to respond authentically. Thus the concept of congruence bridges the gap between getting in touch with ourselves and getting in touch with others. As Rogers sees it, congruence is the basis of good, healthy partnerships, which depend on self-awareness and open communication. It is also necessary for partners to each have a sense of personal well-being, without which sexual experience is likely to be less fulfilling. People who are aware of their inner world of feelings,

[5]Carl Rogers, *Becoming Partners: Marriage and Its Alternatives* (New York: Delacorte Press, 1972), p. 209.

Figure 8–5
Congruence is the bridge between getting in touch with oneself and getting in touch with others. (© Ellen Pines, Woodfin Camp & Associates)

sensations, and emotions and who realize that they do not have to act upon every inner urge can be more accepting of their inner life and its complexities. If they are able to express what they feel to others accurately and appropriately (by being aware of the feelings of others), the sexual experience can be greatly enriched. Alex Comfort, for example, suggests that it is desirable for mature lovers to act out emotions such as anger and dominance in games of bondage, where one partner binds and physically controls the other during sexual play.[6] Without awareness and congruence, such play can be dangerous because one or the other of the partners may take the game too seriously and respond with uncontrolled anger or fear.

Getting in Touch with Others

In our efforts to get in touch with others, most of us place a great deal of importance on words. Once we become aware of our feelings, we want to try and say how we feel. Our overreliance on words may impoverish our communication by reducing most of our interaction to conversation. For example, we may miss the opportunity of being aroused by the voice of our beloved—not by the words or "line" that is uttered, but by the simple sound of the beloved's voice. Other cultures make much more deliberate use of eye contact, body language, touch, and taste in communication than we do. All of us speak with

[6]Alex Comfort, *The Joy of Sex* (New York: Crown Publishing Company, 1975).

our entire being, but most of us are unaware of much of what we say. To the extent that this is so, our communication is confused and our sense of being in touch is reduced.

WORDS

Words are often inadequate in conveying what we feel for one another for a number of reasons. Any language is a collection of symbols with meanings that are universally accepted. But languages describe concrete things better than they do abstract ideas and feelings. Even when our language is adequate, we may be unable to express ourselves accurately.

One of the more obvious problems with language is the fact that the same words mean different things to different people. I may have personal associations with certain words that affect me whenever I hear these words used. If, for example, I was brought up in a family where squabbling was constant and often vicious and painful, the word "argument" may have meanings for me that it will not have for someone else. Indeed, it may well be that if a class of fifteen or twenty students were to discuss the role of arguments in family life, no two of them would be talking about the same thing. For one student, an ar-

Figure 8–6
In our efforts to get in touch with others, we depend greatly on the importance of words;
words, however, can often prove inadequate.
(© Jim Anderson, Woodfin Camp & Associates)

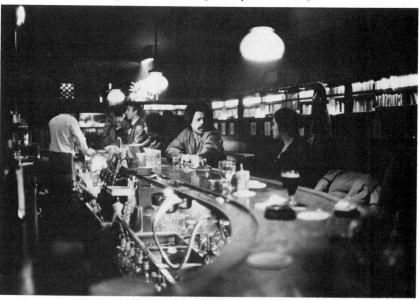

gument would be a healthy airing of differences, while for another it might be a deadly battle of wills that should be avoided at all costs.

In addition to such private meanings, words also have socially determined differences. On this level the associations I have with certain words may be shared by others in my social group, but not by people in different groups. For example, words like "rich," "poor," and even "work" obviously mean different things to people with different levels of income. Words like "liberal," "radical," and "conservative" mean different things to people with different political outlooks. A mother might tell her friends that the young man her daughter is going out with is "a nice boy," but perhaps the daughter wouldn't understand these words in the same way or, if she understood them, might use other words entirely.

Even when such communications problems do not exist, language is often inadequate for conveying our deepest emotions. We all have had the experience of wanting to say something and not knowing how. Indeed, the tenderest, warmest, most human emotions are often the most difficult to express in words. Greeting card companies thrive on the fact that people find it so difficult to say things like, "I care about you and am really sorry to hear that you are sick," and must fall back, in desperation, on prefabricated expressions of emotions. How many of us could find the words to adequately convey to a friend our genuine appreciation of some extraordinary act of consideration?

Because of these inadequacies of language, intimate and caring partnerships tend to develop their own language in which common words come to have very private meanings. Consider the following telephone conversation.

Caller: Hello, Beth, am I disturbing you?
  Beth: Oh no, we were in the meadow. (Giggles)
Caller: The meadow?
  Beth: We were getting up.

Over the years of their marriage, Beth and her husband had come to call their bed "the meadow." Once the association between "bed" and "meadow" is made, however, even an outsider can understand the warmth, the beauty, and the carefreeness that they must have associated with their lovemaking. By the use of one word in their private language, Beth and her husband can convey to each other a rich heritage of experience that is uniquely theirs. This private language enables them to express easily a wide range of feelings and emotions and to recall events in which they have been able to move closer to one another in the past.

Most of us have, at some time, used words with others in this way. Friends develop a common language. Groups of people who live together for any length of time tend to develop a set of words to express important aspects of their lives together. Indeed, for most of us, the type of relationship commonly known as courtship is to a large extent involved with the cultivation of just such a private vocabulary.

Of course, many people are not particularly verbal in their behavior. These people may not invent words or radically change the meanings of common words, but they may rely on nonverbal signs and gestures to supplement their associations with common everyday words like "I love you." For most people, in fact, the language of relationships goes far beyond words. It involves the whole being. We communicate by our tone of voice, by our facial expression, by the use of our eyes. Our whole body is a medium of communication. If we are congruent—that is, if we know how we think and feel about ourselves and our world and can express this to others—the signals that we give off are apt to be clear. If we are not in touch with ourselves or cannot bring ourselves to express what we feel, then we are likely to confuse others by what we communicate.

"It's good to see you," he said with his eyes glued steadfastly to the floor.

In this simple example the lack of eye contact seems to contradict what is said. We wonder if the speaker is just shy or if he really is not very pleased to see us. Even such a simple discrepancy can hinder our ability to understand what is communicated. We have to wait for further information in order to be sure of what is really being said. All of us give off discrepant signals like this from time to time. It is when such behavior becomes a persistent part of a relationship that the relationship itself may be unable to grow and develop. Such discrepancy in what we communicate greatly confuses what we are experiencing in the present. It makes us feel uncertain of what is happening and somewhat out of touch.

BODY LANGUAGE

In sexual encounters body language is particularly powerful when two or more people are rubbing up against one another. The tensing and relaxing of muscles and postures is very apparent to anyone who is aware of their partner's responses. Using the hand to signal displeasure, by gently removing a partner's hand from a particular area of the body as a way of nonverbally indicating that "you're moving too fast" is a common example of body language in sexual contact. But the body speaks before we make such contact and what it has to say increases or decreases the clarity of the verbal communication.

Undoubtedly, we are all aware that a person's posture often betrays feelings not expressed in words. We can tell by the position of someone's body whether he or she is interested or bored. By the same token, it is difficult to say convincingly that you are not tired when your whole body betrays the fact that you are.

Body language is not something that we can either use or not use, as we choose. We are using it all the time, whether we know it or not. And, because of our emphasis on words, most often we don't know it. Thus, if our communication is to be as full as possible, it is important for us to realize what we are saying with our bodies. Consider the following incident.

Your roommate says, "I've got to meet my date in about ten minutes and I don't known what time the movie starts. Do me a favor and call the theater." You don't really want to do it—you're reading and don't want to be interrupted, and you feel your roommate should have taken care of these things without depending on you—but on the other hand you don't think it would be right to refuse. So you decide to do it, but unconsciously you want your roommate to know how you feel. You say "Okay," but you get up very slowly from your chair, like it's a real problem for you to move, and slouch over to the telephone.

Your roommate sees the way you are moving and gets the point. Perhaps he or she says, "Oh, don't bother. You don't feel like doing it and it'll only take me a minute. I'll do it myself." Or perhaps he or she merely makes a mental note that he or she owes you a favor. In any case, the discrepancy between the way your body acted and what you said communicated a complex message: You would do this thing but you didn't really like doing it. There's nothing wrong with such a discrepancy in this case, for the two parts of the communication accurately conveyed the two things you were thinking and feeling.

Problems might arise, however, when one does not pay attention to one's body language, so that one is out of touch with one's own feelings. We all have probably been in situations like the one just described, and at some time or other we probably have reacted by not being open about our communication. The following dialogue is what might result in such a situation.

> *Betty: Do me a favor and call the theater.*
> *Suzanne: Okay. (Moves laboriously toward the phone.)*
> *Betty: Oh, never mind, You don't want to do it, so I'll do it myself.*
> *Suzanne: I said I'll do it.*
> *Betty: I know, but you don't feel like it, and it's no trouble for me.*
> *Suzanne: I didn't say I didn't feel like it. I said I'd do it.*

The result is a kind of double bind. Betty correctly interpreted Suzanne's reluctance to make the call and dropped her request. But Suzanne, who probably felt it was wrong not to want to do this favor and so refused to admit that she felt that way, denied having communicated what her body language clearly said and then got annoyed with Betty for responding to it. The result was one of those little squabbles that almost invariably result from a failure to communicate. Both parties were made unnecessarily uncomfortable.

Our bodies, in short, are almost always communicating our feelings to other people. A large part of this communication is unconscious, but it is important that we try to make ourselves aware of as much of it as possible. Only in this way can we get in touch with our own feelings and be aware of the messages we are sending to other people.

MAKING CONTACT

Communication is a process that involves our whole being. What we say and how we say it is important, but so is the language we speak with our hands, our bodies, and our eyes. Often we make contact with another with our eyes before we speak to them, and so the expression that accompanies the glance and the length of time it persists tell us a great deal about the person looking at us.

Because Americans in general are not a people who take looking into each other's eyes seriously, we tend to reserve eye contact for intimate relationships and to limit its use in public interaction. Nevertheless, our eyes can readily convey our feelings even in a public context. This is why people who want to conceal something about themselves often cover their eyes with dark glasses. These people intuitively sense that it is easier to lie or pretend with the mouth than with the eyes, and they are right.

Gays use eye contact very expertly in what is called *cruising*—looking in a public place for someone with whom to go to bed. It is not uncommon, for example, for two young men to make eye contact in a gay bar and agree to go to bed with one another without saying a word. One will simply exit, and the other will follow. In this case, the meaning of the eye contact is given special significance because of the place in which it occurs and the norms governing the social interaction of gay bars. Nevertheless, a great deal of meaning is conveyed between the particular partners by the intensity with which they look at one another, conveyed largely by the eye contact and facial expression, and the extent to which they maintain eye contact—perhaps in spite of several moves around the room.

Our eyes are a part of our communication equipment that we too often ignore. To experience this more fully, tell someone you care for how you feel about them, using visual contact only. It is not necessary to try and act expressively. Simply sit opposite one another and relax. Then look into each other's eyes. It may require a few seconds in order to relax and allow the feelings to flow, but the power of eye contact can be demonstrated regardless of your ability to use it effectively to communicate how you feel.

Figure 8–7
Touching is a very important part of the communication process. (Joel Gordon)

Touching is also an important part of any complete communication process—so important that psychologist Bruno Bettleheim claims, "The ability to experience touch as pleasant must precede any human relationship.[7] Again, Americans as a people tend to minimize the use of touch in communication. As Sydney Jourard observes:

> *In Paris the average couple came into physical contact 110 times during an hour (and they were just having conversation!), in San Juan, Puerto Rico, couples patted, tickled and caressed 180 times during the same interval; but the typical London couple never touched at all, and Americans studied patted once or twice in an hour's conversation.[8]*

Touching another on the arm or shoulder readily conveys warmth and intimacy, just as the withdrawal from touch conveys distaste. Most people respond positively to being touched, although there are many individuals who typically find touching unpleasant or threatening. Among Americans, touching tends to be considered inappropriate outside one's own home. The use of touch tends to be confined to our intimate and sexual behavior. This is unfortunate.

[7]Quoted in Leonard Zunin and Natalie Zunin, *Contact: The First Four Minutes* (Los Angeles: Nash Publishing Company, 1972), pp. 74–88.

[8]Ibid., p. 85.

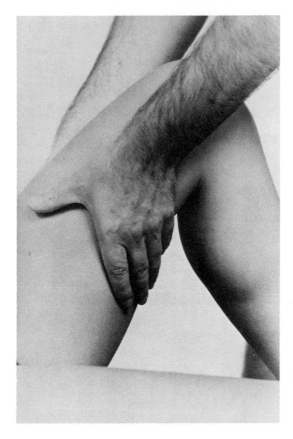

Figure 8–8
An appreciation of the sensual
as well as the sexual appeal of
touch can be acquired by
learning about massage.
(Joel Gordon)

The more that touching is seen as an exclusively sexual mode of communication, the more vigorously it is avoided by people who are not on intimate terms with each other. Initiating an intimate relationship or a close friendship thus becomes more difficult. Touch itself becomes touchy even in intimate sexual encounters. For example, many women resent the fact that their lovers only touch them when they are in bed.

Touch is particularly important to sexual communication because it is fundamental to both sex and love. The work of Harry Harlow and his associates, for example, amply demonstrates that touching and contact are critical in the development of primates.[9] The classic studies of René Spitz further indicate the importance of touch to human babies.[10] Babies in a foundling home who were not picked up

[9]Harry Harlow and Margaret Harlow, "Social Deprivation in Monkeys," *Scientific American* (November 1965).

[10]René Spitz, "Hospitalism," *Psychoanalytic Study of the Child,* vol. 1 (1945), pp. 53–74.

and warmly held were much more likely to die than babies who were warmly handled. Warmth, love, caring, and sexual desire are all closely tied to touch from birth and continue to be throughout our lives. In societies where touching is not common, people are much more likely to be angry and aggressive. Aggressive impulses can be soothed by rubbing or caressing in most cases.

The power of touch can be appreciated by means of a simple exercise. Sit opposite a friend or a willing acquaintance, close your eyes, and explore the face of your partner by gently touching him or her. Becoming more aware of the feelings and sensations involved in holding hands can be equally revealing. It is not necessary to love or feel affection for the other person in order to be moved by touching them. Touch may sometimes elicit these feelings. It is often made magical when the person touched is deeply loved.

Learning about massage can be another way of developing our use of touch in communicating with others. Without elaborate explanations of why it is so, we all recognize that a relaxed body creates a relaxed mind. Given our cultural inclination to keep things like intimate relationships to ourselves (along with our worries and anxieties about beginning them or maintaining them), massage is a good means of making feelings more apparent. It is possible to convey a great deal of caring through how we touch in massage simply by recognizing what pleases the person we are massaging. That pleasure can often be expressed in the way the shoulder or back relaxes and invites our pressure without the necessity of words. Sensitivity to the responses of another's body can be developed through becoming aware of how relaxed muscles feel in contrast to muscles that are tight. The verbal expressions of pleasure or displeasure given off by the person being massaged can also be helpful. There are a number of good books that can help you learn these very pleasant means of finding pleasure with others that go beyond words.[11]

Massage need not be intended to turn people on, but it may. Most books on massage distinguish between regular massage and erotic massage where the genitals are touched with the intent to arouse. In our society, couples who have come to the place in the evening where they have decided to massage one another are probably using this as a prelude to making love. It can certainly be a delightful prelude. But it need not be. It can be enjoyed for its own sake even if the genitals are massaged along with the rest of the body. Being aware of the responses of your partner and aware of your own feelings and intentions can increase the pleasure.

A number of therapy techniques make use of massage in order to effect a lasting change in a client's personality. Reichian therapists,

[11]George Downing, *The Massage Book* (New York: Random House, 1972).

for example, use massage to assist in the dissolution of "body armor." Wilhelm Reich, a former disciple of Freud, found that many individuals subconsciously use muscular constrictions as a defense against repressed emotions. By working on the key regions of the torso, neck, and head, therapists can release these emotions and allow the body to be more receptive to inner feelings.

Rolfing massage, developed over the past few decades by Ida Rolf, attempts to restructure the body by realigning the musculature and connective tissues. It is an intense, often painful massage, mainly administered by means of concentrated pressure of one knuckle on the same spot for several seconds. When the muscles relax, strong emotions are often released, along with painful memories from the past. In some cases, the patient's posture is realigned and equivalent psychological changes occur.

A third technique, polarity therapy, looks like Rolfing but thinks like acupuncture. That is, the technique involves the concentrated pressure of thumb, knuckle, or elbow on one spot for several seconds.

Figure 8–9
Encounter and sensitivity groups
often use touching as a basic tool
to open up communication
between people. (Magnum)

The understanding of what happens as a result of such manipulation, however, depends on an extremely detailed analysis of the body's energy system, much like that used in acupuncture or in some forms of yoga. Other therapy techniques making use of massage include Shiatsu, a technique from Japan, and Proskauer massage, which is also known as breath therapy. All these techniques assume that there is a close interconnection between bodily and psychic states and that the physical relaxation of the body has deep effect on the relaxation of inner processes when properly administered.[12]

Becoming Intimate

Getting in touch with oneself and others can be described in terms of the inner experience of one or both of the partners as congruence, the awareness of feelings and sensations, and the ability to clearly communicate them. It can also be described in terms of an outwardly observable sequence of behaviors. According to Desmond Morris, sexual intimacy develops in the following sequence of behaviors.[13]

EYE-TO-BODY CONTACT

In the most common forms of social contact, one person simply looks another over without making eye contact. The assessment of the general attractiveness and desirability of the other person is very important in those social situations in which there is no reason to expect that they will meet again. If at least one of them is not attracted to the other, it is likely that they will not meet.

EYE-TO-EYE CONTACT

While staring directly into another's eyes is generally an act of aggression or an invasion of privacy between unfamiliar adults in most societies, it can also be an expression of intimacy. The amount of time that eye contact is maintained is important. Breaking it off well involves a sense of timing and a good deal of skill in managing facial expressions. An unacknowledged or expressionless return of an entreating eye contact will normally break off the developing relationship.

VOICE-TO-VOICE CONTACT

In cases where there are no formal introductions and the eye contact has been reciprocated, the next step is normally trivial conversation.

[12]Ibid., pp. 154–58.

[13]Desmond Morris, *Intimate Behavior* (New York: Bantam Books, 1975), pp. 73–78.

What is important is the sound of the voice and the manner and tone of the conversation, not what is said. Moving much beyond small talk in the early stages of a relationship makes it more difficult to disengage should this be desired by either party.

HAND-TO-HAND CONTACT

This stage is something of a quantum jump in our society. Touching marks the beginning of socially recognized intimate behavior. The formal handshake is, of course, the exception. Its very formality prohibits the expression of personal feelings. It is something more, however, to firmly grasp the outstretched hand of another with both hands. It is still more intimate to continue to hold the hand warmly and expectantly for a period of time. Morris observes, therefore, that the first actual body contact aside from the formal handshake is likely to be some form of assistance, a "helping hand." Under ordinary circumstances, when the touching becomes prolonged, it ceases to be helping and unmistakably signals a developing intimacy.

ARM-TO-SHOULDER CONTACT

This is the last act open to friends of the same sex in Morris's scheme. It is the first point at which the two bodies come into contact. It is the simplest introduction to body contact because it can take place in public between friends. It can therefore remain ambiguous in terms of its sexual intent.

ARM-TO-WAIST CONTACT

This is perceived as a slight advance on the arm-to-shoulder stage because it is not something a man would normally do with another man. Women who are friends, however, more frequently touch each other in this fashion. In a heterosexual pair, the behavior signals increasing intimacy because the hand has been placed closer to the genitals.

MOUTH-TO-MOUTH CONTACT

Combined with a full embrace, kissing on the mouth is likely to initiate sexual arousal, especially if prolonged or repeated. The man may feel a slight erection, and the woman's vagina may lubricate. Again, there are some formalities among friends that permit such contact without signalling sexual arousal. But, as a general observation, kissing seems to represent a step forward in a developing relationship.

Figure 8-10
Many types of body contact can be seen as friendly or simply sensual, but intense mouth-to-mouth and body contact is usually part of the sequence of sexual arousal. (© Joan Lifton, Woodfin Camp & Associates)

HAND-TO-HEAD CONTACT

Exploration of the head is covered by no formal rules. It depends on how it is done. Tousling the hair can be a sign of fondness, patting can indicate superiority, and stroking can suggest deep intimacy even if nothing further follows.

HAND-TO-BODY CONTACT

This mode of contact has been vulgarized in the expression, "feeling each other up." And yet, even this vulgarization expresses the mounting emotion such exploration is likely to create. The state of physiological arousal is often so great that further stimulation will make the desire for sex virtually inevitable. For this reason, such behavior marks the dividing line between contacts that may occur in public and those normally performed in privacy.

MOUTH-TO-BREAST CONTACT

Such contact is strictly private in our society. It is clearly part of a lovemaking sequence. It is debatable as to whether there is much of a reliable sequence beyond kissing in the behavior of intimate couples who have had some past sexual experience. But lovers who are discovering each other for the first time probably explore the breast before they get to the genitals.

HAND-TO-GENITAL CONTACT

This marks a significant step, not only because of the contact with the genitals, but also because it is the first step in this sequence in which many people can experience orgasm. Mutual masturbation or the masturbation of one of the partners by the other can readily lead to orgasm in most cases.

GENITALS-TO-GENITALS CONTACT

In this final stage, two irreversible events are possible: the breaking of the hymen, or *maidenhead,* and the conception of a child. Neither of these are inevitable or even likely today, but in the past this was not so. This stage has had a definite specialness about it that has been institutionalized in marriage.

These behavioral sequences are not automatic. They are modified by local custom and interpersonal understandings. Nevertheless, insofar as behavioral cues are to be accepted as indicators of intimacy, this sequence seems roughly descriptive of the way we achieve intimacy in our society. Behaviors that are out of sequence may create problems in the developing relationship. They may signal a lack of sensitivity. They may communicate abuse or disrespect rather than affection. Thus the rapist moves rapidly from eye-to-body contact to genital-to-genital contact with little or no concern for the intervening steps and no regard for the person being used.

Guidelines for Relationships

The capacity of human beings to create situations and develop relationships is very great. For this reason, it is not possible or desirable to try to describe a good relationship. To do so would be to deny each person's capacity to develop his or her own unique relationships. It is better to ask what kind of general guidelines seem to be helpful in most relationships. Carl Rogers has provided a set of four such guidelines.[14]

First, redefine the nature of your commitment to one another, focusing on what is happening between you rather than on the "oughts" that you have been taught about how partners should be-

[14]Carl Rogers, *Becoming Partners,* pp. 201–6.

have toward one another. Rogers says, "We commit ourselves to working together on the changing process of our present relationship because that relationship is currently enriching our love and our life, and we wish it to grow." The emphasis here is upon the partnership itself, which is maintained because it is personally fulfilling to the partners.

Second, keep the channels of communication open. As Rogers says:

I will risk myself by endeavoring to communicate any persisting feeling, positive or negative, to my partner—to the full depth that I understand it myself—as a living, present part of me. Then I will risk further by trying to understand, with all the empathy I can bring to bear, his or her response, whether it is accusatory and critical or sharing and self-revealing.[15]

As we have seen, the communication of feelings is critical to vital relationships. Rogers points out that it is particularly important to communicate persisting feelings because these are the ones that are

[15]Ibid., p. 206.

likely to tell us what parts of our relationship are working well and what parts need adjustment.

Third, "we will live by our own choices, the deepest organismic sensings of which we are capable, but we will not be shaped by the wishes, the rules, the roles which others are all too eager to thrust upon us." This guideline is also known as *role transcendence*. It means that it is possible for people to transcend socially prescribed roles and that such transcendence can lead to personal growth. Open communication is especially important in this area.

Fourth, try to keep in touch with your inner self. Rogers believes that only through a deep awareness of our inner natures can we find authenticity, and only by becoming more authentic ourselves can we participate fully in a growing partnership.

Summary

Getting in touch with oneself involves first of all the effort to become aware of our bodies and our feelings about them. Masturbation is a primary means of self-pleasuring around which very deep feelings are associated in our society. A recognition that pleasure is good in itself, but not the only good in life, can help free us to experience pleasure in our bodies. Learning how to enjoy slow masturbation can improve our capacity to experience pleasure in prolonged lovemaking. Other ways of getting in touch with our bodies involve sense relaxation techniques and meditation. Simply sitting and allowing the flow of whatever thoughts or sensations come to us, without grasping at them or trying to identify them, is a profoundly relaxing experience that can put us in touch with our inner world.

Getting in touch with others is dependent upon being aware of ourselves. Congruence is the capacity to be aware of our deepest feelings and an ability to clearly and appropriately communicate them to others. The sense of appropriateness depends upon our attentiveness to the feelings of others and our awareness of social customs governing our behaviors. When we communicate we speak with our entire being. This is especially true in intimate communication. Touch first defines love and caring to the newborn infant. It underlies all of our understanding of sexuality as well. It is the primary sensation upon which relationships depend. Our tendency to restrict it to private intimate encounters makes it more difficult for us to initiate such encounters and renders us less capable of using touch well.

We can describe the development of intimate relationships in terms of a sequence of observable behaviors and provide guidelines for managing the inner dialogue that must be honored if intimacy is to be experienced and maintained. Morris's twelve steps suggest that there is a culturally defined sequence of behaviors that signal increasing intimacy. If one partner gets out of step, some personal understanding must explain the unexpected rush toward greater intimacy, or it is likely to be misunderstood. We neglect the cultural prescriptions at our risk. We can modify them with awareness to suit our own developing dialogues.

215

Sexual Pleasuring

9

There is but one temple in the Universe,
says the devout Novalis, and that is the
human body. Nothing is holier than that
high form. We touch heaven when we lay
our hand on the human body.

Thomas Carlyle

To most people in the United States, sex has meant heterosexual intercourse for so long that it is difficult for many people to experience and appreciate other forms of sexual pleasuring. The amount of time spent in play prior to intercourse varies greatly in the United States and around the world, but Kinsey found that a half hour's time spent in pre-coital play was common. If no intercourse was intended, and the situation allowed it, such play could go on all night.[1]

Whatever amount of time is spent in sexual pleasuring, such play is generally more like work. Play is done for its own sake, but work typically is done to obtain something else. The intent of sex work is to arouse; the objective is penetration and orgasm. This narrowness is unfortunate. There is a wide range of activities that can afford lovers sexual pleasure whether or not they lead to intercourse. Lovers can also enjoy much sensuous pleasure whether or not they become aroused.

Sexual pleasuring involves more than an activity done by two or more people in privacy. It involves their personal and cultural understandings of what is happening to them as they pleasure one another. Our cultural heritage has been characterized by a woeful ignorance about sex. Medical schools, seminaries, and universities have only begun to plan for course work and training in the study of sexual behavior. Among people who do not have access to such advanced resources, sex education is practically nonexistent. For years, doctors, clergymen, and other professionals have as a whole been uninformed and prudish about human sexuality. Yet these were the people to whom individuals with sexual problems turned for advice. We may indicate through our behavior—and increasingly in our conversation—that we value sexual experimentation, but we are unable or unwilling to change the laws that condemn it. The extent of confusion in this area can be gauged by Alfred Kinsey's informed estimate that if the legal codes governing sexual behavior were ever enforced, something like 95 percent of all American males would be in jail.[2]

It is within this cultural context that we Americans approach love-

[1]Alfred C. Kinsey et al., *Sexual Behavior in the Human Male* (New York: Pocket Books, 1948), p. 259.

[2]Ibid., p. 392.

making. There are signs, however, that many of our ideas may be changing. We seem to have a much more positive attitude toward our sexuality. More and more people are coming to recognize that human sexuality can communicate more than simple erotic attraction. It is becoming increasingly clear that any intimate partnership can be enhanced by an open and genuine sex life.

Factors that Affect the Quality of Sex

Knowing how to make love skillfully enhances the pleasures to be found in sex. But discovering how to truly give each other pleasure in sexual relationships is not simply a matter of technique, however varied and elegant. It is a matter of openness, honesty, and communication as well. The longer and more deeply two partners have known each other and the more vital their love, the more they have to bring to their lovemaking.

Figure 9–1
If words are the only way a couple expresses their feelings
for each other, they have been cheated. (Paul Fusco, © Magnum)

We tend to think of communication, openness, and giving of oneself as occurring primarily through words, but if words are the only way a couple expresses who they are to each other, they have been cheated. The revelation and self-disclosure of two people in love and in bed goes far beyond what can be put into words. This self-disclosure and their joy in finding each other can continue throughout a relationship if a couple does not take their lovemaking for granted. Routine and monotony in lovemaking can easily come to be the pattern in any long-term partnership, but this need not happen.

UNREALISTIC EXPECTATIONS

Although the changes in sexual customs generally described as the sexual revolution have helped many young Americans get over some of their hang-ups, these changes have produced some new problems. People today are coming to understand their sexuality as a rich and rewarding means of communication and as a pleasure in its own right. They also are beginning to understand that women not only can find pleasure in sex, but, indeed, have a much greater physiological potential to enjoy it than men. Most people no longer think of sex in marriage as the man's pleasure and the woman's obligation. The contemporary woman enjoys increased freedom to make her own demands. On the negative side, however, the freedom to make demands has led to fears of being unable to satisfy demands made on us by others. In the last thirty years various self-styled experts—many of whom are no more qualified than the average experienced adult—have offered numerous descriptions of what is expected of both partners in lovemaking. The following is a rather humorous, but basically devastating, description of these changing expectations.

> Once the goal was orgasm for him (essential for health). For her it was "satisfying him" (to keep him at home and preserve the marriage).
> Then the goal was "satisfying her" for him (to prove he was a genuine sexual jock, not a run-of-the-mill athlete). Her goal was reaching orgasm (to prove her feminity). To prove she was also mature, it was necessary for her to reach "vaginal orgasm." That was a change in both rules and goals that unfortunately occurred just after the man had learned to find the clitoris. At first, reaching vaginal orgasm was thought to be her problem. But later, it became his problem, too, as he was expected to keep an erection and keep thrusting (and keep his mind off what he was doing) long enough to bring her to a mature, nonclitoral climax. Otherwise, he wouldn't earn his letter.
> The stakes were later raised to a mutual climax, which if you were a real jock would shake the world. . . . Quantity rather than quality became the basis for scoring, with each player pitting himself against vague and varying national averages or healthful weekly requirements.
> In the meantime, her performance was to be judged in a new way—as if

competing for the Academy Award. She wasn't required to have an orgasm. (She got as much pleasure from pleasuring her partner, the experts said.) But she was required to simulate an orgasm to make his performance look and feel better. To keep either partner from scoring too high, the experts gave him hints to tell if she was faking. Both lost points if her deception was detected.

And then came multiple orgasm (quantity still counts). Now he was able to give her at least three orgasms in the place of one. The first one of several could be clitoral, a pre-intercourse warmup. Then a mature vaginal climax or two after intromission. And finally—back to the mutual orgasm. A truly super performance by two superjocks!

The name of the game is Sexual Freedom, because it has freed sex from the bonds of reproduction, marriage and love. The advertised prizes are health, happiness, and an end to anxiety.[3]

The demands made on both partners by such unrealistic standards for excellent performance may well have contributed to the increasing rates of impotence that are now being recorded. (These increased rates may also reflect a greater willingness to report the problem, now that therapists are better able to treat it.) Masters and Johnson clearly point out that the "fear of inadequacy is the greatest known deterrent to effective sexual functioning" simply because fear gets in the way. An individual who is nervous about possible sexual failure is less likely to pay attention to the arousing qualities of the sexual stimuli that occur naturally in lovemaking.[4]

No set of criteria can adequately measure the sexual performance of a couple except for their own mutual pleasure. In lovemaking, as in all aspects of intimacy, being oneself rather than living up to the expectations of others is more likely to produce such pleasure. As Alex Comfort observes, "The whole joy of *sex-with-love* is that there are no rules so long as you enjoy, and the choice is practically unlimited.[5]

SETTING

The immediate setting in which lovemaking takes place often affects its quality, tone, and meaning.[6] Making love under the pine trees in a

---

[3]Gina Allen and Clement Martin, *Intimacy: Sensitivity, Sex and the Art of Love,* Copyright 1971, with the permission of Contemporary Books, Inc. Chicago.

[4]William H. Masters and Virginia Johnson, *Human Sexual Inadequacy* (Boston: Little, Brown & Company, 1970), p.13.

[5]Alex Comfort, *The Joy of Sex* (New York: Crown Publishing Co., 1975), p. 17.

[6]Setting has always been an important factor in human lovemaking in contrast to animal behavior, which is much less affected by this concern. See Bronislaw Malinowski, *Sexual Life of Savages in North-Western Melanesia* (New York: Harcourt, Brace Jovanovich, 1962); and Margaret Mead, *Sex and Temperament* (New York: Mentor Books, 1952).

Figure 9–2
Having a permanent place to make love is desirable, but varying
the setting can add to a relationship. (Jason Lauré, Woodfin Camp & Associates)

secluded forest, on a sailboat in the privacy of a quiet lagoon, or hurriedly in the back seat of a car can give variety to a relationship. However, people who find it necessary—perhaps because both partners live with their parents—to confine their lovemaking to such unappealing places as motel rooms often find that the setting gives their sexual relationship a somewhat degrading quality. Others feel similarly about the back seat of a car.

Various physical features can be as important in their own way as the general atmosphere of the setting. A waterbed, for example, gives quite different rhythms to lovemaking than a featherbed or a standard mattress. Showering or swimming together during or after lovemaking may contribute to the comfort and pleasure to be found in making love. For some lovers the haste of a clandestine affair seems particularly appetizing, while others relish the intimate leisure of a long Sunday afternoon with the telephone off the hook and no visitors expected.

The couple who has an enduring partnership and the ability to select a permanent place in which to make love has the opportunity to see to it that certain amenities are present in their setting. A bed that is firm and large enough for adequate movement without making undue noise seems to be preferred most of the time, although lovemaking on the floor of the study or living room after the children have gone to sleep is sometimes a refreshing alternative for married couples. Pillows that are full and able to provide support are helpful additions. A chair that is sturdy enough to hold two people can add to the variety of positions that can be enjoyed in intercourse. A great deal of effort can be put into making the bedroom of an ordinary apartment a much more comfortable and esthetically pleasing setting for lovemaking and pleasuring than it ordinarily is. The list of accessories that can enhance sexual relations could be extended indefinitely. The point is simply that where you make love does matter, and that efforts to improve the quality of the setting in which you make love generally will be amply rewarded.

EXPLORATION

A great deal of the joy that two people experience in a sexual encounter is the discovery of each other's bodies. Our sense of touch is as important as the sense of sight in communicating pleasure. Indeed, our bodies are constantly communicating, whether we are aware of it or not. One of the gifts in lovemaking is to make use of the sense of touch in creating physical pleasure and excitement.

Exploring our partner's body heightens our awareness not only of the other person but also of our own inner self. Touching can express tenderness, respect, understanding, trust, and, of course, the sheer

Figure 9–3
(Joel Gordon)

sense of mutual pleasure. When lovers caress, there is fullness that can never be obtained by words. Touching and exploring each other can be an expression of deep self-giving, not simply a mechanical technique of arousal. But, before this can become a reality, one must have developed some awareness of oneself and one's partner.

Most of the time, in the course of our daily interaction, our bodies are covered and held in reserve. Lovers, however, come to each other without their clothing. If they take this condition of nakedness simply as a convenient way to permit access to their sexual organs, they will miss out on the opportunity their intimacy provides for an exploration of each other's body.

People's feelings about their bodies are an important part of their self-images. People who are not comfortable with their bodies may find the openness that is required for exploration and discovery somewhat threatening. They tend to have a reserved attitude in their lovemaking, because their low self-esteem causes them to hold back from giving themselves freely. People who are at ease with their bodies, on the other hand, find it easier to be open with their partners. Often negative self-images are formed quite early in life, but a loving partner who convincingly conveys the sense of excitement he or she feels at discovering his or her partner's body can contribute greatly to repairing the damage done by low self-esteem. A man or woman who fears that he or she is undesirable often can be convinced otherwise by sincere expressions of desire.

PLEASURING

Sex clinics such as Masters and Johnson's are constantly meeting people who are uncomfortable with each other as lovers. They do not know how to give each other pleasure, are fearful of their in-

Figure 9–4
(The Bettmann Archive, Inc.)

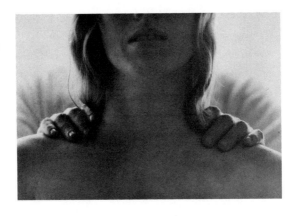

Figure 9–5
Pleasuring, becoming open with each other through touching, is a good general technique for discovering each other sexually.
(Paul Fusco, © Magnum)

adequacies, and come to the clinic seeking help. An important part of the therapy that Masters and Johnson prescribe for many sexual problems is called *pleasuring*. Pleasuring is a simple means by which couples learn to become open to each other through touching. Initially, the couple is asked to engage in nongenital exploration. The man generally rests against a pillowed headboard, and the woman rests against him. If he is to give pleasure to her, she guides his exploring hands over her body and indicates by touch or sound what is pleasurable to her in his touching. Masters and Johnson describe the techinque as follows:

> *The partner who is pleasuring is committed first to do just that; give pleasure. At a second level in the experience, the giver is to explore his or her own component of personal pleasure in doing the touching—to experience and appreciate the sensuous dimensions of hard and soft, smooth and rough, warm and cool, qualities of texture and, finally this somewhat indescribable aura of physical receptivity expressed by the partner being pleasured. After a reasonable length of time . . . the partners are to exchange roles of pleasuring (giving) and being pleasured (getting) and then repeat the procedure in similar detail.[7]*

This technique makes sure that couples learn to communicate with each other at a very basic level. It assumes something that most couples do not assume—that an individual becomes an expert lover not by learning this technique or by reading that manual, but by discovering his or her partner as a unique individual who has specific sexual desires and whose body experiences sexual pleasure in a specific way. This process of discovery depends on having a partner who is willing and able to respond to what is felt as pleasurable, who can say in effect, "I like that." This ability to respond openly to sexual

[7]Masters and Johnson, *Human Sexual Inadequacy,* p. 73.

stimulation is something that many people have never learned to do because of their cultural conditioning.

The most unfortunate misconception our culture has assigned to sexual functioning is the assumption, by both men and women, that men by divine guidance and infallible instinct are able to discover exactly what a woman wants sexually and when she wants it. Probably this fallacy has interfered with natural interaction as much as any other single factor. The second most frequently encountered sexual fallacy, and therefore a constant deterrent to effective sexual expression, is the assumption, again by both men and women, that sexual expertise is the man's responsibility. In truth, no woman can know what type of sexual approach she will respond to at any given opportunity until faced with the absence of a particularly desired stimulative factor. How can a woman possibly expect any man to anticipate her sensual pleasure, when she cannot accomplish this feat with consistency herself? How can any man presume himself an expert in female sexual response under these circumstances? [8]

Pleasuring seems to be a good general technique for discovering

[8]Ibid., p. 87.

Figure 9–6
(Magnum)

each other as lovers. It requires openness about oneself and one's body and willingness to provide the much-needed feedback that increases the pleasures of lovemaking. Many couples discover through pleasuring each other that their entire bodies can become erogenous zones.

Making Love

Knowledge of one's own erogenous zones is essential if one is to move toward one's full capacity for sexual responsiveness. One learns sexual responsiveness through experimentation and experience in a process that begins with acceptance and knowledge of one's own body. The full flavor of sexual responsiveness is discovered only by a person who has developed what Masters and Johnson describe as "a sensuous enjoyment and appreciation for the sight, smell, taste, feel and use of (one's) body in all its infinite capacities."[9] The most common *erogenous zones*—particular places that, when stimulated, produce not only sensual pleasure but also sexual arousal—are the mouth, the genitals, and the anus. In addition, women are likely to be aroused by the gentle stimulation of their breasts, and men often find the stroking of their thighs arousing. Individuals vary enormously in their preference among these zones and in how they prefer to be stimulated. Any part of the body can cause arousal. The fun is in discovering the possibilities.

KISSING

The erotic kiss, the most universal form of human lovemaking, has many variations. A kiss enables the lovers to taste as well as touch each other. During this exploration, lovers come to discover the pleasantness of their own clean body odors. They can smell the fragrance of hair and perfume and enjoy feelings of warmth and closeness. When the kiss becomes a deep kiss, the experience of penetrating and being penetrated becomes a part of their awareness of each other. Light stroking, tentative tongue caressing, gentle nibbling, and sucking all become part of mutual exploration and discovery. Because kissing can be such a varied form of expression, sensitivity and timing become in themselves a show of responsiveness. Kissing can range over the entire body, greatly increasing the feelings of discovery and significantly stimulating both partners. The nape of the neck, the ears, the breasts, the palms of the hands, fingertips, thighs, feet, genitals—indeed, any part of the body—will respond to a lover's kisses.

Some lovers find the genital kiss especially stimulating. The gen-

[9] Ibid., p. 76.

itals are particularly sensitive to erotic stimulation and so the genital kiss often proceeds to further exploration of the genital area. When the female's genitals are taken in the mouth or licked, it is called *cunnilingus*. When the male's genitals are taken in the mouth or licked, it is called *fellatio*. Most adults in the United States have experienced oral sex at some time in their lives as a part of foreplay, or as preparation for intercourse. A minority have experienced orgasm through this means of stimulation. For some lovers, oral sex is psychologically beneficial because it encourages people to become intimate with parts of the body that the Puritan strain in our tradition teaches us to regard as unclean and unacceptable. On the other hand, despite the fact that clean genitals are not hygienically objectionable, some people still find oral-genital stimulation unacceptable.

The kissing of the genitals is thus a very delicate matter. Oral sex can be an expression of the deepest intimacy and self-disclosure. But it can also very quickly cause offense.

In a time in which such sexual pleasuring seems to be increasing, it is not uncommon for some people to hide their discomfort in order to please their partners. Since there is great variation in desire for such caresses, and any individual may feel differently at different times, there is much need for care and tenderness in order for this pleasure to be shared and the intimacy not abused. Openness about such matters need not give offense. There are many ways of sexual pleasuring, and none should be considered mandatory for any individual.

Kissing can proceed from the mouth, ears, and nape of the neck to the shoulders and breasts. Circling the nipples with the tongue and blowing lightly on the moistened breast can have stimulating effects for both partners. Moving slowly down the torso to the navel, the man can lick and kiss tenderly or roughly as the situation seems to demand. The female partner can guide his head with her hands if she so desires, thus encouraging or discouraging his further exploration, depending on her feelings about it.

If the woman is resting on her back and her partner is on top of her and between her legs, her private lips (her labia) can be approached slowly as the mutual feeling of arousal builds.

The mons particularly deserves attention. Since pubic hair is typically rough and wiry and can readily become lodged in the mouth, causing some discomfort, care should be taken to part the hair along with the labia before proceeding to stimulate the clitoris and inner lips. The woman can spread her labia as she further spreads her legs, if she so desires. This invitation is generally highly arousing to her partner, but it is often difficult for her to feel comfortable about making such a gesture. She may prefer to have this particular kind of sexual stimulation happen to her without her having to take an active role. Accordingly, the man may separate the labia with his hands or carefully nudge them apart with his tongue. If the women's legs are widely spread and slightly raised on a pillow, the labia will normally remain open and the man may proceed to further explore the vagina. The tongue is softer, more moist, and considerably more flexible than either the penis or a finger. It can, therefore, provide a much richer variety of stimulating sensations with less danger of causing pain. Nevertheless, the clitoris is extremely sensitive, and too much direct stimulation can cause discomfort. Rapid flicking with the tongue, or sucking, or a tongue massage to the side of the clitoral shaft are commonly pleasurable procedures. The inner lips are also sensitive and can be readily reached with the tongue. The clitoris can be gently sucked. The tongue can penetrate the inner lips. Since any air that might be blown into the vagina can enter the abdominal cavity through the open fallopian tubes, there is an increased risk of infection from what are called "blow jobs." If the women is pregnant, there is great danger that this air will enter the bloodstream through one of the many blood vessels close to the surface of the uterus and be fatal.

Most men also enjoy a tongue bath or kissing of the body, and some find their nipples to be particularly sensitive to touch and tongue. It is also quite easy to suck or lick the penis while in a number of positions. The most sensitive parts of the penis are the head and the frenulum directly beneath it. Licking these areas stimulates through touch and the sensation of cool wetness. The testicles can also be taken gently into the mouth or caressed with the tongue. The head and shaft of the penis can be slowly sucked. There is great variation in the desire of both men and women to orally stimulate a man to orgasm. Many women find the taste of semen offensive. Some, however, enjoy its taste and texture and are excited by the experience of ejaculation because the mouth is more sensitive than the vagina. Some men cannot ejaculate in such situations. Much depends upon the state of arousal. Most likely the lovemaking will proceed to other areas of interest before orgasm occurs.

INTERCOURSE

Intercourse has many forms. Experimentation and discovery of new and satisfying positions enrich the lovemaking of a couple and reveal different aspects of the partners. Initiative, dominance, submission, aggression, tenderness, imagination, and creativity can all be expressed in various positions of lovemaking. In long-term relationships, creative and imaginative couples who are free with each other can deal rather effectively with the threat of boredom and routine in sex. The use of a variety of positions also provides a wide array of different sensations and can enable couples to continue their lovemaking in spite of pregnancy or various types of mild illnesses, which might make intercourse in one particular position uncomfortable for one of the partners.

Although there are many variations in the positions couples can assume while making love, there are four basic positions from which one can improvise by rolling, sitting, or standing. Lovers may assume several positions throughout an evening's lovemaking. There is no normal or natural position, although the so-called "matrimonial" or "missionary's" position enjoys wide acceptance in the United States.

Face-to-Face, Man Above. The face-to-face, man above position is the most commonly employed in the United States, but its use is apt to be rare in many non-Western cultures. In this position, the woman lies on her back with her legs apart, usually with her knees bent. The man, lying above the women and, supporting himself on his elbows and knees, can easily achieve intromission. Once his penis has been inserted, he is basically in control of the body movements, because the weight of his body on the woman tends to restrict her movement to some extent. It is important for him to keep in contact with the clitoris. Since the clitoris withdraws beneath the clitoral hood in the late stages of excitement, this contact is normally achieved indirectly

Figure 9–7
Face-to-face, man above.

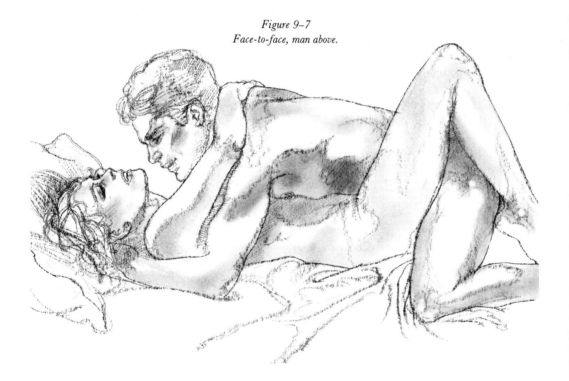

through vibrations of the inner lips and clitoral hood. This may be accomplished by putting pressure on the pubic bone or by the woman's adjusting her position so that the clitoris is stimulated by the tensions in the clitoral hood. (Indeed, the clitoris can be indirectly stimulated in almost all positions of intercourse, including rear entry.)

Although the woman's body movements are somewhat restricted, she is relatively free to vary the position of her legs. During intercourse she may pull her legs up toward her shoulders, she may lock them around her partner's body, she may place her heels behind his knees to give her more control over her pelvic thrusting, or she may place her legs either inside or outside of his. By putting a pillow under her lower back and drawing her knees up toward her shoulders, she can receive the deepest penetration. Thus, by changing the position of her legs, she can alter the depth of penetration, relax, change the rhythm of the thrusting, and vary the amount of tension on the clitoral hood.

The advantages of this position are that it is one of the easiest to learn and one of the most adaptable. In addition, because the partners are facing each other, they may express their feelings with their eyes and may continue their erotic kissing. This is also the position in which couples are most likely to conceive children because of the proper pooling of the ejaculation in the vagina. To increase the possibilities of conception, the woman should remain in this position after intercourse, and the man should not withdraw hurriedly.

There are drawbacks to this position, however. The man's weight can be a burden for the woman, who is hampered in her movements, particularly in the movements of her pelvis. Moreover, because he must support himself, the man's hands are not free to caress, fondle, and stimulate his partner.

Face-to-Face, Woman Above. The woman-above position provides a great deal more freedom for the woman. In this position, she can control and vary the speed of the movement and the depth of penetration. Clitoral contact is frequently more intense in this position because the woman has primary control over this important source of stimulation. It is said that this position is less sexually stimulating to men, yet it does allow the man to be more relaxed. He also has easier access to his partner's body and is able to see, touch, caress, and kiss many more areas of her body than in the man-above position. Because she normally can rest her entire weight on him, she is equally free. The man frequently is able to delay ejaculation for a longer period of time in this position, as he experiences less sexual intensity.

The woman may lie full length against him, with her legs inside or outside of his, attaining a fuller sense of body contact. Or, she may more or less sit astride him. In this approach, the man also may vary his position. By resting on his elbows he may raise himself closer to her body. By raising his legs, he can provide his partner with a back rest.

An advantage of this position is that many women find it easier to experience an orgasm. On the other hand, there are certain psychological disadvantages. With the woman on top, some men feel threatened because they feel they are being placed in a passive or subordinate position. There are certain indications, however, that this attitude is far less common than it used to be.

Face-to-Face, Side Position. The face-to-face, side position offers both partners the opportunity to control their own body movements during intercourse. The partners lie on their sides, facing each other. Often this position is arrived at by rolling from the man-above position. A thoughtful couple who plan ahead will have the freedom of their

Figure 9–8
Face-to-face, woman above.

arms, legs, and hands after they have rolled over. With the arms, legs, and hands free, the couple has an infinite variety of opportunities for touching, caressing, and exploring. Because this is the most relaxing position for both partners, it is often possible to engage in intercourse for longer periods of time while in this position. After intercourse in this position, a couple can lie together in the warmth of each other's body and may even fall asleep without separating.

A variation of this position (see Figure 9–9) is declared to be most satisfactory by Masters and Johnson, who encourage couples to try it because it permits the woman to vary her pelvic thrusting with more ease, while at the same time allowing the man greater ejaculatory control.[10] Despite the fact that this position may be difficult to get into for inexperienced couples, it has the advantage of neither partner's having to support the weight of the other. This position is especially advantageous if one partner is considerably taller than the other. Although penetration is normally shallower and the movements less active, the leisure and tenderness normally associated with this position make it a desirable variation.

Rear-Entry Position. Because animals typically copulate from a rear-entry position, many people feel that this is an inappropriate position for human beings.[11] Nevertheless, this position can offer a great deal of pleasure to both partners. Many variations are possible: the woman sitting on a man's lap with her back to him; the woman lying on her stomach or kneeling; or both partners lying on their sides. The rear entry position offers the man greater freedom to caress the woman's breasts, clitoris, back, buttocks, legs, and almost all of her upper body. In this position the man can massage and caress his partner's back with much greater ease than in any other position. It also offers a wide variety of depth of penetration, depending on the variation employed. As the couple moves from a stretched out position to a more seated position, the depth of penetration increases. Even in those variations that offer only slight penetration, some women find great pleasure in the stimulation of the front part of the vagina and either partner is able to compensate manually for any stimulation of the clitoris that may be felt to be lacking. The position is restful in most of its variants, and, although there is lack of eye-to-eye contact, many of the other satisfactions can compensate for this.

These four basic positions in lovemaking can be almost infinitely varied to suit the couple's taste. The variations are very subtle. They cannot possibly be adequately described in terms of simple mechanics

[10]Ibid., pp. 310–11.

[11]In the Kinsey study, *Sexual Behavior in the Human Male,* only about 15 percent of the respondents reported having used this position.

Figure 9–9
Face-to-face, side position.

and techniques. They must be arrived at by exploration, discovery, and sensitive communication between loving couples.

Part of the great joy of lovemaking comes from bathing in the afterglow. Being together, recognizing what has happened to each other, caressing, and lying in the warmth of each other's body are all part of the total experience of loving—a feeling well captured the the poet Dylan Thomas, who wrote, "Let me lie shipwrecked between thy thighs." It may sometimes be the case that the aftermath of one orgasmic experience may lead imperceptibly to another beginning.

One of the warm and endearing attributes that can be brought to a partnership is the experience of anticipating, planning, and preparing for lovemaking yet to come.

Lovemaking Roles

So much of our lovemaking in the past has been tied up with our understanding of masculine and feminine roles. Our culture traditionally has ascribed dominance to males and submissiveness to females.

This sort of role stereotyping can be very crippling.[12] A man and a woman in a partnership should be free to define their own roles in terms of their own and each other's needs. Fortunately, there are some indications that this is becoming possible for an ever-increasing number of people—thanks in no small part to the efforts of the women's liberation movement, which has succeeded in making large numbers of men and women sensitive to the problems created by restrictive definitions of sex roles.

These restricted definitions are the stereotypes of sexual behavior. For example, men are supposed to initiate sexual encounters. Women who "ask for it" are prostitutes. Men are endowed with a higher sex drive that must be expressed. Sexually frustrated males will suffer such physiological symptoms as "blue balls," which are supposedly caused by the backing up of semen. The notions that men must spend their semen while women should conserve their virginity has contributed much to the sexual frustrations of the past. It is commonly believed that women are much slower to achieve orgasm than men, but we now know that when properly stimulated there is little difference between the sexes in their capacity to achieve orgasm or in their rates of achieving it. The common sex role stereotypes have it that men are much more genitally oriented in their sexuality, while women are

[12]Masters and Johnson, *Human Sexual Inadequacy,* pp. 159–60.

Figure 9–10
Rear entry position.

more sensual. This has probably been something of a self-fulfilling prophecy in the past, but both sexes are converging in their appreciation of sensuality in all its forms. Men are supposed to be more preoccupied with sex and to fantasize about it in cruder terms than women, who are supposed to be more romantic. However, as we have seen in our investigation of fantasy, women have virtually equal capacity to enjoy a rich fantasy life.

To the extent that these stereotypes have persisted, they have served to perpetuate the behaviors they define. Evidence is growing that the sexes are much more similar than dissimilar in their erotic life. Whatever their similarities or dissimilarities as a group, however, in making love it is very important to turn on the particular pleasures of your partner rather than assume that you know what pleases him or her. So varied is the human sexual appetite that the same person may respond quite differently on different occasions. Old pleasures become worn when used as a technique. New pleasures vary the menu and increase the likelihood that sexual relationships will not become a bore or simply a matter of social obligation.

Figure 9–11
A couple should be free to define their own roles in terms of their own and each other's
needs in sex as well as in their other activities. (Paul Fusco, © Magnum)

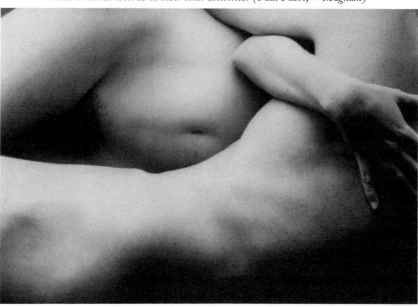

Summary

Most Americans think of intercourse when they think of sex and view other forms of sexual activity as ways of achieving the goal of intercourse. More and more people are coming to realize, however, that there are many things two people can do with each other that are valuable in their own right, even if they do not lead to arousal, let alone intercourse.

Lovemaking involves much more than good technique. Open communication, realistic expectations, a pleasant setting, and a willingness to explore and to give and receive pleasure are all essential to enjoyable sex.

Making love is based on the stimulation of people's erogenous zones. People differ in which parts of their bodies are the most sensitive and in the kind of stimulation they prefer. Thus, sensitivity and responsiveness to one's partner are probably the most important qualities in a good lover.

The erotic kiss is the most universal form of human lovemaking. Any part of the body can be orally stimulated, though the mouth, breasts, and genitals are the most sensitive. Most Americans have had some experience with cunnilingus and fellatio. Many still find it uncomfortable, but many others have learned to enjoy it.

There are four basic positions used in intercourse: man above, woman above, side-to-side, and rear-entry. Subtle variations on all these can assure a couple sufficient variety, even in a long-term relationship.

Rigid stereotypes limit our sexual activity as well as our social behavior. The sexes are much more alike in their erotic needs than we once thought. People in bed together should try to be themselves rather than live up to some abstract idea of what is appropriate behavior for a man or a woman.

Homosexuality and Bisexuality

10

Homosexuality is assuredly no advantage,
but it is nothing to be ashamed of, no
vice, no degradation, it cannot be classified
as an illness; we consider it to be
a variation of the sexual functions produced
by a certain arrest of sexual development.

Sigmund Freud

People who have been labeled as homosexual because they have been arrested, or those who consider themselves to be members of the gay community (the overt homosexual subculture), are in fact a small minority of those who have felt an attraction for a person of the same sex. An erotic attraction for a person of the same sex is a common part of human sexual experience. Most people have felt such an attraction at some time during their lives. Some choose to act on it; others are content to fantasize about it. A person who experiences such an attraction may not even recognize it as homosexual. Most men and a significant minority of women have had sexual relations with a person of the same sex at least once in their lives. The experience may have been considered simply as an experiment to find out what it was like to make love with someone of the same sex, or it may have been part of a continuing relationship. Oral and anal intercourse, which were once considered strictly homosexual behaviors, are now commonly enjoyed by heterosexual couples. In fact, homosexuals can be distinguished from heterosexuals mainly in terms of the gender of the of person they choose to have sex with, not in terms of what they do together.

A simple way to describe the varieties of sexual preferences is to set up a continuum. At one end are those heterosexuals who have never had homosexual feelings. They are followed by those heterosexuals who have had some homosexual experience. Bisexuals, those who find people of both sexes sexually attractive, would be in the middle, followed by homosexuals who have had some heterosexual experience. Homosexuals who have never had any heterosexual feelings would be at the other end. Since individuals may occupy different places on this scale at different times in their lives, it is not possible to determine the number of people who typically behave in a homosexual or heterosexual way. But it is possible to determine how many individuals fall into these categories at any particular time. Kinsey anticipated that future research would determine that all people were capable of homosexual arousal under some circumstances. He nevertheless classified most of his respondents as heterosexual. In some societies all men enjoy homosexual relationships while away from home and resume heterosexual relationships when they return. In other societies, there is no trace of homosexual attraction or behavior, even though the society is quite permissive in its regulation of sexual behavior. Because homosexuality has been severely punished in the past, we cannot study it in our society without recognizing that "homosexual" is a negative label to pin on a person, even today.

Far from being a single class of human beings, homosexuals represent many different styles of life. Homosexuality is a complex phenomenon because it results from many different factors and can mean quite different things to different people.

Problems of Definition

The complexity of homosexuality begins with the problem of definition. No definition is totally adequate to its task, but any definition of homosexuality can be useful as a means of focusing attention. In common usage, the term *homosexual* usually refers to males, and the term *Lesbian* is used to refer to female homosexuals. Webster defines *homosexual* as "relating to, or exhibiting sexual desire toward, a member of one's own sex." But does desire alone make a person homosexual, or does it need to be expressed in behavior? Irving Bieber, a psychoanalyst, defines a homosexual as an adult who engages repeatedly in overt sexual relations with a member or members of the same sex.[1] Bieber's emphasis is clearly on the behavior. Although Freud did not think of homosexuality as a sickness, he did see it as evidence of arrested development. Freud was convinced that even if a person had developed past the homosexual stage, certain vestiges of this stage could remain as latent homosexuality. These hidden homosexual feelings could be reflected in expressions of friendship with members of one's own sex that would be more appropriately expressed to the opposite sex. Thus, Freud saw homosexuality as a conglomerate of feelings, attitudes, and behaviors that exist in varying degrees in all human beings.[2]

More recently, homosexuality has come to be seen as a social status and role rather than as an aspect of an individual's personality. The focus on social roles rather than personality traits enables the emphasis to be shifted somewhat from specifically sexual acts or attitudes toward the way a person lives in society. In this view, a person does not need to define himself or herself as gay or straight, but may well know how to perform either or both of these roles in a variety of styles.

To some people, a homosexual is any person who has been so la-

[1]Irving Bieber, "Clinical Aspects of Male Homosexuality," in *Sexual Inversion: The Multiple Roots of Homosexuality,* ed. Judd Marmor (New York: Basic Books, 1965), pp. 248–67.

[2]Judd Marmor, "Introduction" in Marmor, *Sexual Inversion,* p. 2.

beled by society. It is assumed that this person prefers to have sex with a person of the same sex, although in the case of some bisexuals this is not true. This preference, which is deemed so important by society, is less significant in shaping the pattern of a homosexual's daily life than the the label itself. Regardless of how such a person came to have such a preference, he or she is clearly stigmatized by the label "homosexual" which often has ill effects above and beyond any that might result from simply having a sexual orientation toward a person of the same sex. A large number of people have such preferences, but do not become labeled as homosexuals because they have never expressed such preferences in their behavior, or because they have managed to avoid detection and have adequately established themselves in straight society. As a result, their problems are different from those who have acquired the label. We know less about them because they are difficult to locate and to study. The focus of this chapter is largely on the person who has been labeled homosexual or gay.

Historical and Cultural Contexts

Because homosexuality is a many-faceted phenomenon, it is not possible to make clear historical and cross-cultural comparisons. Homosexuality is one thing among the ancient Greeks, another in the Bible, and yet another in modern San Francisco. More useful comparisons can be made between contemporary industrialized societies, but care must be taken in each case to preserve the cultural context and its unique definitions.

Figure 10–1
(Photo Trends)

Homosexuals arrested by the police are often charged with the crime of sodomy. The word "sodomy" comes from the infamous town, Sodom, in the book of Genesis that was destroyed by God because of its corruption. It is commonly thought that Sodom was destroyed because its inhabitants enjoyed a particular sex act (anal intercourse), which came to be called *sodomy*. According to the Bible, the Israelite patriarch, Lot, was entertaining strangers under his roof (in accordance with Semitic custom) when the men of the town, the Sodomites, came to his door and shouted, "Where are the men who came to you tonight? Bring them out to us, that we may know them." Now the word "know" sometimes suggests carnal knowledge, or intercourse, in the Old Testament, so the inference is that the Sodomites wanted to have anal intercourse with these strangers. Unfortunately for the Sodomites, these strangers were angels (messengers) of the Lord, in disguise. In the biblical story, this insult to Lot's angel guests was the crowning touch to a long history of outrageous behavior. God lost his patience, and the Sodomites were justly punished.

But there are complications to this interpretation. In the King James version of the Bible, the Hebrew word *kedeshim* is translated as "Sodomite" when the word is masculine. In the feminine version, however, it is sometimes rendered as "harlot." In fact, the original meaning of the word is "temple prostitute," which could be either a male or a female. The nomadic Israelites made a great effort to dissociate themselves from the native populations and their worship of various fertility cults. It is possible, therefore, that the condemnations of homosexuality in Deuteronomy, Leviticus, and Kings reflects the Israelites' aversion to practices that were part of some of these religions. However, another interpretation of this story could be that the abomination of Sodom was not anal intercourse, but simply the flagrant violation of the code of hospitality. This interpretation becomes more plausible when it is recognized that in all other cases in the Bible where "know" means carnal knowledge, it clearly refers to heterosexual intercourse.

It is important to remember, however, that the term homosexual has an expanded meaning today both in common usage and in the law. Common Hebraic practices, such as the patriarch's placing his hand on the genitals of another male as a form of blessing, would be considered homosexual by some people today. There also can be little doubt that the ancient Hebrews were much more physically expressive of affection to people of both sexes than we are. But, in any case, the record seems clear that homosexuality was strongly condemned: "Thou shalt not lie with a man as with a woman" (Leviticus 20:13). This condemnation applied to men. Female homosexuality was apparently winked at. The scriptures do not tell us precisely what homosexuality is, however. We must infer behaviors that are not explicitly described.

The Greek tradition stands in marked contrast. The Greeks idealized the love of a man for a young boy (*pederasty*). "In the dialogues of Plato love is always pederasty or homosexual love."[3] While Socrates found the companionship of young boys a delight, the evidence suggests that he practiced abstinence as far as any form of intercourse was concerned. We do not know if this behavior of Socrates was typical or not. The Spartans and Thebans were noted for their armies, which were made up of homosexual lovers. The Athenian aristocracy at least was quite accepting of bisexuality. A man's love for a young man was not thought of as incompatible with his love for a woman.

How extensive homosexuality was among the ancient Greeks is hotly contested today. The prevalence of phallic worship (worship of the male genitals) suggests to some that it was widespread. Phallic images date back to the Stone Age in Greece, as well as in many other countries. Representations of the phallus were common in the festivals and processions of Dionysus, who was called both *phalles* and *paederastes*. According to Vangaard, linking worship of the phallus to the love for young boys makes both more understandable. The phallus symbolized the full force of manliness, not just the ability to impregnate a woman. The god or the tutor could transfer his full manliness to the worshipper or student through the act of anal intercourse.[4] Women, of course, could receive the penis, but not maleness.

Pederastry was not as much a part of Athenian culture as it was in the Dorian world. Vangaard contends that "the love of boys remained in Athens a more personal, erotic, and aesthetic phenomenon . . . among the Dorians the typical predicate for the beloved boy was agathos meaning good in an ethical sense, while in Athens the word was kalos, beautiful, handsome with an aesthetic-erotic bias."[5]

However, according to Robert Flaceliere, an authority on Greek sexual life, "inversion was never very prevalent except in one class and over a quite limited period . . . there is no evidence that homosexuality met with any general social approval. . . . The Greeks never 'canonized' the physical act of sodomy. They always kept up the fiction of 'educational' pederasty."[6] Nevertheless, though it was probably not prevalent throughout Greek culture, it did contribute im-

---

[3]Robert Flaceliere, *Love in Ancient Greece,* trans. James Cleugh (New York: Crown Publisher, 1962), p. 168.

[4]Thorkil Vangaard, *Phallos: A Symbol and its History in the Male World* (New York: International Universities Press, Inc., 1972), p. 62.

[5]Ibid., p. 67.

[6]Quoted in Arno Harlen, *Sexuality and Homosexuality: A New View* (New York: W. W. Norton and Company, Inc., 1971), p. 33.

measurably to the lives of many aristocrats—"the leisured, literate elite from which artists and statesmen came."[7]

Greek literature, in the writings of Sappho, also provides evidence of the existence of female homosexuality, the love of one woman for another. Sappho lived in the sixth century B.C. She ran a school for girls and fell in love with some of her students. Sappho was called a Lesbian because she lived on the island of Lesbos, and that term has since been applied to all female homosexuals. Sappho herself was probably a bisexual, however, having been married and given birth to a daughter. Her sensuous poems describing her homosexual desires earned her the title of the "Tenth Muse" among the later Greeks. Her "Ode to Atthis" was written on the occasion of the departure of one of her favorite students who was intent upon marriage. This expression of homosexual love has become the definition of heterosexual lovesickness for the Western mind.

> *Peer of Gods he seemeth to me, the blissful*
> *Man who sits and gazes at thee before him.*
> *Close beside thee sits, and in silence hears*
>   *thee silvery speaking,*
> *Laughing love's low laughter. Oh this, this only*
> *Stirs the troubled heart in my breast to tremble!*
> *For should I but see thee a little moment,*
>   *Straight is my voice hushed;*
> *Yea, my tongue is broken, and through and through me*
> *'Neath the flesh, impalapable fire runs tingling;*
> *Nothing see mine eyes, and a voice of roaring waves in my ear sounds;*
> *Sweat runs down in rivers, a tremor seizes*
> *All my limbs, and paler than grass in autumn,*
> *Caught by pains of menacing death, I falter,*
>   *Lost in the love-trance.*[8]

It must not be forgotten that sexuality in all its aspects was much more a part of Greek society than it is of ours. The Greeks were not at all uncomfortable about their erotic feelings. In this sense, they represent a break in the heritage of Western civilization. From the early period of Christianity on, sex and the flesh have been seen as sinful. For example, Origen castrated himself in order to become a eunuch for the kingdom of heaven's sake, and Saint Jerome flagellated his flesh in order to drive out the devil.

Homosexuality reached its high point under the Romans. It became popularized by the emperors. "Roman life was, in fact, marked

[7]Ibid., p. 38.

[8]"Ode to Atthis," quoted in Harlen, *Sexuality and Homosexuality* p. 45.

by bisexuality, homosexuality, brutality, and emotional caprice."[9] Catullus, a lyric poet who is usually credited with the development of heterosexual romantic love, was also a lover of boys. The emperor Nero was introduced to homosexuality by his tutor, Seneca. Female homosexuality is mentioned in Roman literature, but not as extensively as male homosexuality.

The Roman Bacchanalia, officially stamped out in the second century because of its sexual excesses, provided an occasion for homosexual intercourse. The Roman historian Livy observed that, "the men were guilty of more immoral acts amongst themselves than the women."[10] The mystery cults of Isis, Mithra, and the Great Mother in her castrating forms (Cybele, Atargatis, Astarte) also fostered homosexual love. Petronius's *Satyricon* tends to equate eunuchism (the custom of castrating the male harem guards), homosexuality, and Eastern religious cults. The *Satyricon* is a fragment of a larger work intended to satirize the love affairs of the Emperor Nero. Indeed, it was in association with these cults that the Roman emperor's sexual deviance became most flagrant.[11]

The most renowned imperial homosexual was the Emperor Elegabalus who began his rule at the age of 14, in A.D. 218.

> . . . "He entered Rome amid Syrian priests and eunuchs, dressed in silks, his cheeks painted scarlet and his eyes made up. . . . he assembled the homosexuals of Rome and addressed them garbed as a boy prostitute; put on a wig and solicited at the door of a brothel; tried to get doctors to turn him into a woman; offered himself for buggery while playing the role of Venus in a court mime; kissed his male favorites' genitals in public and, like Nero, formally married one of them. The phallic sun cult of Baal, like the Great Mother cults, demanded the service of effeminates who joined themselves as in marriage, to the deity. Elegabalus erected in Rome the great phallic asherim which the Hebrew kings had kept trying to purge from their land. . . . Until his madness became insupportable to enough people, he was very popular among the masses, and the cult of Baal was welcomed by large crowds.[12]

Sexual expression and worship of the gods were closely interrelated in the religious cults of the Mediterranean world, particularly in the pre-Christian period. Indeed, it took three centuries of struggling to define itself over and against these mystery cults before Christianity became established in the Roman Empire under Constantine in A.D.

[9]Ibid., p. 48.

[10]Ibid., p. 58.

[11]Ibid., p. 62.

[12]Ibid., p. 62.

312. It seems reasonable to infer that a good portion of the early Christians' antisexuality derived in response to the sexual excesses of such pagan cults. Augustine was among the first to link homosexuality (or sodomy) with sins against nature, and by the fourth century, homosexuals were to be burned at the stake. Novella 77 of the Code of Justinian written in A.D. 538 declares that earthquake, famine, plague, and even total destruction would be the fate of cities that harbored homosexuals. One ancient historian, Procopius, asserts that the prosecution of homosexuals under this code was carried out in reckless fashion.[13]

Unquestionably, the law of the Church strongly condemned homosexuality, but the enforcement of this law has varied, depending on the circumstances. In its efforts to expand, the Church absorbed various pagan cultures, which had different understandings of sexuality. Harlan concludes that "premarital sex, adultery, homosexuality and oral and anal intercourse may have been practiced, but they were frowned upon and perhaps severely punished. The Church and the barbarians probably inherited these values from common cultural ancestors, and have passed them on to us."[14] The Church of the Middle Ages "was intensely preoccupied with homosexuality. To what extent it constituted a genuine problem is hard to say, but in all probability the menace was vastly exaggerated."[15] The Church did not single out homosexuality as especially bad. Homosexuality was only one part of the Church's ban on any sexual practice that did not lead to procreation. "Homosexuality was thus condemned as much because it was a source of pleasure as because it was unnatural."[16]

The first writings about Lesbian love in the Christian West appeared in the Renaissance, which saw something of a rebirth of women's rights in general. "Lesbianism existed, in fact was common, in Rennaissance erotic writings, but how widely it was practiced is a mystery."[17] In most cases the focus was on cross-dressing or transvestism, rather than on lovemaking. Transvestism need not imply sexual relations and is normally distinguished from homosexuality today.

Homosexuality was apparently widespread in urban Victorian England. London brothels of the age featured both male and female prostitutes. The most famous case, the trial of Oscar Wilde for homosexuality, was no isolated phenomenon.

[13]Ibid., p. 78.

[14]Ibid., p. 81.

[15]Gordon Rattray-Taylor, *Sex in History* (New York: Vanguard Press, 1954), pp. 45–46.

[16]Ibid.

[17]Harlan, *Sexuality and Homosexuality*, p. 123.

The historical record can tell us little more than that homosexuals have always been with us. What homosexuality meant to the people accused of it is rarely recorded. Attempts to determine the incidence of homosexuality were not systematically undertaken until well into the twentieth century.

An examination of the data collected by anthropologists indicates that most societies today do not prohibit homosexual behavior. Nevertheless, people who exclusively or nearly exclusively prefer partners of the same sex are more rare in preliterate societies. Among the Siriono of Brazil, for example, homosexual behavior appears to be totally absent, even though there are no norms against it. There is also no homosexuality among the Mangians, even though the society is very sexually permissive.

Among the Sewans of Africa, *all* men and boys engage in anal intercourse, but are not exclusively committed to such contact. In other societies such as the Iatmul of New Guinea, work boys are actively homosexual with men from other tribes while on the job. At home, however, they remain completely heterosexual within a society that strongly condemns homosexuality. Cases such as these are used as proof that genetic or hormonal factors do not exclusively determine homosexual behavior, though they may have an effect.

Homosexual behavior among women is rare in other cultures. In Australia, however, the Aranda women commonly engage in mutual stimulation. Women in some cultures characteristically use a penis substitute when engaging in homosexual intercourse.

> *The Chuckchee women of Siberia use an artificial penis made from the large calf muscle of the reindeer, but its mode of use is not described. In Africa, Moundu and Nama women use an artificial penis in mutual masturbation. Women among the Azande, particularly wives of important men, use a wooden phallus, or occasionally a banana, manioc or sweet potato which is tied around the waist of one of the women who stimulates copulation with her partner. Among the Dahomeans, the common practice of homosexuality on the part of women is believed to be a cause of frigidity in marriage. Interestingly, the Haitians put it just the other way: the frigid women who cannot please her husband seeks another woman as a sex partner.*[18]

Ford and Beach report that information on female homosexual behavior is available for only seventeen of the seventy-six societies in their sample.[19] They conclude that if sanctions against homosexuality were lifted in some future hypothetical society, heterosexual inter-

[18]Clellan S. Ford and Frank A. Beach, *Patterns of Sexual Behavior* (New York: Harper and Brothers, Publishers, 1951), p. 123.

[19]Ibid., p. 123.

course would still remain the most common sexual practice, though homosexual contact would undoubtedly increase.

This lack of information about homosexuality and especially about its nonerotic dimensions, affects our understanding of it even in the more modern, industralized societies.

The Homosexual in the Modern World

A study of homosexuals in the United States, Holland, and Denmark, done by Martin Weinberg and Colin Williams, provides an opportunity to compare three contemporary societies.[20] Homosexuality is not a criminal offense in Holland and Denmark, as it is in America. The Dutch and the Danes do not necessarily approve of homosexuality, but they clearly have more tolerant attitudes toward it. For example, almost half of all respondents from large cities in the United States agreed very much that homosexuality was vulgar and obscene. In Copenhagen, 11.8 percent so agreed, and in Amsterdam only 5.4 percent did so. In Amsterdam, over half (54.1 percent) declared that homosexuality was not at all obscene and vulgar. In a similar fashion, 30.3 percent of American respondents replied that they would have nothing more to do with a friend who was discovered to be a homosexual, while only 3 percent of the respondents in Copenhagen and 2.7 percent in Amsterdam so replied.

Dutch officials have taken a positive stand toward the alleviation of the problems faced by homosexuals. In the United States, however, official assistance at the national level is completely absent. Probably for just that reason, *homophile*[21] organizations are much better developed in the United States, and the gay community is better established. San Francisco seems to be the most tolerant locale for gay life in the United States, but even here authorities have not shown any great concern for the homosexual's situation—though they may directly appeal to the homosexuals for votes. In spite of the more favorable official attitude toward homosexuals in Holland, people do have negative images of homosexuals and there is a lack of social acceptance that does cause problems.[22]

Homosexuals have the same needs as heterosexuals do and they attempt to satisfy those needs in much the same way. Homosexuals eat

[20]Martin S. Weinberg and Colin J. Williams, *Male Homosexuals: Their Problems and Adaptations* (New York: Oxford University Press, 1974).

[21]The term "homophile" means "lover of men" and is preferred by many gays to the term "homosexual," which puts too much stress on sex.

[22]Weinberg and Williams, *op. cit.,* p. 86.

the same food, live in the same sort of homes, and generally wear the same sorts of clothes as heterosexuals do. There is no such thing as *the* homosexual or *the* homosexual life style. However, in most modern societies, homosexuals must live their lives in some degree of social isolation. Because most heterosexuals do not want to associate with them, homosexuals are apt to cluster together for comfort and companionship. Because they cannot be themselves in the places provided for heterosexuals, homosexuals are able to meet like-minded people in places that cater to homosexuals. One such place is the homosexual or gay bar.

GAY BARS

The gay bar is a central part of the gay community in industrial societies. Establishing and operating a gay bar can be made more difficult because public officials are not inclined to open them in the first place and may seek ways of harassing those involved once such bars are established. As a common means of harassment, gay bars are subject to inspection for violation of one municipal code or another much more often than other sorts of public facilities. In New York, as a result, gay bars are much more likely to be run by organized crime, which can afford the pay-offs and also has the muscle to keep officials in check.[23] Bars in San Francisco are much less involved in such pay-offs because the officials there are more open about such things. In the Netherlands, gay bars are legal, but the procedures for their establishment are strictly enforced. Permission to operate must be sought from several sources in the hopes that the red tape will discourage people. Copenhagen, which is sometimes described as a good scene for homosexuals, has a very depressing bar area, according to Weinberg and Williams. It is separated from the central entertainment district and is gloomy, run-down, and potentially dangerous.[24]

Gay bars are places where homosexuals meet for friendly conversation, entertainment, and sexual contact. Some of these bars are also frequented by straights. One-night stands are set up most often in gay bars. Evelyn Hooker conceives of gay bars as "free markets" in which "leisure is retailed in the form of liquor and legitimate entertainment" and negotiations for an exchange of sexual services are conducted.[25] The atmosphere of the gay bar colors straight people's attitudes toward homosexuals.

Most people focus their complaints about homosexuality on the cruising that takes place in gay bars. Homosexuals are looked down

[23]Ibid., p. 57.

[24]Ibid., p 82.

[25]Evelyn Hooker, "Male Homosexuals and Their 'Worlds' " in Marmor, *Sexual Inversion*, p. 96. © 1965 Basic Books, Inc., Publishers, New York.

on because they meet their lovers in a bar, rather than at a more socially acceptable place, such as a private party, museum, or on the job. Leaving the issue of sex aside for the moment, one wonders how

Figure 10–2
Many observers believe that if homosexual marriages were
legalized, homosexuals would not depend so much on one-night stands for
companionship and sex. (© George W. Gardner)

people would feel about gays if they typically congregated at coffee shops, bowling alleys, or poetry readings.

People object to gay bars mainly because, in most cities, they are the public expression of an activity that most people would like to pretend doesn't exist. But, when looked at in terms of social rather than sexual activity, most people would have to admit that the scene at most heterosexual singles bars is essentially the same as in most gay bars. For both heterosexuals and homosexuals, a bar can be a place to meet people. Homosexual social activity is concentrated in the gay bar; society provides heterosexuals with other ways to make friends not available to homosexuals. Making a date at work could end a homosexual's career. A homosexual cannot walk up to a stranger at a museum and make sexual overtures as a heterosexual can. But in a gay bar, where he feels safe, the homosexual can open himself up to the search for companionship. The common expectation in encounters in both singles and gay bars is that sex can be had without commitment. The homosexual is often charged with being more promiscuous than most heterosexuals because of his greater reliance on one-night stands, but many have observed that he is promiscuous because society forces him to be. Homosexual partnerships are unstable because society places so many impediments in their way. No small part of the problem is the illegality of homosexual marriages.

The market environment of the gay bar encourages an emphasis on the "cosmetic self." The way people dress, behave, and look is extremely important. This is also true in heterosexual singles bars, which have been described as "body shops" and "meat markets." However, once heterosexuals do meet, they are apt to freely exchange information about themselves—where they live, what they do, and so on. Soon the people can come to know each other and may turn their encounter into a deeper relationship. But, in the homosexual world, to provide such information might increase the risk of exposure and blackmail. The exchange must be impersonal; it is contracted typically in the holding of a glance, which may be followed by a brief conversation, and then leaving together in a casual and unobtrusive manner. Out of fear, they may be as unknown to each other after the sex act as they were before. Heterosexual encounters under similar conditions produce similar results.

But gay bars should not be thought of simply as markets for the exchange of sexual favors. About half of the clientele of a typical gay bar gather with friends to exchange gossip, share advice on how to cope with the problems of the gay world, and to simply relax without having to wear the mask required by "respectable" straight society.

Gay bars also serve as induction centers for people entering the gay world for the first time. In the context of a bar, people who have been unwilling to identify themselves as homosexuals may find sufficient support to "come out." In the bar, a cross section of occupations and life styles provides a much broader conception of the homosexual scene, as well as specific models with whom the homosexual can more readily identify.

As is the case with heterosexuals, the bar world is most exciting for the young. Homosexuals who are over thirty find crusing more difficult, the pace more hectic, and tend to prefer more sedate private parties. They typically frequent the bars only occasionally.

Contrary to common persuasion, homosexuals of either gender are less sexually active than heterosexuals. Younger gays may be hyperactive after coming out—like young heterosexuals after they have lost their virginity—but this phase soon passes. Because these young gays are the most visible aspect of the gay life, outsiders tend to think of them as representative of that life. Gays, in fact, vary considerably in the extent to which sexuality is seen as an organizing principle of their lives. The same, of course, is true for heterosexuals, but heterosexuals do not have to constantly defend their sexual preference (though they may of course have to defend their sexual behavior if it is perceived of as too unacceptable to their community).

Gay men enjoy a wide variety of lovemaking techniques. Much of their lovemaking follows the same pattern as heterosexual pair lovemaking: kissing and petting, leading to genital contact and orgasm. Oral-genital and anal-genital intercourse are both common techniques that can be utilized in a variety of positions. The partners may rub their penises against each other and experience orgasm without penetration. Hunt found that mutual masturbation was the most common means by which homosexual males experienced orgasm. He also concluded that oral-genital intercourse was more common than anal-genital intercourse. In marked contrast to Lesbians, who may enjoy sensuous pleasuring and massage without genital contact or orgasm, homosexual males virtually always experience orgasm in sexual relationships.[26] Yet, in Kinsey's findings, bisexual males were less likely than bisexual females to report their homosexual experiences as more satisfying.[27]

The bar world represents but the tip of the iceberg of the gay community. Present estimates assume that there are about 4 to 5 million males in the United States who are exclusively homosexual. Kinsey found that up to 37 percent of all males had experienced orgasm in a homosexual relationship at least once in their lives.

---

[26]Morton Hunt *Sexual Behavior in the 1970's* (New York Dell Publishing Co., 1974)., p. 318–19; Alfred C. Kinsey *et. al., Sexual Behavior in the Human Female* (New York: Pocket Book, 1965), p. 488.

[27]Kinsey *op. cit.,* p. 488.

Figure 10–3
(Joel Gordon)

LIVING ARRANGEMENTS

A broader perspective on the gay life styles can be obtained by considering the various types of living arrangements. In Weinberg and William's sample of 1,865 American homosexuals, 45 percent of the Americans were living alone, 38 percent with a roommate or lover, 13 percent with parents, and 4 percent with their wives. In Amsterdam and Copenhagen, most homosexuals lived with a roommate.[28]

Living With A Homosexual Lover. This would seem to be the desired living arrangement for most homosexuals and is more likely to be realized in practice when the social climate permits it. The ideal is to live with someone who is loved and with whom one's life is shared; in short, to live in marriage. People who choose to live in this fashion are, according to Weinberg and Williams, less likely to fear being labeled as homosexual and less likely to be socially involved with heterosexuals. Most significantly, those homosexuals who were living to-

[28]Derived from Weinberg and Williams, *op. cit.*, Table 1, p. 341.

gether were least likely to be depressed, lonely, or experienced guilt, shame, or anxiety regarding their homosexuality.[29]

Living Alone. In the United States, in particular, it is probable that most homosexuals live alone. It is perceived as unseemly for grown men to live together. Less suspicion is apt to fall on two women who happen to be sharing an apartment because they can be thought of as banding together for protection. Homosexuals who live alone are older than the typical gay of the bar scene. They are more likely to experience loneliness and anxiety about their homosexuality, are less well integrated into the gay community, and anticipate more discrimination compared to those gays living with a gay roommate. Such people are also less apt to be considered homosexual by their straight friends and acquaintances.

Living With Parents. Most gays who live with their parents are dependents and, therefore, are younger than the average member of the gay community. Parents seem to be inclined to force their gay children into therapy, or simply kick them out of the house. (There is, however, a national organization for parents of gays, which does not

[29]Ibid., pp. 235–36.

Figure 10–4
A national organization formed by parents of gay men and women urge other parents not to
add to their children's problems by rejecting them because they are homosexual.
(© Sepp Seitz, Woodfin Camp & Associates)

condone such behavior.) The problem of maintaining a straight facade is thus particularly acute for these men. They may be forced to show an interest in girls, to date, and to invent heterosexual friends in order to allay parental suspicions. As a result of the pressures placed on them, these homosexuals are least likely of all to have close friends. Only men who live with their wives are less involved in the gay community and have less homosexual contact. Those living with parents have less self-acceptance, less stable self-concepts, and more depression than other gays.[30]

Living With Wife. Homosexuals who live with their wives are as a group the most fearful of being detected, have the least association with the gay community, and, in spite of their occasional homoerotic experiences, may choose not to define themselves as homosexual. On the other hand, some of these men may be more actively homosexual than heterosexual and may have entered marriage for camouflage, through a desire to have children, or simply through giving in to the social pressure to marry.

Often the man in such cases may best be described as a bisexual because he has an erotic interest in both men and women. In some cases, the wife knows of her spouse's homoerotic preference. In others, she does not. There are a few marriages of convenience in which the wife is also gay. A common meeting ground for married homosexuals is the public rest room (called a tearoom) or park. Apparently these encounters are rewarding enough for some men to cause them to repeat the risks involved in such "bush" encounters.[31]

Dwight, a married bisexual, had intercourse with his wife three or four times a week and stepped out on her with other women on occasion. He also claimed to visit the tearooms almost daily.

> *I guess you might say I'm pretty highly sexed (he chuckled a little), but I really don't think that's why I go to tearooms. That's really not sex. Sex is something I have with my wife in bed. It's not as if I were committing adultery by getting my rocks off—or going down on some guy—in a tearoom. I get a kick out of it. Some of my friends go out for handball. I'd rather cruise the park. Does that sound perverse to you?*[32]

Laud Humphreys has described four main types of homosexuals: the trade, the ambisexual, the gay, and the closet queen. The men who are classified as "in the trade" are the most lonely and isolated of all. They are largely Roman Catholic males whose wives will not en-

---

[30]Ibid., pp. 237–38.

[31]Laud Humphreys, *Tearoom Trade,* 2nd. ed. (Chicago: Aldine Publishing Company, 1975) pp. 149–66.

[32]Ibid., p. 119.

gage in intercourse for fear of having another child, and are generally unsuccessful at their job. In the impersonal sex of the tearoom, they will only play the insertor role because it is against their sense of masculinity to use their mouth as a substitute for the female organ. Dwight who enjoys sex with both men and women, is an example of an *ambisexual*. *Gays* are openly homosexual, live with their male lovers, and make use of the tearoom only when they are horny or when their lovers are away. The tearoom does not become the focus of their sexual lives. The last group in Humphrey's sample, the *closet queens,* parallel the trade group in some ways. They too have very few friends, are mainly Roman Catholic, tend to play the insertor role, are not particularly successful on the job, and are mostly high school graduates. As a group they are more lonely than those in the trade and are distinguished even more by their preference for young boys. "Closet queen" is a generally prejorative term in the gay community, in part because these men tend to become involved in the public scandals that do so much damage to the image of gay life.

It is Humphrey's conviction that tearooms provide important outlets for what otherwise would be pent-up frustrations. He feels that public policy would best be served by easing up the police vice-squad surveillance of tearooms and encouraging the covert homosexual to come out.

LIFE CYCLE

There are important variations in the life style of the homosexual that can be related to particular stages in the life cycle.[33] Everyone has problems or crises in life that pertain to tasks that must be done at a certain time in one's development. In the case of the homosexual, a particularly tense and exciting time is associated with the period of his life when he "comes out." This period, during which he publicly acknowledges his homoerotic preference, is a time of comparatively high sexual activity, very much likened to the heterosexual's early dating. Coming out legitimates their homosexual desires, within the homosexual subculture at least, and the feelings they have struggled with for so long may now be expressed at last.

It is during this period, shortly after coming out, that homosexuals are most likely to dress in women's clothing, ("go drag") and to act in effeminate ways in relatively public places. The very core of their masculine identity is called into question. "A few males remain in this commitment to pseudofeminity, a few others emerge masquerad-

[33]John H. Gagnon and William Simon, "The Sociological Perspective on Homosexuality," *The Dublin Review* (Summer, 1967), pp. 96–114.

[34]Ibid., pp. 104–5.

ing as female prostitutes to males, and still others pursue careers as female impersonators."[34] The fact that this stage in the homosexual's life is likely to be most visible to the general public helps account for the tendency of straights to think of all gays as effeminate.

Coming to terms with aging is an important transition for all of us. For the homosexual, however, it is particularly difficult. The emphasis on youth in the straight world is greatly exceeded among homosexuals. By his mid-thirties, a homosexual is considered much less attractive, sexually. His ability to find companionship by cruising has declined dramatically, and he is inclined to participate less in the gay community. The homosexual has generally fewer resources with which to deal with this problem. He ordinarily has no wife or children. If he is living alone, he may have very few friends. However, even though they are more apt to be on their own, like most heterosexuals, they come to accept the inevitable.

Lesbian Worlds

William Acton, the leading authority on sexual matters in Victorian England and America, declared that respectable women were not inclined toward sexual arousal or the seeking of sexual pleasure in marriage. They were wives and mothers—not lovers—and, therefore, a young man contemplating marriage need not worry about his ability to satisfy his wife sexually because she wouldn't expect him to. Queen Victoria herself, when confronted with the suggestion that English common law should include sexual acts between women as crimes against nature, was appalled that anyone should think that ladies could do anything like that and refused to consider the matter further.

Perhaps it is the affront to the male ego in the suggestion that women can find sexual satisfaction without male services that accounts for the fact that the law rarely defines lesbianism as a crime. Law enforcement officials are most inclined to harass men, whom they suspect to be homosexual, rather than women. Until recently, it has been assumed that women, simply because they are women, adjust more naturally to celibacy than men do. The lesbian deals with a double problem in developing her sexuality: her sexual preference and her status as a woman.

In spite of the fact that her sexual preference is less likely to cause her to be labeled as a homosexual, the lesbian knows that she is different even if others do not perceive her as being so. She becomes a chameleon creature, skilled in cover-up and concealment. Consequently, less is known about lesbians than about male homosexuals. Lesbians are not inclined to discuss their sexuality, even with other lesbians, and most investigators are males who find it hard to listen. Therefore, much of what is said about the lesbian at present is somewhat tentative and suggestive.

Furthermore, even though they may recognize lesbianism as a way of life, many people assume that whatever can be said about male homosexuals applies equally as well to lesbians, but this is apparently not so. A lesbian is neither necessarily a heterosexual reject—a woman too unattractive to make it with men—nor a woman inclined to seek "masculine" love in another woman. A lesbian is a woman who loves another woman because she is a woman.[35]

Del Martin and Phyllis Lyons are lesbians who have been living together for over twenty years. They co-founded the Daughters of Bilitis, a leading homophile organization based in San Francisco. As a result of their interviews with hundreds of lesbians, they argue that the most important element in the lesbian partnership is mutual love, not sexual satisfaction. Simon and Gagnon's impressions generally concur with Martin and Lyons's. "Almost all of the women we interviewed saw themselves as women who wanted to become emotionally and sexually attached to another woman who, in turn, respond to them as a woman."[36]

Most straights have difficulty accepting the presence of love in a homosexual relationship. Homosexuals and lesbians are not seen as normal and therefore are not expected to have the same feelings straight people do. Constant use of the term homosexual reinforces this excessive focus on sexual behavior rather than on emotions. The clearest expression of this reluctance to acknowledge homosexual love is the unwillingness to legalize homosexual marriages in our society.

In spite of the fact that lesbians generally want to love and be loved as women, there are a few for whom the masculine identification is important. Sometimes this is manifested in wearing men's clothes, smoking cigars, using foul language, and assuming an aggressive stance toward people. These women are sometimes called "dykes," or "bull dykes." It is also apparently true that lesbians go through a phase in their development during which they are inclined to try out one or the other stereotype of the heterosexual roles in their partnerships. The butch/femme partnership may mimic or even caricature the heterosexual masculine/feminine sterotypes in great detail, or may simply follow them generally as one way of dividing up the responsibilities of a common household. Martin and Lyons feel that most older lesbians have gone through the butch/femme pattern be-

[35]Del Martin and Phyllis Lyons, *Lesbian/Woman* (San Francisco: Glide Publications, 1972) p. 1.

[36]William Simon and John Gagnon, "The Lesbian: A Preliminary Overview," in *Sexual Deviance*, John Gagnon and William Simon, eds. (New York: Harper & Row, 1967), p. 265.

cause that was the only model that they had for working out a long-term partnership. Younger lesbians today are less inclined to follow these roles and seek a more egalitarian model for their partnerships. Simon and Gagnon point out that imitating heterosexual roles can provide security for some lesbians who are having difficulty coping with their deviant identities. They may also be useful as a way of getting a relationship going. As one young lesbian has commented,

When I first got into the gay world with the first girl, there was no butch or fem. We didn't know, though I was slightly more aggressive. (In making love?) No, I mean in taking care of things, managing, planning. When we made love, there was a kind of flow, a sharing. So I eventually came out in the gay world as a kind of butch. Mostly because I felt you had to be somewhere. Later, if someone asked, I said I was butch, but mostly because I didn't want any of these bull dykes coming to me. [37]

Another woman whose first two lesbian contacts were both "butch" declared,

They didn't like me to touch them, or anything. They had to do everything. Just like most men, but if that's what you want you might as well go "straight." [38]

Most lesbians have made love with men, many have been married, and many are married still. While some prefer to act out masculine roles, most complain about the masculine way of doing everything, from making love to managing household tasks, and consciously seek an alternative. This alternative does not seem to be the femme caricature of heterosexual femininity, but a more liberated view of women, stressing equality in interpersonal relationships and valuing a style of lovemaking that places much less emphasis upon the genitals than is common in heterosexual lovemaking.

Just what lesbians do when they make love is often a mystery to women who find themselves attracted to other women. Little is available in print about the subject, and much of what is in print follows the heterosexual fantasies and stereotypes. Martin and Lyons assert that lesbians have three basic styles of lovemaking: mutual stimulation, cunnilingus, and tribadism.[39] Cunnilingus can be enjoyed by one partner at a time, or mutually, in the "69" position. Tribadism is a technique that may fulfill butch/femme fantasies, but that demands considerable skill in order to achieve orgasm. In tribadism, one partner stimulates the other's clitoris by rubbing her own genitals

---

[37]Ibid., p. 265.

[38]Ibid., p. 266.

[39]Martin and Lyons, *Lesbian/Woman*, p. 63.

against it. A number of variations are possible, just as in heterosexual intercourse.

There are two additional techniques that are rarely used, but deserve comment because of the fantasies of the heterosexual world. The use of a penis substitute or dildo made of rubber or some other material shaped to resemble a penis is very rare. According to Martin and Lyons the dildo is most apt to be used by heterosexual women in masturbation, and is rare even then.[40] Those few lesbians who feel the need to experience fullness in their vagina are inclined to use some other object, such as a cucumber, banana, or candle. Anilingus is the stimulation of the anus by means of the tongue (in slang, called "rimming"). Both penis substitutes and anilingus are also enjoyed by some heterosexual couples.

[40]Ibid., p. 63.

The listing of such techniques should not imply that lesbians are inclined to go directly to the genitals in their lovemaking. On the contrary, the evidence is strongly suggestive that great value is placed upon the entire body as an erogenous zone and that many lesbians find sex between women more rewarding because it is much less focused on the genitals. At the same time, the problems in coping with their sexual identities, their displeasure in heterosexual lovemaking experiences, and their problems in growing up have made many lesbians unable to achieve orgasm.[41] While most lesbians make love to each other, some either refuse to make love or only allow themselves to be made love to. There is, in short, a wide range of roles and techniques employed by lesbians in making love and a common recognition that the love between partners is more important than any technique that may be employed to achieve sexual satisfaction.

The available evidence strongly suggests that lesbians do not become lesbians in order to satisfy some strong urge for sexual excitement. As in the case of heterosexual women, lesbians more commonly discover that they are in love before they become involved in sexual behavior. "One might say that for females the 'discovery' of love relations regardless of sex precedes the 'discovery' of sexuality while the reverse is generally true for males."[42] A common example of this romantic drift into lesbianism is provided by a young woman whose previous experience was some mild homosexual play with a cousin during mid-adolescence. Her second attachment to another woman was similarly overtly sexual only to a limited extent.

> We met at the (a residential hotel for women). We started out just being friends and then it became something special. She taught me a lot of things. I love music and she taught me how to listen to it and appreciate it. She liked things like I liked, like walking. We read a lot together. We read the Bible, we read verses to each other. We shared things together. We caressed each other and kissed. I think it was a need to have someone there. And I was there and she was there and we just held on to each other. (Did you ever become sexually involved on a more physical level?) Not to the fullest and when I say not to the fullest extent I mean we didn't take off our clothes and lie in the nude with each other. I enjoyed being with her. I got something from her without going through the actions of sex.[43]

Lesbians are not as inclined to be as active in the gay community as are male homosexuals. They come from all parts of the country and are found in all occupational niches of the class structure that are available to women. The impression one gains from the data is that

[41]Ibid., p. 71. The suggestion of causes here is not intended to be exhaustive.

[42]Simon and Gagnon, "The Lesbian," p. 251.

[43]Ibid., pp. 252–53.

Figure 10–6
It is important to keep in mind
that except for their sexual
preference, lesbians are no
different than other women.
(© 1976 Sherry Suris)

lesbian relationships tend to last longer than male homosexual relationships, though cruising is not unknown among lesbians, and there
are some gay bars that cater strictly to lesbians.

Are such women happy? Martin and Lyons contend that happiness
is a poor measure to apply to lesbians.

> *A lesbian who is struggling with her identity or who may be trying to re-*
> *press her sexuality will, of course, be unhappy during that period of her*
> *life. The woman who has come to terms with her identity and has crossed*
> *the bridge of self-acceptance may have gained self-confidence but not yet a*
> *lover, and so feels lonely and unhappy for a time. The lesbian who has*
> *hurdled the identity crises and established a meaningful and satisfying*
> *relationship with another woman may still feel somewhat unhappy on oc-*
> *casion because of society's structures. Happiness is not stationary; it is*
> *fluid; it fluctuates. As lesbians we have experienced great joy and hap-*
> *piness and love. We have also know despair, conflict and unhappiness.*
> *This is the human condition.*[44]

Finally, in spite of our focus on the more explicit sexual aspects of

[44]Martin and Lyons, *Lesbian/Woman*, p. 25.

lesbianism, it should not be forgotten that in most respects lesbians are no different from other women. A woman can be a lesbian and still be a woman who is warm, loving, and nurturing. Thus, lesbians may not have as much violence done to their self-esteem and their sex identity as male homosexuals have. A lesbian is a person whose sexual preference creates a problem for her because it is not the common pattern. In some instances, this sexual preference may become the center of a distinctive life style in which everything else is subordinated to it, but this is not the common case. Of the 2 to 3 percent of the female population that is probably exclusively homosexual, most are very inconspicuous simply because they are no different from everyone else except for their sexual preference, which is generally considered a personal and private matter.[45]

Becoming Homosexual

Some people contend that trying to find out how people become homosexual or come to do homosexual things is futile. Homosexuality is evidently not caused by any single factor. It often involves conscious choice, though the decision, as in the case of many lesbians, may be to love another woman rather than to become a homosexual. It may take a number of years to reconcile that choice with one's sense of identity. Nevertheless, the study of homosexuality to date has mainly focused on what causes homosexuality. A great deal of this emphasis is motivated by a desire to prevent others from becoming homosexual, if possible. There are a number of explanations of homosexuality that have been offered. None of these have been confirmed by research, but all of them have been supported by some evidence.

The classic Freudian explanation still influences clinical attitudes toward homosexuality. In this view, homosexuality is a normal stage in the development of every child—a stage in the evolution of heterosexuality. Freud contended that homosexuality was the result of an arrest of normal development or was a regression to an earlier stage of development as a result of castration-anxiety. Such anxiety was usually brought about by an unhealthy childhood. Many Freudians, however, do not accept the idea that we are all potentially bisexual, or the notion that homosexuality is an arrested stage in the devel-

[45]The 2 to 3 percent figure is from Gagnon, *Human Sexualities* (Glenview, Ill.: Scott, Foresman and Company, 1977), p. 254. An estimated additional 2 to 3 percent of the female population have had both mixed homosexual and heterosexual experiences. Unlike many men, women do not tend to have homosexual contact in adolescence. Such experimentation typically comes later in life, when they are in their twenties, or later.

opment of heterosexuality. They see homosexuality as caused by an unconscious fear of the opposite sex. While some clinical evidence supports these views, there is no reason to believe that they are the only or most significant factors in the development of homosexuality.

Others see homosexuality as the result of continuous or presistent positive rewards for a sexual preference for the same sex. Prison populations, for example, have high incidences of homosexual behavior because inmates are not able to find heterosexual partners. Some people find it difficult to form or resume heterosexual relationships once they are released from prison. However, most people who experience such situationally induced behavior have no trouble with heterosexual relations when they become possible.

Some people contend that homosexuality is caused by an avoidance of heterosexual contacts because of the fear of commitment that is assumed to go with heterosexual sex. In this line of reasoning, the homosexual is attracted to the gay world because the typical relationships that develop are unstable and short-term. I have argued earlier, however, that the more probable explanation for the instability of these relationships is the unwillingness of straight society to legalize homosexual marriages and the many social rebuffs that gays must endure.

Social and cultural factors undoubtedly contribute to the incidence of homosexuality in a particular society and are sometimes considered causes. For example, societies that have female deities conceive of incest as the major taboo, while homosexuality is treated with little significance.[46] Third sex, or *berdache,* roles, are legitimized in societies such as those of the American Plains Indians. Males may dress like and assume the responsibilities of women because they do not want to become warriors or because their vision quest revealed that they were destined for that sort of role. Among the Chuckchee Eskimo, homosexuality seems related to the inability of the male to acquire enough wealth to provide for a wife. Westermark, an antropologist, contends that homosexuality appears to increase with urbanization and also during periods of high civilization.

A view that has recently been revived as a result of increased precision in the measurement of hormone levels in the body is that homosexuality is caused by an abnormal hormone level, particularly of testosterone. Male homosexuals have been shown to have lower levels of testosterone than normal heterosexual males in some studies. But males subjected to stress, as in combat, for example, have levels of testosterone equally as low. Also, it is impossible to say whether homosexuals have lower testosterone levels before they became homo-

---

[46]Gordon Rattray-Taylor, *Sex in History* (New York: Vangaard Press, 1954). p. 80ff.

sexuals or after they became exposed to the stresses of homosexual life.

The assumption underlying these theories is that psychosexual differentiation should normally produce heterosexuality. Homosexuality means that something has gone wrong with the process. Researchers are inclined to find evidence to support the contention that male homosexuals are effeminate men and female homosexuals are masculine women. While some homosexuals undoubtedly do fit these descriptions, many, if not most, appear not to. The underlying assumption that heterosexuality is normal and homosexuality is not is supported by the conviction that reproduction is the norm, goal, or purpose of human sexual behavior.

However, evidence is beginning to accumulate in support of the view that homosexuality is a normal variant of human sexuality. The trials and tribulations of homosexuals can better be explained in terms of the cultural norms that make it more difficult for them to achieve a satisfactory sex identity and a satisfactory degree of self-esteem, as well as by the harassment they must endure because of their "deviant" life style. In view of the greater burdens imposed on homosexuals, it is remarkable indeed that many, if not most, seem to be well-adjusted individuals who are able to cope with the society that finds them so offensive.

Summary

The evidence is growing that homosexuality is a normal variation of human sexuality. Homosexual attraction and homosexual behavior is widespread in the industrial societies of the world, being more common among men than women. The historical record can only tell us that homosexuals have been around for a long time and are found in every age. We cannot determine precisely what homosexuality meant in each of these eras, however, because in most cases the information is too sparse. Holy scripture is particularly difficult to interpret, precisely because very little detailed information is presented as to what was meant by homosexuality at various times in Biblical history. Comparative studies of other cultures can tell us that there are some societies in which there is no homosexuality even though there is no norm against it; there are some societies in which all males at some time or another have had sex with other males; and there are some societies in which it is possible for men to assume the female role, which may or may not involve sexually relating to other men as a woman. Less information is known about lesbians.

Contemporary research favors the view that there are many causes for a person to become labeled as a homosexual or lesbian. About 2 to 4 percent of all men in the United States are exclusively homosexual, and another 4 to 6 percent are almost entirely so in their sexual preference. About 2 to 3 percent of all women are exclusively homosexual, and about the same percentage is almost exclusively homosexual in their sexual preference.

The gay life is a complex, changing phenomenon for which stereotypes are most misleading. The effeminate closet queen may be more visible to the straight world, but in fact represents a small percentage of the homosexual world. The gay community itself is but a small portion of all those who regularly enjoy homosexual behavior. Whatever causes we may find to help account for the occurrence of homosexuals, it is evident that a great deal of damage is done to these people because of the negative label society attaches to them. To be openly recognized as a homosexual or Lesbian is to risk considerable abuse.

Sexual Dysfunction and Sexual Therapy

11

It is a measure of human ignorance that nobody knows
how many couples endure serious sexual problems.
There are only the educated guesses of qualified
medical authorities. According to their estimates,
at least one-half and possibly as many as three-fourths
of all marriages are more or less chronically crippled
by sexual disabilities.

Peter and Barbara Wyden

Once any sex was better than no sex, but now only the best will do. In the past, if a person found it hard to enjoy sex, it was assumed that it was because he or she had some other psychological problem. The situation has reversed somewhat; now a person's lack of a satisfying sexual life is more apt to be seen as contributing to his or her other problems. The change in American sexual attitudes and behavior is dramatically seen in the rise of sex therapy. This change has occurred quite recently and in no small measure derives from the work of William Masters and Virginia Johnson.

Until recently, the most common sexual dysfunctions or disorders—premature ejaculation and impotence in men, and inability to achieve orgasm in women—were considered to be psychological in origin. However, psychoanalysis had been remarkably ineffective in treating them. A completely new approach to these and other sexual dysfunctions, which has become the backbone of what is now called the new sex therapy, was begun by Masters and Johnson. Masters and Johnson's approach involves no drugs, no surgery, and no psychoanalysis. It is primarily an intensive relearning experience that can normally be accomplished in a ten- to fourteen-day crash program. Other therapists, such as Joseph Wolpe, Donald Hastings, and Albert Ellis, had previously developed a remarkably successful therapy based on learning principles (cure rates of 60 to 80 percent were reported), but this radical approach was not made known to the general public until the publication of Masters and Johnson's *Human Sexual Inadequacy* in 1970.[1] Although the book was written for other professionals and much of its language is virtually incomprehensible to the average reader, the book has sold over a quarter of a million copies.

Masters and Johnson's technique was appealing to people because it was fast and it worked. People may be willing to spend five years in analysis to find out why they don't like their fathers, but waiting five years for help with a sexual problem would try the patience of Job. Since 1970, there has been an enormous increase in the demand for

[1] Joseph LoPiccolo, "From Psychotherapy to Sex Therapy," *Society/Transactions* (July/August, 1977), p. 61.

Figure 11–1
William Masters and Virginia
Johnson. (© Elliot Erwitt,
Magnum Photos, Inc.)

sex therapy. Such a rapid increase in demand has created problems in the training and regulation of sex therapists and raises a number of questions regarding the new role of sexuality in our lives.

Common Sexual Dysfunctions and Therapies

No one hits a home run every time at bat. Sex may be terrific one night and blah the next. People have a tendency to want to blame someone or something for these normal variations in response. For most people, having more realistic expectations can help. In most cases, getting more rest, sharing some fun, having more privacy, and taking more time can do a lot to banish the blahs. But when sex is not fun and is something to be nervous about over a long period of time, then a problem exists. Both men and women can have problems enjoying sex. Male problems involve difficulty in achieving and maintaining an erection and ejaculating too soon or too late. Being unable to have orgasm is the primary reason women seek sex therapy. In general, a *sexual dysfunction* is a sexual behavioral problem that makes sex consistently unsatisfying for an individual.

IMPOTENCE

There are two basic kinds of impotence. A man with *primary impotence* has never been able to have an erection lasting long enough to allow him to have intercourse. This condition is extremely rare. Every man can expect to have a problem getting an erection at one time or another in his life, as the result of fatigue, distraction, excessive drinking, or a poor relationship with his partner. While such occasional episodes of impotence can be upsetting and embarrassing, it is not considered a problem unless it goes on for a long time. When an otherwise healthy man cannot achieve an erection consistently, he is said to have *secondary impotence.*

"There is probably no other medical condition which is as potentially frustrating, humiliating, and devastating as impotence."[2] Because almost all cultures place so much value on the male's ability to have an erection, the impotent male frequently experiences secondary depression. However, since depression can also cause impotence, it must first be determined if the depression preceded or followed the impotence. In similar fashion, marital discord can be both a cause and consequence of impotence. Finally, some men are able to achieve erection in unusual situations (for example, by watching young girls undress, by exposing their penis to an unsuspecting passerby, by dressing in women's clothing, or through watching people urinate), but remain impotent in more typical heterosexual situations. These men are not really susceptible to the new therapy, but most impotent men can benefit from professional help.

Depending on the therapist's theoretical orientation and training, a number of treatments may be offered for impotence. Masters and Johnson have identified three primary goals in treating impotence: to help the man regain his sexual self-confidence; to make sex something he enjoys being involved in, rather than passively takes part in; and to assure the woman that they can do it if they try.[3]

Most sex therapists assign a number of sexual tasks in order to achieve these goals. The basic attitude of these pleasuring techniques is expressed in the "give-to-get" principle. Briefly, the male learns to concentrate on giving his partner pleasure—not in order to achieve an erection, but simply in order to give her pleasure. So that such pleasuring can occur without stress, intercourse is usually forbidden by the therapists. Erection is not expected, but may occur. Kaplan and her colleagues instruct the couples not to worry if the man fails to get an erection during such sessions, she simply advises them to try again later. The basic premise behind this program is that the ability to regain an erection can be learned, and the learning reduces the fear of failure. Helping to avoid the feeling of being pressured to perform can help the man relax enough to relearn the ability.

Masters and Johnson place heavy emphasis on opening up commu-

[2]Helen Kaplan, *The New Sex Therapy: Active Treatment of Sexual Dysfunction* (New York: Brunner/Mazel, 1974), p. 257.

[3]William Masters and Virginia Johnson, *Human Sexual Inadequacy* (Boston: Little, Brown & Co., Inc., 1970), p. 196.

nication between sexual partners. They believe that there is no such thing as an uninvolved partner in the case of sexual inadequacy and that the condition of the couple's relationship can strongly affect either partner's sexual adequacy. Open communication is encouraged in joint therapy sessions in which the couple meet with the therapy teams. Masters and Johnson believe that the teams must be composed of a man and a woman if the therapy is to be most beneficial.

Distraction is an enemy to good sex. A number of suggestions to defeat distraction are offered, such as getting lost in the pleasuring of one's partner, getting lost in one's favorite sexual fantasy, and focusing on one's own erotic sensations. Often the most distracting thoughts center around fears that are quite deep in the unconscious. For example, an overconcern for one's partner, born of feelings of guilt and a deep-seated fear of rejection, can interfere with sexual functioning. To overcome this, the couple is encouraged to take turns. He proceeds at his own pace when pleasuring and is not afraid to feel good about receiving pleasure, knowing that his partner's turn will come. The pleasuring sessions also foster confidence in that they allow the couple to establish unambiguously what they like and dislike. "There is positive reinforcement for any man learning what really pleases the woman of his choice by having her quietly show him the specifics of her sensual interest."[4] This is also accomplished in the sharing of sexual fantasies in some treatments.

After establishing considerable success in achieving erection, the couple moves on to intercourse. Because these initial sessions are critical, a common approach is to place the woman on top and instruct her to mount his erect penis and move her hips up and down in a nondemanding fashion. She is told to separate before ejaculation occurs. After several such couplings, he may be encouraged to thrust to orgasm.

Kaplan finds that the male hormone testosterone can be used effectively in the treatment of some cases of impotence. It relieves the vicious circle of depression by giving the man a psychological boost. The man may then be able to achieve some degree of erection and restore some of his confidence, regardless of the effects of the drug itself. It does not work in all cases, however.

Over half of all cases of primary impotence and nearly three quarters of all cases of secondary impotence, among those who seek therapy, are cured.

PREMATURE EJACULATION

Premature ejaculation seems to be the most common sexual dysfunction. Fundamentally, it is an inability to control the ejaculatory reflex, causing ejaculation before one's partner can achieve satisfactory

[4]Ibid., p. 204.

stimulation. Masters and Johnson define it as the "inability of a man to delay ejaculation long enough to penetrate *and satisfy* his partner at least fifty percent of the time.[5]

Kaplan contends that most premature ejaculators will ejaculate as soon as they enter the vagina. But men vary considerably in their ability to postpone ejaculation after penetration.[6] Some men with relatively poor ability to control ejaculation may be able to satisfy their partners most of the time by adequate attention to foreplay and arousal. Nevertheless, it is normally the woman, not the man, who sees premature ejaculation as a problem.

Premature ejaculation may be the result of behavior patterns learned in the man's early experiences with intercourse—in the back seat of a car, before one's parents come home, for the sake of the girl's reputation. A series of such exposures to pressures to perform can be sufficient in establishing a life-long pattern of premature ejaculation in some males. Early masturbating habits in which the male hurries to ejaculate before he is discovered can also contribute to the problem.

The treatment of premature ejaculation proposed by Masters and Johnson begins with the assurance during the initial discussions that there is a very good prospect for cure (failure rate is only 2.2 percent). In such a situation, the woman is usually quite cooperative. She realizes that she has much to gain if the man's difficulties are resolved and that it is quite likely that she can be satisfied if they both work at it.

The man is taught to focus his attention on the moment of ejaculatory inevitability (the moment when the semen enters the urethra), which normally occurs 2 to 4 seconds before ejaculation. When this stage is reached, no man can control his ejaculation. But the man can learn to delay this feeling of inevitability. In contrast to the instructions not to touch the genitals in the first stages of therapy involving most other types of sexual dysfunction, those involving premature ejaculators emphasize early genital stimulation. In these early sessions, the man lies on his back and the woman sits facing him with her legs straddling his body. She approaches his genitals directly and strives to stimulate him to erection. As soon as full erection is achieved, the *squeeze technique* is employed. In this technique, the woman tightly squeezes the coronal ridge of the penis for several seconds. This somewhat powerful pressure causes the man to immediately lose his urge to ejaculate. He may also partially lose his erection. With proper instruction, however, the man will gain the ability to delay the urge to ejaculate. Focusing on this common task can help the

[5]Ibid., p. 92.

[6]Kaplan, *The New Sex Therapy, p. 290.*

couple to improve their sexual communication. He tells her when to squeeze (just before he feels he is going to ejaculate). After sufficient confidence has been established, a nondemanding form of intercourse may be attempted. The woman is again on top, but instead of sitting directly down on the penis, she sits back on it from about a forty-five degree angle and moves slowly back and forth. This sort of pressure on the penis shaft helps retard ejaculation.

Masters and Johnson report that most couples are so delighted with the results of their crash program that they dramatically increase their frequency of intercourse. The male may have a brief episode of secondary impotence immediately after the acute phase of therapy, but this can normally be taken in stride by a forewarned couple who have found new delights in one another.

Kaplan prefers the Seman's stop-start approach to ejaculatory control to the squeeze method advocated by Masters and Johnson. In the Seman's approach, the man lies on his back and concentrates on the sensations produced by the woman's stimulation of his erect penis. When he feels that he is about to ejaculate, he signals her to stop. Before his erection is completely lost, he instructs her to restimulate him until the moment of inevitability again approaches. Then he again signals her to stop. Such a simple technique, properly carried out, has been quite effective in the treatment of premature ejaculation.

Figure 11–2
Demonstration of "squeeze technique."

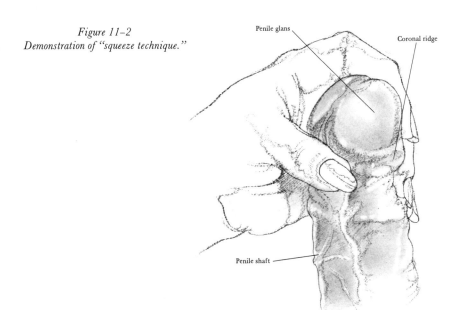

Penile glans

Coronal ridge

Penile shaft

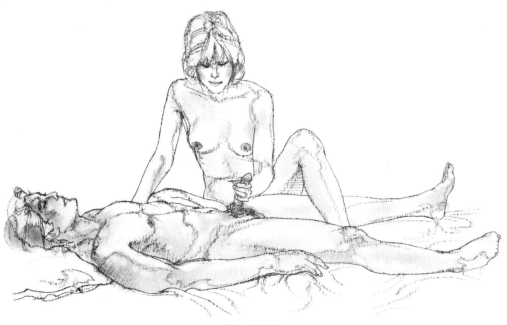

Figure 11–3
The Semans Procedure for the Treatment
of Premature Ejaculation

RETARDED EJACULATION

Masters and Johnson found that only a small percentage of their clients had this problem, but Kaplan and others contend that at least mild forms of it may be much more widespread than at first thought. Retarded ejaculators are men who have difficulty ejaculating. They can respond to sexual stimuli, achieve a full erection, and strive for ejaculatory release, but such men fail to achieve it completely or only after much effort. The problem ranges from those cases of occasional retardation, which can readily be overcome by the use of a little fantasy or additional stimulation, to those in which the man has never ejaculated in his life. Retarded ejaculation may result from injury or surgical error as well as from situational or psychological causes. In its mildest form, it is situationally conditioned; for example, a man may have problems only with a particular partner. The most common clinical case, however, is the man who complains that he can never achieve ejaculation during intercourse, though he may readily accomplish it through manual or oral stimulation. Women usually find retarded ejaculation as disturbing as men do, although one might expect them to rejoice in their partner's staying power.

In the Masters and Johnson approach, after the initial discussion, the first sexual task is for the women to manually force the man to ejaculate. Because this may take days, lubricating creams will be necessary to prevent the penis from becoming bruised. There is no rush in the accomplishment of this task, but the mere accomplishment of it goes a long way toward a cure. In some cases, retarded ejaculation may be the man's way of psychologically punishing the woman. Once she is able to get him to ejaculate by any means of stimulation, the man's defenses may break down. Once ejaculation has been experienced, the couple use a technique similar to the exercise employed with premature ejaculators, except, in this case, the man learns to hasten the moment of inevitability. Kaplan concentrates more on generally helping the man to be more comfortable in psychologically threatening situations, but agrees with Masters and Johnson that ejaculation achieved with a female partner by whatever means is a major breakthrough in the treatment. Fantasy often helps in the early stages of treatment to excite and hasten ejaculation.

Figure 11–4
Manual Stimulation of the Penis During Coitus
This method is used in the treatment of retarded ejaculation. In the male-above position, the female places her hand as shown in the drawing, which allows her to stroke the penis during coitus.

ORGASMIC DYSFUNCTION

The woman's inability to have an orgasm has only recently come to be seen as something to be concerned about. Women in the past were not expected to particularly enjoy sex. As a matter of fact, in those days, having an orgasm could damage a woman's reputation. We now know, however, that prolonged sexual activity without orgasm can and should be treated as a problem.

Primary orgasmic dysfunction in the female is defined as never having experienced an orgasm through any form of sexual stimulation. *Situational orgasmic dysfunction* is defined as any orgasmic failure that is not primary. Thus, a woman who reports inability to experience orgasm with her partner will be diagnosed as suffering from secondary orgasmic failure if she has ever experienced orgasm with a different partner or as a result of masturbation.

The inability of women to achieve orgasm through intercourse is apparently widespread. Fisher indicates that, while only 5 to 6 percent of his sample never experienced orgasm, up to 60 percent said that they could not consistently achieve it.[7] On the other hand, Masters and Johnson found that all of their female clients could achieve orgasm through some form of stimulation.[8] Most women experience such inability at some time in their lives. Masters and Johnson contend that a major cause of such inability is the fact that our culture has traditionally made it very difficult for a woman to express her sexual feelings.[9] Therefore a considerable portion of the therapy for such dysfunction is a reorientation of the woman's social attitudes as well as her sexual value system. Women entering therapy for orgasmic dysfunction had typically had a significantly harsher religious background. According to Masters and Johnson, while there is no single cause of sexual inadequacy, a strict religious upbringing figures in almost all forms of it.[10]

One of the frequent causes for orgasmic dysfunction is related to how the women feels about her partner and their relationship. The relevant questions here, according to Masters and Johnson, are:

What value has the male partner in the woman's eyes? Does the male maintain his image of masculinity? Regardless of his acknowledged faults, does he meet the woman's requirements of character, intelligence, ego

---

[7]Seymour Fisher, *The Female Orgasm: Psychology, Physiology, Fantasy* (New York: Basic Books, 1973) p. 185.

[8]William Masters and Virginia Johnson, *Human Sexual Response* (Boston: Little, Brown & Co., Inc., 1966), p. 139.

[9]Masters and Johnson, *Human Sexual Inadequacy*, p. 218.

[10]Ibid., pp. 229–30.

Figure 11–5
Treatment for orgasmic dysfunction involves sensual rather than
sexual pleasuring. The partners gently stimulate each other, with
direction as to what does and doesn't please. The drawing above
depicts the position generally advised, but variations may be used.

strength, drive, physical characteristics, etc.? Obviously, every woman's re-
quirements for a partner vary with her age, personal experience, confidence,
and the requisities of her sexual value system.[11]

The key to therapy in Masters and Johnson's view is for the co-
therapists to seek out those things that the man does or does not do
that may not adequately meet the woman's needs as defined by her
sexual value system. This system, of course, has been shaped by her
past experience, both real or imagined. In most cases, therefore, the
therapy sessions aim at modifying both the husband's behavior and
the wife's expectations. The simpler cases of orgasmic dysfunction

[11]Ibid., p.241.

Figure 11–6
Face-to-Face, Woman Above, with Clitoral Stimulation
This position is used for the treatment of premature ejaculation, orgasmic dysfunction, and impotence. As the
illustration shows, the female-above position allows for greater freedom of movement.

may often result from the man's inability to properly pleasure the woman because he is clumsy in manipulating her clitoris.

According to Kaplan, women exhibit a far greater range of response to orgasmic dysfunction than men do to impotence.[12] Some women are convinced that not having an orgasm is normal. Some women accept the role of pleasing their partner mechanically during intercourse without pleasing themselves, but most come to resent this approach. Orgasmic failure also evokes feelings of self-hatred and depression in women. Men react very differently to their partner's inability to achieve orgasm. Some contend that it is normal that she should not experience such feelings. Some men blame their own inadequacies as a lover for the woman's problems. Kaplan also acknowledges that, for some people, sexual satisfaction is genuinely not

[12]Kaplan, *The New Sex Therapy*, p. 363.

important.[13] The notion that abstinence need not be psychologically damaging points to a major difference in sex therapy as opposed to other forms of treatment. What constitutes an adequate sex life must be defined in most cases by the people themselves and may vary situationally from partner to partner. A delicate interchange must transpire between client and therapist before the therapist can determine if a cure has been affected, because cure for one person may not be satisfying for another.

Treatment of orgasmic dysfunction commonly consists of discussions and sessions devoted to sensual rather than sexual pleasuring. A common task is to have the woman pleasure the man first and then receive pleasure herself. She is instructed to lean back against her reclining partner and guide his hands over her body, giving him direct instructions in what pleases her and what does not. Normally, being able to give each other pleasure without having to worry about having an orgasm is enough to change the partners' attitude toward each other. Then they can move on toward nondemanding forms of intercourse. Sometimes, however, the woman objects to the man's clumsiness in touching her, she feels ticklish rather than turned on, or she does not recognize a sensual experience when she has one. These experiences are discussed with the therapists, and she is instructed more precisely in what to expect. Some women may turn off their sexual feelings as a result of deep-seated psychological problems. These inner conflicts must be explored if such women are to feel free to experience sexual pleasure.

Different therapists have different ideas about what defines sexual adequacy for women. Kaplan distinguishes between what she calls a general sexual dysfunction and orgasmic dysfunction. She feels that it may be normal for some women to experience sexual arousal without experiencing orgasm and that it is quite possible that they should not be considered inadequate in any way. Masters and Johnson do not make this distinction. The issue is further complicated by the fact that women experience orgasm differently. Masters and Johnson tend to de-emphasize this difference by contending that there is no physiological difference between the vaginal and clitoral orgasm.[14] Thus, though women may report that they experience each sort of orgasm differently, Masters and Johnson say that an orgasm is an orgasm is an orgasm.

Masters and Johnson claim a 19.3 percent failure rate for orgasmic dysfunction after their intensive two-week program. Kaplan does not report a cure or failure rate.

[13]Ibid., p. 365.

[14]Masters and Johnson, *Human Sexual Response;* Kaplan, *The New Sex Therapy,* pp. 375–84; Seymour Fisher, *The Female Orgasm: Psychology, Physiology, Fantasy.*

VAGINISMUS

In vaginismus, a woman reacts to having her vagina penetrated by reflexively tightening the muscles around the entrance to the vagina. She does not do this on purpose, but cannot will herself to relax. Clients with vaginismus typically suffer from fear of intercourse, and thus vaginismus can be seen as a classic example of a psychosomatic illness. Its symptoms can be simply and successfully treated, but its causes may be deep and complex. Vaginismus is commonly seen as a conditioned response resulting from the association of pain with vaginal penetration. A wide variety of factors—real and imagined—can play a role in this conditioning (rape, unpleasant surgical procedures, deformities in the pelvic region, strict religious upbringing, an impotent sex partner, and so on).

Vaginismus is rarely tolerated lightly, but is often endured for long periods of time. For example, marriages may remain unconsummated for many years because the wife is vaginismic. Any attempt to penetrate the vagina may result in severe pain and humiliation. The partner of a vaginismic woman may become secondarily impotent. Vaginismus produces extreme anxiety and can lead to a phobic avoidance of intercourse. This pattern of avoidance presents the main obstacle to therapy.

The treatment of vaginismus is aimed at relieving the conditioned response. If nothing else is physically wrong with the woman, the procedure is simple. Dilators of successively larger diameter are clinically inserted into the vagina until an adequate size can comfortably be accommodated. This procedure is not attempted by psychoanalysts, who are generally more concerned with the underlying causes than with the relief of their symptoms. Most sex therapists, however, take the view that it is far preferable to be a neurotic without the symptoms of vaginismus. They argue, further, that the increased pleasure and confidence that come when the symptoms are relieved can go a long way toward helping the person cope with whatever underlying problems might remain. Thus, the underlying psychological causes are treated only when they present obstacles to the reconditioning. Normally, a women suffering from vaginismus is able to participate in intercourse after only four to ten dilation treatments. During the initial penetration experiences, the women guides her partner's penis into her vagina, and he is instructed not to engage in demanding thrusting until she has had several such experiences and has become comfortable with them.

When the woman has become phobic about sex, however, the treatment is more complex. In the Masters and Johnson procedure, it begins with the demonstration of the conditioned response of the vaginal sphincter (the muscle that surrounds the vaginal opening).

This helps to remove the mystery surrounding the phenomenon. The man can see that the woman has no control over the response and is not deliberately shutting him out. A mutual investigation of both partners' genitals help overcome some of the phobic reaction, since, in most cases of phobic avoidance, the people understand very little about the genital area. Vaginismic women are advised to expect some unpleasant sensations. The success of the treatment depends on the woman's being able to insert something into her own vagina—an act she cannot possibly accomplish without feeling some psychic discomfort. Normally, the physical discomfort is minimal. Women are encouraged not to avoid these unpleasant sensations, but to stay with them and work them through.

Masters and Johnson report 100 percent success in ridding their clients of the symptoms of vaginismus.

Sexual Dysfunctions and Psychological Disorders

Sex therapy is most successful when applied to the sexual dysfunctions we have discussed. In many cases, the relief of these specific symptoms is all that is necessary to ensure sexual adequacy. It is not uncommon, however, for these common dysfunctions to be associated with other problems. For example, vaginismus may be associated with fear reactions, and impotence may be related to depressions of various sorts. Therefore, depending on the underlying psychological causes, the relief of the symptoms of vaginismus, for example, may have a positive effect on the fear of penetration, it may have no effect, or it may worsen the condition. In similar fashion, the relief of the symptom of impotence may result in the disappearance of the associated depression. It may also have no effect. The man may be potent, but may remain depressed for other reasons. Or, if the impotence was a part of a much more pervasive defense mechanism that should not have been dismantled until the person was able to cope without it, curing his impotence may make the depression worse.

These are very complex matters, and therapists handle them quite differently. Sometimes they attempt to screen these other problems out by refusing to treat people who manifest certain symptoms. The therapist, however, may feel competent to treat the person on several levels or may refer the person to another specialist while treating the sexual dysfunction simultaneously. In the view of some analysts, the following two conditions should be met before sex therapy is begun: The person must be in a stable psychological state when seeking therapy, and the sexual dysfunction should not be a part of a more pervasive defense against psychic disturbances. This second condition is difficult to determine in some cases.

Because the new sex therapy has enjoyed considerable success in treating sexual dysfunctions, there is a tendency on the part of some therapists to conclude that sex therapy is valuable in all cases. Those therapists who have psychoanalytic training are apt to be more cautious. They admit the often surprising benefits derived from curing sexual dysfunctions, but point out that in some cases, the curing of these symptoms may well worsen an underlying neurosis or may trigger a psychotic episode—a "break with reality."

In general only about 1 percent of the population experience psychotic breakdowns. Neuroses, however, merge imperceptibly with normal psychological functioning and require more skill to diagnose. In the view of psychoanalytically oriented therapists, underlying neurotic conditions may also be worsened by the cure of sexual dysfunctions. Some sex therapists disagree. This disagreement has led to a continuing, often heated debate about the qualifications necessary to be a sex therapist and the screening procedures that should be established for selecting appropriate clients for therapy.

For example, a young married couple (wife age twenty-three, husband twenty-five) sought treatment because the wife was not responsive to sexual stimulation. She accepted intercourse, but was never aroused and never experienced orgasm. While in college, the wife had experienced a brief episode of acute paranoid schizophrenia and had been hospitalized for three months. The husband had no history of previous problems. They had been married for a year and seemed to have a good relationship.

Treatment began by focusing on sensual enjoyment. He enjoyed these sessions, but she remained tense and felt nothing. They were advised to engage in gentle touching and caressing exercises. He enjoyed the experience, but his wife was enraged. The next day at work she felt depersonalized, and experienced grandiose and hostile fantasies. Being a very insightful person, she recognized the significance of these symptoms and asked the therapist to discontinue treatment on the grounds that she was once again experiencing "schizophrenic" feelings. The therapist concurred in her judgment, gave her antipsychotic medication, and referred her to her former psychotherapist for treatment.

The analyst concluded that although there was no evidence of a current psychological problem when the couple first sought treatment and, both partners seemed close to each other, there was in fact considerable hostility. The wife was really quite withdrawn and isolated. Her unresponsiveness to sexual stimulation was part of her defense against her fear of another psychotic episode. The intimacy produced in the therapeutic exercises threatened this defense.

The therapist's sensitivity to the possible disorganizing effects of sex therapy can, in some cases, make it possible to modify the treatment in order to avoid unduly threatening a person's defense mechanisms. For example, a forty-two-year-old bachelor with a history of psychotic episodes sought treatment for impotence. He had established a warm relationship with a woman whose company he enjoyed, but he was unable to achieve an erection. Since he was in a stable psychological state when seeking treatment, and since the sexual symptom did not seem to be part of a defense against his schizophrenia, he was admitted to treatment. He was treated alone because he was afraid to ask his partner to participate with him for fear of losing her. However, she cooperated well with the instructions given by the therapist. The man was given permission to use any erotic fantasy that aroused him and was instructed in the techniques of bringing his partner to orgasm by clitoral stimulation. During therapy the effects of pleasuring on himself and his partner and his fears of failure were discussed. Threatening material was avoided as far as possible, and the patient responded well. After three weeks he was enjoying intercourse twice a week and his anxiety about his relationship markedly decreased.

Sexual dysfunctions are also associated with discord and conflict in partnerships such as marriage. There is disagreement among therapists about whether both partners should be treated in such cases. Masters and Johnson have held the position that it is absolutely necessary to treat both members of a couple. Kaplan, LoPiccolo, and others say that it is not. There should probably be no hard-and-fast rules about this. Sexual dysfunctions do not necessarily represent symptoms of marital discord. A marriage may be unconsummated for many years and still be a caring, loving partnership. On the other hand, a sexual dysfunction may be a symptom of more pervasive problems within the partnership. Sometimes these other problems may be so acute that they sabotage the therapy.

For example, a married couple was referred for sex therapy because of the husband's premature ejaculation. The wife had previously left home, presumably because of her sexual frustration, but was now reconciled to her husband. Treatment went well for two sessions. Then the wife, contrary to instructions, urged her husband to enter her. He did so and ejaculated prematurely, thus bringing on a sense of failure and depression. When asked why she had disregarded the instructions, the wife simply said that she was only trying to help. The wife continued to sabotage the treatment in various ways, and the results left the husband frustrated and enraged. It soon became apparent that the wife's actions were determined by underlying feelings of hostility, which were too well protected to be dealt with quickly. The couple was advised to discontinue therapy. Both spouses seemed relieved and elected to stop. The husband later called for an appointment and asked if the therapist would see him with another partner. He had been considering divorce and had apparently used sex therapy to test his wife's motivation to make their marriage work. When she continued to treat him cruelly he became confirmed in his conviction to seek divorce.

The treatment of a single symptom as is commonly done in sex therapy is contrary to the traditional approach of psychoanalysis, which seeks to treat the whole person. Nevertheless, surprising results have been obtained from such specialized therapy. The conditions under which positive results are most likely to be achieved and remain lasting in their effect are not well understood at present. Obviously, extensive cooperation between partners seeking sex therapy is essential. Sometimes they cannot cooperate in the therapy because of underlying psychic disorders or discord in their relationship that do not become evident until therapy has begun.

Effectiveness of Sex Therapy

The major difficulty in evaluating the effectiveness of sex therapy is that evaluation research has lagged far behind the mushrooming practice. The cure and failure rates reported by the practitioners are not strictly comparable because the therapy package is not identical, the criterion for the selection of clients is not always clearly set forth, and the criteria for establishing a cure are different. When the program works, it probably works for many interrelated reasons that are very difficult to separate out and evaluate. For example, a part of the effectiveness of the Masters and Johnson approach may derive from their high visibility and good reputation. People come to them with great confidence that they will be able to be helped. Therapy may be effective because of the techniques employed, the therapists who use the techniques, or the methods that they choose for excluding some people from treatment in the first place. It is quite possible that a portion of the cure results from the simple fact that the clients have finally decided to do something about their problem.

The best that can be done toward answering the question of why sex therapy works when it works is to look at the techniques that seem effective in varied contexts and to carefully consider the few controlled evaluations that do exist. Most therapists utilize various structured sexual experiences with a high degree of success. These pleasuring experiences normally begin with sensual massages, hugs and kisses, and move up gradually to more threatening situations involving masturbation and intercourse. Some therapists show clients films of sexual behavior until they are relaxed enough to engage in it themselves, or they instruct the clients to construct fantasies of sexual activities they would like to engage in and to fantasize about these activities until they feel comfortable, as part of a desensitization technique. The available evidence suggests that the pleasuring procedures, if properly administered, are highly effective. It is less clear that the various anxiety-reducing and attention-focusing techniques are as effective, though case studies suggest that they can be very useful.[15]

The basic elements of the new sex therapy as LoPiccolo sees them are:

1. The assumption that sexual problems mostly occur in long-term relationships rather than one-night stands.
2. The instruction in sex education and technique that importantly involves an authoritative permission to experiment in previously untried behaviors.
3. The assumption that sexual attitudes must be changed.
4. The need for procedures to reduce anxiety about sexual performance.
5. The inclusion of techniques to increase effectiveness in both verbal and nonverbal communication.
6. The effort to change destructive elements of life styles and family interaction patterns.
7. The change of sexual behavior through training in sensual enjoyment.

These sensual enjoyment sessions have so attracted the attention of the press that it is widely assumed that they are the major element in the therapy. In fact they are only one technique in the total package.

Many common sexual problems are caused by misinformation about sexual functioning. Education, not therapy, is the cure for such problems. People are becoming more aware of the importance of accurate knowledge, and the number of people seeking help who are grossly misinformed about their sexuality is diminishing. Even with more complex problems, a minimum amount of basic and accurate information about sexual functioning is necessary for any therapeutic technique to be effective. Films are often good ways of providing instruction, and a number of excellent films are now on the market.[16]

Interestingly enough, although communication training is strongly recommended by many sex therapists, there is no evidence support-

[15]Douglas Hogan, "Sex Therapy," *Society/Transactions* (July/August, 1977), p. 410. This section is heavily indebted to Hogan's analysis.

[16]Some major producers of such educational films are EDCOA, an affiliate of Ormont Pharmaceuticals; and the National Sex Forum, Glide Memorial Methodist Church, San Francisco.

ing its effectiveness. The only controlled study of the effects of such procedures to date found no difference between programs that used communication training and those that did not.[17] Kaplan and others sometime combine marital therapy with sex therapy. Group therapy has been used successfully in the treatment of impotence and premature ejaculation, but there is no controlled evaluation of its effectiveness.

Masters and Johnson strongly argue that sex therapy must be undertaken by a dual-sex team, and that both partners must be treated simultaneously if the treatment is to be successful. Other clinicians, however, have effectively treated most dysfunctions without either of these elements in their therapy package.[18]

It must be noted, finally, that sex therapy has thus far been practiced almost exclusively on upper-middle-class, affluent, white couples. A broader population including racial minorities, homosexuals, and lower-class whites would be necessary to demonstrate the general effectiveness of any technique. The high cost of treatment is, of course, a major reason why most people are unable to obtain sex therapy. The studies of Kinsey and others strongly indicate, however, that the sexual styles of these other groups are quite distinctive in a number of ways and may present the therapist with a host of different problems. Certainly the therapist will be confronted with different tastes and values regarding what is normal in sexual behavior.

The Notion of Normal Sexuality

The question about what constitutes normal sexual response is never more clearly raised than when we are considering sex therapy. Sex therapy must be concerned with what is adequate from the client's point of view, rather than what is normal or typical of the population at large. As we have suggested, the definition of adequacy will vary from couple to couple. For example, one woman may want her partner to satisfy her by intercourse, while another woman may be content to be satisfied by manual stimulation or oral sex before she and her partner have intercourse.

This brings up another fundamental issue: Is there only one proper type of female orgasm? Some psychoanalysts still insist that the only

[17]J. R. Husted, "Effect of Method of Systematic Desensitization and Presence of Sexual Communication in the Treatment of Sexual Anxiety by Counter-conditioning." Procdings of the 80th Annual Convention of the American Psychological Association, Honolulu, Hawaii, 1972, pp. 325–26. Hogan "Sex Therapy," p. 41.

[18]Hogan, "Sex Therapy," p. 42.

true female orgasm is the orgasm achieved through intercourse and experienced vaginally. They consider a woman who is capable of experiencing multiple orgasms from direct clitoral stimulation but who cannot achieve orgasm during intercourse to be dysfunctional. Feminists are in revolt against this position. They claim that it reflects male chauvinism on the part of the analysts and further contend that the vaginal orgasm as such does not exist. They contend that the true female orgasm is the clitoral orgasm and frequently quote Masters and Johnson to support their views. However, Kaplan points out that Masters and Johnson research has established that there is only one kind of physiological orgasm, which in fact has both clitoral and vaginal elements. For example, direct or indirect stimulation of the clitoris is necessary, but so apparently are vaginal contractions. Thus, while we do not yet fully understand the female orgasm, the separation between the vaginal and clitoral orgasm is clearly false.[19]

Kaplan asserts that women have a broad range of responses to stimulation (see Figure 11–7). Where does one draw the line and consider

[19]Kaplan, *The New Sex Therapy*, p. 376.

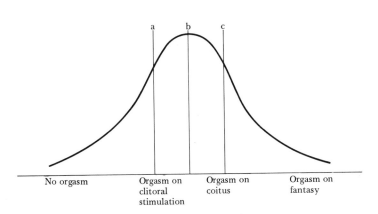

Figure 11–7
Hypothetical Distribution of the Female Orgasm
The actual distribution of the female orgasm is unknown.
Therapists who are psychoanalytically oriented would consider as
normal only those who achieve orgasm on coitus; other therapists
would consider the normal range as falling between points (a)
and (c).

a woman's performance inadequate? This depends on what the woman considers to be adequate for her needs. In part it must reflect some minimal notion of a basic sexual response. In practice, Kaplan does not consider her therapy to be a failure if she can help the woman to achieve orgasm by whatever means. She has never failed to help a woman who has never experienced orgasm to achieve it. She has also never failed to improve the threshold of orgasmic sensitivity so that, for example, women who were only able to experience orgasm by masturbation were able to do so in the presence of their partner; or a woman who was only able to experience orgasm through masturbation to experience it while in the woman-above position; and so on. She has, however, not been able to help all of her female clients to experience orgasm during intercourse. She concludes that perhaps some women simply cannot.

In similar fashion, if sex becomes more than just intercourse, and a much broader range of behaviors becomes part of normal, healthy sexuality, then many of the problems of impotency or premature ejaculation would be eliminated or greatly reduced in importance. As Albert Ellis dramatically pointed out, "the great coital myth" (the only "real" sex is heterosexual intercourse) is responsible for many of our problems in sexually relating to one another. As we move in the direction of accepting greater variety of sexual behaviors, sex therapy

Figure 11–8
Some women can only experience
orgasm through self-stimulation;
this can be done with a partner.

may find that its greatest contribution is toward the enhancement of sexual pleasure rather than in the cure of problems. In fact, some therapists use their techniques for this purpose today, and much of what others call therapy can best be seen as an enhancement rather than a cure. Strangely enough, one factor that would operate against such a redefinition of sex therapy is the criteria governing eligibility for coverage by various health-care programs. At present, sex therapy as such is generally not covered, but the argument that it affects a cure with consequences as dramatic as other forms of therapy now being covered is being made. Were sex therapists to be widely seen as enrichers rather than physicians affecting cure, there is little likelihood that health-care programs would cover them. Perhaps, however, such treatment could be considered as a form of preventive medicine.

Problems of Professionalization

The high demand for sex therapy since 1970 and the shortage of trained personnel has created what might be called the problems of professionalization of sex therapy.[20] The argument has hinged around the issue of whether sex therapy should properly be seen as a subspeciality of psychoanalysis or should be considered as a set of techniques that can effectively be administered by people who don't have psychoanalytic or similar medical training. Many professionals have a stake in the issue not only because of their disciplinary concerns but also because sex therapy has rapidly become a most lucrative enterprise. Society has a stake in seeing that people are not swindled by incompetent practitioners.

While mental health practitioners tend to argue that sex therapy is a specialization of psychotherapy, sex therapists argue that it is a new profession. William Masters and Virginia Johnson, for example, are not trained in psychotherapy. At present, there is no evidence that any particular professional training improves the effectiveness of the therapy. However, this research is not conclusive because of the poor quality of the evaluation procedures now applied to treatment. "Outside the sex area, comparisons of effectiveness of therapy for emotional problems have generally *not* provided strong evidence that professional psychotherapists do better than nonprofessional psychotherapists (for example, ministers, family doctors, and so on)".[21] It is also clear that, in some cases, written programs, such as in

[20]LoPiccolo, "From Psychotherapy to Sex Therapy," p. 61. This section is heavily indebted to the analysis of Joseph LoPiccolo as presented in the above article.

[21]Ibid., p. 62.

the treatment of premature ejaculation or some cases of orgasmic dysfunction, without any personal contact with a sex therapist, can be effective.[22]

The problem can perhaps be resolved by a better matching of client and therapist. Some people don't need any therapy. Some need sex therapy, some need psychotherapy, and some need both. As a first step, everyone with sex problems might first try do-it-yourself techniques of therapy, which can be found in several books. If they try these and they do not work, they can then seek more professional help. But to whom should they turn? If sex therapy is less expensive than psychotherapy, a recognized sex therapist might be the next logical stop. Those people who can not be effectively treated by sex therapy, or who feel the need of getting further help beyond the elimination of their symptoms, might then seek the help of professional psychotherapists, who presumably can help them with their underlying problems. Unfortunately, such an ideal screening procedure is unlikely for a host of reasons. Also it assumes that the most effective therapist is the one with the most professional training—that is, the psychotherapist. There is little evidence at present to support this assumption.

The current state of affairs is further complicated by the fact that there are virtually no regulations governing the licensing or practice of sex therapists. In most states, there are very minimal qualifications regulating who can be a sex therapist. Some of these poorly trained sex therapists are well-intentioned people, but some are simply charlatans. The heavy demand for therapy also encourages institutions and individuals to offer brief courses in sex therapy training, which invites others to enter the field. They may be poorly prepared, but at least they are minimally certified.

As one concrete example, one sex therapy group offers a one-day workshop in a number of cities each year. The admission requirements for this workshop are minimal. After sitting in a large room with one hundred others for a total of eight hours, the graduate receives an impressive diploma (complete with blue ribbon and gold seal) certifying status as a trained sex therapist. There is no examination to see if the trainee was awake and learning everything (or even physically present) during the course; if you

[22]See, for example, the programs proposed by Julia Heiman, Leslie LoPiccolo, and Joseph LoPiccolo, *Becoming Orgasmic: A Sexual Growth Program for Women* (Englewood Cliffs, N.J.: Prentice-Hall, Inc., 1976); and Patricia E. Haley, *Making Love: How to Be Your Own Sex Therapist* (New York: Dial Press, 1976). The line between therapy and enhancement merges imperceptibly in such works as Alex Comfort, *The Joy of Sex* (New York: Crown Publishing Company, 1972), and *More Joy* (New York: Crown Publishing Company, 1974); and Betty Dodson, *Liberating Masturbation* (New York: Bodysex Designs, 1974).

pay your $85.00 fee in advance, you can merely show up Sunday afternoon to pick up your diploma.[23]

Some of the practices adopted by the new sex therapists are quite questionable because they can be abused and are of unproven effectiveness. The use of a surrogate partner (a person hired to have sex with the client) creates the problems of professional direction of the procedure on the one hand (some surrogates, for example, have set up shop as therapists), and offers the possibility of treatment that is effective in the clinic but may or may not generalize to another partner. Treatment with a surrogate may cure the patient, but only as long as he has sex with the surrogate. Intercourse with some other person might still be difficult. It has not yet been established just how much of the new behavior learned with a surrogate generalizes, but a number of competent and long-established therapists are persuaded that such a procedure is justified at least on the grounds of effectiveness if not on some notions of morality. They support the use of surrogates, but with caution.

Of less value and much more open to abuse, however, are those cases in which the therapist directly engages in sexual activities with the client. The extent to which some therapists participate in the therapy may range from nudity, to sensual massage to arousing the client through intercourse. Masters and Johnson note that their files are filled with cases in which professionals of every kind have engaged in such activities with their clients. There is strong opposition to such practice.

In all procedures involving nudity, touching, and sexual activity between patient and therapist, even the most charitable observer must question the therapist's motives for using such procedures. Is there a theoretical rationale or actual data to support the utility of such risky procedures? Is the enjoyment and gratification of the therapist, rather than patient's welfare, a major factor in the decision to use such procedures?[24]

LoPiccolo suggests the following as guidelines for those seeking the services of a sex therapists.[25]

1. Do not respond to *paid advertising* in any media. Most professional organizations advise their members not to use such a means of making their services available.

2. News coverage of successful therapy programs, on the other hand, are good ways of locating programs. Institutional clinics,

[23]LoPiccolo, "From Psychotherapy to Sex Therapy," p. 64. Published by permission of Transaction, Inc. from *Society,* vol. 14, #5, copyright © 1977 by Transaction, Inc.

[24]Ibid., p. 65.

[25]Ibid., pp. 67–68.

in general, can offer broader services at lower costs than private programs and are more likely to exercise quality control over their procedures.

3. Licensing as a psychiatrist, psychologist, or social worker provides the consumer with certain legal protection not available in the case of unlicensed professionals.

4. References by university departments of psychiatry, psychology, or social work are preferred over local medical society or state psychological associations because the latter are required to offer three names without prejudice from their membership rosters, while the university departments may be more discriminative in their recommendation.

5. Consider referrals from a family doctor or minister as starting points to be checked out, rather than uncritically accepted.

The only attempt thus far to certify sex therapists as such is being carried out under the auspices of *The Association of Sex Educators Counselors & Therapists* (ASECT). Not all practicing therapists are accredited by ASECT. Some feel that ASECT standards are not adequate.

Summary

The rapid increase in demand for sex therapy has been occasioned both by the sexual revolution that has caused people to expect much more competence in sexual performance and technique as more people value their sexuality and by the widespread advertisement of the effectiveness of such therapy. Whether we consider treatment an enhancement or a cure, there is evidence that some of the techniques of the new therapy work. Why they work is not always clear, nor are we at present sure of their effectiveness because of the inadequate controls over evaluation procedures.

It may well be that as we move away from a focus on intercourse as the sexual act and enjoy a wider range of sexually gratifying activities, the character of sex therapy will change. The plasticity of sexual response makes it seem reasonable that such a cultural transformation in our expectations about adequate sexual expression would have far-reaching effects.

At the present time, however, it is well to be cautious in seeking out professional help from those who label themselves sex therapists. Until it is possible to better regulate the training and practice of such persons, the consumer is well advised to be wary.

Section Three

Sex and Society

There are three major concerns to be addressed when considering how sex interacts with social institutions. The first is the extent to which the expression of human sexuality changes from one cultural tradition to another. The second is how the expression of human sexuality varies with one tradition over time. The third concern is to specify how, within our own culture at the present time, the expression of human sexuality is influenced by various types of socially acknowledged patterns of commitment, one of which is marriage.

As we look at our past and at the tradition of other cultures, it will become clear that our traditional understanding of the role of marriage in the regulation of human sexual behavior is quite unique. Our very negative view of sex, coupled with the very high value we place on human life, has created a number of complications that have historically been resolved in the institution of marriage. Within the context of marriage, sexual passion could be released because the end of the activity was the production of a child and the passion was blessed by the sacrament of Holy Matrimony. Therefore, it has been obligatory for Christians of fundamentalist ascetic persuasion to not only refrain from reproducing a child outside of marriage (which is widely condemned around the world), but also to refrain from enjoying intercourse outside of it (which is widely permitted around the world). In the strictest sense, such Christians were also to avoid experiencing sexual desire and passion as much as was humanly possible, either inside or outside of marriage. Fortunately, this view of marriage is losing ground, but its effect upon our view of human sexuality has been great.

Whatever our view of marriage is, it remains true that most of our sexual activity takes place within the context of some understanding or commitment. The commitment may be to enjoy the moment without future expectations, or it may involve more elaborate speculation about the future implications of this enjoyable moment. The commitment may be established by the social situation, as is the case in a singles' bar, where it is expected that one can enjoy sex with a comparative stranger without commitment. Commitment in this broad sense of the term is a shared understanding of what is happening.

In this section, chapter 12 explores our changing beliefs about sex. Chapter 13 considers sex in a variety of cultural contexts, and chapter 14 examines the costs and benefits of various patterns of commitment as they affect the expression of human sexuality.

Changing Beliefs About Sex

12

The disordered sexuality of the Western cultures is
surely due to the fact that the sexual relationship
has never been seriously integrated with and illuminated
by a philosophy of life. It has had no effective
contact with the realm of spiritual experience.
It has never achieved the dignity of an art, as in the
Indian Kamasutra, and would thus seem to rank in our
estimation far below cookery. Theoretically, the
Christian sacrament of Holy Matrimony is supposed to
satisfy the relationship, but in practice it does so
only by indirection and by prohibitions.

Alan Watts

How we behave sexually is at least in part a function of what we believe about sex. In our Western tradition, the common beliefs about sex have changed a great deal. In the preface to *The Joy of Sex,* Alex Comfort points out that "instead of worrying if sex is sinful, most people now worry about whether they are 'getting satisfaction'—one can worry about anything given the determination."[1] Comfort provides us with a gourmet cookbook approach to the art of lovemaking because he is convinced that enough people have gotten beyond the basics of sexually relating and need really detailed information, "not simple reassurance." In terms of the experience of most people, Comfort deals with sex as it could be rather than describes it as it is. He is looking forward to new possibilities of sexual and sensual delight that are now not widely shared, in part because of past repressive beliefs about sex. In the present there are a number of different beliefs about sex, each of which have their strong advocates. We live in a pluralistic age.

Some perspective on this pluralism can be obtained by looking back over our heritage and observing how people in other times have thought about sex and how our beliefs have changed. We are a part of the Western tradition in world civilization and our current views about sex are based on elements that can be traced back to the writings of the ancient Hebrews, Greeks, Romans, and early Christians. Romantic poets and secular philosophers have made their contribution. The Industrial Revolution has not only provided the leisure and affluence that has made our sexual revolution possible, but has also contributed fundamentally to a kind of sexual work ethic. Scientific research on human sexuality is very recent, but it seems to be a prominent element now shaping our beliefs about sex.

This chapter will pick out basic threads that tie together the changing pattern of our beliefs about sex. Some attempt will be made to suggest why others in our tradition believed what they believed about sex. We will look briefly at the basic thoughts of Sigmund Freud, Havelock Ellis, and Alfred Kinsey in the context of their times.

---

[1]Alex Comfort, *The Joy of Sex* (New York: Crown Publisher, 1975) p. 8.

Two Ancient Views on Sex

The Greek and Hebraic traditions take a quite different stance toward sex. In the Hebraic culture, sex is most intimately linked to reproduction. Children are the fulfillment of God's blessing—"be fruitful and multiply",—and are a kind of immortality. Because in Hebraic thought the flesh is in no sense evil, it can be enjoyed for its own sake as well. The Hebraic husband expected to find sexual pleasure with his wife, while the classical Greek husband typically did not. He expected to find sexual pleasure with courtesans or prostitutes. Lovemaking was much less associated with reproduction among the Greeks. For example, sex became a mode of worship in Dionysian rites, something never legitimized among the Hebrew peoples. The Greek emphasis upon contests or games as a way of giving value to the self also established a tone in Greek sexual adventures that is not found in Hebraic literature. Sex as conquest is much more typical of Greek than Hebraic thinking.

Greek and Hebrew thought came into close contact in New Testament times. Jesus and his disciples spoke out of a Hebraic background to a predominantly Hellenized world.[2] The fact that Greek thought dominated Hebraic thought in the Christian mainstream helps account for Christian asceticism. The Greeks thought of the body as a tomb in which the spirit was trapped. The Hebrews did not. Christian asceticism accepted the Greek perspective more than the Hebraic, and Christians have struggled in a peculiar way with the sins of the flesh ever since.

New Testament Christianity

One way of looking at the Bible is to see it as a love story. As such, it is a story of God's love for his creation, written over a period of about 1,400 years. During this long period of history, the images of God changed. During the last two centuries of this period, these images become focused around an historical person, Jesus of Nazareth.

While there are many images of Jesus and various accounts of his work and significance, perhaps the most dominant image in Western Christianity is the one that can be traced from Saint Paul, through Saint Augustine and Saint Thomas Aquinas down to the papal encyclicals and fundamentalist revivals of today. These two modern ex-

[2]The entire Bible was translated into Greek in 250 A.D. The Gospel according to St. John was written in Greek in about 110 A.D.

pressions of Christianity are different in many ways, but they both tend to share the same image of Jesus.

In this view, Jesus was an *ascetic,* a person who practiced strict self-denial, especially in regard to the sins of the flesh. Jesus is typically portrayed as a long-haired, pale-skinned, immaculately clean person of tender, refined features and intensely blue eyes that look into your very soul. It is hard to imagine him laughing about anything, though his rage at the money changers and his grief at Gethsemane show him to have been a man with strong feelings. Jesus endured the mortification of the flesh, but apparently experienced little of its joys.

Some people find it equally possible to picture a robust Jesus, son of a carpenter, used to the plane and the lathe, striding the dusty roads of Galilee, talking to fishermen, listening to the townsfolk talk, and cursing the fig tree because it was not bearing fruit in the right season. This Jesus, associated with prostitutes and thieves, healed the sick, ate and drank on the Sabbath, and fed the multitude from the abundance of his life. He was indeed a "Lord of all hopefulness, Lord of all joy." Yet it is still very difficult to look at Jesus and not see him as an ascetic in matters of sex, not so much because of what the New Testament tells us, but because of what it does not tell us.

We know little about his birth, less about his childhood, and nothing at all about his young adulthood. The biblical account of his life is confined almost exclusively to the three or four years of his ministry when he was presumably in his early thirties. He never married. So far as we know he never physically desired a woman. He had very little to say about sex or marriage and nothing at all about the art of lovemaking—advanced or otherwise. Those who talk about imitating Jesus in their lives are inclined toward celibacy and the association of sexual desire with sin. But, in fact, we do not know why Jesus never married or how he felt about sexual desire, or even if these matters were very important to him.

While the worshippers of Dionysus could readily think of their god with an erect penis, the average Christian would feel very uncomfortable thinking such thoughts about Jesus. In our mythology, Satan has an erect penis, not Christ. Those who contend that modesty has its place even in a liberated age and that we should not undress our gods, even in our heads, have a point. One obvious advantage of a sexless image of Jesus is that at least it avoids the male chauvinism of phallic worship.

But the failure of Christian thought to widely affirm the warmth of human lovemaking demands correction. This lack of affirmation derives from only a part of the New Testament image of Christ. We must also remember that the New Testament was closed (no further material was to be considered as Holy Scripture) during a time when Christians were doing everything possible to distinguish the image of

Figure 12–1
Disgust at the Romans' sexual excesses may have helped establish Christian asceticism. (Culver Pictures, Inc.)

the Christ from various other cultic gods.[3] What was omitted from our understanding of Jesus as a result of this effort? It seems apparent that the books that were not chosen to be Holy Scripture were generally more affirmative of the flesh.[4] They were certainly much more accepting of women as leaders in the church. As a result of the exclusion of these books, Christianity has established a male-dominated, largely ascetic religion in the West. Because of its ascetic elements, Christianity has had to deal with the whole of human sexuality largely through its understanding of marriage.

The bible is silent on many points of sociological concern and much must be inferred about the structure of marriage and the fam-

[3]The books now recognized as the New Testament were not the only books written about Jesus. They were selected in 250 A.D. by a process not fully known to modern researchers and undoubtedly reflect the biases of an ascetically oriented, patriarchially organized Christianity. The canonical books were supposedly selected to represent the most accurate (most orthodox) picture of Jesus—but Christianity's battles with a whole host of heresies undoubtedly affected the choice.

[4]Mary Daly, *Beyond God the Father* (Boston: Beacon Press, 1976).

ily from about 225 verses in the New Testament. It may seem evident to the modern reader that Jesus was talking about monogamous marriage, since the singular (a man and his wife) is used in Matthew 19,[5] but this passage could also reasonably refer to one of the several possible relationships that occur in polygamous marriages. This is more likely because there were many kinds of marriages and households in the first century—Christians in Jerusalem practiced a form of communalism, for example. Further, polygyny was permitted in the Old Testament tradition out of which Jesus and the Pharisees spoke. If Jesus was so concerned about monogamy as an element of the Christian faith, why did he not establish the practice unambiguously? It is established unambiguously in the Christian tradition, but this took time—about five centuries. That it is not an essential aspect of the Christian faith is acknowledged by those denominations who recognize polygamous marriages in Africa as valid.[6]

The Christian understanding about marriage was strongly influenced by another bachelor, Saint Paul. While it is true that Paul sees marriage as symbolizing the union between Christ and his Church, it is clearly a concession to the flesh in his view. According to Paul, the husband is divinely intended to be the head over his wife and that she should obey his authority. But for all his asceticism, Paul sees lovemaking as capable of expressing the whole personality, and he regards it as an essential obligation of both husband and wife.

From Paul's pastoral advice, the early Church, derived a scriptural basis for celibacy. The early Church fathers also found in Paul justification for male dominance in the Church. Paul's warnings about the sins of the flesh, plus Jesus's silence on most sexual matters set the tone of Christian asceticism. But the whole elaborate structure of celibate male clergy worshipping God the Father and fearing the private parts of women rests on shaky scriptural inferences and has had to be constantly defended from the very beginning.

Christian Asceticism Established

An early expression of Christian asceticism is found in the lives of the desert fathers, those who ran off into the wilderness seeking the kingdom of God. They abstained from sexual intercourse and set their

[5]This passage in Matthew's Gospel is primarily a teaching about divorce which has been used as a statement about the form of marriage. It begins with the question put to Jesus by the Pharisees, "is it lawful to divorce one's wife for any cause?"

[6]Adrian Hastings, *Christian Marriage in Africa* (London: SPCK, 1973), p. 22.

hearts and minds on higher things. One famous monk, named Amon, was so convinced that celibacy was the highest state for a Christian that when his parents arranged his marriage—as was often done in those days—he convinced his wife not to consummate it. Amon and his wife lived in the desert in separate huts, and people came from miles around to bask in the purity of their celibacy.[7]

An Alexandrian named Carpocrates declared that matter was so evil that we must rise above it. Unlike Paul, Carpocrates believed that it was possible for people to do this and become perfect. His gnostic (cults claiming secret knowledge as a means of salvation) son, Epiphanes, advocated sexual communism. In keeping with his father's teaching, however, orgies were not for the purpose of enjoying the flesh but rather were undertaken to demonstrate the filth and vileness of the flesh.[8] Gnosticism also departed from the Christian mainstream in worshipping God as Mother as well as Father and in permitting women to exercise all of the offices of the ministry. Gnosticism was declared heretical (in error of the true faith) early in church history.

Another early heretic's thought entered the mainstream at the same time that his followers were being publicly persecuted. Mani lived from 215 to 275 A.D. He taught that Jesus, Plato, Zoroaster, and Buddha were all equally great teachers. He was convinced that the creation of the world was only an episode in the struggle between the powers of darkness and light and that lovemaking was evil because it imprisoned particles of light (human spirit) in babies. His followers, who were called Manicheans, believed that it was better to let one's light return to God than to propagate the species and continue the imprisonment of light. Adam's sin—for which he was exiled from the Garden of Eden—was having intercourse with Eve. All men sin insofar as they desire women. Manicheans attempted to conquer this desire by abstaining from having intercourse.

LOVE GOD AND DO AS YOU PLEASE

Mani's thought entered the Christian mainstream through one of its most revered theologians, Saint Augustine (354–430 A.D.).[9] Augustine is a central figure in the history of Western ideas about love and

[7]Morton Hunt, *The Natural History of Love* (New York: Alfred Knopf, 1959), p. 38 ff., Wayland Young, *Eros Denied* (New York: Groves Press, Inc. 1964), p. 52 ff.

[8]A vivid account of a gnostic agape (love) feast is provided by Saint Epiphanius (second century) in his *Panarion* 26.4.1. Saint Epiphanius was a gnostic before he became orthodox and renounced his former evil ways. See also the analysis in Joseph Campbell, *The Masks of God: Creative Mythology* (New York: Penguin Books, 1977), p. 159 ff.

[9]Anders Nygren, *Agape and Eros* (Philadelphia: Westminster Press, 1953), pp. 499–562.

sex. In him, Plato, Mani, and the Christian gospel are synthesized. One way of looking at what he accomplished is to say that he set forth the Christian conception of love as the answer to the persistent question of antiquity, "What is the highest good?" He also solved the problem of passionate desire by justifying its expression in holy matrimony.

It is relatively easy for modern readers to find Augustine's teaching about sexual love funny or absurd, or to simply dismiss him as irrelevant. Having struggled hard to overcome the shackles Victorianism placed on sexuality, modern readers are inclined to look at Augustine's *Confessions* as an early and mild form of pornography (if they understand his language well enough to get turned on by it) and his *City of God* as an unfortunate reaction to the excesses of his youth. But considering that he lived toward the end of the fourth century, Augustine established an accommodation with the things of this world that was generally most affirmative. In an age inclined toward the gratification of the senses and seeking the joy of sex, it is difficult to understand what a celibate bishop means when he declared, "The sweetness of pleasure must be vanquished by something yet sweeter."[10]

The problem that sexual pleasure poses to the good person is fundamentally that it is such a near-at-hand delight. It is no further away than the sensuous delight in one's own body. Along with eating and drinking, sex is a good and necessary thing, but because of the intense pleasure it can provide, it is tempting to make more of it than it deserves. People all around Augustine had even worshiped sexual excess as though it were a god.[11] Orgasm, in particular, represented an occasion in which the higher love of God was completely obliterated, if only momentarily.

Augustine felt that the ability to reason distinguished men from animals. The most notable aspect of his conversion experience, for example, was that it enabled him to embrace new ideas—the teachings of Saint Ambrose. But rationality was also obliterated in orgasm. Indeed, the fact that an erection was an involuntary response troubled Augustine. He speculated in his *City of God* that before the fall, Adam had voluntary control over both his passion and his penis.

Those members, like the rest, would be moved by the command of his will, and the husband would be mingled with the loins of his wife without the seductive stimulus of passion, with calmness of mind and with no corruption of the innocence of the body. . . . Because the wild heat of passion would not activate those parts of the body but, as would be proper, a volun-

[10]Saint Augustine, *Confessions,* Book 9, Ch. 1.

[11]Saint Augustine, *City of God,* Book 15, Ch. 7.

tary control would employ them. Thus it would then have been possible to inject the semen into the womb through the female genitalia as innocently as the menstrual flow is now ejected.[12]

Thus, Augustine did not oppose sexual intercourse as such. Sex was obviously necessary for the procreation of the species. It is the overvaluing of the passion associated with the act that concerned him.

The apparent dilemma posed by the close association of a sinful passion and a necessary biological act is resolved by Augustine in his conception of marriage. By making what had been a secular contract into a sacrament of the Church, Augustine felt that it was possible to protect the married couple from *cupiditas*—finding their good in the wrong place. Marriage was a public statement of the intent to have children. The sex act itself would be redeemed for its natural end (procreation) by the sacrament of Holy Matrimony. Later corruption of this notion compared the situation of the person experiencing orgasm to that of a person sneezing—the assumption in both cases is that the soul escapes the body and needs to be protected from the evil one. In sneezing, the protection is supplied by "God Bless You!" In sex-in-marriage, it is protected by the sacrament.

However, Augustine's primary message about our sexuality is to see it in its proper place. Don't make too much of it. Love it for what it is and use it as a means to a higher end. Not having a body, finally, but thinking of oneself as the highest good is the deepest root of sin. If one truly loves God and rests in Him through his grace, doing what one pleases will, therefore, please God.

The Middle Ages

In the Middle Ages, Saint Thomas Aquinas carried Augustine's concern that people could not act rationally in the sexual realm even further. The evil element in intercourse for Aquinas was not sexual pleasure or desire, not the act itself, but simply its irrationality. Husband and wife were not morally responsible for this irrationality, however. Within marriage, intercourse was not sinful.

Augustine said that sex in marriage was all right as long as nobody got very excited about it. Aquinas made even more judgments about sex by establishing that there was only one proper way to have it. Because the only accepted purpose of sex was procreation, the worst thing people could do was have nongenital sex (even with their spouses). Nongenital sex and other practices that did not lead to procreation, such as masturbation, bestiality, and homosexuality, were

[12]Ibid.

considered by Aquinas to be crimes against nature. Rape, adultery, and incest were considered much less serious offenses. Much of our legal tradition has been directly affected by the language of Aquinas and his concern about "crimes against nature."

While Aquinas was formulating the classic Christian understanding of marriage, eleventh-century troubadours were at work on the image of romantic love. The troubadour's model for romantic love was the relationship of a noble man and his beloved, who was commonly someone else's wife. The man's nobility and respect for the sacrament of marriage meant that the relationship could not be consummated. The passionate yearning, the feeling of exaltation in the beloved, and the sense of faithfulness to her would all be spoiled by sexually possessing her. The image and the quest were ends in themselves to the romantic lover. Our common understanding of marriage today incorporates elements of both the ascetic and romantic traditions, but tends toward the romantic conception of love as a personal commitment.

Romantic love thus offered an alternative to the mundane relationship of marriage. It was a safe way to play around. Lovers fought with their rivals, performed many acts of bravery and self-sacrifice, and yearned mightily and publically for their beloved. The fact that the union could never be consummated only added to its appeal. Although the rewards seem basically to lie in the suffering, striving, and yearning of an unrequited love, romantic love introduced for the first time into the emotional relationships between men and women in the West many elements familiar to us today.

It brought into them tenderness and gentleness, exaggerated and sometimes absurd in form, but important nevertheless. It operated within a framework of adultery, yet it stressed as never before the importance of the fidelity of one man and one woman each to each.[13]

Romanticism began as an ethic governing courtly love among the nobility of southern France in the eleventh century, was spread by troubadours and poets, and finally became the ideal of the European middle classes. The essence of this love was its distinction between true love and false love. True lovers could kiss, touch, fondle, even lie naked together, but they could not enjoy intercourse. Should a lady give herself to her lover in intercourse, she was no longer an appropriate object of his adoration. Intercourse was confined to marriage—in keeping with the teachings of Christian asceticism—but was pronounced by the troubadours to be inferior to true love, which did not allow intercourse at all.

---

[13]Hunt, *The Natural History of Love,* p. 192.

The Renaissance and Reformation

By the middle of the sixteenth century, church authority was irrevocably challenged in the Reformation. The freedom and rights of the individual believer became a concern of an increasing number of Protestant groups. Some have argued that this escape from the chrysalis of Christendom was a premature birth and that post-reformation Western humanity tries continually to escape from freedom into one or another conformist movement.[14] Be that as it may, the rebirth that began in the sixteenth century loosened some heavy fetters from the hearts and minds of men and women, but not without cost. It is indeed fitting that the transition should have been described as a rebirth (a Renaissance), for a changing understanding of human sexuality was very much involved in what was happening.

Wayland Young contends that "the first female nudes in Christian iconography were the mermaids on churches of the dark ages." They were not affirmations of human sensuality, but rather a way of putting sexuality in its proper place. "Look these creatures do it, funny little things, but people don't. Never make that mistake, nakedness and copulation are all right for satyrs and mermaids and things like that, but not for people."[15]

By the middle of the sixteenth century, Baroque altars in Christian churches briefly acknowledged that even saints could be erotic. Saint Theresa of Avila (1515–1582) wrote of a vision she had had in which an angel of the Lord came to her bearing a long golden spear. She saw the angel plunge the sword several times "into my deepest inward. When he drew it out, I thought my entrails would have been torn out too, and when he left me I glowed in the hot fire of love for God. The pain was so strong, and the sweetness thereof was so passing great that no one could wish ever to lose it."[16] The sculptor Bernini immortalized this moment in his rendering of the altar of the Church of Santa Maria della Vittoria in Rome. In white and glowing marble, the angel is poised, spear in hand, over the saint who is supine in orgasmic ecstasy.

The dominant image of femininity within the Church was still the Virgin Mary. However, a sinister countertheme with elements of Eve, the temptress, developed during the early Renaissance. While the early Church fathers had written about succubi—evil female spirits who come to men in their sleep—the belief that women could voluntarily join the legions of the Devil did not become widespread until

---

[14]See, for example, Erich Fromm, *Escape from Freedom* (New York: Avon, 1965), pp. 52–53.

[15]Young, *Eros Denied*, p. 290.

[16]Quoted in Young, *Eros Denied*, p. 306.

the fifteenth century. Civil trials began against witches in 1400. By 1450 it had become accepted opinion that witches could fly in the night. The great study of witchcraft, *The Malleus Maleficarum,* was written during the trials and tortures of the late fifteenth century by two Dominican brothers and professors of sacred theology, Jacob Sprenger and Henry Kramer, who personally took part in the Inquisition. The seductive role of woman and the fear of intercourse were never more dramatically presented in the West.

A woman is beautiful to look upon, contaminating to the touch and deadly to keep . . . a foe to friendship . . . a necessary evil, a natural temptation . . . a domestic danger . . . an evil of nature, painted with fair color . . . a liar by nature. (She) seethes with anger and impatience in her soul. . . . There is not wrath above the wrath of woman. . . . Since (women) are feebler both in mind and body, it is not surprising that they should come under the spell of witchcraft (more than men). . . . A woman is more carnal than a man. . . . All witchcraft comes from carnal lust which is in woman unsatiable. . . . These women satisfy their filthy lusts not only in themselves but even in the mighty ones of the age, of whatever sort and condi-

Figure 12–2
The ecstacy of Saint Theresa, as sculpted by Bernini, has an erotic as well as a spiritual flavor.
(The Bettmann Archive, Inc.)

tion, causing by all sorts of witchcraft the death of their souls through the excessive infatuation of carnal love.[17]

Feminine eroticism was thus expressed in several images during the centuries of rebirth. Most commonly within the Church, the woman was pictured as nonerotic Mary, the ever-virgin (St. Theresa's ecstasy was but a minor cord). She was the idealized beloved or the true love of romantics who could indeed induce erotic passion, but should not consummate it. The most open portrayal of her eroticism was brutally denounced in the trials of witches.

Yet strangely enough the joy of sexual love was proclaimed by people who called themselves Christian even in this age. A century later the Reformation furthered their spread. Sects such as the Homines Intelligentiae (sixteenth-century Germany) elevated lovemaking to a sacrament and made the communion an orgy of celebration of the flesh. The Ranters, an English sect of the sixteenth century, contended that it was only necessary to be reconciled with oneself in order to be reconciled with God and warmly affirmed erotic lovemaking as a form of worship.

These sixteenth-century attacks on celibacy sound quite modern in many respects. They remind us once again of the complexity of Christian belief and behavior with regard to erotic love. Laurence Clarkson, a Ranter, declared in his book *The Single Eye* (1650) that no man could be free from sin till he had acted out that so-called sin and experienced it as no sin. Dostoevski observed over two centuries later that some acts come to us from the father wrapped in a cocoon called sin as long as it is wrapped, we are condemned both to ignorance and to curiosity. No act has been more enclosed in the cocoon of sin by Christian asceticism than sexual intercourse.

The major Reformation leaders took a much more positive view toward sex and marriage than was generally true of Christianity. Martin Luther enthusiastically embraced the idea of the married state. Marriage is "God's gift to man, a heavenly and spiritual state, a school of faith in love in which every menial task, every trouble and hardship, is a means of religious education."[18] Although Luther still saw sexual intercourse as a source of temptation that could lead people to forget the joys of spirituality, his thinking on marriage represents an advance on asceticism insofar as it emphasizes the companionship between the partners. In any case, Luther's concerns about sexual sin were in a different context because he did not believe that anyone could live the good life (except the Christ). Jesus may have redeemed the flesh, but he did not perfect it.

---

[17]Quoted in Hunt, *The Natural History of Love,* p. 177.

[18]Derrick Sherwin Bailey, "Sexual Ethics in Christian Tradition," in *Sexual Ethics and Christian Responsibility,* John Charles Wynn, ed. (New York: Association Press, 1970), p. 148.

John Calvin was more original in his view of marriage. For Calvin, sexual intercourse was holy, not unclean. Marriage was a high calling, the primary purpose of which was to fulfill people's needs for belonging and acceptance. It was important to Calvin that each adult person belong to a family, for families were the elemental building block from which the religious community was built. In this system, woman was ordained to be man's companion through the gamut of his experience, though her specific calling was motherhood.

Both Luther and Calvin repudiated the notion of the indissolubility of marriage, permitted divorce, and conceded authority over all matrimonial issues to the state. Since Calvin regarded the state as governed by God, however, in his view the Church retained essential control over the institution of marriage.[19]

Perhaps the greatest contribution of seventeenth-century thought to our understanding was the conviction expressed by a number of theologians that "cohabitation—the common life of husband and wife at bed and board—is the essence of marriage."[20] When this common life is permanently disrupted, the marriage no longer exists. Simply put, this is the modern view of marriage as essentially a personal relationship—not a sacrament of the Church or a civil contract.

Revolution and Response

The eighteenth century was a century of excesses. The wealth of monarchs and aristocrats allowed them to do things undreamt of by peasants and the new middle class. But the main keynote of the eighteenth century was enlightenment—the infinite capacity of reason to illuminate the workings of the universe. Newton's scientific breakthroughs and Descartes's philosophy ("I think, therefore I am") led to a respect for individual achievement in secular fields. Scientists and philosophers became secular saints. This respect for the products of individual minds led to a respect for the rights of individuals. The individual human being assumed increasing significance, culminating in the American and French Revolutions.

The revolutions in science, philosophy, and government were paralleled by a sexual revolution of sorts.

At the beginning of the eighteenth century, the religious libertines, who from the first century onward opposed Christian asceticism, were now in open defiance of the whole of Christianity. Libertines of the seventeenth and eighteenth century did not celebrate sexuality for its

[19]Ibid., p. 152.

[20]Ibid., p. 152.

own sake so much as they engaged in excesses of all sorts as a form of revolt. French libertines were most often aristocrats who had the leisure and the money to live as they pleased. They tried hard to make intercourse an end in itself. Extremists among them, such as de Sade (1740–1814), found no fulfillment in such activity, however. The end of de Sade's philosophy was not the celebration of life, but rather its destruction. His orgiastic excesses included the eating of excrement, suicide, and murder. He found no fulfillment in any of his experiences however much he tried to satiate his desire. A full understanding of his sexual views is made more difficult, however, by the fact that his writing was politically motivated. How much his sexual images reflected his personal attitudes and behavior and how much they served as metaphors for his political ideas is hard to tell.

Pornography had its origins in the seventeenth century, but it came into its own in the latter part of the eighteenth century and flourished in the nineteenth. Victorian morality, which was as much informed by science as by Christianity, and had deep roots in romanticism, assumed that proper women were asexual and that sexual desire should be suppressed in men. What purity excluded, pornography exalted.

Sexuality to the pornographer is primarily "organ grinding." It glories in the repetition of technique, not in the development of a relationship. Steven Marcus contends that pornography owes its development to the growth of cities, the spread of literacy, and the increasing possibilities for private experience.[21] In the middle of the nineteenth century pornography became a minor industry.

For every warning against masturbation issued by the official voice of culture, another work of pornography was published; for every cautionary statement against the harmful effects of sexual excess uttered by medical men, pornography represented copulation in excelsis, endless orgies, infinite daisy chains of inexhaustibility; for every assertion about the delicacy and frigidity of respectable women made by the official culture, pornography represented legions of maenads, universes of palpitating females; for every effort made by the official culture to minimize the importance of sexuality, pornography cried out—or whispered—that it was the only thing in the world of any importance at all.[22]

The official culture against which pornography was defined was the Victorian ethos of the upper-middle classes. The spokesmen for this ethos on sexual matters were likely to be doctors. Perhaps the most celebrated of all such spokesmen was William Acton, a London physician. Acton wrote on prostitution with a keen eye towards clearing up much of the mystique attached to the subject. The net effect of

---

[21]Steven Marcus, *The Other Victorians: A Study of Sexuality and Pornography in Mid-Nineteenth-Century England*, © 1964, 1965, 1966 by Steven Marcus, Basic Books, Inc., Publishers, New York, p. 282.

[22]Ibid., p. 283–84.

this work was a kind of enlightenment much needed in his day. However, his most famous work is entitled *The Function and Disorders of the Reproductive Organs.* It was published in 1857. The book was so popular it remained in print twenty years after Acton's death. It contains a clear picture of the Victorian understanding of human sexuality. It warns of the dire consequences of masturbation, advises continence, and fears spermatorrhea, the loss of semen. The following account is typical.

A medical man called on me, saying he found himself suffering from spermatorrhea. There was general debility, inaptitude to work, disinclination for sexual intercourse, in fact, he thought he was losing his senses. The sight of one eye was affected. The only way in which he lost semen was, as he thought, by a slight occasional oozing from the penis. I asked him at once if he had ever committed excesses. As a boy, he acknowledged having abused himself, but he married seven years ago, being then a hearty, healthy man, and it was only lately that he had been complaining. In answer to my further inquiry, he stated that since his marriage he had had connection two or three times a week, and often more than once a night! This one fact, I was obliged to tell him, sufficiently accounted for all his troubles. *The symptoms he complained of were similar to those we find in boys who abuse themselves. It is true that it may take years to reduce some strong healthy men, just as it might be a long time before some boys are prejudically influenced, but the ill effects of excesses are sooner or later sure to follow.*[23]

In the understanding of Victorians, the conservation of semen was the essential element in sexual practice. The notion that semen should be conserved is clearly based on the model of a monied economy. Indeed, the chief English colloquial expression for orgasm up until the end of the nineteenth century was "to spend." One conserved semen like money because of its inherent scarcity. The body was a productive system with only a limited amount of resources at its disposal. In contrast to this economics of scarcity, pornography portrays an abundant world. In "porn-utopia," all men were abundantly endowed with a universal fluid that could be spent without worrying about running dry.

Acton also spoke eloquently on the Victorian view of the sexuality of women.

I should say that the majority of women (happily for them) are not very much troubled with sexual feeling of any kind. What men are habitually, women are only exceptionally. It is too true, I admit, as the divorce courts show, that there are some few women who have sexual desires so strong that they surpass those of men. (but) The best mothers, wives and man-

[23]Ibid., p. 26.

agers of households, know little or nothing of sexual indulgences. Love of home, children, and domestic duties, are the only passions they feel.

As a general rule, a modest woman seldom desires any sexual gratification for herself. She submits to her husband, but only to please him; and, but for the desire of maternity, would far rather be relieved from his attentions. No nervous or feeble young man need, therefore, be deterred from marriage by any exaggerated notion of the duties required from him. The married woman has no wish to be treated on the footing of a mistress.[24]

Acton claimed as medical knowledge derived from his clinical practice what was accepted as common sense among the upper-middle class of his day. Men were sexual beings, women were not. Men, therefore, could be expected to find mistresses or prostitutes useful, although they must be wary of excessive loss of semen. Acton was apparently totally oblivious to the fact that he was reporting what might be better called an ideology. That ideology so completely clouded his perception that he tended to see what he wanted to see. In any case, the opinions of this accredited physician reflected the tone of his time. Although it took over a century for the sexual capacity of women to be empirically explored in the works of Masters and Johnson, the scientific study of human sexuality began in the nineteenth century with the work of Sigmund Freud.

SIGMUND FREUD

Sigmund Freud was, indeed, a great emancipator. He examined human sexual experience with a clinical thoroughness and most forcefully theorized on the pervasiveness of sexual energy or libido in all aspects of human behavior. He shocked his contemporaries by formulating a theory of childhood sexuality and by suggesting that sexual perversions were only extreme expressions of tendencies found in all of us. His conceptualization of the Oedipal stage of sexual development—when the male child struggles with his desire to make love to his mother and to kill his father—remains shocking to many people.

And yet in other ways Freud was very much a Victorian gentleman. He never doubted that heterosexual intercourse expressed the proper aim and object of sexual desire. He firmly argued that homosexuality, which he saw as a stage in normal sexual development, should be overcome. He asserted that women are naturally asexual and that the nuclear family is both an essential element of social structure and a major shaper of the human psyche.

At the core of Freud's understanding of human sexual motivation was his libido theory. *Libido* is instinctive sexual energy that can be described in terms of its source, its aim, and its object. The source of

[24]Ibid., p. 31.

Figure 12–3
Sigmund Freud was the first to study
sexuality in a scientific way. (National
Library of Medicine)

this energy lies in the excitement of a bodily organ—particularly the skin and mucus membranes of the erogenous zones surrounding the mouth, anus, and genitals. While Freud recognized that any part of the body was capable of becoming an erogenous zone, he defined normal eroticism as developing through a predictable pattern because of the associations made in childhood with the primary gratification derived through eating and defecating. The normal progression of sexual expression goes from oral to anal to phallic and finally matures in the genital stage.

The aim of sexuality in childhood is the simple gratification achieved through the stimulation of the erogenous zones. At puberty, when the sexual organs become fully developed, a new aim appears. In men, the new sexual aim becomes "the discharge of sexual products," accompanied by the highest sense of pleasure. In women the new aim becomes the stimulation of the vagina. This view is the source of the idea that the ability to have a vaginal orgasm is the mark of a mature woman. According to Freud, after puberty, "the (woman's) sexual instinct is now subordinated to the reproductive function; it becomes, so to say, altruistic."[25]

The object of sexual energy may be a part of the person's own

[25]Humberto Nagera, ed., *Basic Psychoanalytic Concepts on the Libido Theory* (New York: Basic Books, 1969), p. 23. See also, *The Complete Psychological Works of Sigmund Freud,* vol. 12, pp. 174–222.

body, another person, or a thing. Freud uses the term "object" in two ways: first, "as the thing in regard to which or through which the instinct is able to achieve its aim," and, second, in the sense of the love object as a whole person. The child's first understanding of love arises through the parent's (or caretaker's) stimulation of its erogenous zones in the process of caring for it. The infant's first object is normally the mother's breast. After a while, this primary object is lost (through weaning). The instinct can then become autoerotic in the form of thumb sucking.

Freud is to be credited with making our image of human sexuality much more complete, even if we do not agree with all of his conjectures. Both Freud and Darwin firmly established our continuity with the rest of organic life. It was difficult to talk about the special creation of humankind after Darwin. We must deal with the interaction between nature and culture in human sexuality because of Freud. He studied sexuality intensely, while, at the same time, he tried to relate it to the rest of life. His lesser known contemporary, Havelock Ellis, also tried to keep his intense interest in human sexuality within some broader context.

HAVELOCK ELLIS

Unlike Freud, who was interested in the manifestations of a sexual instinct, Ellis devoted his life to the study of the "art of love."[26] Freud sought to help his patients to adjust to the cultural constraints of their time, particularly those arising from family life. Ellis was a social researcher, not a clinician. He recommended dramatic—some thought utopian—transformations of the institutions of marriage and the family. Freud's focus in his sexual studies was largely on the pathological; Ellis sought out the normal. In short, Freud was quite concerned with the preservation of civilization, while Ellis was at least equally concerned with its transformation.

The revolutionary aspect of Ellis's thought can be seen in his attention to the works of Galton on eugenics. Ellis argued in *The Task of Social Hygiene* that it was an act of cruelty to bring an inferior child into the world. The commitment to the ideal of selective breeding in the human species would eventually become fixed in the conscience of the community in such a fashion that only the fit would appear sexually attractive.[27] With all of his radicalness, he retained a devotion to parenthood. He was convinced that the erotic life was apt to suffer in the absence of children. Today, many are inclined to argue that the erotic life suffers by the presence of children.

[26]Havelock Ellis's major work is the collection, *Studies in the Psychology of Sex* (Philadelphia, Pa.: F. A. Davis, 1924–28), vols. 1–7.

[27]Havelock Ellis, "Autoeroticism," Vol. 4 in *Studies in the Psychology of Sex.*

Figure 12–4
Havelock Ellis contributed to greater
acceptance of sexual variation because of
his belief of sexual normalcy.
(The Bettmann Archive, Inc.)

Like Freud, Ellis retains the Victorian image of women to a considerable extent. Even though Ellis established the nonreproductive elements of human sexuality, he did not wish to divorce them completely from the reproductive function. In his earlier writing especially, he was convinced that, just as men are designed to make history, women are designed to make children. The mother, being more "naturally" nurturant, was the child's supreme parent and was thus the proper person to educate the child in matters of sex. Ellis further argued that a woman could not achieve psychological fulfillment without the experience of maternity. In his later writings, however, he acknowledged that some women could be exceptions. He was by then convinced of the need to control the world's exploding population.

Ellis did not really develop a theory of human sexuality. He came closest to a general theory in his notion of erotic symbolism. According to Ellis, all sexual deviations were in reality an imitation of the actions and the emotions of normal sexual intercourse. Ellis saw the exhibitionist, for example, as feeling that "he has effected a psychic defloration" of his victim.[28] He exposes himself with the intention of shocking—but ultimately of pleasing—his victim. This assertion was plausible to Ellis because he contended that sexual arousal was a two-stage phenomenon. The first stage, *tumescence,* is the consciously pur-

[28]Havelock Ellis, *Sex and Marriage* (New York: Random House, 1952).

sued accumulation of sexual tension. Thus, courtship and exposure both represent the pursuit of arousal. The second stage, *detumenescence,* is the release of this built-up tension as in the case of the consummation of a courtship. The exhibitionists seeks, and sometimes finds, such release in exposure.

In conceiving of the "pervert" as a sexual symbolist, Ellis contributed to greater public acceptance of sexual variation. More significantly, in his conceptualization of the two stages of erotic arousal, he called attention to sex as an intentional pursuit of pleasure, rather than as a response to some powerful instinct or drive.

Ellis held a newly popular conviction that the art of love demanded both a prolonged erotic relationship and sexual variety. Marriage could satisfy the former need, but not the latter in most cases. While prostitution functioned to remedy the situation somewhat, it was a poor solution because of the ill effects upon both client and practitioner. A far better—but also far riskier—solution was for married couples to learn to have affairs. Ellis firmly believed that men and women were fully capable of desiring, and erotically loving, more than one person at the same time. Ellis was not glib about this assertion, however. He reckoned that jealousy would remain intractable in the emotional life of the human species, but that it could be managed if it were handled frankly and openly. In true romantic fashion, he did not advocate sexual promiscuity. He contended most fervently that affairs could be justified only if intense physical and personal attraction were involved. The relationship justified the expression of sex, not the other way around.

The Sexual Revolution in the Post-Industrial World

The Industrial Revolution has had great, if indirect, effects on human sexuality through changing the status of the family and through creating a relatively abundant world. Included in the cornucopia of abundance are such items as contraceptives, automobiles, and rock music, as well as medical science and sanitary cities, which have increased our life expectancy. Technology is providing increasing control over sexual development as well as over life itself.

The Industrial Revolution has had far-reaching and profound effects on the expression of human sexuality in the United States over the past century. Most important of these is the establishment of economic opportunity for women, the social isolation of the conjugal family, and the creation of an impersonal, if not antipersonal, society. It has helped us develop alternatives to the conjugal family and improve our communication skills. Finally, the automobile, which liber-

Figure 12–5
It is possible to appreciate changing perspectives regarding sexual beliefs with this study
of sexuality in films. (Opposite, top left, The Kiss, *1896; top right,* Gone With the
Wind; *Middle,* From Here to Eternity; *bottom left,* Gidget; *bottom right,* Women
in Love; *this page, top,* Pillow Talk; *and bottom,* Coming Home, *1978.*
All photos courtesy of The Museum of Modern Art/ Film Stills Archive)

ated much of our lovemaking from the confines of the family parlor, and adequate contraceptives, which permit women to have control over their reproductive capacity for the first time in history, have directly influenced the style of our lovemaking—especially since the advent of the pill in 1960. Only the last item on this selective list was intended to have anything at all to do with how we behave sexually. Yet the rest provide us with some of the most significant opportunities (and constraints) within which we must fashion our personal styles of lovemaking.

The net effect of the Industrial Revolution upon family structure has been toward increasing its isolation from daily contact with kin as the small conjugal family moves around the country and up the social ladder in search of even better jobs and careers. World War II created jobs for 8 million women that did not go away when the war was over. Today over half of all married women work, and over 60 percent of all married women with dependent children over the age of six are working. Marriage is not the same economic transaction for women that it once was.

The small, relatively isolated conjugal family (more characteristic of the middle class) is subjected to enormous stress and strain at the same time that more and more of its functions are being taken over by other institutions in our society. Both husbands and wives are expected to keep house as well as work. Cut off from close contact with intimate friends, spouses are expected to provide each other, and their children, if any, with all the emotional support that they are likely to receive outside of professional hands. The idea of "Open marriage" begins with the premise that spouses cannot adequately meet all of their partner's needs.[29]

The psychological impact of the work world is great. It rewards individual skills more than group efforts. People are expected to be competitive, competent, and cool. Emotions are used first to demonstrate control, then to sell products, but rarely to simply express one's true feelings. It is difficult to place this emotional control aside and be spontaneous in intimate relationships. To date our family life has suffered emotionally while it has prospered economically. The work world and the intimate world of human relationships are not well wedded in our society. The multimillion dollar business in sensitivity training and encounter groups of various sorts provide the upper-middle class individual with some awareness of the issues in interpersonal relationships, some communication skills, and an opportunity to explore some private time with others away from the home.

[29]Nena O'Neill and George O'Neill, *Open Marriage* (New York: M. Evans & Company, Inc., 1972). The term is used to describe a kind of marriage in which the couple are free to develop intimate friendships—which may or may not include sexual relationships—outside of marriage.

The hope of many such programs is to increase the capacity to enrich and fulfill intimate friendships and marriage. Such groups often provide the major occasion for upper-middle class people to feel free enough to become intimate. Whatever the merits of creating such special environments for intimacy, it remains true that they are not widely affordable.

To what extent the sexual revolution is a simple function of the affluence and leisure generated by an expanding economy remains to be seen. At present, the United States leads the world in sex research simply because our country can afford it. Worrying about the nonreproductive aspects of human sexuality is a privilege. Experimentation with alternative life styles and the open expansion of the erotic community are much more prevalent in the upper-middle class, where affluence provides couples with greater opportunity to experiment.

Marriage as a personal contract has a greater obligation to be personally fulfilling. If it does not meet such expectation—and we expect more of marriage in this regard than any other generation in Western experience—there are fewer social constraints to help hold it together until the partners resolve their difficulties. What we as individuals have agreed to, we as individuals have the right to dissolve. We tend to think that sexual difficulties—or loving—can be worked out through the learning of new techniques, but there is much to suggest that loving relationships are anything but efficient ways of relating to others. The more we attempt to improve our performance, the more we run the risk of devaluing the relationship.

ALFRED C. KINSEY

Kinsey's studies of human sexual behavior are very much a reflection of this scientific, secular, industrial age.[30] While Freud considered human sexuality to be hedged with danger and potential psychic catastrophe, and Ellis saw it as the central problem of life, Kinsey treats it in a quite matter-of-fact fashion.

Kinsey received a good deal of criticism not simply because of his findings as such, but because he delighted in pulling the rug out from under established wisdom. Even more than Freud and Ellis, Kinsey believed that sexual differences are more a matter of degree than kind. He assumed this not only within the human species, but between human and animal species as well. Thus, "abnormality" became a meaningless term in his classification of sexual variety. In his report on *Males,* Kinsey boldly asserted, "It is not possible to insist that any departure from the sexual mores, or any participation in so-

[30]Alfred C. Kinsey *et al., Sexual Behavior in the Human Male* (Philadelphia: W. B. Saunders, 1948); and Kinsey, *Sexual Behavior in the Human Female* (Philadelphia: W. B. Saunders, 1952).

Figure 12–6
Our attitudes toward premarital sex, homosexuality, and masturbation have not been the
same since Alfred Kinsey showed us that the majority of Americans had experienced them.
(© 1953, Institute for Sex Research Photo from United Press)

cially taboo activities, always, or even usually, involves a neurosis or a psychosis, for case histories abundantly demonstrate that most individuals who engage in taboo activities make satisfactory social adjustments."[31] Indeed, it is not against social convention that Kinsey measures his sexual deviation, but rather against the basic sexual patterns of other mammals.[32]

In his study of the *Human Male,* Kinsey reduces sexual behavior to those acts leading to orgasm, which he rather dispassionately calls an "outlet." Under the term "outlet," he discusses masturbation, nocturnal emission (wet dreams), heterosexual petting, heterosexual intercourse, homosexual relations, and intercourse with animals—in that order. Significantly, heterosexual intercourse is fourth on the list. Marital outlets are given about one-third as much space as homosexual outlets and are placed near the end of the book. This ordering and variation in coverage suggests that Kinsey's set of values differed drastically from the traditional view.

Kinsey did not hesitate to sum up all outlets achieved through

[31]Paul Robinson, *The Modernization of Sex* (New York: Harper & Row, 1976), p. 3.

[32]Kinsey, *Sexual Behavior in the Human Male,* p. 201–2.

whatever means under the phrase "total sexual outlet." This calculation means that, for some purposes at least, Kinsey considered all outlets equal. Kinsey's view is related to Freud's libido theory, Ellis's concept of tumescence, and the Victorians' spermatic economy. But Kinsey's sexual economy is somewhat more open than most. For example, more sexual activity before marriage did not mean less after marriage. Indeed, Kinsey believed the reverse was often true.

Kinsey's documentation of the extent of homosexual experience as a part of adult life in America has made it very difficult to claim that homosexuality is a pathology. Fifty percent of his male sample had responded to orgasm to homosexual stimulation at some time in their life. He concluded that homosexuality, because of its widespread occurrence, needed no explanation.

Under the concept of "factor," Kinsey discussed how sexual behavior—measured in outlets—was affected by nonsexual phenomena. Under the general label of "public opinion factors" he discussed the impact of marriage, religion, and history on sexual behavior. But in his *Male* study, the age and socioeconomic class of his subjects seemed to him to be by far the most important factors. Kinsey loved to hobnob with the lower class. He championed their life style as more straightforward and direct than the sophisticated lovemaking of the upper class. The lower class "slam, bam, thank you, ma'am" seemed somehow more natural to him.

In his study of the *Human Female,* Kinsey payed more attention to emotions and attitudes and less to orgasm as such. "Factors" were not as important as sources of explanation for female sexual patterns. Indeed, only religion seemed to make a significant difference in female sexual behavior. The more devout women (as measured by church attendance) had considerably less total sexual outlet. He concludes that upper class females were more likely than upper class males to be homosexual. He made comparisons between the genders in the *Female* volume. Female sexuality, he argued, was less conditional than male sexuality, since few of his factors proved important in the female study. Kinsey claimed that he could document differences between male and female sexual behavior, but was more inclined to stress the similarities between the sexes.

Kinsey made a tremendous contribution to our modern understanding of human sexuality. He inclined us to believe that homosexuality exists—at least as a potential—in most of us. He argued forcefully for greater sexual freedom for the young, and especially the young male, whom he saw as a veritable sexual dynamo who suffered greatly even under the double standard. He said that masturbation is to be greatly valued—especially by women—as a means of self-pleasuring. Only repressed masturbation is harmful. He continued the demystification of sex begun by Freud. His sexual outlet was quantitative, morally indifferent, and colorless.[33] Such a term for sexual behaviors, ranging from heterosexual intercourse to bestiality, could only be conceived by a person who made every effort to look at sex dispassionately. Kinsey made that effort.

A NEW SPIRITUALITY

The great attention that has been given in academic, social, religious, and philosophical writings and discussions to the question of "violations" of the traditional sexual mores since the turn of the century has frequently obscured the fact that the sexual revolution includes the development of a new social system with respect to the erotic relations of men and women. Much of this life style seems at first glance little more than rebellion against the mores of the established society. Yet at its core is an attempt to rediscover human sexuality not as an act of "doing it" for the sake of ego enhancement or even simply for the erotic pleasure that is to be found in making love. Rather, sexuality is seen as an expression of the whole of a life style and as a manner of worship after some traditions of the East.

A number of works have caught the ideology of a cultural revolu-

[33]See Robinson, *The Modernization of Sex,* p. 55.

Figure 12–7
(Henry Moore, King and
Queen, *1952–53, Hirschhorn
Museum and Sculpture Garden,
Smithsonian Institution*)

tion.[34] One recent attempt to define the character of what is happening is Anna Francoeur and Robert T. Francoeur's *Hot and Cool Sex: Cultures in Conflict*.[35] Francoeur and Francouer define our culture as predominantly a "hot sex" culture with enclaves of the coming "cool sex" culture. By "hot sex" they mean "genital interlocking" and nothing else. Hot sex is isolated from everyday life, confined to the "groins." Sex roles are commonly accepted stereotypes. Women have no identity as individuals, but tend to be defined as sex objects. In marriage they are the property of their husbands. Sexuality is "screwing." It focuses on technique, a means of proving oneself, a fear of nudity, possessiveness, and exclusiveness—at least for the woman.

In contrast, Francoeur and Francoeur contend that a "cool sex" culture is beginning to form. Cool sex culture diffuses and defuses sexuality. It reduces sex role distinctions, encourages the expression of sexual behavior beyond the genitals—to touching, sleeping with, and the affectionate courting of people. In a cool sex culture, sexual satisfaction is effectively separated from an exclusive involvement in procreation and is developing an ethic based on sexuality as a means of communication and growth. Marriages are not expected to fulfill all the partners' basic needs, and a variety of satellite relationships are allowed to develop to supplement the primary marital bond. Above all, spirituality and sexuality are not the incompatible forces they have been made out to be in the ascetic Christian tradition. This notion is captured in the concept of maithuna.

> *The general idea of maithuna in Tantric Yoga is that sexual love and intercourse can be transformed into a type of worship in which the partners are, for each other, incarnations of the divine. In the Buddhist and Taoist counterpart—since the notion of worship is foreign to them—maithuna is more a contemplation of nature in its true state.*[36]

It would indeed be one of the wonders of our age if, as Western technology spans the globe, Eastern religion and philosophy spreads westward to rehumanize our living and our loving.

[34]For example, see Robert H. Rimmer, *The Harrad Experiment* (New York: Bantam Books, 1968); Robert H. Rimmer, *Proposition 31* (New York: New American Library, 1968); Robert H. Rimmer, ed., *Adventures in Loving* (New York: New American Library, 1973); Robert A. Heinlein, *Stranger in a Strange Land* (New York: Berkley, 1961); Nena O'Neil and George O'Neil, *Open Marriage* (New York: Evans, 1972); and Nena O'Neill, and George O'Neill, *Shifting Gears* (New York: Evans, 1974).

[35]Anna K. Francoeur and Robert T. Francoeur, *Hot and Cool Sex: Cultures in Conflict* (New York: Harcourt Brace Jovanovich, Inc., 1974).

[36]Ibid., p. 58.

Summary

This chapter has attempted to reconstruct some of the major elements in our changing beliefs about human sexuality. It could not be exhaustive, only suggestive. The central threads that were traced were fundamentalist Christian asceticism, Romanticism, and the popularization of science through some of the classic studies of human sexuality. These threads were partially woven together at various critical times in our history, particularly in the first century, the sixteenth century, the nineteenth century and mid-twentieth century.

While at all times it was possible to point to instances in which we have placed a high positive value on sex in our belief system, the dominant conviction has been that human sexuality, as such, was essentially bad, at best a necessary evil. This conviction has been nurtured by the dominant element of the Christian tradition that has been labeled fundamentalist Christian asceticism. It has been supported by much of romanticism as well. Even Freud, who for all intents and purposes, can be said to have begun the scientific study of human sexuality, thought of it throughout most of his work as a powerful instinct that had to be socialized and controlled by social institutions such as marriage or it would destroy civilization. Havelock Ellis was much more positively inclined toward sexuality, even though he was strongly influenced by his Victorian beliefs in regard to the family.

Our beliefs about sexuality determine to a considerable extent what we experience when we experience sex. To the extent that we believe in them or simply take them for granted as natural, they define what sex is for us. Sex is what it is for many of us because our beliefs tell us that as an emotion or passion it is dangerous or bad, that its primary purpose is the reproduction of children, and that this purpose should be carried out in marriage through the means of heterosexual intercourse as the primary means of sexual behavior. All of this seems so evident to many people that they cannot consider it to be otherwise. In this chapter we have partially traced out the origins of such a belief system.

What is called a sexual revolution is the accumulating evidence that this belief system is being replaced by a system of beliefs about sex that is apparently much more positive. While the sustaining source of the old belief system seems to have been fundamentalist Christian asceticism, the sustaining source of the new belief system is the scientific study of sexuality as it has developed since Freud.

In the new belief system human sexuality is essentially good. It is to be enjoyed for the purpose of the recreation of persons as well as for the purpose of making babies. An individual may enjoy this sexuality alone, with another person of either sex by means of a wide array of techniques, or in groups of three or more persons. While group sex and homosexuality are still not widely accepted in our society, the new belief system encourages their acceptance. Certainly, the expression of human sexuality is no longer effectively regulated by the institution of marriage. Among a small number of people, the new stance toward sexuality has been taken to its logical conclusion within a belief system. Human sexuality for them, has become, once again, a means of worship.

Cultural Variations in Sexual Attitudes and Behavior

13

> The sexual freedom which we find among the
> Trobriand Islanders must not be mis-called
> "immorality," and placed in a non-existent
> category. "Immorality," in the sense of
> an absence of all restraints, rules, and values,
> cannot exist in any culture, however debased or
> perverted it may be. "Immorality," on the other
> hand, in the sense of morals different from
> those which we pretend to practice, must be
> anticipated in every society other than our own
> or those which are under the influence of
> Christian and Western culture.
>
> *Bronislaw Malinowski*

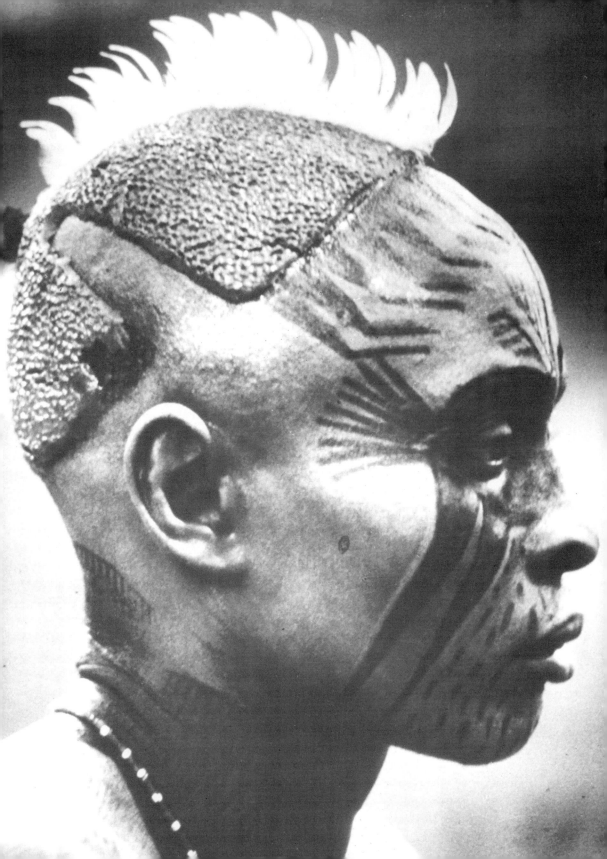

332

CULTURAL
VARIATIONS IN
SEXUAL
ATTITUDES
AND BEHAVIOR

In the nineteenth and twentieth centuries, anthropologists and other social scientists began to discover what human sexuality was like in other cultures. As a result of their studies, the richness of human sexuality became more and more apparent. Things Westerners considered to be abnormal, other cultures found quite normal. While parents in industrialized societies thought of masturbation as an extreme form of abuse, parents in other cultures openly taught their children how to pleasure themselves by means of masturbation. Some of these differences seemed not only to defy Western cultural preferences, but to go against nature itself. For example, the natives of the Trobriand Islands believed that the spirits of female ancestors were responsible for impregnating women and not the men of the tribe. What is to be made of all this?

This chapter examines how sex is expressed in other cultures. It also considers some of the variations in the style of lovemaking that have been found by anthropologists. Finally, it considers three contemporary societies, Ireland, Sweden, and Mangaia, in order to provide a clearer picture of how sexuality is related to other aspects of a people's way of life.

The Institutional Regulation of Human Sexuality

George Peter Murdock wrote in the 1940s that the United States was one of only three societies in his study that had what he called a "general taboo against sex."[1] By this he meant that we have a taboo about sexuality in any form. In contrast to our attempt to regulate sexuality itself, most other societies regulate sex to protect such social institutions as marriage, the family, and social stratification (including ethnic differences). Historically, the influence of Christian fundamentalist asceticism and some aspects of romanticism have been responsible for this difference in attitudes. Many people in the United States today still believe that sexuality itself is sinful.

In their analysis of other cultures' regulation of sexual behavior,

---

[1]George Peter Murdock, *Social Structure* (New York: Free Press, 1965), p. 262.

most anthropologists focus on the regulation of sexual intercourse to the exclusion of much of the rest of human sexuality. Furthermore, most of the information concerning the regulation of sexual intercourse focuses on the norms rather than upon actual behavior. Thus the analysis examines the occurence of taboos against adultery, incest, breach of caste, class, or racial boundaries, the violation of special offices such as the priesthood, and simple fornication (sexual intercourse between unmarried persons). While the behavior may be the same in all cases (heterosexual intercourse), it is placed into different boxes because it has a different social significance, depending on which norm it has violated. The individuals engaged in the act of intercourse may interpret what they are doing as "having fun," "making love," "getting even with someone," or what have you. A more complete understanding of what is happening must include a description of the behavior, its social significance, and what it means to the people involved. But such a degree of completeness is rarely found in studies of sexual behavior.

333

CULTURAL
VARIATIONS IN
SEXUAL
ATTITUDES
AND BEHAVIOR

MARRIAGE

Western cultures have tried to regulate sexual behavior almost exclusively by means of the institution of marriage. Even modern researchers tend to assume that the classification of sexual behavior according to how it impinges on marriage is the best way of considering its social significance. Thus we talk about premarital, marital, extramarital, postmarital, and even nonmarital intercourse as though all sexual behavior ought to be considered in its relationship to marriage, when this may very well be more misleading than helpful. Nevertheless, the categories persist, and we must make use of them because the data has been collected in these categories.

Premarital Intercourse. Murdock declared that men and women who are unmarried and who are not close blood relatives are forbidden to have intercourse in about 18 percent of the societies in his sample. Such activity is approved for both sexes in varying degrees in 45 percent of the societies. "In the rest the taboo falls primarily upon females and appears to be largely a precaution against childbearing out of wedlock rather than a moral requirement."[2] In his much smaller sample, Stephens calculated that premarital intercourse was permitted in 52 percent of the societies, ineffectively proscribed in 21 percent, and effectively prohibited in 15 percent. In 10 percent of his societies, women are severely restricted, but not men.[3]

[2]Ibid, p. 265.

[3]William F. Stephens, *The Family in Cross Cultural Perspective* (New York: Holt, Rinehart and Winston, 1969), p. 246.

Figure 13–1
Regardless of the type of ceremony, most societies rely
on marriage in the regulation of sexual behavior.
(Top left, © Micha Bar-Am, Magnum Photos, Inc.;
top right and bottom, United Press
International Photo)

Such an account of societies thought to be more or less permissive in their norms does not, however, give us an adequate account of how each might go about controlling premarital intercourse. Normally only those persons who are eligible to be one's spouse can be eligible to be one's partner in sex. Such a requirement may exclude the majority of people otherwise potentially available as sexual partners. On the other hand, prostitutes may be permissibly used in societies that otherwise prohibit premarital intercourse. Furthermore, relatively simple matters such as the formal regulation of public behavior may be so restricting in practice that the range of people one might reasonably expect to seduce is severely limited. Finally, other social ceremonies, such as the initiation ceremonies of the Tiwi that require the young man to be away from the village for months, may effectively remove significant segments of the youthful male population and prevent contact with females not otherwise restricted.

335

CULTURAL
VARIATIONS IN
SEXUAL
ATTITUDES
AND BEHAVIOR

The situation is further complicated by the fact that societies are not consistent in their efforts to control intercourse before marriage. We might think that norms against premarital sex should be reinforced by expecting formal behavior to prevent intimacy between the sexes, but this is only roughly the case. Premarital intercourse may be permitted in societies that, rather incongruously, also value virgin brides. For example, Kluckholn found that 99 percent of the Navaho men and 50 percent of the women had experienced sexual intercourse before marriage.[4]

Something of the range of effective control over premarital intercourse can be seen by considering the Cheyenne, the Kaoka Speakers of Guadacanal, and the Alorese, all of whom value virgin brides. The Cheyenne had explicit rules prohibiting fornication, severely punished both male and female violators, and reinforced their attitudes and behavior in myths and ceremonies. Cheyenne women were famous among all the Western tribes for their chastity. The Kaoka Speakers also had a norm against intercourse before marriage, but it applied most directly to women who wished to remain respectable. Men might indulge as they saw fit in the services of prostitutes who were "fallen women" or captives. Prostitutes never married, and so a portion of the Kaoka women were sacrificed for the sake of preserving the virginity of the "good" women of the tribe. The Alorese also valued virgin brides, but they were much less concerned about enforcing the taboos on premarital intercourse. Thus "both men and women feel free in that respect as long as they are careful not to be caught."[5]

In societies that permit or prescribe premarital intercourse, almost everyone, especially males, has experience before they are married. It

[4]Clyde Kluckholn and Dorothea Leighton, *The Navaho* (Cambridge, Mass. Harvard University Press, 1948).

[5]See the brief ethnographies of these peoples presented in Ian Hogbin, *A Guadacana Society: The Kaoka Speakers* (New York: Holt, Rinehart and Winston, 1966); E. Adamson Hoebel, *The Cheyenne Indians of the Great Plains* (New York: Holt, Rinehart and Winston, 1966); and Cora DuBois, John C. Messenger, "Sex and Repression in an Irish Folk Community," in *Human Sexual Behavior: Variations in the Ethnographic Spectrum,* eds. Donald S. Marshall and Robert C. Suggs, © 1971 by the Institute for Sex Research, Inc., Basic Books, Inc., Publishers, New York.

is much more difficult to determine the incidence of such behavior in societies that prohibit premarital intercourse. Messenger contends that none of the people on the Irish island he studied had made love before they married.[6] In the United States, on the other hand, about half of the females and two-thirds of the males have had intercourse before marriage, and the incidence of premarital sex seems to be increasing.[7] In small permissive societies the number of actual premarital sexual partners for any one individual might approach a substantial percentage of unmarried persons of the opposite sex whom that society defines as potential marriage partners. In the United States there is great variation between socioeconomic classes, the upper class having fewer potential partners.[8]

336

CULTURAL
VARIATIONS IN
SEXUAL
ATTITUDES
AND BEHAVIOR

Most anthropological records do not contain data on the frequency with which individuals engage in premarital intercourse. Some records indicate that it is nearly daily for some individuals in permissive societies. The frequency seems to diminish as social control increases. In the United States, the average female who has intercourse before marriage does so about once a month, and the average male does so about twice a month.

Marital Intercourse. Other societies are more formally restrictive of marital intercourse than we are. Most of them prohibit intercourse during menstruation, during at least a part of pregnancy and for a period of time after childbirth, and during or just preceding certain rituals.[9] While many Americans tend to restrict lovemaking during menstruation, in some stages of pregnancy, and for a time after childbirth, no formal rules, except those suggested by doctors, prevent such behaviors.

Gebhard reports that—excluding the first weeks of marriage—most married couples make love about two to five times a week in our society. But there is great cultural variation in frequency of marital intercourse. The Basongye average more than seven times a week, even when they are in their late fifties and sixties. In contrast, the Cayapa feel that a frequency of twice a week is something to boast of. Ordinarily, frequency declines with age. Thus there are some general patterns governing human preferences in lovemaking.

The most common setting for marital intercourse is at home, before

[6]Donald Marshall and Robert C. Suggs, eds., *Human Sexual Behavior: Variations in the Ethnographic Spectrum* (New York: Basic Books, Inc., 1971) pp. 9–38.

[7]Morton Hunt, *Sexual Behavior in the 1970s* (New York: Dell Publishing Co. Inc., 1974), pp. 146–47.

[8]Paul Gebhard, "Human Sexual Behavior: A Summary Statement," in *Human Sexual Behavior,* Marshall and Suggs, eds., p. 210.

[9]Ibid., p. 212.

going to bed. Privacy is usually valued and, where walls are thin or privacy difficult to obtain, sex often occurs out of doors.[10]

Extramarital Intercourse. The lovemaking of a married person with someone other than his or her spouse is much less permitted than premarital lovemaking. Murdock reported that in 79 percent of his sample, societies had a rule against such activity; Ford and Beach found that 61 percent of their sample had such a rule—although in 16 percent it applied only to women—and Stephens found that 16 percent had an ineffective rule against it. More than one observer has noted with Murdock that the rule is honored "more in the breach than in the observance."[11]

337

CULTURAL
VARIATIONS IN
SEXUAL
ATTITUDES
AND BEHAVIOR

Frequently, extramarital intercourse is reserved for special occasions, such as wife lending among the Copper Eskimo, or the periods of orgiastic celebration, such as occur among the Murngin, Kwoma, or Marquesan peoples. In general, the husband is allowed more freedom in such matters than the wife is. In Mexican and Mexican-American society, the husband's right to demonstrate his machismo seems to permit adultery for him and deny it to his wife. But even in such cases, the husband is not free to do as he likes. Above all he should not allow his outside activities to interfere with his marital obligations to his wife and family. Custom fully decrees that an exaggerated dedication to intercourse at the expense of cultivating friendships demonstrates a lack of intellectual ability in social interaction. Finally, the fear of venereal disease tends to reduce such adventuring.[12]

> *One can generalize that in most human societies the regulatory concern is not with the extramarital coital act itself but is rather with its social implications. Does it constitute a defiance of the spouse and society? Will it involve neglect of duties and obligations? Will it spoil prestige? Will it cause pregnancy and complicate inheritance? Will it weaken kinship ties and loyalties? Will it endanger disruptive jealousy.*[13]

It may be difficult to think of cases in which extramarital sexual intercourse would not create any of these problems. Nevertheless, some societies do permit such behavior, and others are apparently willing to put up with the problems it creates.

[10]Ibid., p. 211.

[11]Murdock, *Social Structure,* p. 265; Clellan S. Ford and Frank A. Beach, *Patterns of Sexual Behavior,* (New York: Harper & Row Publishers, Inc., 1951), p. 115; and Stephens, *The Family in Cross Cultural Perspective,* pp. 251–52.

[12]William Madison, *The Mexican American of South Texas* (New York: Holt, Rinehart and Winston, 1964), pp. 49–50.

[13]Gebhard, "Human Sexual Behavior," pp. 212–13.

The matter of jealousy deserves separate treatment. It appears to be a part of the human experience of most people in most cultures regardless of the norms governing sexual fidelity. Thus the Mexican wife may feel jealous of her husband, even though she expects him to express his machismo in adultery. Jealousy is found even among co-wives of African polygamous households and, as modern observers such as Carl Rogers note, it can be a part of an experimental marital contract in which the couple does not contract for sexual fidelity. Jealousy is a common experience when marital fidelity is broken, but it is treated differently in different societies. Many societies try to overcome it, but we tend to make it a sign of love.

338

CULTURAL
VARIATIONS IN
SEXUAL
ATTITUDES
AND BEHAVIOR

The incidence of extramarital intercourse is difficult to estimate. It seems to vary from culture to culture with the severity of sanctions imposed against it, but it does occur even in the strictest society. In the United States, which is generally a prohibitive society, socio-economic class makes a difference. About one-quarter of the females and about one-half of the males in the middle and upper classes have experienced sexual intercourse outside of marriage. In the lower classes the incidence among males is higher.[14]

Postmarital Intercourse. In most preliterate societies, people who are divorced or widowed are expected to remarry in a very short time. The Tiwi, for example, remarry widows at the grave side of their husbands and thus totally avoid the issue of postmarital intercourse. In societies where remarriage is difficult, it is common for divorced, separated, or widowed people to become prostitutes. Societies that are quite rigid regarding intercourse outside of marriage may ignore or even condone postmarital intercourse. In the United States, almost all men and about three-quarters of all women who have been divorced, separated, or widowed have continued to have sexual intercourse after their marriage ended.[15]

In summary, then, the majority of the peoples of the world prescribe or permit premarital intercourse, proscribe extramarital intercourse, prefer marital intercourse, and tend to ignore postmarital intercourse in their norms. Nevertheless, intercourse outside of marriage is, and apparently has always been, a common feature of the human sexual experience.

[14]Alfred Kinsey, *Sexual Behavior in the Human Female* (Philadelphia: W. B. Saunders, 1958), p. 437.

[15]Paul H. Gebhard, W. B. Pomery, C. E. Morlin, and C. V. Christenson, *Pregnancy, Birth and Abortion* (New York: Harper and Row Publishers, Inc., 1958), p. 143.

FAMILY

Family and kinship structures are other social institutions that societies attempt to protect through the regulation of intercourse. The incest taboos prohibit intercourse between people who are thought to be inappropriate sexual partners because of their family or kinship status. In some societies, these prohibited people may constitute over half of the population. Thus, even in societies that have permissive norms regarding nonmarital intercourse, the number of permissible partners may be so drastically reduced by kinship considerations that the frequency of nonmarital intercourse is much lower than might be the case if the society did not care about the family.

There is continuous discussion among anthropologists over the origin and function of the incest taboo, since it seems to be the most universal of all of our norms governing sexual behavior. Murdock and others argue that the primary function of the incest taboo is to protect the nuclear family (husband, wife, and their children).[16] Goody and others contend, on the other hand, that it is the larger kinship group, the lineage, that is being protected.[17] Those favoring the nuclear family tend to argue that it is primarily the reproductive and socialization functions of this family form that are being preserved because of the obvious survival value both functions have for the society. Those favoring the kin group tend to take the position that what is being preserved is the social structure of a society through the reciprocal exchange of women. In any case, the incest taboo tends to exclude those people as sexual partners who could not become marriage partners under the norms of a particular society.

Whatever the function of this taboo, the surprising thing is that, while all societies ever known have incest taboos, it seems that only parent-child incest is universally prohibited. Brother-sister incest is prescribed in a few cultures, and outside of the conjugal family there is great variation in the persons one is prohibited from having intercourse with under incest taboos.

Another notable aspect of the incest taboo is that it evokes intense emotion. Murdock speaks of the "grisly horror" with which most people respond to the very idea of incest. In *Oedipus Rex,* for example, Oedipus puts out his eyes when he discovers that he has killed his father and married his mother, an idea that Freud used to illustrate some aspects of the Oedipal complex. Our own attitudes toward incest are thus not a great deal different from those of primitive

339

CULTURAL
VARIATIONS IN
SEXUAL
ATTITUDES
AND BEHAVIOR

[16]Murdock, *Social Structure,* p. 285.

[17]Jack Goody, "A Comparative Approach to Incest and Adultery," in *Marriage, Family and Residence,* Paul Bohannon and John Middleton, eds. (New York: The Natural History Press, 1968), p. 45.

peoples. In spite of this, there is recent evidence that incest in our society may be much more common than we think.

OFFICES AND CEREMONIES

The regulation of intercourse can also be seen as a way to preserve or make special certain offices and occasions. Thus, Roman Catholic priests are pledged to celibacy and some Christians abstain from intercourse during periods of fasting, such as Lent. While these practices in our culture are more likely to be considered as matters of discipline, in preliterate societies they are associated with fears of contamination.

In the Tiwi culture off the coast of Australia, young males during their puberty rite (which might last over a year's time) were expected to abstain from intercourse. Plains Indians on vision quests, shamans preparing for special ceremonies, and warriors getting ready for battle were often expected to abstain. The Cheyenne, who fiercely restricted intercourse to marriage, permitted extramarital intercourse on special occasions such as the arrow renewal ceremony.

For most people in most cultures, however, these kinds of ceremonial restrictions are very minor influences on their sexual activity.

340

CULTURAL
VARIATIONS IN
SEXUAL
ATTITUDES
AND BEHAVIOR

Patterns of Sexual Behavior

Most societies regulate sex through norms aimed at protecting their major social institutions. In these cases, the norms are somewhat distant from the behavior in that their focus is on the preservation of the institution, not the regulation of behavior. In some cases the norms regulate sexual behavior more closely and directly. This occurs in the prescription of the sexual partner.

PERMITTED, PREFERRED, AND PROSCRIBED PARTNERS

Few societies are indifferent as to whether sexual behavior takes place between people of the opposite sex, the same sex, in solitary, or with an animal.

Heterosexual Contact. In the cultures studied by anthropologists, there is a strong preference for heterosexual contact above all others. To be more specific, heterosexual intercourse is generally seen as the most desirable form of sexual behavior. It would seem reasonable to assume that this preference exists because of the need for children. But the preference also exists in societies such as that of the

Trobriand Islanders, who had no knowledge of the role played by the male in reproduction. Many primitive societies were ignorant of the reproductive role of intercourse and some remain so. We must not, therefore, prematurely conclude that intercourse is naturally repro-ductive—much less that it should be.

Nevertheless, the fact remains that there is a strong preference for heterosexual intercourse over other forms of sexual expression, though many other modes of sexual expression may be permitted in varying degrees. Indeed, there is no sexual act that is not permitted or pre-ferred in some cultures around the world under some conditions.

Homosexual Contact. Homosexuality is one case in point. At times, within the tradition of a particular society, in certain societies on spe-cial occasions, and for the subcultures of most societies most of the time, homosexual behavior is permitted if not preferred. Within some subcultures of most societies homosexuality is preferred most of the time.

Most societies do not prohibit homosexual behavior. Over two-thirds of the seventy-six societies in Ford and Beach's sample ap-proved of at least some forms of homosexual behavior.[18] Thirty-seven percent of the societies (for which there is adequate data) have norms prohibiting homosexual contact as we do. It is probable, however, that homosexual behavior does exist in spite of the norms against it. Among the Siriono, however, homosexual behavior appears to be to-tally absent, even though there are no social pressures against such behavior.

Homosexual contact is also permitted between transvestites or be-tween older males and adolescent males. Among the Plains Indians of North America, a male might forsake the role of a warrior, assume the dress of a squaw, and be permitted homosexual contact. Such men were called *berdaches.* Male homosexuals sometime achieved high status as shamans and might share a husband with another wife.[19] Data on Lesbians, however, are scarce.

Gebhard concludes that,

Exclusive or near-exclusive homosexuality appears to be more rare in pre-literate societies than in the more complex civilizations. Homosexuality is less common in females than in males. Anal coitus is the usual technique employed by male homosexuals in preliterate societies; data regarding tech-niques used by females are too inadequate to generalize.

In the United States, about one-quarter of the females and one-third of the males experience at least one overt homosexual contact, generally prior

341

CULTURAL
VARIATIONS IN
SEXUAL
ATTITUDES
AND BEHAVIOR

[18]Ford and Beach, *Patterns of Sexual Behavior,* p. 130.

[19]Ibid., p. 130.

to marriage. Persons who are exclusively or almost exclusively homosexual throughout their lives are rare, constituting less than 5 percent of the population. Oral-genital contact is more common than anal coitus.[20]

Masturbation is apparently rare among adults in preliterate societies, though it is often permitted for children through adolescence. Although American norms have long described self-stimulation as abuse of the body, Kinsey found the behavior to be quite common, and sex therapists now encourage it.

342

CULTURAL
VARIATIONS IN
SEXUAL
ATTITUDES
AND BEHAVIOR

In the United States, about nine-tenths of the males and one-half to two-thirds of the females have masturbated. Unmarried males masturbate about once or twice a week when younger and less when older. Married males normally do so only a few times a year. In contrast, unmarried females who masturbate do so about once or twice a month, while married women masturbate about half as often. Thus, married women masturbate more often than married men.[21]

In preliterate societies, on the other hand, self-stimulation may not be as common because other forms of sexual expression are more available. For example, the Trobriand Islanders were quite permissive about heterosexual activities, but strongly condemned masturbation along with other forms of nonheterosexual contact. "To ask a man seriously whether he had indulged in such practices would deeply wound his vanity and self-regard, as well as shock his natural inclinations."[22]

Bestiality. Having sex with animals is a common theme in preliterate mythology and folk tales. Such practice in most societies is strongly tabooed, but even this mode of sexual expression receives support in some societies. Some express bestiality only in their folk lore, others strongly condemn even infrequent occurrences, and some societies do not condemn the practice at all. In the United States, about 4 percent of all adult males report having had some sexual contacts with animals. In preliterate societies, it seems to be even rarer.[23]

Paraphilia. The term *paraphilia* is commonly used to indicate all sexual interests that are not common in a culture. It is superior to terms such as "perversion" and "abnormality" because pathology may not be present.

[20]Gebhard, "Human Sexual Behavior," p. 215.

[21]Ibid., p. 208. See also Hunt, *Sexual Behavior in the 1970s,* pp. 76–77; and Kinsey, *Sexual Behavior in the Human Female,* pp. 173–75.

[22]Bronislaw Malinowski, *The Sexual Life of Savages* (New York: Harcourt Brace Jovanovich, Inc. 1929), p. 469.

[23]Ford and Beach, *Patterns of Sexual Behavior,* p. 147.

With increasing sexual permissiveness, many behaviors once thought to be exclusively in the deviant category are now incorporated into the lovemaking of normal couples. Oral-genital sex, anal intercourse, and the use of vibrators are now common practices. It was once thought that nudity in the home was a form of exhibitionism[24] and that other members of the family were thereby turned into voyeur's, or "Peeping Toms." The extent to which the unusual behavior dominates a person's sexual life is the important factor in deciding whether or not that behavior is a true paraphilia. For example, some exhibitionists ("flashers") and voyeurs may practice this variant form of sexual arousal along with an otherwise conventional sexual life style. For some, however, exhibitionism or voyeurism may be their primary sexual activity. Exhibitionists and voyeurs are not typically dangerous. They may masturbate after exposure or while peeping, but rarely attempt to molest the victim in any way.

Sadomasochism (the derivation of sexual pleasure from inflicting or receiving pain), *fetishism* (being aroused by an inanimate object or a particular part of the body), and *pedophilia* (being aroused by a sexually immature partner) can also be considered paraphilia when they come to dominate a person's life.

Kinsey concluded that about a quarter of the men and women in his sample were aroused by being mildly bitten, or by bitting, while making love.[25] Many primitive peoples engage in very violent lovemaking by comparison to our standards. The Mundugamor of New Guinea, for example, bite their lovers until they bleed, tear their clothes, and rip ear ornaments from their pierced ears while engaging in violent bush encounters that will likely leave both partners bedraggled and bruised.[26] Violence is ordinarily not necessary in order for these people to be aroused and to enjoy sex, but it seems to add zest to their excitement. Criminals like the Boston Strangler are sometimes called sadists, but it is not at all clear that such people kill to achieve sexual pleasure. In similar fashion, rape is in many instances best understood not as a crime of passion, but as a crime of violence and an antisocial act. It is not easy to differentiate passion from aggression in all instances.

In true sadomasochism, a remarkable transformation must occur. Pain is converted to pleasure, and the achievement of arousal depends on inflicting or receiving pain. The nonpathological use of mild pain, playfully and mutually inflicted as a part of a robust ex-

343

CULTURAL
VARIATIONS IN
SEXUAL
ATTITUDES
AND BEHAVIOR

[24]See, for example, the discussion in Frank S. Caprio, *Variations in Sexual Behavior* (New York: Grove Press, 1955), pp. 222 ff.

[25]Kinsey, *Sexual Behavior in the Human Female,* p. 678.

[26]Margaret Mead, *Sex and Temperament in Three Primitive Societies* (New York: Mentor Books, 1950), pp. 152–53.

pression of love must be distinguished from pathological forms in which the pain is intense (involving, for example, the tearing and burning of tissues, painful bondage, and other forms of mutilation that may even kill on occasion). Such pain is usually nonmutually inflicted. The victim does not have a turn either, because it is not wanted or it is not given. It is violently, not playfully, inflicted. The Mundugamor love-play, while violent by our standards, was mutually inflicted and incorporated into a socially recognized form of courtship. Loveplay, however aggressive, has a definable turning point in orgasm and the reasonable hope that with good fortune and good will it can begin again. The extreme of sadomasochism is unconsciousness and death.

344

CULTURAL
VARIATIONS IN
SEXUAL
ATTITUDES
AND BEHAVIOR

It is difficult, however, to justify the pathological form of sexual expression even among consenting adults because the behavior is so damaging to one or both individuals. It might be argued that the persons who inflict or receive such pain are not to be considered adults in any legal definition and thus not able to give consent. But when should society intervene in such behavior? In the case of murder or its threat, intervention is clearly justified, but short of this, when is it so? The issue is extremely difficult to handle in terms of general principles. A great deal of attention must be given to individual cases in order to determine if consent was truly given. More difficult to establish is the extent to which society should condone the mutilation of even consenting adults. We might not want to intervene in their behavior, as long as it was in private, but we need not encourage others to follow their example. Because a common means of inflicting such pain is through whipping with a rod, some analysts conclude that some sadomasochistic tendencies are learned through corporal punishment in school.[27] But the origin of this kind of sexual behavior is undoubtedly complex and poorly understood at present.

Fetishism takes many forms. Most commonly a piece of clothing—usually an undergarment—is used as a part of masturbation. Shoes are commonly arousing for fetishists. The soft fluffy kind are suggestive of the female genitals; the smooth, pointed kind symbolize the male genitals. It is assumed that these objects become arousing because of early association with sexually arousing events in childhood—seeing a sister's or mother's genitals while they were undressing and associating the shoes or undergarments on the floor with the genitals and the pleasant sense of arousal. Men are much more likely to be fetishists than women.

Pedophilia, the love of youth or young children, has been recorded throughout history. Pedophilia is a serious legal offense. It is not true that only homosexuals engage in this practice. The vast majority of

[27] Hunt, *Sexual Behavior in the 1970s*, p. 328.

individuals who are arrested for this sex offense are heterosexual men. Most know the young girl that they molest, and most molestations occur in the child's home. In only 2 percent of reported cases is the child physically damaged, and in only about 6 percent of the cases is intercourse attempted. In most cases the young victim takes the matter less seriously than the parents, who may cause some psychological difficulties for their child by their overreaction.[28]

The anthropolgical data on paraphilia is very sparse, and the following generalizations are only suggestive. The intense interest in a portion of the anatomy such as a foot or breast (which is called *partialism*) is very common among preliterates, but fetishism, a comparable intense interest in an inanimate object, is apparently rare. Very few people in preliterate societies derive their sexual pleasure from seeing others nude such as voyeurs do in our own country.

While sexual intercourse occurs between people of widely differing ages in some regularity in preliterate societies, a preference for a particular age group, such as in pedophilia or gerontophilia (desire for sex with old people), does not seem to be common. Similarly, while sadomasochistic behavior is fairly common on certain occasions, such as puberty rites in preliterate societies, situations in which pain is necessary for sexual satisfaction are absent or rare. Thus, we can conclude that "large complex societies, where individuals can evade sanctions through anonymity, are conducive to the development of paraphilias."[29]

345

CULTURAL
VARIATIONS IN
SEXUAL
ATTITUDES
AND BEHAVIOR

Variations in the Sexual Scenario

Animals have distinctive behaviors that set the stage for copulation. Human societies have likewise adorned intercourse with a vast array of associated behaviors and embedded it in myth and fantasy. Individuals further modify cultural traditions with their own distinctive interpretations. However, unlike most animal courtship rituals, human courting is very difficult to capture in terms of stimulus and response. The social script normally leading up to intercourse, even if ritually followed, will not guarantee that either partner will copulate. On the other hand, if either partner widely diverges from what is considered culturally acceptable courtship behavior, the other partner is likely to be offended or turned off. Making up one's sexual script from

[28]See Paul Gebhard, John H. Gagnon, Wardell Pomeroy, and C. V. Christensen, *Sex Offenders* (New York: Harper and Row Publishers, Inc., 1965) for a fuller discussion.

[29]Gebhard, "Human Sexual Behavior," p. 216.

scratch—without using the common cultural guidelines—is thus a delicate art indeed.

ATTRACTION

346

CULTURAL
VARIATIONS IN
SEXUAL
ATTITUDES
AND BEHAVIOR

The preferred sexual partner in most societies is thought of as beautiful or at least attractive. But what is considered sexually attractive is so diverse that a truly universal beauty contest would make the task of judging impossible. For example, at one time the Chinese considered very small feet to be beautiful. Most Chinese women deformed their feet so that they would be beautiful, even if they couldn't walk when the bindings were removed. The Alorese blacken and file the teeth of their beautiful maidens to sharp points. Traditionally, Burmese beauties elongated their necks with brass rings from childhood on so that, if the rings were removed in adulthood, they could not hold up their heads. Many peoples find beauty in the scars they inscribe on the face and body. The Bushmen think huge buttocks are a sign of beauty. And so it goes. One can say that beauty is universally valued, but that wide disagreement exists over what it is.

While much of the Western world relies on eye contact to initiate the sexual scenario, it is probable that odor plays a much more central role in sexual attraction. Filthiness is generally considered repulsive, but body odors themselves are regarded as attractive in some societies.[30] In preliterate cultures, clean bodies may or may not be adorned with perfumes, flowers, herbs, and scented oils. In our cosmetic age, we try to cover up these odors and may thus deaden our sensitivity to the influence of odors in sexual arousal.

We normally conceal the genitals until late in the sequence of events leading to lovemaking because the exposure of the genitals to a person of the opposite sex is an unmistakable invitation. Although speech is undoubtedly a very important medium of sexual solicitation among human beings, gestures play a significant role as well. Thus, in the west central Carolinas, the man invites a woman to make love, and she consents by moving her hand downward from her forehead over her face. Among the Marshall Islanders, men solicit sexual partners by rolling their eyes and pronouncing the name of the sexual organs.[31]

Love magic is an almost universal form of attracting a sexual partner. We can understand something of the feeling thought appropriate to sexual love by considering the following example of love magic from the Trobriand Islands.

[30]Ford and Beach, *Patterns of Sexual Behavior*, p. 85.

[31]Ibid., p. 33.

O, her sensual excitement,
O, her erotic swoon,
O, desire, O feminine swoon,
My clasping, thy clasping, kindle our erotic swooning,
My embraces, thy embraces, kindle our erotic swooning,
My copulation, thy copulation, kindle our erotic swooning.

The last sequence is repeated with the insertion of words indicating appropriate erotic behaviors such as "erotic scratching, erotic biting, nose rubbing, eyelash biting, lousing, rubbing each other's lips," and so forth. Then comes:

Thou goest my way, crying for me,
Thou enterest my house, smiling at me,
The house is shaken with joy as thou treadest my floor.
Tease and tear out my hair,
Drink my blood,
So that my feelings are glad.[32]

347

CULTURAL
VARIATIONS IN
SEXUAL
ATTITUDES
AND BEHAVIOR

As with most magic, these words meant to be a formula that must be precisely followed if the desired seduction is to take place. It may be practiced by attractive, experienced, and skillful lovers, or by people who feel left out of the sexual swirl. When the conquest has not been made yet, the formula is chanted over a mint plant boiled in coconut oil. The scent of the boiling ambrosia entering the beloved's nostrils while she sleeps is thought to cause her to dream about the magic maker. If the formula is practiced over someone who has already been subdued, the oil is used to anoint the beloved. Both men and women may make use of love magic in the Trobriand society. In general, women are given more freedom to initiate sexual encounters in other cultures than in our own.[33]

SETTING

Most people care about where lovemaking takes place. Where households are one-room affairs, the preferred location for making love is likely to be out of doors. In those societies where living quarters afford a sufficient degree of privacy, a few societies decree that the only place to make love is indoors. But even here unmarried lovers may seek an encounter in the bush. The style of lovemaking may vary according to whether it takes place indoors or outdoors. Public copulation is extremely rare in most of the world, but is occasionally permitted as a part of a public ritual.

In our society, intercourse for most couples takes place at night.

[32]Malinowski, *The Sexual Life of Savages,* pp. 371–72.

[33]Ford and Beach, *Patterns of Sexual Behavior,* p. 101.

Figure 13–2
Since time immemorial, women have experimented with make-up and ornaments to increase their attractiveness to others. In some societies, this same privilege is extended to men. (Below, United Nations, Jerry Frank; opposite, top, Olivier Rebbot, Woodfin Camp & Associates; bottom, Marc & Evelyne Bernheim, Woodfin Camp & Associates)

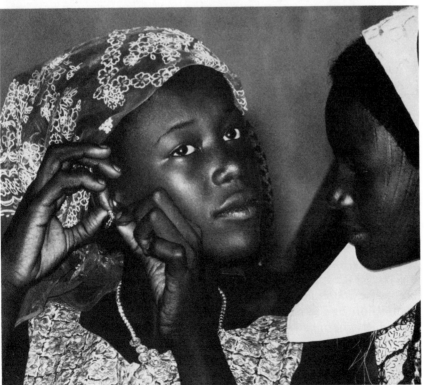

350

CULTURAL
VARIATIONS IN
SEXUAL
ATTITUDES
AND BEHAVIOR

Figure 13—3
Many young Americans, who are limited to making love in the back seat of a car, would see
this vehicle as the answer to their prayers.

Some people prefer the night because they feel that copulation is shameful or that daytime copulation is too risky. Some societies prefer the daytime, and some have no preference. Kinsey determined from his sample that males tend to prefer to make love in the light and females in the dark.[34] But there is little cross-cultural evidence to support Kinsey's findings about American preferences in this regard.

SEX ROLES IN LOVEMAKING

While we might be able to see some of our emotional responses to lovemaking reflected in Trobriand love magic, there is great cultural variation in people's attitudes toward intercourse itself. Among the Arapesh, for example, either sex may initiate sexual encounters. Because sex is conceived of as dangerous even within marriage, the fear of coercion is ever present. Arapesh males are not thought of as dominant in sexual encounters and take great care to avoid any sense of compulsion in their sexual adventures. "A man must approach his wife gently, he must make 'good little talk,' he must be sure that she is well prepared to receive his advances. . . . It is as customary for the woman as for the man to say, 'Shall I lay the bed?' or 'let us sleep.'" What is stressed is mutual readiness and mutual ease. Orgasm is not recognized among Arapesh women. Sexual intercourse arises from the

[34]Kinsey, *Sexual Behavior in the Human Female,* p. 665.

same order of feeling of affection that is to be found between parent and child. There is no conception of a sex drive that has to be controlled lest children experiment inappropriately with sex. The Arapesh, finally, do not recognize any temperamental difference in sexual drive between men and women. If spontaneous sexual desire does occur, the Arapesh feel that women are more likely to experience it.[35]

The Mundugamor, on the other hand express a great deal of aggression in their copulation. Their intercourse is violent and may be used as a means of expressing aggression against neighbors. For instance, copulating in a neighbor's yam garden is seen as a way to spoil the crop.[36]

The Tchambuli completely reverse our taken-for-granted conception of sexuality. Women are thought to be the more naturally sexed. They choose their mates. Young women are expected to be married and to remarry shortly after the termination of marriage. "Has she not a vulva? they ask. . . . Are women passive creatures who can be expected to wait upon the dilly dallying of formal considerations of bride price?" Because men are not so urgently sexed, they can wait for the formal discipline of precedence. Women cannot.[37]

Margaret Mead found the Samoans to have the "sunniest and the easiest attitudes toward sex, putting their whole emphasis on the specific interpersonality of the sexual act." Lovemaking is approached slowly and engaged in langorously. The girl's body must be prepared by proper stimulation, and the good lover rapidly loses his concern about his performance in his sensitivity to his relationship with his beloved. Samoans engage in intercourse at an early age and continue throughout life to develop their artistry. "Love between the sexes is a light and pleasant dance, in which one may be either very graceful, or alas, awkward and so lacking partners." The awkward lover resorts to "sleep crawling," taking advantage of the natural readiness of a young woman to receive a lover by disguising himself and coming to her bed under the cover of darkness.[38]

TECHNIQUE

Some sexologists distinguish between petting and foreplay reserving the term "foreplay" for heterosexual stimulation that leads to intercourse. Because most people put a lot of emphasis on intercourse, petting is assumed to be inferior to foreplay. In our culture, adolescents

351

CULTURAL
VARIATIONS IN
SEXUAL
ATTITUDES
AND BEHAVIOR

[35]Margaret Mead, *Sex and Temperament in Three Primitive Societies* (New York: Mentor Books, 1950), p. 103.

[36]Ibid., p. 154.

[37]Ibid., p. 178–79.

[38]Margaret Mead, *Male and Female* (New York: Mentor Books, 1955), p. 160. Copyright 1949, 1967 by Margaret Mead. By permission of William Morrow & Company.

spend an enormous amount of time "necking." This takes on quite a different significance if it is seen as frustrated foreplay or as a gratifying activity in its own right. Gebhard concludes that in the cross-cultural data "seldom is petting an end in itself or a substitute for coitus."[39] Males usually initiate petting and females respond in varying degrees from culture to culture. Among the Manu, women respond little. Among the Trobriand Islanders women are equally active in lovemaking. In the United States, petting may take hours, but foreplay (even in the case of experienced lovers) rarely lasts longer than thirty minutes.[40]

352

CULTURAL
VARIATIONS IN
SEXUAL
ATTITUDES
AND BEHAVIOR

While kissing on the mouth is common to all European and American societies, it is rare among preliterate peoples. Males are apt to place their hands on the female breast when making love in all known cultures, but rarely do they place their mouth on the breast, as is common in our culture. Males are somewhat more likely to place their hands on the female's genitals than women are to touch the male's genitals, but both are nearly universal practices.

In parts of Oceania and Asia, it is common for males to practice cunnilingus. In the United States, this is common practice in the upper class, but is much more infrequent among the lower classes. The fact that the practice of cunnilingus is common implies that the practice of fellatio should also be considered; but in fact, it is not.

The placing of the penis between the female's thighs (femoral coitus) and rubbing the genitals together without penetration seem to be primarily characteristic of some African tribes. In the United States, one-sixth to two-thirds of the various subgroups examined in the Kinsey studies shared these practices. Data on anal intercourse is sparse, which suggests that the practice is rare, though perhaps not uncommon.[41]

Orgasmic Response

Because ejaculation is almost everywhere identified with orgasm in the male, male orgasmic response is culturally universal (there are, of course, a few individuals who cannot experience orgasm). Female orgasmic response, on the other hand, is much more of a learned behavior. In societies such as Mangaia, females quickly learn to achieve orgasm and experience it often in intercourse thereafter. In Inis Baeg, near Ireland, where sex is severely repressed, females seldom achieve

[39]Gebhard, "Human Sexuality," p. 209.

[40]Ibid., p. 209.

[41]Ibid., p. 210.

orgasm.[42] Females everywhere require somewhat more time to achieve orgasm in lovemaking than males. A number of studies have reported that males deliberately delay orgasm in order to satisfy the slower female, but others have recorded complaints by women that men come too quickly.[43] Multiple orgasms are rarely mentioned in the anthropological records.

Mead concludes from her studies that the male response is best over all when it is more automatic.

353

CULTURAL
VARIATIONS IN
SEXUAL
ATTITUDES
AND BEHAVIOR

> *Male sexual functioning seems to work most easily when it is most automatic, when the response is to a simple set of signals that have been defined as sexually exciting, whether those signals be bodily exposure, a special perfume, a woman's reputation for compliancy, or simply a woman alone in a bush, path or in an empty apartment. Once male sex functioning is complicated by sets of ideas about sentimental love or by prestige, moral qualms, theories of the relationship between sex activity and athletic prowess or religious vocation, or between virility and creativity, then sex functioning may become that much less automatic and reliable. It is not an accident that in the elite groups—the aristocrats, the intellectuals, the artists—of all cultures there have developed a variety of subsidiary and supplementary practices designed to stimulate male desire, whether these be perversions, a new concubine every night, homosexuality, or dramatizations of obscure daydreams, they occur with startling regularity, while in those portions of the population, where there is less choice, less taste, and fewer confusing ideas, copulation is a simple matter.[44]*

Masters and Johnson's study of sexual response in the United States seems to agree with the anthropological evidence on orgasmic frequency. They add another dimension to these observations, however, by noting that while all women registered an orgasmic response on their recording instruments, not all were aware that they had actually achieved orgasm.

> *The ability to achieve orgasm in response to effective sexual stimulation was the only constant factor demonstrated by all active female participants. This observation might be considered to support the concept that sexual response to orgasm is the physiologic prerogative of most women, but its achievement in our culture may be more dependent upon psychological acceptance of sexuality than overtly aggressive behavior.[45]*

[42]Messenger, "Sexual Repression in an Irish Folk Community."

[43]Gebhard, "Human Sexuality," p. 214.

[44]Mead, *Male and Female,* p. 151.

[45]William H. Masters and Virginia E. Johnson, *Human Sexual Response* (Boston: Little, Brown & Co., Inc., 1966), p. 139.

Masters and Johnson found that, as Mead had said earlier, social factors also seem to affect sexual response in the case of the male.

> *Cultural demand has played a strange trick on the two sexes. Fears of performance in the female have been directed toward orgasmic attainment, while in the male the fears of performance have been related toward the attainment and maintenance of penile erection, and orgasmic faculty always has been presumed.*[46]

354

CULTURAL
VARIATIONS IN
SEXUAL
ATTITUDES
AND BEHAVIOR

But some men are not able to experience orgasm, even though they readily attain erection. In such comparatively rare cases, the partners frequently report that the woman is able to achieve many orgasms while copulating. Surprisingly, these women are not commonly pleased with this situation.

Sex and Society: Three Contemporary Cases

Studying the sexual attitudes and behaviors of other cultures tells us something about the range and variation of the human sexual experience, but little about how it is related to other aspects of a people's way of life. In the following three examples, I will examine a contemporary society in which sexual expression is strongly repressed (Ireland), one in which it is much more permitted (Sweden), and one (Mangaia) which is very permissive. Even these brief accounts can suggest how economics, religion, politics—indeed the whole heritage of a people—impinge upon sexual expression.

SEX AND REPRESSION IN IRELAND

An example of extreme sexual repression can be found in the study of a small island off the coast of Ireland, which shall be called "Inis Beag."[47] The two square mile island currently has a population of about 350, which is a decline from its peak population of 532 in 1861. The islanders are in touch with the mainland through radio, television (two sets were introduced in 1963), newspapers, magazines, and personal contacts with tourists or neighbors who infrequently travel to Ireland. The effect of all of these contacts has been minimal. In fact, the culture of this folk or peasant community can be said to have been stable over the past 200 years. It has not been noticeably contaminated by outside influence during this period. The men of

[46]Ibid., p. 218.

[47]This account is taken from Messenger, "Sex and Repression in an Irish Folk Community," pp. 3–38.

Inis Beag spend most of their time fishing at sea or tilling small plots of arable land. The women are mostly confined to the house. Some elderly women have not walked to the beaches on the lee side of their island in over thirty years.

There is no evidence that adults are ignorant about what must be done in order to have babies, as some adults are even today in some sections of Ireland, but sex is not discussed in front of children. Boys are better informed about sex than girls because they can learn from older men and boys and from watching animals. Girls are often frightened by their first menstrual bleeding because they are not prepared for it, and their mothers can rarely offer an adequate explanation of what is happening to them. Most islanders believe that after marriage "nature will take its course."

Nudity is abhorred. Only babies are completely washed once a week. All others wash only their faces, necks, lower arms, hands, lower legs, and feet. The abhorrence of nudity even prevents men from learning to swim, though they spend a good portion of their lives at sea in fragile boats.

Inis Beag lacks a "dirty joke" tradition. Mild phrases in ballads such as "dreaming perhaps of a beautiful mate" were observed to cause blushing when sung in the local pub. Natives permit set dancing in which rigid body postures shift attention below the hips and contact with another body is minimal. Even so, some girls refuse to dance because it involves touching a boy, and the local priest appears at dances to show his displeasure.

Sexual technique seems quite limited on the island. There was no evidence of deep kissing, oral stimulation of the female breast or genitals, anal or oral intercourse, overt homosexuality, bestiality, fetishism, or sadomasochistic behavior. There was also no evidence of extramarital intercourse. Indeed intercourse outside of marriage seems to be confined to contacts made between single males and female tourists.

Messenger attributes sexual repression on Inis Beag to a number of historical socio-cultural and psychological factors. Irish Catholicism represents perhaps the extreme of Christian asceticism, which in this case has been exaggerated by Jansenism. Jansenism entered Ireland with the establishment of the Roman Catholic seminary at Maynooth in 1795. In its rigid and gloomy doctrine, people are helpless, doomed beings who must endure rigorous penances to demonstrate their love for God. Jansenism was denounced by the Jesuits, but it became popular because it reinforced the basic tendencies of the Irish. Jansenism produced in Ireland the most severe denunciation of the flesh. Sex and marriage are seen as rather regrettable means of propagating the species.

On Inis Beag, the local clergyman's denunciation of the sins of the

355

CULTURAL
VARIATIONS IN
SEXUAL
ATTITUDES
AND BEHAVIOR

flesh takes subtle forms in addition to his hell-fire and damnation sermons. Some of the more extreme forms of clerical control include employing informers, allocating indulgences (attendance at missions is a means of reducing time in purgatory), refusing the sacrament to known sinners, and in some instances actually placing curses on people. The school joins with the church in its support of asceticism. "The adult Irish person is rare, who, although anticlerical, and even agnostic or atheistic, can transcend these early enculturative experiences."[48] Curates at the local church have supressed dancing and have roamed the fields at night in search of young lovers, even though their intrusion in such matters is often resented by the villagers.

Parents reinforce the teachings of national church and school by numerous rewards and punishments. Warm handling and kissing of the young is rare in Inis Beag. Words even indirectly suggestive of sexual arousal and sensual activity are severely punished. Breastfeeding is rare. On such a small island, gossip is a major means of social control, and women will not walk in the fields for fear that "they" will "wonder why I wasn't home tending my chores." Courting is suppressed, as are all efforts of even husband and wives to "share themselves." Messenger contends that mothers in Inis Beag "display the extreme of Oedipal attachment when they rejoice in their son's decision to join the priesthood; not only are spiritual blessings and prestige brought to the family as a result, but their sons are at last removed from potential wives."

Islanders marry late (between the ages of twenty-four and forty-five in the case of men, and eighteen and thirty-two for women). Many factors account for this. The most prominent seems to be the pattern of inheritance, wherein the eldest son must wait until his own siblings have married. He inherits the family farm from his father (who is often loath to give it up). The siblings, because they cannot inherit the land, normally move away to marry. It is not, therefore, uncommon for a man in his late twenties to have a mother who acts in most ways as a wife, and who becomes reluctant to marry because he enjoys "running with the lads." Marriage on the island is also difficult because girls find their future more gloomy there than boys and tend to emigrate at even younger ages. The collapse of the kelp-making and fishing industries in recent years has contributed somewhat to the decline in the island's population, but Messenger concludes that "by far the most important reason . . . is the total cultural impact of sexual puritanism and the secular 'excesses' of the clergy." Blanchard concludes for the whole of Ireland, "when all the reasons for a flight from Ireland have been mentioned, there still remains a suspicion that Irish young people are leaving their nation largely because it is a

356

CULTURAL
VARIATIONS IN
SEXUAL
ATTITUDES
AND BEHAVIOR

[48]Ibid., p. 28.

poor place in which to be happy and free. Have the priests created a civilization in which the chief values of youth and love are subordinate to Catholic discipline?"[49]

SEX AND SOCIETY IN SWEDEN

The uninformed American tends to think of Sweden as a sexually promisucous society in which almost anything goes. This is far from the truth. As Lester Kirkendahl remarks in his preface to Birgitta Linner's book, *Sex and Society in Sweden*, "The philosophy underlying Swedish sex laws is not the prevention of sin, but the intent to allow mature individuals to choose their own patterns of sexual behavior so long as they do not infringe upon the rights of others."[50]

Swedish society is a quite different environment from our own, and the sexual attitudes and behaviors of any society can be better understood when they are placed in their own cultural context. For example, the Swedes are far more committed as a people to the rational planning of their entire social life than we are. Sweden's mixed economy has quite different objectives than our own. People who can work have a right to work, and the government sees to it that industry employs and retrains its workers with government assistance. (We have more people currently unemployed than now live in Sweden, and yet we accept 4 to 5 percent unemployment as normal.) Swedish families further enjoy the security of a workable national health program, and the standard of living is higher for the average Swede than for the average American.

Sweden, however, is still more of a nation of small towns and farms than the United States. The large extended family is thus more functional in Sweden than in the United States. The conjugal family is much more of a direct concern of public policy in Sweden. For over twenty years the public school system of Sweden has supported sex education. Its official handbook, however, does not condone sexual intercourse before marriage. The church of Sweden, the Lutheran establishment, officially has a very restrictive view of morality in sexual relationships, limiting them to marriage and discouraging the widespread sale of contraceptives. The Church even contends that "every marriage in which husband and wife . . . do not desire to have children is misdirected."[51] In keeping with this emphasis on the reproductive aspects of sex, the Church teaches that homosexuality is morally wrong, but does not encourage the imprisonment of homosexuals. In spite of this, youngsters can readily obtain contraceptives in Sweden,

357

CULTURAL
VARIATIONS IN
SEXUAL
ATTITUDES
AND BEHAVIOR

[49]Paul Blanchard, *The Irish and Catholic Power* (London: Derek Verschoyle, 1959), p. 154.

[50]Birgitta Linner and Richard J. Litell, *Sex and Society in Sweden* (New York: Random House, 1967), p. vi.

[51]Ibid., p. 69.

have ready access to free clinical treatment of venereal disease and can obtain abortion on demand. Perhaps the most astonishing thing about the Swedish approach to human sexuality is the extent to which it can be discussed openly as a public policy issue. The farcical treatment of Jimmy Carter's interview with *Playboy* during the 1976 election, in which he declared that he had lusted after women in his heart, suggests the distance that separates the United States from Sweden in this regard.

358

CULTURAL
VARIATIONS IN
SEXUAL
ATTITUDES
AND BEHAVIOR

Sexual attitudes in Sweden are not anxiously focused on the incidence of certain behaviors such as the trends in premarital or extramarital intercourse. They are couched in a more embracing concern for equality between the sexes. Much of Swedish policy on sexual matters has been adopted explicitly to reduce sexual inequality. In sexual matters, the most obvious inequality is the double standard, which allows men to sow their wild oats, while women are expected to remain sexually ignorant. The traditional ethic of the established church tries to reduce the inequality by supporting abstinence outside of marriage. The Swedish people, especially the younger Swedes, attempt to reduce the inequality between the sexes by permitting both men and women to responsibly and freely express their sexuality.

Obviously this means that women must not be especially penalized should they become pregnant, either before or after marriage. Contraceptive clinics, sex education classes, abortion clinics, childcare centers, and various other forms of government assistance aim at reducing the adverse effects of pregnancy, which are normally borne by women. Official government policy, while protecting the rights of women, also aims at guaranteeing equal opportunity to every child born in Sweden, regardless of the circumstances of its birth. Every child should be wanted, but every child should have equal rights in a free society. In addition to its concern about reproductive sexuality, more and more recognition is officially given to nonreproductive sexuality as an expression of intimacy. Thus, in most instances, prisoners are permitted to engage in sexual relationships with their spouses or lovers while remaining in prison or while being released on special privileges.

The major change in sexual behavior in today's Sweden seems to be in the area of premarital intercourse. More and more young people are experiencing it, particularly in the case of the college-educated population. Studies of students in various schools in the 1960s reveal significant increases in the percentage of unmarried men and women who have experienced intercourse. The percentage of a sample of male students from four Peoples Colleges who had experienced premarital intercourse increased from 72 percent in 1960 to 81 percent in 1965, and the percentage of women who had sexual experience before marriage increased from 40 to 65 percent. The average age at first intercourse for men declined over these years from 18 to 17 and, comparably for women, from 18 to 17.6.[52] Unfortunately, Sweden has no study as broad in scope as the Kinsey studies and little is known of the behavior of the rest of the population. However, a 1953 study of Danish women, twenty to thirty-five, found that the average age of the 88 percent who had experienced intercourse was 19.1 years and that only 1.4 percent were married at the time. Twenty-four percent were formally engaged when they experienced their first intercourse, 44.7 were dating their partner steadily, and 1.8 copulated with a casual acquaintance.[53]

One difference in attitude between Swedish and American women in regard to sexual intercourse is that American women are much more likely to flirt and pet, but less willing to "go all the way," while Swedish women seem more reluctant to flirt if they do not desire intercourse. If this is a true characterization, it would seem to reflect the differences in the social consequences of premarital sex in both societies. Studies indicate that Swedish couples are likely to cultivate their sexual relationships in the context of increasing intimacy and are not as likely to be forced into marriage by pregnancy as American couples. Nevertheless, in about 30 to 35 percent of all marriages, children are born either before the wedding or during the first seven months.

Sentiment against extramarital intercourse seems stronger in Sweden than in the United States. Fully 90 percent of a 1947 public opinion poll affirmed that marital fidelity was absolutely necessary for a happy marriage. In a 1952 poll, 94 percent believed that "fidelity was among the most important values in a marriage." There is no reason to believe that the behavior should be more frequent there than in other Western countries. It may well be less.

Masturbation is very common among Swedish adolescents, though somewhat lower rates are to be found among women than among men. About half of the males in a 1954 sample continued to masturbate into adulthood, and about 33 percent of the young women continued to masturbate after they had experienced intercourse.[54]

Prostitution is virtually unknown in Sweden, and sexual crimes constitute less than 17 percent of all crimes. On the other hand, the most dismal aspect of the greater permissiveness in Sweden is the increasing rates of venereal disease. Gonorrhea, in particular, is showing alarming rates of increase since 1960. In 1965, 23,928 cases of gon-

359

CULTURAL
VARIATIONS IN
SEXUAL
ATTITUDES
AND BEHAVIOR

[52]Ibid., p. 19.

[53]Ibid., p. 21.

[54]Ibid., p. 25.

orrhea and 476 cases of syphilis were registered—the highest annual incidence since the current legislation went into effect in 1919.[55] In spite of the open attitude toward sexuality among the young, and in spite of all government efforts to control the spread of veneral disease to date it remains a sad fact that little has been effectively done to curb the spread of these health hazards. Permissiveness has its costs as well as its benefits.

360

CULTURAL
VARIATIONS IN
SEXUAL
ATTITUDES
AND BEHAVIOR

SEX IN MANGAIA

Lovemaking in Mangaia, a small island in the Cook Islands that is some 650 miles southwest of Tahiti in the very center of Polynesia, is markedly different from that in Inis Baeg and Sweden.[56] Although the natives have been exposed to the Christian religion since 1822, their pre-Christian culture retains a considerable degree of its integrity. The Mangaians have an earthy sense of humor and an elaborate vocabulary of sexual terms. They generally enjoy talking about their sex life, and much of it is lived out on a relatively narrow strip of land, shore, and sea that is readily observable.

While the small conjugal family has increased in importance since the advent of Christianity, the Mangaian, like most Polynesians, lives surrounded by a large extended family. The birth of a child is a welcomed event signaling the continued existence of the family. The birth of a child also strengthens the sexual relations between its parents.

Mangaian couples copulate regularly until the onset of labor pains. Some men prefer intercourse during pregnancy, believing that the woman then has wetter, softer, fatter, and larger genitals. Folk custom contends that copulation during pregnancy eases the path of the child at the time of delivery. Lovemaking is resumed a few days after delivery in some cases, though the common preference is to wait a number of months.

Public displays of affection between lovers and kin are discouraged, even though their private relationships may be intense. In spite of the fact that sexual activities regularly take place in often crowded, one-room houses where all can see, it is impolite to discuss sex within the family. However, much information can be obtained outside of the house.

Both boys and girls masturbate from an early age. Adults often manipulate the genitals of young children when caressing them. Parents may attempt to stop children from masturbating, but usually do not severely punish them for it. Early entry into sexual relationships with

[55]Ibid., p. 86.

[56]See Donald S. Marshall, "Sexual Behavior on Mangaia," in *Human Sexual Behavior,* Marshall and Suggs, eds., pp. 103–69. © 1971 by The Institute for Sex Research, Inc., Basic Books, Inc., Publishers, New York.

the opposite sex usually diverts sexual interest elsewhere. When adults are deprived of sexual partners for any extended period of time, they typically resort to masturbation.

Most girls begin their sexual adventures once their menses have begun. Most boys begin their sexual adventures at about the age of thirteen or fourteen, following the ritual act of superincision (ritual scarring of the penis), which initiates them into adulthood. The superincision of the boy is encouraged for aesthetic reasons (an uncircumcized organ is a "stinking penis," but a circumsized one—provided that the operation is performed properly—is a beautiful organ). The experts in charge of this ceremonial operation also instruct the boy in the ways of women and in the art of lovemaking. The boy learns how to locate a "good girl," how to perform cunnilingus, how to suck the breasts, engage in coitus, achieve mutual orgasm, how to bring the woman to several climaxes before he achieves orgasm, and much else. After this period of formal instruction, an older woman of the village initiates the young man into the pleasures of intercourse and ritually removes the scar of his operation during the act. The father acknowledges the help given to his son by killing a pig and presenting the appropriate parts to the appropriate experts. The feast is a signal for the boy to be called a man.

Mangaians do not date. They make use of a go-between to inform the chosen person of their desire to copulate. Folk custom asserts that having intercourse with many women in succession will prevent pregnancy. Pregnancy, it is believed, results from perseverance in a monogamous relationship. Nevertheless, about 13 percent of all births on the island in the past 100 years were out of wedlock, and most marriages are contracted after the woman is pregnant. Children born to unwed mothers are considered part of the mother's family. All children born to a married woman are considered to be her husband's, unless he protests.

Mangaian males admit to being stimulated by music, the nude body of the female, and from observing certain big-hipped women who are able to rotate their hips vigorously in the dance (and presumably in intercourse as well). Female passiveness definitely dampens male arousal. "Personal affection may or may not result from sets of sexual intimacy, but the latter are requisite to the former—exactly the reverse of the ideals of Western society."[57] The female tests the desire and virility of the male very early in the relationship. A common test is to require the lover to have successful intercourse without making contact with any part of the body other than the genitals.

One woman went several days without washing her genitals, then required her lover to perform cunnilingus before admitting him to

361

CULTURAL
VARIATIONS IN
SEXUAL
ATTITUDES
AND BEHAVIOR

[57]Ibid., p. 119.

the more intimate pleasures of intercourse. Clearly the focus of Mangaian lovemaking is on "going in and out." While there is considerable loveplay, this usually occurs after the first coital episode in preparation for the next. The brief episode of foreplay before the first coital episode is, however, usually adequate to bring the woman to sufficient heights of arousal so that she can achieve orgasm. The ideal male pattern is to defer orgasm for two or three episodes.

Mangaians believe that the really important aspect of sexual intercourse for the male is to give pleasure to his partner. Next to his own orgasm, the male accounts his pleasure in observing his partner's orgasm to be the greatest. Indeed, a woman will test her lover to see if he is still in love with her after they have had an argument by his ability to give her an orgasm. A young male assumes that he will have coitus every night of the week in his youth. When he reaches thirty or forty, however, he may begin to miss a night. He judges his potency by his ability to get the same woman pregnant twice in the same year. While certain physical characteristics of women—light skin, big hips, and so on—are something to talk about, they are not as important as having a sexual partner. No one is deprived of a sexual partner in this society.

It is common for adolescents to copulate with older people who are more experienced. Young men also visit old men to learn about their sexual adventures and techniques. It is said among the Polynesian peoples that the name of an island "travels on a man's penis." The sexual adventures of virile young men are thus much encouraged. European erotica has been introduced into the island through these adventures, but very little use is made of various artificial devices in Mangaian lovemaking.

With all of the sexual adventuring and explicit sex education, public propriety must be observed. A young man may sleep with a girl for several years and give her several children, but if he is not married to her or regularly mated with the approval of the family, he must leave her home before dawn so as not to offend the dignity of the community. Matters are complicated somewhat by the official courtship ritual of *motoro,* or "sleep crawling." It is considered best form for a young man to court the woman he intends to marry by going into her house and making love to her while her family sleeps. Mangaians believe that girls will not call out to their fathers if the lover sweet-talks her and achieves penetration, but that a girl will call out if he tries force. Overly vigilant parents will destroy their daughter's chances for marriage, and so, if awakened, they commonly listen for sounds of enjoyment signifying that the couple is potentially a good match.

Marriage in Mangaia is still arranged by some high-status families in order to maintain the high standing of the family or to increase its

362

CULTURAL
VARIATIONS IN
SEXUAL
ATTITUDES
AND BEHAVIOR

wealth. In most cases, however, the choice of the young person is considered important. Marriage takes place after considerable sexual experience has been obtained, and a young man knows that a certain female will suit him. Many factors enter into the choice of a mate—a pretty face or beautiful skin, wealth, cooking ability, good family, intelligence. The element most often triggering marriage, however, is the conception of a child. Kinsmen commonly have some word in the choice of a mate, and this complicates the arrangement, since many factors must be balanced in the consideration of a good match.

363

CULTURAL
VARIATIONS IN
SEXUAL
ATTITUDES
AND BEHAVIOR

Marriage marks the termination of a major stage in a man's life—his youth or "his time," when he was strongest in work and strongest in chasing women. Folk custom has it that marriage gives a man the right to have intercourse any time he pleases, and a male's rating of his sexual ability shifts from the number of times he can bring his partner to orgasm to the number of nights he can have intercourse with her. Keeping her pregnant is another test. Since men want to copulate more than women, it is necessary for them to pursue their wives until they give in—even if this involves beating her. It is commonly believed that husbands and wives come together only to copulate. There is no public display of affection, little small talk at the table, and no culturally patterned time for husband and wife to simply sit together to talk. Marital quarrels are common and often result in one partner, usually the wife, spitting on herself as a way of getting rid of her anger.
Marriage remains much more of an effective economic arrangement than a means of personal fulfillment.

Sexual jealousy, however, is commonly felt on the island. Men who travel will ask their family to keep an eye on their wives who remain behind, and the wives will write ahead telling any kin they might have on the island their husband is visiting to do the same.

Extramarital sexual relationships are common, though disapproved of. There are ways of publicly making amends with an offended husband; one method is sitting on his porch until asked to come in and eat. This may take all day, during which time the offended man does not notice the suppliant figures on his porch. In spite of church teaching against premarital intercourse, the traditional ways are coming back. Local pastors interfere very little with the youthful beer schools, where young people drink and learn about sex. However, there is still a nine o'clock curfew, at which time all unmarried people are supposed to be off the streets.

Mangaian women reach menopause at about age forty-five. In contrast to their periods of pregnancy, when they are culturally inclined toward being bad-tempered, menopause usually passes unobtrusively. A woman becomes "like a man"—unable to bear children. Some Mangaians feel that a husband and wife get closer to each other after they are fifty. Old age gradually sneaks up on the Polynesian. Death is a traumatic event for the surviving mate. The survivor may live with the partner's family if that were the case before death, unless he or she becomes a problem and is sent home to his or her own family. Widowers remarry more readily than widows.

Mangaian culture places a very high value on sexual experience and pleasure. Though much of this favors the male, no adult is deprived of a sexual partner. It is probable that Mangaian men copulate more frequently and more vigorously than the average European. However, they are also probably more likely to experience impotence and sterility in their later years. Even though Mangaia is a very permissive society, there is no evidence that homosexuality exists amongst the 2,000 Mangaians. However, there are few men who prefer to dress like women and assume their sex role. All Mangaian women seem able to achieve orgasm. This appears to be learned in the process of lovemaking. The Mangaian male's interest in pleasing his partner and the cultural expectation that she be active in the pursuit of such sexual pleasure no doubt helps account for her success. The fact that orgasm is universally achieved in one society suggests that it can be so achieved in other societies if the proper learning conditions are established.

364

CULTURAL
VARIATIONS IN
SEXUAL
ATTITUDES
AND BEHAVIOR

Summary

From a cross-cultural perspective, the United States is most conspicuous to the extent that we retain our general taboo against sex. We are also in the minority of societies that place as much importance on confining sexual intercourse to the institution of marriage. While most societies prohibit the conception of a child outside of marriage, most also permit sexual intercourse to occur outside of it, though normally only with those people whom culture defines as potential mates. Premarital intercourse is much more widely accepted than extramarital intercourse. The concern in the latter seems to be mostly with the preservation of the family and its patterns of inheritance that would be disrupted by a child born outside, rather than by any disdain for sexuality itself.

While human lovemaking undoubtedly assumes a virtually limitless variety in its expression, certain preferences suggest patterns of behavior. Heterosexual intercourse is preferred, although homosexual contact and masturbation are widely permitted. While eye contact usually initiates sexual adventures, odors play a much more central role in other cultures. The most common time for making love around the world is in the evening, before going to bed. The most common preference is for privacy in such matters, although public sexual encounters have ceremonial significance in many cultures. There is general agreement that the male is the more sexed of the sexes, but Mead established early in this century that this is a cultural preference, not a dictation of "nature." Her studies of the Mundugamor, Tchambuli, Arapesh and Samoans demonstrate that either sex may be the "most sexed" in a particular culture and that some cultures make no apparent distinction. Since orgasmic response is almost universally equated with ejaculation in the male, there is no society in which males do not commonly experience orgasm. There are some cultures in which women are not trained in orgasmic response and some, like our own, in which they have some difficulty in achieving it because of past cultural proscriptions against it. Among the Mangaian, apparently all women achieve orgasm. The nature of orgasm is not fully understood in either sex.

365

CULTURAL
VARIATIONS IN
SEXUAL
ATTITUDES
AND BEHAVIOR

The more detailed studies of Ines Beag, Sweden, and Mangaia indicate the extent to which legislation and ecclesiastical practice can curb or express sexuality among a particular population. The Irish example seems almost to define the limits of repression under a rarefied Christian asceticism, while the case of Sweden is much less clear in its implications. The goal of Swedish policy seems admirable, the reality of Swedish life a bit less so. Clearly Sweden is not a nation of promiscuous people, but is rather a people trying to encourage the expression of sexual love in the context of intimate relationships with the proper precaution against the conception of unwanted children. We have much to learn about how Swedish practice follows policy. The Church has had its impact in Mangaia as well, but here the native culture seems more resistant and the native clergy more accepting of common sexual customs. Mangaia remains one of the more sexually permissive societies known to anthropologists.

Patterns of Commitment

14

Can't you go to bed with a woman
without loving her, and can't you
love her without going
to bed with her?

M. deSade

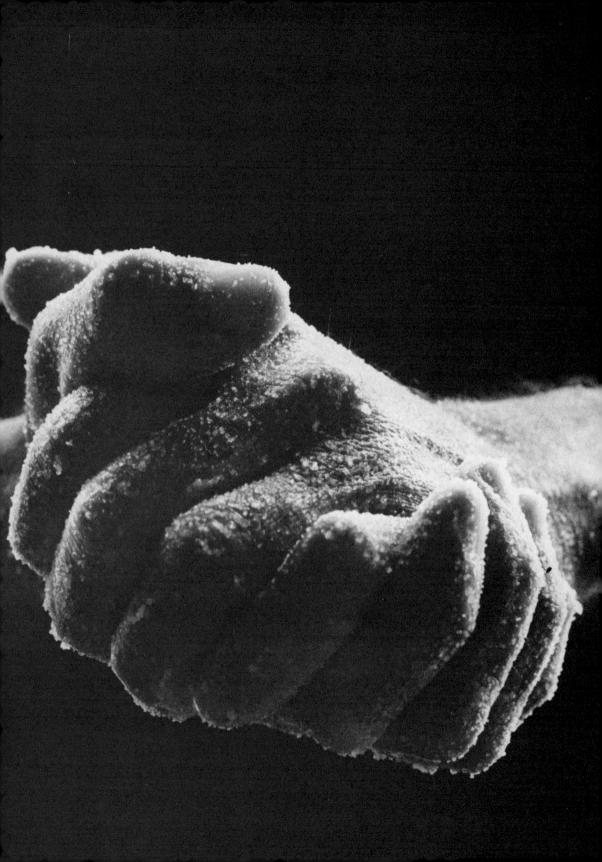

Human sexual behavior commonly involves a commitment to another person. This commitment may be a shared understanding that sex without commitment is best. It may be elaborated into a sexual life style called "swinging" or be confined to a single one-night stand. The commitment may be negotiated between two or more people. It may be socially recognized as in the case of marriage, or it may reflect a very personal set of values. The common element is a shared understanding of what is expected.

Obviously, sexual behavior does not need to be bound by commitment as we have defined it. It can occur alone or with others and not be shared. Sex without commitment is not necessarily bad, nor less pleasurable. It is simply another way in which sexual activity can be experienced. It has its costs as well as its benefits.

Some common patterns of commitment will not be approved of by some readers. This is an important consideration. Those people who find pleasure in unusual commitments will have a more difficult time finding role models to guide their development, and greater difficulty finding help if they need it. They may also experience a more invigorating sex life because the breaking of convention in and of itself may add zest to their sexual experience. Similarly, those who prefer the more conventional commitments may find that they must struggle to maintain a high level of pleasure and satisfaction because their sex lives become too routine and repetitious. They may decide that sex is not all that important after all and may permit their sex life to become inactive.

By looking at some of the commitments that have been stabilized enough over time so that they can be called a life style, we do not mean to imply that people with a describable sexual life style always honor their commitments, or even that they retain a single commitment throughout most of their lives. Indeed, part of the game of sex is the effort to discover if another person, whom you find sexually exciting, is on the level with you about what is at stake, or simply giving you a line. Being clear about the character of the commitment, whatever it is, is a very important aspect of human sexual behavior.

We begin by describing some of the established patterns of commitment—both marital and nonmarital—that can be observed in our society. Marriage is a social institution, but there are distinctive class, ethnic, and regional variations in the way actual marriages are made and carried on. The same is true for established nonmarital patterns such as love affairs or cheating on one's spouse. While we do not know everything that there is to know about these patterns of commitment, they have been around long enough for people who engage in them to know in general what to expect. They know how to behave even if they have not had prior personal experience, because there is precedent in our tradition and role models to whom they can readily turn if they want to do so. We know less about the more unconventional patterns of commitment or sexual life styles. These unconventional sexual life styles or patterns of commitment are part of a vast experiment in alternative life styles. They have not been around long enough for us to feel that we know what to expect if we decide to try one out. There are not many consistent role models and little professional understanding of how to help if anything should go wrong with the partnership.

Marriage as a Social Institution

Marriage is the pattern of commitment that most affects the expression of human sexuality in the United States. The vast majority of people in our society want to get married, and it is fair to say that a considerable portion of their early sexual experience is thought of as sowing their wild oats before they find the right person, settle down, get married, and raise a family. Most sexual behavior before marriage probably occurs between two people who, at the time, were at least thinking about marrying each other.

One study concluded that the major effect of the sexual revolution is found in the greater frequency and variety of sexual behavior within marriage.[1] Having said this, we must also go on to say that the character of marriage is changing. Where it was once a sacrament that could not be broken, it is now a personal commitment that people feel should be broken when it ceases to be personally satisfying. Once married people felt obligated to have children, but there is not as much pressure to do so today. While once it was not permissible to engage in sexual intercourse with someone other than your spouse, it is becoming more common to do so, often with the spouse's knowledge and consent. We do not know how many monogamous marriages are sexually exclusive because sex outside of marriage isn't something people are likely to talk to census takers about.

[1]Morton Hunt: *Sex in the Seventies* (New York: Dell, 1974).

We can begin to establish some rough idea of the different kinds of marital commitments that are to be found in the United States by looking at the variety of family types that can be found in the 1970 census data.[2]

Adults heading single parent families	16%
Other single, widowed, separated, or divorced adults	21
Adults living in childless or post-child rearing marriages	23
Adults living in extended families	6
Adults living in "experimental" families	4
Adults living in dual-breadwinner families with children	16
Adults living in single-breadwinner conjugal families	13
Adults living in no-wage-earner nuclear families	1
	100%

When Americans think of marriage and the family, they commonly think of the *conjugal* family—the small unit composed of a husband, wife, and their children, who live apart from other relatives and have a single breadwinner. In fact, this ideal conjugal family is not at all common: Only 13 percent of all adults live in conjugal families. Yet we have taken it for granted that such a family structure should regulate the proper expression of sexual desire throughout most of our adult life.

Some people have pointed out that many of the alternatives are not particularly dramatic departures from this norm. The shift to a dual-breadwinner family, for example, should not have significant impact on the sexual life of family members. But women in such families have greater economic as well as sexual independence and, of necessity, spend less time regulating the lives of their children than women who don't work. So also, the fact that 23 percent of all adults live in childless families may not seem to be a radical departure from the traditional form, but the fact remains that for most of these people sexuality has lost (or never attained) its connection with reproduction. Sex must become something else for these people. The nearly one-third of the adult population who head single parent families or who live alone probably have the greatest freedom to express their sexual preferences of any group, except possibly for some of those living in experimental alternatives. This experimental group, however, is made up of such a variety of sexual life styles that it is impossible to cover them under a single heading. Among the experimenters are those who live communally, but who retain exclusive sexual relationships with their spouses; and those who practice free love as a sexual sharing, either in some form of group marriage or simply as a con-

[2]James Ramey, "Alternative Life Styles," *Society* (July/August, 1977), pp. 43–47.

Figure 14–1
The conjugal family, whether large or small, is the traditional and expected pattern of commitment in most Western societies. (Top, © Joan Liftin, Woodfin Camp & Associates; bottom, © 1973 Linda Ferrer Rogers, Woodfin Camp & Associates)

sequence of not wanting to control the sexual behavior of the group any more than is absolutely necessary. There are those who practice abstinence from intercourse as a part of their experiment.

For good or ill there are—and always have been—many ways of contracting a marriage in the United States. Some of them represent quite dramatic departures from the traditional norm. Others are less dramatic, but in the long run may lead to even more powerful transformations of marriage. The dual career family or the various modifications of conjugal roles to permit greater equality between the

Figure 14–2
The top graph illustrates first-marriage and remarriage rates from 1920 to 1980; the bottom illustrates the divorce rate for the same period. (From "Marital Instability: Past, Present, and Future," by Arthur J. Norton and Paul C. Glick, in Divorce and Separation: Conditions, Causes, and Consequences, *eds. George Levinger and Oliver Moles, © 1979 by Basic Books, Inc., Publishers, New York.)*

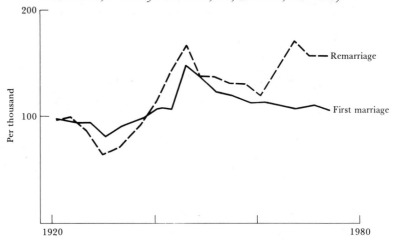

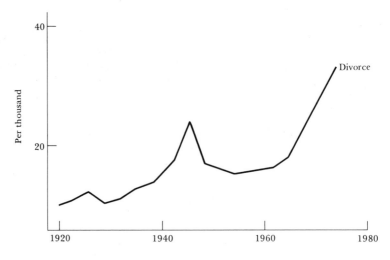

Figure 14–3
A divorce clinic is one method that can be used to help us deal with the changing patterns of commitment. (Wayne Miller, © Magnum Photos, Inc.)

spouses are cases in point. The tendency seems to be toward even greater variety within as well as outside of marriage.

Another perspective on what is happening can be obtained by looking at a few statistical trends. The most notable of these are displayed in Figure 14–2. Fewer people are getting married for the first time. Indeed, the first-marriage rate is approaching an all-time low. This fact has been somewhat disguised by the second trend, which, until recently, was approaching an all-time high—namely, the remarriage rate. It, however, is off slightly in the 1970s. Finally, the divorce rate is at an all-time high. Such statistics tell us little about the quality of marital life, but the strong inference must be that, whatever its quality, marriage is changing its character. Regardless of the partners' expectations when they married, marriage is becoming less of a lifetime commitment. Serial monogamy—more than one spouse but only one at a time—is not likely to be carried beyond the second partner. This has led to an increase in the number of people who are likely to have two marriages. A smaller but growing number of people will intentionally choose not to marry at all. To marry or not, to stay married or not, are much more a matter of personal choice today than ever before in our history. At least so the statistics—and some supportive studies—suggest.

Other trends are worth noting. Working mothers are becoming increasingly common. In 1948, 26 percent of all mothers with dependent children (between the ages of six and seventeen) were working. By 1974, that figure had risen to 51 percent. More than 60 percent of all married women work. The most dramatic increase has been among those mothers with preschool children. In 1948, one out of every nine such mothers worked; by 1974 one out of every three was working. Finally, two-thirds of all working mothers had full-time jobs in 1974.[3]

These trends suggest that the intimate environment within which our sexuality is expressed is rapidly changing. The individual, not the family, may now be the basic unit of society.[4] Personal happiness is thus becoming an increasingly important consideration in whatever life style is chosen, and good sex is often closely associated with personal happiness.

Feeling free to put oneself first has been psychologically beneficial for many people. But some observers point out that the emphasis on the individual can be costly for the society. In Urie Bronfenbrenner's view, for example, we have focused so much on a search for personal satisfaction that we are about to sacrifice family obligations completely. "Today what matters most for many people is their own growth and happiness, their own self-fulfillment, doing their own thing, finding themselves. We seem to be sunk in individualism. We so much want to make it for ourselves that we have almost stopped being a society that cares for others. We seem to be hesitant about making a commitment to anyone or anything, including our own flesh and blood.[5]

In addition to these individualistic attitudes, Bronfenbrenner feels

[3]Heather Ross and Isabel V. Sawhill, "The Family as an Economic Unit," *The Wilson Quarterly* (Winter, 1977), p. 87.

[4]Ramey, "Alternative Life Styles," p. 47.

[5]Urie Bronfenbrenner, "Family Breakup," *The Washington Post* (Jan. 2, 1977) p. C 2.

Figure 14–4
(© Arthur Tress,
Magnum Photos, Inc.)

that the structure of our society tends to further separate and fragment us. In our work schemes, social dances, travel patterns, and through the use of telephones and other technical apparatus we place rules, routines, and hardware above face-to-face interaction. As a result, we know each other more in terms of the social roles we are called upon to play than in the terms of the people we are.

The work world, especially that created by the corporations and government bureaucracy, tends to depersonalize interaction. Some of this depersonalization (contracts instead of personal agreements, money instead of bartered exchange) seems essential to the operation of an industrialized society, and a radical change in these seems counterproductive. Other types of depersonalization however, are more subtle and more pernicious. For example, many people, particularly those in the professions, may be said to derive intrinsic satisfaction out of their work, but that work often requires them to use their emotions and feelings in order to sell themselves or a product rather than to indicate how they really feel. It is taken for granted that people should have their professional emotions under control, but this need for control on the job often trains people to be insensitive at home as well. The conjugal family is expected to fulfill the very specialized roles of emotional support and interpersonal nurturance. But the working members of this family are less able to meet these needs because they spend most of their time behaving in an impersonal way. They find it difficult to shift gears when they are at home.

In such circumstances, people sometimes turn to sexual pleasures in an attempt to recover the sense of an intimate world in which their feelings count. But most people are not able to use sex as a means of getting in touch with either themselves or another person. Sex is experienced predominately as a tension release.[6] For many, even this pleasurable sense of release is clouded over with a deep sense of guilt. This is particularly true of masturbation, but it also applies to other sexual situations.[7] Many people have experienced a great deal of sexual behavior, but find it unsatisfying. This is exactly the reverse of the typical problem faced by Freud.[8] Clearly, there is nothing wrong with experiencing sex as a tension release, but if you expect such an experience to resolve your interpersonal problems, you are likely to be disappointed.

This particular pattern of sex and commitment is more common in the upper classes. In order to see this more clearly, we turn now to a

[6]William H. Masters and Virginia Johnson, *Human Sexual Inadequacy* (Boston: Little, Brown & Co., 1974).

[7]Sherie Hite, *The Hite Report* (New York: Macmillan Publishing Co., 1977).

[8]Rollo May, *Love and Will* (New York: W. W. Norton & Company, Inc. Copyright © 1969 by W. W. Norton & Company, Inc.).

consideration of some of the ways in which patterns of commitment and sexual behavior vary by class.

Class and Commitment

A social class is a large group of people who share a similar way of life because they have similar economic opportunities. Money is a very important thing to have in our society, not only because of what you can buy with it to make you comfortable, but also because we have a strong tendency to think that people's importance depends on how much money they have. What people do to earn their money is also very important from a sociological point of view because the work experience establishes certain persistent patterns of behavior and reinforces certain beliefs about the world. It makes a difference if the two people in a particular situation are rich or poor. Their understanding of what they are doing, their preference for some techniques over others, their expectations of pleasure, and their attempt to relate sex to other aspects of their lives will all be affected by their social class.

UPPER-MIDDLE-CLASS PATTERNS

The upper classes establish the preferred patterns of behavior for the entire society, and they do so out of the context of a tradition largely shaped by people of similar economic background. As a result, not only has the social institution of marriage enjoyed a dominant role in the regulation of sexual behavior, but marriage has been thought of in terms of a very limited ideal type.

Our view of marital commitment has been strongly shaped by the history of upper-middle-class marriages. The Victorian husband was expected to fulfill his parental obligations by siring children, but he expected his sexual pleasures to come from elsewhere—most commonly from prostitutes or mistresses. The mistress has enjoyed very high status in Western civilization. *Hetarae* or courtesans strongly shaped the culture of classical Athens. The romantic's true love was expressed as a peculiarly spiritual panting after his beloved mistress (normally someone else's wife) without the expectation that his passion would be consummated. Passionate intercourse has simply not been a commonly expected part of Western marriage, except possibly during the honeymoon.[9]

Therefore, we should not be surprised when we learn that the most intensive in-depth study of man-woman relationships among professionals—Cuber and Harroff's, *The Signigicant Americans*—found that

[9]Denis de Roguemont, *Love in the Western World* (New York: Harper & Row, Publishers, Inc., 1974).

about 80 percent of the sample felt that sex was not an important part of marriage.[10] It is as though the sexual revolution has passed these people by.

Cuber and Harroff found that most of these relationships were in fact utilitarian marriages or marriages of convenience. Cuber and Harroff broke these relationships down into three main types. The *conflict-habituated relationship* is characterized by much controlled tension and conflict. It seems strange to realize that the management of this conflict can in itself be a basis for commitment in a marriage. Such relationships may last for a lifetime, even though it is unlikely that the partners would say that they have a satisfactory relationship. The *devitalized relationship* is perceptibly devoid of zest. Although no serious tension or conflict may exist and some aspects of the marriage may be satisfying, the interplay between the partners is apathetic and lifeless. It will continue partly out of habit and partly out of the recognition that "something" is there. The *passive-congenial relationship* is often characterized by the partners as satisfying or even very satisfying. But the most distinguishing feature of this type of marriage is the recognition that the relationship is comfortably adequate. "We both like classical music." "We agree completely on religion and politics." "We both love the country and our quaint ex-urban neighbors." "We are both lawyers." These, common interests, rather than emotional commitment or physical passion, serve as the focus for this type of marriage.

About 20 percent of the significant Americans were classified as having *intrinsic relationships.* For these people, the relationship itself was most important, not the convenience it provided. Cuber and Harroff described two types of intrinsic relationships. The *vital relationship* made up about 15 percent of the sample. In these relationships, there is a "vibrant exciting sharing of some important life experience—sex comes immediately to the mind, but the vitality need not surround the sexual focus or any aspect of it. . . . The clue that their relationship is vital and significant derives from the feelings of importance about it and that the importance is shared."[11] *Total relationships* accounted for about 5 percent of the sample. These were like the vital relationship in that the relationship itself was intrinsically satisfying, but differed from it in that a wider spectrum of experiences was shared and the marriage was sexually exclusive. Many of the vital relationships were nonmarital.

There are very few good man-woman relationships at these ages (35–55) in this class (upper-middle class). We mean by good . . . deeply satisfying

---

[10]John F. Cuber and Peggy B. Harroff, *Sex and the Significant Americans.* Copyright © 1968 by John F. Cuber and Peggy B. Harroff. All rights reserved. By permission of Hawthorne Books, Inc.

[11]Ibid., p. 99.

man-woman relationships as appraised by the people themselves. . . . Further, of the good relationships that do exist, there is a surprisingly high incidence of them outside of marriage . . . either as enduring, relatively total associations among the unmarried, or as is more often the case, extramarital in the sense that one or both in the pair are married to someone else.[12]

This assessment must be disturbing to young people hoping to find personal fulfillment in a life-long commitment to marriage. In fact, young people from upper-middle-class families formed the dominant element in the counterculture of the 60s and 70s. Confronted with the largely utilitarian marriages of their parents and desperately in need of love and intimacy, these young people sought to redefine marriage so that sexual fulfillment had a more prominent place and the structure of marriage was more flexible. Because parental careers may be blamed for the lack of vitality in their parents' marriage, children may place lower values on success, status seeking, and career opportunities. In any case, it is clear that the ideal of an intrinsically satisfying lifelong relationship was rarely realized among the significant Americans.

It is also clear that extramarital sexual encounters were common. The meaning of these outside relationships, however, differs depending on the type. In the conflict-habituated relationship, they are definitely seen as infidelity and seem to be little more than another outlet for hostility. Among people in passive-congenial marriages, these outside relationships are typically in line with the stereotype of the middle-aged man who "strayed out of sheer boredom with the uneventful deadly prose" of his private life. People whose marriages have become devitalized are typically trying to recapture a lost mood. But even the vital relationships have their share of outside relationships. Some are simply "emancipated—almost bohemian." To some, sexual freedom is an accepted fact of life. "Frequently the infidelity is condoned by the partner and in some instances even provided an indirect (through empathy) kind of gratification. The act of infidelity in such cases is not construed as disloyality, nor is it a threat to continuity of the relationship. . . . It is simply a basic 'human right' which the loved one ought to be permitted to have—and which the other perhaps also wants for himself or herself."[13]

The 15 percent who lived out a vital relationship were clearly a mixed group. All undoubtedly found sexual pleasure to be an important part of life, but they were mixed on whether or not it should be linked to some sort of commitment outside of marriage. Some went so far as to redefine commitment itself so that it made sense to speak of

[12]Ibid., p. 100–2.

[13]Ibid., p. 102.

commitment both inside and outside of marriage. Some placed the emphasis on sexual pleasure both inside and outside of marriage as a matter of right to both partners. The few people involved in the total marriage represent those for whom both sexual pleasure and commitment were very important, but only within marriage.

LOWER-CLASS PATTERNS

Now let us look at the patterns of commitment that are observable in the underclass of black America.[14] Only about 15 percent of all black Americans are in this class. The life styles of those blacks are based on conditions of deprivation and exclusion from the mainstream of American life. Therefore, these styles are less a matter of personal choice than those of the affluent. They may be quite functional. For example, because it is difficult to keep a job and earn a dependable income, it is difficult to stay married. Nevertheless, about two-thirds of poor black families are intact. Marriage is remarkably durable even under such conditions. What has happened is that a number of alternative kinds of partnerships have developed. Most of these are acceptable in some degree among underclass blacks, but traditional marriage is still preferred.

Since the black male is more vulnerable in the marriage market (if we assume that he ought to be the major provider), we can develop some patterns of commitment by looking at how he relates to his wife, lovers, and children. His commitment can be measured by the extent to which he cares for a woman and her children. Caring means taking care of the children, providing income for the family, and disciplining and playing with the whole household instead of simply confining his attentions to the woman. A very crude typology can be set up like a continuum, with the traditional type of husband at one end and the pimp, who totally ignores traditional values, on the other. The interrelationships between love, sex, and commitment are given a slightly different emphasis in each case.

The *traditional monogamous father* is characterized as having a commitment to marriage. He does not believe in "cutting out" on his wife, although sexual pleasure may or may not be part of his expectations of marriage. He doesn't talk much about sex as a rule. His emphasis is on fidelity and on taking care of his family as best he can. He is a moral man, first and foremost.

> *. . . If your child can't say they seen you doing this or that you're bound to be holding a good program for them. I don't let my children see me do no*

---

[14]See Andrew Billingsley, *Black Families in White America* (Englewood Cliffs, N.J.: Prentice-Hall, Inc., 1968). The underclass is the lowest level of the black lower class in Billingsley's classification.

things wrong. Not one thing. I'm not playing (cutting out with other women). I ain't got none that can tell you that today. They ain't never seen daddy come in here drunk, cussing, clowning or nothing. They'll tell you that right now. Daddy is going to come in here as he leaves. . . . I ain't going to come in here drunk and beating my wife over my kids. Of course I don't jump on her and beat her no how.[15]

The traditional monogamous father has the most complete commitment to his wife and children of any male in this class, as measured by his fidelity to his wife and his support for his children. He seems to seek a total relationship with his spouse, but what he can share with her is severely constrained by poverty. The language they use to describe their relationship suggests more of a comfortable than a vital mode of adjustment.

But extramarital sexual encounters are very much a part of underclass life—just as they are a part of upper-middle-class life. It all depends on how they are handled. One type of man, the *discreet free man,* resembles the professional male in that he values such encounters as a basic right—although he is not inclined to grant the same privilege to his wife. He honors her, however, by being discreet about his outside relationships. He may be caring for two or more families at the same time, but his wife and children are clearly primary. In contrast, the *indiscreet free man* makes a point of playing up the other woman. Della Mae Patterson says this about her husband, Edward:

Well before we came to (the city) my husband and I were separated three times on the sake of fighting. He used to fight me all the time. He was in the city about nine months before I came. When I came up he was living with another woman at my uncle's house. . . . I have never walked out in front of him. But this lady he used to live with, he have had her right out in front of my door. . . . The first time he brought her down there I didn't say anything so I asked him not to do it again, because he seemed like he was boasting about it. And the next time he did it . . . I got a gun and started down the steps and he ran down there by the car. By the time I got down under the building he had done pulled off.[16]

Edward remarks, "You can't run in the house and what's on the outside of the house both at the same time. . . . I take whatever it is and go along with it as long as it's not hurting me."[17]

The involvement of these husbands in the affairs of other women and their children seem to make them more marginal to their wives

[15]David A. Schulz, *Coming Up Black: Patterns of Ghetto Socialization* (Englewood Cliffs, N.J.: Prentice-Hall, Inc., © 1969), pp. 113, 126.

[16]Ibid., p. 113.

[17]Ibid., p. 113.

than the traditional monogamous husband. The indiscreet husband is less committed to his wife because of his boasting about his outside affairs. Whether through lack of skill, split allegiance, or both, the indiscreet free man is torn between two worlds, while the discreet free man manages to live reasonably well in both. The outside adventuring of both, however, is clearly not simply sexual adventuring. Both types of men are concerned with more than simple pleasure outside of their marriages. They care for their other women and their children.

Indeed, the greater acceptance of sex as something natural among underclass people generally makes it less of an important issue. The tradition that sex is sinful has not affected the poor in the same way that it has affected working-and middle-class Americans. In this sense, the poor have greater freedom to create alternative life styles. But these life styles are fashioned on the horns of a dilemma. They are intentional adaptations to poverty and exclusion, but they sometimes make it more difficult for these people to get into the mainstream. They are likely to be acceptable life styles, but not preferred ones.

There are four nonmarital types of relationships that seem to be distinctive styles of the underclass. Because marriage is difficult under any circumstances and next to impossible when you are regularly unemployed, a goodly number of underclass men have "boyfriend" relationships with women by whom they may or may not have children. One type, the *quasi-father,* is a father in all but the legal sense of the word. His woman's children may or may not be his, but he cares for them, disciplines them, entertains them, and seeks companionship in the context of the family rather than simply in the context of a man-woman relationship. The *supportive biological father,* is a man who is concerned about the children he has brought into the world, but has long since lost interest in their mother. In contrast, the *supportive companion* is interested in his woman, but not in her children. He provides her with money, but only to buy dresses for herself or to fix herself up. They seek entertainment outside of her household, and weekends away from home are desirable whenever possible.

Finally, the *pimp* really cares for no one but himself. He uses a woman and lives off of her income. He provides her sexual pleasure in return. Just to show that he doesn't really care for her, he might take her money and spend it on another woman. While a man who lives off the earnings of prostitutes is commonly called a pimp, in the underclass neighborhood, pimp is also used to refer to any man who lives off a woman's income and uses her in the way a pimp might use a prostitute. Sexual exploitation with a minimal commitment outside of marriage is the pimp's ideal. The woman might be in love with him, or may tolerate being used simply because good men are hard to find.

The boyfriend relationships (except for the pimp) allow the woman to have a chance to test out a man before marrying him. At least this is a commonly mentioned motivation for entering into such relationships. In a poor neighborhood, this testing has a very high value. As one woman put it, "If he don't love your kids, he don't love you." By caring for a woman and her children, a boyfriend demonstrates what love means in a culture in which "love is an everyday word."

These patterns of commitment are persistent, although a man may change styles during his lifetime. It is not a simple matter to assume responsibility for another's welfare, especially when it is difficult to secure your own. A more certain source of income increases the likelihood that marriage will be contracted and maintained, but, as is the case of professional people, a steady job does not guarantee the style of the partnership that will result.

Sexual Behavior and Marital Satisfaction

Kinsey was not at all concerned with patterns of commitment, but he did make note of how sexual behavior varied by class. He once quipped, "Lower-class males copulate, upper-class males masturbate." Drawing on his two studies of sexual behavior, the following patterns emerge.[18] Among upper-class youth in the 1940s and 1950s, Kinsey discovered much less sexual intercourse, but a greater amount of petting. These young people tended to reserve intercourse for someone for whom they felt affection. Most people of the upper class tended to prolong the sexual play leading up to intercourse and to make use of a much wider array of techniques and positions. Oral-genital behavior was much more common at this social level. There was, Kinsey felt, a greater equality between the sexes. Women were more active sexually. Both sexes masturbated to a greater extent than people of the lower classes. There was also a lower incidence of homosexuality.

In contrast, people at the lower socioeconomic levels were more direct about sex. Males were much more likely to experience intercourse before marriage, and while fewer females participated, those who did, did so at a much higher frequency than upper-class females. There was a greater tendency to distinguish between "good" and "bad" girls in these classes. Males, did not tend to see sex as a part of an affectionate relationship. It was a part of their role as a man to experience sex. Sex was a male-oriented affair. Such men were more impatient with petting and were less likely to bring their partner to orgasm. Intercourse was much simpler, with less foreplay, less

[18]Alfred C. Kinsey et al., *Sexual Behavior in the Human Female* (Philadelphia: W. B. Saunders 1953).

elaboration of style and technique, and was shorter in duration. Masturbation was not as prevalent as in the upper classes, but homosexuality, especially among high school graduates with no college, was higher.

A number of studies have looked at sexual satisfaction in lower-class marriages. Mira Komarovsky found that 30 percent of her sample of working-class women were highly satisfied with their sexual adjustment in marriage; 40 percent were moderately satisfied, and 30 percent expressed serious dissatisfaction. Fifteen percent of these wives felt that it was the wife's duty to "give it to her husband whether she like it or not."[19] There was little detailed investigation of what was considered to be a satisfactory sexual adjustment in each case. But we can reasonably assume from the suggestion of the Cuber and Harroff study that many of these satisfactory sexual adjustments involved little actual sexual satisfaction. Working-class women typically expect less pleasure from their sexual relationships than upper-class women.

Lee Rainwater suggests that sexual satisfaction in marriage is related to the degree of role segregation in the marriage.[20] By this he means the extent to which husband and wife share their activities. It is more common in the lower classes for husbands and wives not to expect much sharing in marriage. Men do things with other men, while the women turn to other women for companionship. While social class still has some influence on sexual satisfaction in marriage, its effect is much reduced when role segregation is taken into account. Thus Rainwater found that the husband's assessment of his wife's enjoyment of their sexual relationship was consistent with hers all of the time in the upper-middle-class couples he studied, 79 percent of the time in the lower-middle-class couples who had an intermediate level of role segregation, and 49 percent of the time in the case of couples who had a highly segregated role relationship. He also found that women living in highly segregated role relationships were much more likely to reject sexual relationships with their husbands. Finally, the expression of enjoyment in sexual relationships was higher in less segregated role relationships.

Marital and sexual satisfaction are based on personal preferences as well as the class a person belongs to. For men, marital satisfaction seems to be based on the quality of their sex life. For women, however, the quality of their sex life depends more on how they feel about the marriage in general.[21] Religious conviction, which is normally measured by church attendance, can make sex less of an issue for

[19]Mirra Komarovsky, *Blue Collar Marriage* (New York: Random House, Inc., 1964), p. 85.

[20]Lee Rainwater, *Family Design* (Chicago: Aldine, 1963).

[21]Richard Udry, *The Social Context of Marriage*, 3rd ed. (Philadelphia: J. P. Lippincott, 1974), p. 321.

some women. Church-attending women are less likely to be negatively affected in their marital satisfaction by sexual dissatisfaction. Men are not similarly affected. These findings can be seen to support the traditional conception of what a marriage ought to be. They will probably be less appropriate guides in the future, as the social conditions affecting marriage continue to change and as the younger generation experiments with different marital contracts.

We know, of course, that marital satisfaction is affected by other considerations besides sexual satisfaction. There is evidence that couples find greater satisfaction in the pre- and post-childbearing stages of their marriage, which suggests that parenting (or the increased role strain introduced by extra people in the household) decreases marital satisfaction.

Income has a mixed effect. It increases the rewards in marriage, but can lead to increased tensions as well. While Rainwater and others have shown that higher status families have life styles that are more companionable and mutually responsive than lower status families, the tensions induced by the job create their own problems.[22] Therefore, both husband and wife may consider that they are satisfied in their marriage, while not being particularly active in or satisfied with their sex lives. We must remember that marital satisfaction means different things to different people and that researchers rarely determine what, specifically, the term means to a particular couple.

In some of these less conventional relationships, role models are more difficult to find and the social consequences are not yet well known. These relationships are social experiments for which we have no agreed-upon name. Here we find such words and phrases as "wife swapping," "swinging," "open marriage," "satellite relationships," and "triads." They are hailed on the one hand as manifestations of the "new intimacy" or "honest sex," and on the other denounced as "sexual suicide" or the "new narcissism." More neutrally they are often simply called, "alternative life styles." Robert Rimmer calls them "adventures in loving."[23]

[22]Ibid., p. 324

[23]Rimmer, *Adventures in Loving* (New York: New American Library, 1974). See also Larry and Joan Constantine, *Group Marriage* (New York: Macmillan Publishing Comany, Inc., 1973); Carl Rogers, *Becoming Partners: Marriage and Its Alternatives* (New York: Delacorte Press, 1973); Rosabeth Kanter, *Commitment and Community: Communes and Utopias in Sociological Perspective* (Cambridge: Harvard University Press, 1972); Kathleen Kincade, *A Walden Two Experiment: The First Five Years of Twin Oaks* (New York: William Morrow, 1972); Tom Hatfield, *Sandstone Experience* (New York: New American Library, 1975); Judson Jerome, *Families of Eden* (New York: Seabury Press, 1974); James Ramey, *Intimate Friendships* (Englewood Cliffs, N.J.: Prentice-Hall, Inc., 1976); Gordon Clanton and Chris Downing, *Face to Face to Face: An Experiment in Intimacy* (New York: Dutton, 1975); and Jerome R. Smith and Lynn G. Smith, *Beyond Monogamy: Recent Studies of Sexual Alienation in Marriage* (Baltimore: The Johns Hopkins University Press, 1974).

If permanence is a desirable element in such adventures—and sometimes it is not—then commitment needs to be redefined. Carl Rogers has suggested this way of redefining commitment.

We commit ourselves to working together on the changing process of our present relationship because that relationship is currently enriching our love and our life and we wish it to grow.[24]

The shift in emphasis from commitment to a marriage contract or to a set of roles (being a good husband or a good wife as conventionally understood) to commitment to a person or persons in the process of growth is an important one. But such a definition is not particularly helpful to people who are having grave difficulties with their partnerships. It assumes that the current relationship is an enriching one and that love is experienced now—not simply known about as an abstract ideal. For relationships to be growing, it is necessary to be open to the processes of growth and to be sensitive to other people. Rogers provides us with several helpful guidelines for maintaining growing relationships, but these rules cannot replace the basic commitment. They are nourished by it. Notice also that commitment and love are not commonly thought of as the same. Love is more a matter of emotion and feeling; commitment is more a matter of will. Given this understanding, it is possible that any of the following patterns could be adventures in loving, though none of them necessarily need be so evaluated.

A number of people, primarily from the upper-middle class, are involved in intimate friendships. Many of these people do so with the consent of their spouse. George O'Neill and Nena O'Neill have called these relationships "open marriages."[25] The adventure in open marriage concerns a number of renegotiations of the traditional contract. These changes all seem to center around whether or not it is permissible to enjoy intercourse with someone other than one's spouse, while the spouse knows about it and not only accepts, but approves of it. But intercourse is only a *potential* in these relationships. The more important aspect is the acceptance of both married partners that intimate friendships (which often involve considerable time and resources being spent outside of the home) are desirable for both of them. To say this much is to accept the possibility—but not the inevitability—that such friendships will be expressed in erotic love that may include intercourse. Open marriage is a radical experiment based on the proposition that sexual pleasure and commitment are desirable both outside and inside of marriage. It is the exploration of

[24]Rogers, *Becoming Partners,* p. 201.

[25]George O'Neill and Nena O'Neill, *Open Marriage* (New York: M. Evans & Co., Inc. 1972).

the idea that it is possible and even desirable to erotically love more than one person at the same time.

In open marriage, the relationships outside the marriage are based on friendship. Thus, whether sex occurs in these relationships or not, they represent an involvement outside the home. Swinging, on the other hand, is the proposition that it is desirable to enjoy sexual pleasures outside of marriage with the spouse's approval and the understanding that you will not get involved with these outsiders. The commitment is to the adventure and to the marriage, but it is not to extend beyond the limits of courtesy and consideration to others who might properly be called "playmates." Swingers can meet desirable playmates through clubs, magazines, as well as through personal ads in tabloid newspapers and magazines.

Reports on the amount of commitment actually manifested in swinging encounters varies. Those researchers who do not consider themselves to be swingers see very little concern for others in swinging. Those who admit to being swingers themselves, on the other hand, find a good deal of care and consideration given to others in spite of the rule of no commitment.

Aside from their sexual lives, swingers are typically quite conservative middle-class couples. It sometimes happens that couples drop out of the swinging scene as they get older, become tired of the routine, or seek more durable friendships. Some move from swinging to complex living arrangements or to intimate friendships in which commitment does become an important element.

Multiple marriages are one form of complex living arrangement. *Triads* (groups of three people) are particularly durable in comparison to other kinds of group marriages. A detailed account of one such adventure that lasted about six months is provided in *Face to Face to Face.*[26]

Rich and Amy were in their late twenties when they invited Karen to come and live with them and share living space, money, psychic support, sexual expression, and long-range plans. They kept diaries of their experiment, which later provided the basis of the book. Rich and Amy and Karen were unusual people. Rich and Amy had had a sexually open marriage for over six years before Karen came. Both had participated actively in swinging. All three recognized bisexual elements in their natures, and Amy and Karen had had lesbian experiences before entering into the triad. Rich experienced some homosexual relationships afterwards.

Rich was clearly the binding element in the relationship. He was, by his own assessment, highly sexed and philosophically inclined. He also had a tendency toward male chauvinism supported by a pygma-

[26]Gordon Clanton and Chris Downing, *Face to Face to Face* (New York: E. P. Dutton & Co., 1975). Paperback, New York, Ballantine Book, 1976.

lion complex that inclined him to change women into his own ideal. The triad was his experiment. He wanted Karen to continue her education and join Amy and him at their work. Nevertheless, their accounts indicate that all three wanted the experiment to work and were committed to it, though each had different investments.

Considerable discussion and correspondence preceded the joint venture. Rich had known Karen before he married Amy. Karen had always felt that she was in love with Rich. The threesome, when they came together, went through five discernable stages, according to researchers who studied the case: first, a honeymoon period colored by a sense of beginning and anticipation (about a month and a half); second, a period of peaceful consolidation during which all three felt at home in their new arrangement (about one month); third, a time of testing, during which time drug trips revealed, among other things, a growing hostility between Karen and Rich (about two months); fourth, a climax in hostility reached between Thanksgiving and New Year symbolized by a furtive attempt to celebrate Christmas; and fifth, disentanglement and disengagement.

All three seemed to have been dramatically changed by their experience. Amy has gained some independence from Rich and is thinking of a separation, at least for a while. Rich has begun to make some adjustments to accommodate the new Amy he helped to liberate. While both need breathing room, both feel that their relationship is basically sound. They remain comfortable with its openness to other sexual encounters—although somewhat less than before Karen's arrival. A new person, Eileen, has joined Amy and Rich, participating in an undefined way in their intimate relationship. Karen is living with her former boyfriend, and feels that somehow she is responsible for the breakup because of her own insecurities. After several months, Karen and Rich and Amy have begun to see one another again.

What seems clearly evident from *Face to Face to Face* is that such marriages are exceedingly difficult undertakings. Even if both partners have had considerable experience in open sexuality, a marriage involving the investment of love and concern in at least two other people is another matter. These three sexual sophisticates weren't up to it, and it is likely that most of us aren't either.

Finally, communes provide a variety of settings within which sex, love, and commitment can be negotiated. Multiple marriages focus on the redefinition of marriage, but communes attempt to refashion an entire way of life. A personal guide to a select number of communes is provided by Richard Fairfield in *Communes U.S.A.*[27] However, few of these have been as totally dedicated to creating a sexual

---

[27]Richard Fairchild, *Communes U.S.A.: A Personal Tour* (Baltimore: Penquin Press, 1971); See also, Kanter, *Commitment and Community;* Jerome, *Families of Eden;* and Rimmer, *Adventures in Loving.*

paradise as Sandstone, a community near Los Angeles. The community was composed of five or more individuals and was open to hundreds of others for swinging parties that took place about once a week during the peak of the community's life. It began in the late 1960s and closed December 28, 1973. New owners opened it for a few months after 1973, but it is now closed again.

People within the Sandstone inner community normally maintained primary relationships while openly relating to other intimate friends around them. Some of these primary relationships survived the four years of the community's existence, and some did not. As with all utopias, Sandstone was a bold adventure with high risk and great promise.

The Nature of Love

It is possible to examine our patterns of commitment in a much more interpersonal context by looking at what people think love is. Our expectations about love are internalized norms that we have made our own. These norms are based on patterns that can be traced back in history, have been celebrated in philosophy and literature, and are shared in the present by lovers. However, in the game of love, we do not always recognize that we operate out of a set of expectations about what we are doing that is different from that of our beloved. It is not a simple matter to adjust our behavior in order to more easily communicate with those whom we love, because we expect them to behave as we behave when we say "I love you." When they do not, we become angry or disappointed. We may thus break off the relationship before we find out that they were in love too. Sex is valued differently in each love style and plays a different role in energizing each kind of a relationship.

The Chinese call love a many splendored thing. Almost all cultures have more than one word to describe love. We are impoverished in this regard because we try to make one word cover a multitude of feelings, behaviors, and commitments. Let us distinguish four principal kinds of love: affection (storge), friendship (philias), eros, and agape.[28] If Rollo May is correct, a major problem of our sexual liber-

[28]This classification is after C. S. Lewis, *The Four Loves* (New York: Harcourt, Brace, Jovanovich, Inc., 1960). Other typologies of interest include Rollo May's four-fold division of love into sex (lust or libido). Eros, Philia, and Caritas in May, *Love and Will,* p. 37; and John Alan Lee's characterization of six *Love Styles* (not types of love necessarily) as Eros, Ludus (playful love), and storge as primary love styles and mania (jealous, obsessive, possessive love), pragma (common sense, compatible love) once commonly expressed in arranged marriages and agape (charitas or gentle unselfish, dutiful love) as secondary love styles. See John Alan Lee, *The Colors of Love* (Don Mills, Ontario: New Press, 1976), pp. 9, 10.

Figure 14–5
Affection is the basic love out of
which others are born. (Burk
Uzzle, © Magnum Photos, Inc.)

ation is that we have attempted to make sex carry the entire load of our feelings for others. This has resulted in the banalization of sex and the increase in loneliness so characteristic of our age.

AFFECTION

The love that the Greeks called storge, which we roughly translate as "affection," is a low-profile love. It is a bond commonly felt between kin, especially between parents and children.

> *Affection . . . is the humblest love. It gives itself no airs. People can be proud of being "in love," or of friendship. . . . It usually needs absence or bereavement to set us praising those to whom Affection binds us. We take them for granted.*[29]

Nevertheless, this is a basic love out of which others spring. Our experiencing this fundamental love gives most of us the first sense of self-confidence, the sense of being loved, that later critically affects how we love others. Affection is often found intermixed with the other kinds of love.

Lee contends that storgic lovers never consciously select a love partner. Storgic love is love without fever or folly. Storgic lovers are likely to treat each other as old friends, even though they may have met as strangers. It is slow-burning and sexual contact of any extent is likely to develop late in the relationship. The constant emphasis upon sex in the media makes it difficult for the storgic lovers to persist in their belief that sex is not all that important in love, but they do.

While affection is the most unassuming form of love, it can become an all-consuming demand, as in the case of the mother who lives for her children or the animal lover who pampers his pet. The distortion

---

[29]C. S. Lewis, *The Four Loves*, p. 56.

of affection is readily observable in the case of the teacher who affectionately nourishes a student toward independent thought and then becomes offended when the student achieves a degree of independence and thinks for himself or herself.

FRIENDSHIP

Friendship, or philias, is characterized by common interests and is founded on a common devotion to causes. Friends are characterized by their ability to relax in each other's presence because they share more or less the same world view and take the same things for granted. While it is possible to experience an erotic love and a friendship with the same person, nothing is less like a friendship than a love affair. Lovers are always talking to each other about their love affair, but friends rarely say to one another, "you are my best friend." Lovers are normally face-to-face, absorbed in one another. Friends are side-by-side absorbed in a common interest. Erotic love is best expressed between two people, in Lewis's view, but two is far from the best number of friends. Friendship is the least biological of the natural loves. It is not homosexual or abnormal when friends treat each other affectionately. And yet, because of our often frantic fear of being considered homosexual, we often treat our friends less affectionately than we might otherwise.

Friendship becomes perverse when it creates an in-group that is insensitive to anyone else. Friends share the same jokes, support each other's advance in business, and in many ways define themselves as

Figure 14–6
*One characteristic of friendship
is an involvement in common
interests. (© Joan Liftin,
Woodfin Camp & Associates)*

different from the rest of the world because they care about the same truths. They can be a threat to government when they have the power to assert their exclusiveness. Yet, throughout all ages, little bands of friends have turned their backs on the world and have often transformed it. The snobbish elite from the outside is often a group of friends from the inside.

EROS

The form of love called eros is partially expressed when two people feel they have fallen in love. The Greeks thought of it as a passion or fascination for ideal beauty—a search for the one ideal beloved. In our time, however, we have tended to reduce eros to sexual attraction, as shown in our use of the word "erotic." But it is of the utmost importance that we distinguish between sex and eros. Ruddick and others contend that eros evolves or can evolve out of sexual attraction, but others disagree. C. S. Lewis, for example, sees the process of falling in love somewhat differently. Some people may feel sexually attracted toward another and then go on to fall in love, but Lewis thinks this is not the common case. What is more common is that there is at first a delighted preoccupation with the beloved. A man lusting for sexual satisfaction doesn't want the woman in her totality, but only the pleasure that she can provide as an instrument. Eros is not primarily a gratification of desire, a release of tension, or a pursuit of pleasure, although all of these elements may be a part of erotic love.

"Eros is a kind of loving motivated by great appreciation of beauty. Of course, the particular bodily forms which each lover considers beautiful vary a good deal."[30] Such a lover may be unable to find a truly suitable partner because of a rigid commitment to a particularly scarce ideal form of beauty. Erotic lovers must frequently compromise or live a life of unfulfilled love.

Because this image of the beloved is idealized, the erotic lover will want to discover as quickly as possible if the real flesh-and-blood partner is what he or she seems. Hence, the rush into bed and the frequent confrontation with disillusionment that gives erotic love its trials and tribulations. One of Lee's erotic lovers remarked, however, "Our sex is good, sometimes its really great, but it was never the thing that held us together. We make love; sex doesn't make us love."[31]

Erotic lovers often have difficulty controlling the sensation of touch. They are powerfully drawn to each other's bodies, and yet mere sexual intimacy soon becomes blunted. Therefore, they are more apt than others to employ fantasy and to enjoy the cultivation

[30] Lee, *The Colors of Love*, p. 12. Used by permission of the author John Alan Lee.

[31] Ibid., p. 36.

of techniques to preserve their delight in the partner's body. Lee contends, in contrast to Lewis, that erotic lovers typically launch into intercourse early in their relationship because they must directly and intensely experience the embodied personality of the beloved. Growth in erotic love is achieved by expanding the base of erotic intimacy and self-disclosure. And yet, how often can you reveal your deepest feelings and ideas without the very act of revelation becoming boring?

Nonjealous erotic lovers, Lee finds, are those who have not been disappointed in their previous loves and whose current erotic needs are fulfilled by the partner. Because the ecstacy of Eros cannot be maintained, the continuing problem facing the erotic lover is how to combine eros with the other forms of love, without allowing those other forms to take over. Lee contends that although eros could readily be transformed into others, he found no erotic lover that began loving with another love style.[32]

Sex for the erotic lover is primarily a means of knowing the beloved. But because it is an art that most of us must cultivate in order to be at ease and achieve adequate communication with the beloved, the unskilled or inexperienced erotic lover may be turned off by a potentially compatible partner because of the clumsiness of their lovemaking.

> *The rapid disclosure of self, early sexual experience, honesty of emotion, and intensity of feelings all make this a difficult lovestyle. Of course, these qualities also make it the most ecstatic, exilerating, and challenging kind of love for some people.*
>
> *Your chances of successfully enjoying Eros are substantially reduced when you lack some of the important qualities of self-confidence, self-esteem, and social stability. A would-be erotic lover should first put his own psychological house in order, enjoy his work, surround himself with good close friends, and have a good relationship with his parents, if possible, before attempting an erotic approach to love.*
>
> *You might well say, 'If a person has all of these advantages he doesn't need a love anyway,' precisely. The successful erotic lover must not need to be in love. Rather he finds the right person to love and then allows himself to need that person. Eros is not a way of being happy, but of being happier.[33]*

The demonic characteristic of Eros is not so much to be found in its sensuousness or its sexuality, but rather in its tendency to demand unconditional devotion from the lovers. It is not the idolization of the beloved, nor the idolization of sensual pleasure, but rather the eleva-

[32]Ibid., p. 34.

[33]Ibid., p. 37.

tion of erotic love to a law in its own right that threatens the greatest danger to the lovers. "The pair can say to one another in an almost sacrificial spirit, it is for love's sake that I have neglected my parents, left my children, cheated my partner, failed my friend at his greatest needs. These reasons in love's law have passed for good."[34] Theologically, God is love, but the reverse is not true. Love is not God.

AGAPE

Agape is defined as "esteem for the other, the concern for the other's welfare beyond any gain that one can get out of it; disinterested love, typically the love of God for man."[35] The New Testament usage of the word "charity" is really a poor translation of agape, though it retains an element of selfless giving. Agape is gift-love, and it implies an obligation or duty to love whether or not the other is lovable. Lee laments,

> Unfortunately, I have yet to interview any respondent involved in even a relatively short-term affiliative love relationship which I could classify without qualification as an example of agape. I have encountered brief agapetic episodes in continuing love relationships.[36]

Altruism, much less agapetic love, has failed to make much of an impression on social science models of human love. There is so little evidence of the existence of such behavior. If we try hard enough, it is always possible to come up with a motive, a vested interest that motivates our behavior. Sexual behavior and human loving are no exceptions. And yet, agape is an answer to the questions posed by the other loves and, paradoxically, we must receive it as a free gift. We cannot actively create it, though we may hunger and thirst after it. Its effectiveness in our lives depends on the extent to which we are open to receive it. Agape, however, is not a substitute for the other loves. It is best to say that it can enrich all of them.[37]

Agape is more akin to the expression of intentionality or will than it is to emotions or sensations. In the Christian view it is commanded, "Thou shalt love the Lord thy God, with all thy heart and all thy soul and all thy mind. This is the first and great commandment, and the second is like unto it, Thou shalt love thy neighbor as thyself." This commanded love is to include all people, enemies as well as friends, the leper as well as the healthy person. Christian theologians do not

[34] Lewis, *The Four Loves,* p. 157.

[35] May, *Love and Will,* p. 316.

[36] Lee, *The Colors of Love,* p. 156.

[37] See, for example, the discussion in Rustum Roy and Della Roy, *Honest Sex: A Revolutionary Sex Ethic By and For Concerned Christians* (New York: New American Library, 1968), pp. 34–46.

claim that it is often realized in the lives of human beings. Lewis remarks, "It is dangerous to press upon a man the duty of getting beyond the earthly love when his real difficulty lies in getting so far."[38]

According to Erich Fromm, the lover must love out of duty with care, knowledge, responsibility, and respect. The lover must strive to love rather than to be loved or to become lovable.

> . . . *love is exclusively an act of will and commitment, and therefore fundamentally it does not matter who the two persons are . . . We are all one— yet each one of us is a unique, unduplicable entity. Inasmuch as we are all one we can love everybody in the same way in the sense of brotherly love. But inasmuch as we are all also different, erotic love requires certain specific highly individual differences.*[39]

Theologians tell us that we are all one family of brothers and sisters because God is our father. This is a mystical unity, not an apparent one. Our differences seem to divide us more than our similarities unite us. If, however, it is possible to become open to this gift-love, then we can love others out of an abundance of love rather than out of a scarcity.

Summary

In this chapter we have seen how sexual behavior is understood and expressed in terms of the various patterns of commitment. In the past, a rather narrow ideal image of marriage and family life was expected to regulate the legitimate expression of sexual behavior in our society. This conjugal family, in which marriage was a sacrament that could not be broken, has gradually diminished in importance. Even so, most Americans wish to marry and eventually do. We have always, in fact, had a variety of types of marriage contracts in the past. We are now beginning to feel more comfortable with this variety. Sexual satisfaction is becoming a more important element in marriage of whatever sort.

The types of commitments men and women make are affected by social status, ethnic background, and other social patterns. There were very few good commitments—good being defined by the partners themselves—in the upper-middle-class relationships studied by Cuber and Harroff. In all but one type of commitment, sex was engaged in outside of the commitment in the majority of cases. It was

[38]Lewis, *The Four Loves*, p. 165.

[39]Erich Fromm, *The Art of Loving* (New York: Bantam Books, Inc., 1970), quoted here in Lee, *The Colors of Love*, p. 159.

experienced differently depending upon the type of commitment. So, for example, in the conflict habituated type of commitment, sex outside of it was a further means of expressing hostility. In the vital relationship, it was considered to be the right of the partner to do so. We concluded that among these couples between the ages of thirty-three and fifty-five in the upper-middle class, sex was not very important. Most couples, nevertheless, will report that they are satisfied with their relationships.

Sex was even less related to intimate relationships in the commitment patterns of the lower class. It was more male-centered, less elaborated in love play and coital positions, and not expected to provide the woman with pleasure. In the lower class, sexual behavior is a much more important form of recreation and means of income than it is in the upper classes because of the deprivation experienced by the poor.

The alternative life styles that we called adventures in loving are new experiments for the most part. It is not clear how they will develop though it is clear that a large number of people are trying them. Swinging, open marriage, and communal living are all quite different contexts within which to enjoy sex or not. In swinging, no commitment is to be made beyond the marriage. According to the rules of the game, swinging takes place with the knowledge of the spouse in most cases, and with playmates with whom one is not expected to get serious. In open marriage, intimate friendships are encouraged outside, which may or may not involve sexual relationships, under the conviction that the spouse cannot possibly fulfill all of one's needs. Intimate friends can help meet these unfulfilled needs with the expectation that this will have a positive effect upon the marriage. Communards mix sex and commitment in a multitude of ways.

At the interpersonal level, sexual satisfaction is valued differently, depending upon the accepted style of love one takes for granted. The affectionate lover develops a slow-burning relationship that may eventually or never develop into a sexual encounter. The erotic lover, in contrast, is eager to bed the beloved because carnal knowledge is a vital means of knowing and an élan in life. Such a love style is characterized by highs and lows and may never result in marriage because the ideal beloved cannot be found.

Section Four

Sex and
Social Issues

In this section some of the ways in which sex becomes a social issue are discussed. What is defined as a social issue in one culture is not necessarily so defined in another. Indeed, within a culture, what is considered to be a social issue in regard to sex changes, as attitudes and the conditions of life change. The notion of what to do about sexual issues such as prostitution, pornography, and venereal disease also changes.

Chapter 15 discusses some aspects of the commercialization of sex. Sex is said to be pervasive in advertising and yet its expression in mass media in this fashion is most subdued. A customer offended is a customer lost. Advertising must be very sensitive to the changing climate of sexual opinions and beliefs. Prostitutes openly advertise and yet even they must be quite cautious in their solicitation. Within "the life" they are able to let their hair down, but in confronting potential customers they must put the best foot forward or suffer a reduction in their trade. Even after they have successfully solicited a client, or "John," they must not let their negative feelings or personal preferences about sexual tastes interfere with their giving the John what he wants. Most prostitutes depend upon a core of customers to sustain their enterprise and these must be pleased or the prostitute will lose her clientele. Even pornography is subject to censure by the dominant cultural beliefs. Its distribution, if not always its content, is at least partially regulated by law and custom. The basic problem of pornography is its pretension to show everything, when, in fact, it reveals little. Nevertheless, it has played an important role in sex education and still serves a role in the sexual life of many people.

In Chapter 16 the legal regulation of sexual behavior will be discussed. In the past the law has assumed a single sexual ethic to be widely held by all Americans. This has become increasingly less tenable. At present the legal regulation of human sexual behavior is an embarrassment to any sensitive attorney. Accordingly, there is some movement to reform the law along the lines suggested by the Model Penal Code. The essence of this modification is that any sexual behavior between consenting adults in private should not be the concern of the law.

The last chapter in this section, chapter 17, describes some of the health problems associated with sexual behavior. These are most often limited to a discussion of venereal disease, meaning syphilis and gonorrhea. There are several other common diseases that are associated with human sexuality that are discussed here as well. In the past, the fear of getting a venereal disease or of getting pregnant was used to bolster the argument that sexual intercourse should occur only in marriage. This is a spurious—if often convincing—argument. Nevertheless, given the increasing expression of sexual behavior of all sorts, it becomes important for everyone to understand more about these diseases. Knowledge about them, plus really caring for others, can help control their spread. Fear or ignorance cannot.

The Commercialization of Sex

15

I saw both girls daily for nearly a fortnight, and
Sophy had my seminal libations more frequently than
Nelly—but I could not talk to her; her language was
indescribably common and coarse, and whether eating,
drinking, speaking, washing or even pissing, her
vulgarity and idiocy were intolerable. She was . . . a
magnificant bit of fucking flesh but nothing more.

My Secret Life, Annoymous

Sex can be used to make money in a number of ways. In the most ancient way the prostitute offers sexual pleasure for a price. The pornographer makes money by sexually stimulating the human mind through words and images made available to the public in bookstores, movies, and peep shows. Both the prostitute and the pornographer are very direct about what they are selling. Other merchants use sex in less open ways. Sex sells products like automobiles and cigarettes and undoubtedly increases the size of the viewing audiences of legitimate movies and television programs as well as the circulation of newspapers, magazines, and books. Television's emphasis on violence is only slightly more obvious than its emphasis on sex.

In this chapter, we look at some of the ways in which sex makes money in our society. First sex in advertising is described. Prostitution is also considered, as is pornography. In each case, some of the functions apparently served by sex in such contexts are pointed out and the apparent costs and benefits of using sex in these ways are examined. Finally, some suggestions are made about the regulation of commercialized sex.

Sex in Advertising

Perhaps the most widespread commercialized aspect of human sexuality in the industrial societies of the world is the extent to which sexual themes are used to sell consumer products, ranging from underclothing and toiletries to cigarettes, liquors, and automobiles. So many ads have sexual themes that our immediate response might be to say that sex will sell anything. It is becoming apparent, however, that the interplay between sexual themes and images in advertising and the sexual ethos of the culture at large is complex and poorly understood. It is clear that the female bust or male torso is likely to attract attention, but will it necessarily increase the sale of a product?

Sex in advertising is really quite restrained. Great care is taken not to offend because every offended person is a lost customer. Advertising has not caught up with the change that has occurred elsewhere in the media. When Kinsey released his famous studies of human sexual

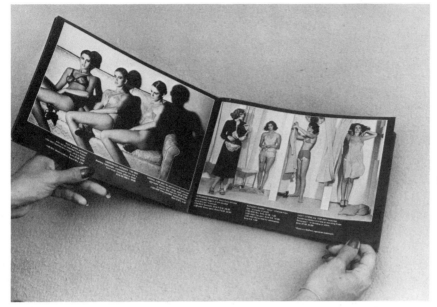

Figure 15–1
Sexual themes are used to sell many consumer products, ranging from lingerie to automobiles.
(Michal Heron)

behavior, the respectable skin book was *Esquire* magazine. Its pin-ups of semi-nude women were much more appealing than the explicit-edly portrayed sex in the "Eight Page Bibles" (small poorly drawn booklets, illustrating sexual behavior in a crude and jocular style) that made the rounds in grade schools and high schools of the 40s and 50s. In what must be a classic case of sour grapes, the November, 1976 *Esquire* pointed to the current skin-book boom and asked, "What have they done to the girl next door?"[1] They have not only taken off her clothes, opened up her legs and deflowered her, they have photo-graphed her frolicking in everything from semen to shackles. The boy next door is rapidly following suit. The long protected female pubic hair made its debut in slick-paper magazines in 1972. We may now look inside. Male nudity was legitimated in 1973 by *Playgirl*. These magazines sell millions of copies each month to men and women from all walks of life, costing $1.25 and up. The top three—*Playboy, Penthouse,* and *Hustler*—have a combined monthly circulation exceed-ing 11 million, and the last of the trio expected a $20,000,000 profit in 1977. *Hustler's* Larry Flynt comments on *Penthouse*, "Bob Guccione is just selling tits and ass and is ashamed to admit it. Hustler is selling

[1]"The Skin Book Boom: What Have They Done to the Girl Next Door?", *Esquire* (Nov. 1976), pp. 92–97.

the same thing, but we are proud of it. Because we aren't repressed."[2] Flynt is currently fighting an obscenity charge in the courts and paralysis from a gun shot wound inflicted in Alabama, where he was brought to trial.

Television editing remains much more restrictive, but even this media is being modified to permit more explicitedly sexual themes to be discussed—if not fully shown—under a "parental guidance may be required" warning. The porn film came of age in *Deep Throat* (1972), which probably did as much to promote and refine oral sex among the general population as any erotica.[3]

In literature, the 1959 court decision permitting D. H. Lawrence's *Lady Chatterly's Lover* to be sent through the mails in this country opened the door to a host of paperback editions of erotica classics.[4] The language of the popular novel changed along with the explicitness of its description. Thus Norman Mailer was thought bold indeed for repeatedly using the euphemism "fug" in *The Naked and the Dead* (1948), but by 1972 "fuck" appeared in the supplement to the *Oxford English Dictionary*.[5]

In contrast to the increasing explicitness about sexual themes in the rest of media, advertising is much more indirect and suggestive. Very few nudes enjoy full exposure, even in situations in which it might be appropriate to do so such, as in the sale of soaps and other toiletries. Instead we are tantalized. In television ads, the camera moves from an arm uplifted in sudsy enjoyment, to a face delighting in the pleasure of it all, to feet receiving the cascading suds and shower. In magazines, a profile of the female breast may be softly suggested, but a towel most often discretely covers the genitals, or a shower curtain is pulled coyly around the showering male.

There is evidence that when sexual themes do not match the image of a product (for example, when female models are used to sell computers), the themes are remembered, but the product is more often forgotten than when it is advertised without use of sexual themes.[6] Steadman found that this response was particularly true for those individuals who disapproved of the use of sexual themes in advertising generally, but that it also had a negative effect even when people approved of sex in advertising.

Sexual themes in advertising present another problem for the pro-

[2]Ibid., p. 92.

[3]Morton Hunt, *Sexual Behavior in the 1970s* (New York: Dell Publishing Co., 1974), p. 6.

[4]Ibid., p. 7.

[5]Ibid., p. 7.

[6]Major Steadman, "How Sexy Illustrations Affect Brand Recall," *Journal of Advertising Research,* *9* (1969), 19.

ducer. They tend to segregate the market into masculine and feminine sectors. Rudolph found that ads featuring pictures of women were more often read by women and those with pictures of men were more often read by men.[7] Some products (cigarettes, deodorants, cigars, and hair spray) explored an almost exclusively masculine or feminine market. Finally advertisers realized that they were missing their targets and sought to move their products out of an exclusively sex-typed market by changing their ads.[8]

In any case, sex enters advertising as much in terms of its contributing to a sense of sex role and identity as it does as an erotic element intent to arouse or suggest sexual passion. In this context, it mingles subtly with status symbolism, an equally appealing theme in advertising. A major part of the advertising effort seems to be concentrated on providing the viewer with suggestions of valuable and widely recognized symbols of who he or she is in society. It is because sex roles and a sense of gender identity are so large a part of the average person's sense of personal identity, that these themes can be exploited. Wouldn't it be simple indeed, if you could establish who you are in society just by buying the right car, smoking the right cigarette, using the correct deodorant, and drinking the best liquor? Given the impersonality of most public life in industrial societies, these highly publicized cues are obviously appealing. Brand names are status symbols as much as they indicate superior products.

Since males have generally more status in the United States than females, it has been suggested that the process an advertiser must use to move a product from a predominantly female market to a predominantly male market is different than one required to move it from a predominantly male market into a female market. For example, in Europe, the cigarette was associated with females and foppish dandies, but Americans saw it differently. Its conveyance rapidly attracted males to the market, especially after their experience in the trench warfare of World War I.

The automobile's increasing popularity boosted cigarette sales because cigars and chewing tobacco were too unsightly, and cumbersome in automobiles. As a result, males soon dominated the American cigarette market. Then, the effort was explictly made to attract the female by means of advertising. Lucky Strike suggested that women "reach for a Lucky instead of a sweet." Armed with this excuse, women bought cigarettes in large numbers for the first time in the United States.[9] They were gradually attracted to cigars by such

[7] H. J. Rudolph, *Attention and Interest Factors in Advertising* (New York: Funk and Wagnalls, 1947).

[8] John R. Stuteville, "Sexually Polarized Products and Advertising Strategy," *Journal of Retailing,* 47 (Summer 1971), 3–13.

[9] Ibid., p. 6.

techniques as was recently attempted by Tiparillo ("Should a gentleman offer a Tiparillo to a lady?").

In contrast to the gradual suggestion involved in attracting women to cigarettes, men were rather quickly enticed into using hair spray. The dominant male, the theory goes, is not prevented by status consideration from entering this market.[10] Producers simply scented the product with masculine odors (spice, pine, or leather), packaged it in bold colored containers emblazoned with cannons, crossed swords, and the like, and introduced advertisements in which an obviously athletic he-man pushed the product. These ads seemed to say, "If you say I'm not masculine because I use hair spray, I'll beat the crap out of you!"[11] Stuteville speculates that with increasing equality between the sexes such problems will cease to exist.[12]

Even when sexual themes suggest erotic desire in advertising, they suggest rather than explicitedly display it. The lovely reclining blond suggests that you slip into a smooth black velvet scotch—not crotch. Perfume ads run the gamut of suggestion from the notion that a particular fragrance will attract a man's attention to a warning that another may be too powerful for some women to handle. Most of these ads that are aimed at women are more romantic than sexual in their presentation.

Sexual themes are very important elements of many ads selling products to a sexually awakening society. They seem most effective in increasing sales when they are appropriate to the product being sold, but the basis for determing this congruence is often difficult to determine. Thus, the use of sex in advertising is a subtle business requiring constant attention to changing fads and foibles.

Sex is more directly commercialized in prostitution, but even here there are a large number of constraints that make it impossible for most prostitutes to be completely explicit about their wares.

Prostitution

Although there are call boys and gigolos, prostitution is predominantly a woman's world. It is humorously called the world's oldest profession. Of course, it is not ordinarily thought of as a profession because accepting money for sexual services is counter to conventional norms governing sexual behavior, and training is thought to be minimal. Like homosexuality, prostitution is usually studied as a form of deviant sexual behavior, even though it has been with us throughout recorded history.

[10]Ibid., pp. 8–9.

[11]Ibid., p. 9.

[12] Ibid., p. 4.

The standard definition of prostitution is the indulgence in promiscuous sexual relations in return for money. For the prostitute, sex is not only without love or feelings, it is for money. The ordinary mind boggles at the thought of a single woman servicing thirty or forty clients in one night—a good night's work by any account. In London during the 1960s, each customer, or trick, returned about three pounds. In Los Angeles or New York during the same decade the fee was about twenty dollars. The price in the 70s is around thirty dollars a trick. Six to eight hundred dollars for one night's work is a lot of money. However, not all of this is clear profit because the prostitute relies on others to provide her with customers, and not every night will be as good as the next one. Young call girls make more money than old streetwalkers. But, even so, as the old saying of the prostitute has it, "every woman is sitting on a fortune if she would only realize it."

A great many people benefit economically from the prostitute's earnings. Those who provide her with clients for a fee (pimps, madams, steerers, fellow prostitutes, and so on) probably take the biggest cut. Those who rent her the apartment where she works—and the one where she lives—also get their share. The righteously outraged depend on the prostitute, since they need someone to be outraged about in order to stay in business. The efforts of the criminal justice system—

police, lawyers, social workers, judges, bail bondsman, and the like—to control prostitution are often richly rewarded by funding from those who are righteously outraged by it. In some cases, credit card companies have allowed such services to be charged, although a word such as "entertainment" is usually written on the bill. Much more indirectly, convention centers and entire sections of cities benefit from the services prostitutes provide to men who are away from home and want a night on the town. In such European cities as Amsterdam and Copenhagen, red-light districts, where prostitution is legal, have become tourist attractions.

What type of person would pay for sex? The answer is anyone who wants it and cannot get it for nothing. From this perspective, all sex can be seen fundamentally as a commercial transaction. According to Marx and Engles, for example, a housewife differs from a prostitute only because she has sold herself into slavery once and for all. Less abstractly, however, people who feel that their sexual desires are too kinky, who are ashamed of their bodies because of physical handicaps, who are convinced that sex is dirty and should not be inflicted on good women, or who are away from home and lonely or seeking excitement are most likely to become the prostitute's "John," or customer. The wealthy playboy out for a night on the town and the business executive trying to make an impression by hiring the services of an attractive call girl are also typical customers. Finally, any man who finds the customary procedures of courtship or seduction too time-consuming or complex will pay for sex because of the simplicity of the transaction. Thus, the potential clientele is enormous. Contact with a prostitute is a rare experience for most men today. It is probable that every man has thought of paying for sex at one time or another even if he has not done so. It has been observed that one effect of the sexual revolution has been to change the middle-class male's sexual partner from a prostitute to a peer.

Because prostitution is illegal, people involved in it are naturally rather secretive and self-protective. Thus, there is great difficulty getting an accurate picture of what the world of the prostitute is like. In fact, few researchers have looked at prostitution to any extent. Most studies are of fifteen to thirty prostitutes from a single city at a particular point in time. There is much written about prostitution, but there is little extensive research.

ENTERING THE LIFE

In the past it was common for young women to be forced into prostitution because of economic destitution. Today this is less so. Most women who become prostitutes do so over a period of time. They sort of drift into the life. They are commonly isolated from society. They are usually at odds with their parents. Many come from small towns and find themselves more or less alone in the city. In the city, the only work they can find is usually unskilled and low-paying. They may become attracted to the possibility of selling themselves after a man whom they casually dated, and then went to bed with, left behind a twenty-dollar bill. Even though they did not solicit the fee, having been paid seems to start the process. It is not so bad being paid for something that required less effort than they exert on their job.

It is essential that such a woman make contact with someone who can set her up. Most women cannot suddenly start charging men they have known for sexual services. The men don't understand and are inclined to take it as a joke. Even solicited or referred customers cheat and refuse to pay on occasion. The contact who refers clients establishes the businesslike tone of the transaction before the prostitute meets the John. Finding a brothel and moving in is no longer the way

Figure 15–3
Call girls do not pick up Johns on the street, and so have higher status than the common prostitute. In many cases, a call girl will have a madam, who acts essentially as an agent.
(© Bob Adelman, distributed by Magnum)

that a girl moves into prostitution. Most brothels do not keep women for any period of time, a week is a common stay. After all, the customers like variety.

A part of the difficulty in getting into the life derives from the prostitute's need to keep her identity a secret from almost everyone except fellow prostitutes and customers. Knowledge of a prostitute's identity could be used to blackmail her. Even people who sometimes refer customers to her abuse her in this way by expecting free sex. They may openly threaten exposure or subtly imply it, but the threat is real enough. Many prostitutes live in apartments in which the landlord does not know or does not choose to be aware of the fact that they are prostitutes. Should their occupation be brought to his attention, they might be evicted. The problem of disclosure of identity is particularly acute for the streetwalker, the prostitute that directly solicits her Johns on the street. She must be able to judge a potential customer quickly, disclose enough to entice, but avoid making a direct offer until she is sure that the John isn't a cop or someone else who could harm her. She is not always right in her assessment, but she is right often enough to enable her to survive. The call girl has the potential customer referred to her. He may come to her apartment, or more often she goes to his hotel room. But even in this case, she must be able to discern ulterior motives if she is to avoid being arrested or blackmailed. This need for secrecy makes it more difficult for an inexperienced girl to find an experienced prostitute who will show her the ropes, though most who are intent on becoming prostitutes eventually do.

LEARNING THE ROPES

Call girls, most of whom are relatively sophisticated and can pass readily in upper-class society, undergo a training period of about four to eight months. The purpose of this training period is to build up a clientele, a group of regulars, and to familiarize the new girl with the culture of the prostitute's world. The new girl is not taught very much about sexual techniques. Training is usually under the guidance of an experienced call girl or, less frequently, a pimp. The experienced woman listens to the new girl proposition her potential customer and offers suggestions on how to handle the transaction efficiently. This open solicitation is most difficult for new prostitutes to learn since it goes against the feminine role that has governed the expression of most of their sexuality.

The experienced prostitute may also listen to how the new girl handles her John during the sex act itself. In general, she advises the new girl to pretend pleasure and "bang it about a bit" so that he comes sooner and you can get on to the next one. There may be some instruction in techniques of oral sex, but this is about all that the new girl is likely to pick up in the way of sexual technique. The rest she learns on her own. Whatever the feelings of the prostitute may be, her job is to sexually please her John. If her act is not convincing, she does not develop the regular clientele on which her career heavily depends.

The continued practice of the trade further isolates the prostitute from the larger society. The hours she keeps, the people she meets, and the beliefs she fosters in order to rationalize her profession all serve to reinforce her conviction that respectable people are no good and that she is right to take their money. The prostitute who feels affection for her customer, or allows herself to experience sexual pleasure renders herself more vulnerable to the John.

PROBLEMS IN TURNING TRICKS

There seem to be two common problems that prostitutes face in their dealings with their customers. The first is to get the money before the sex is delivered. Often new girls feel uncomfortable about making the deal first. Getting swindled by a sexually satisfied customer who simply walks out on them is the way most of them learn to overcome this problem. The second common problem is a failure to perceive soon enough what they are being asked to do sexually. This might be surprising, since one of the functions of sex for a price is to reduce the uncertainty about obtaining sexual experience, and yet, the very men who have the greatest need to have this uncertainty reduced are also most likely to be unable to precisely express what they desire. The prostitute who can read between the lines and become sensitive to what actually pleases her customer is likely to be more successful in her trade.

The transfer of money serves to emphasize the businesslike character of the transaction. The customer is buying a service that the prostitute is willing to provide for a price. The acceptance of the fee labels her a prostitute and signals to him that, within limits, she can be treated as an object. For many men, this is a liberating experience. They can explore and express their erotic feelings without guilt or worry about future complications or their partner's feelings. For the prostitute, the fee serves to detach her emotions from her actions—she is just doing her job. She works to maximize her profits and can use her money to enjoy life somewhere else. Usually she enjoys life with her pimp, who is, for all intents, the prostitute's husband. In some instances they may even be married.

While the pimp pushes the prostitute out on the street or sees to it that her bed is always full, the policeman is constantly trying to keep her off the street. Arrests are routine. In most cities, prostitutes are arrested, tried, and convicted, and dismissed after paying a fine all in the same evening. The fines are not high enough to make prostitution unprofitable. There may even be a rotation system established so that only certain girls are arrested at a particular time. Prostitutes may resent such an arrangement as a rotation schedule, but when they do, it's usually because they have been arrested out of turn.

The relationship between pimp and prostitute is variously described. Most commonly a prostitute claims to be in love with her pimp. He manages her books, saves money for her, provides bail bond, solicits her customers, enjoys her body, and generally treats her well, as long as she does not cross him. He lives high off her income. Indeed, the style of dress and state of luxury of her pimp is a status symbol for a prostitute because it signifies how well she is doing in her trade.

Generally, only the lower status prostitute are dependent on pimps. In the more modern apartment buildings in our big cities where the new breed of call girl establishes her place of business, the madam is

Figure 15–4
There have been changing trends in prostitution in the past years; Nevada, like some countries in Western Europe, has legalized prostitution. (© Marvin Newman, Woodfin Camp & Associates)

Figure 15–5
Margo St. James started Coyote ("Cast Off Your Old Tired Ethics") as part of her campaign to urge other prostitutes to assert their civil rights and to regain their self-respect. (Woodfin Camp & Associates)

commonly little more than a housekeeper and pimps are virtually un-heard of. These girls are in business for themselves.

While the call girl may go anywhere in a city, the streetwalker commonly solicits in particular parts of a city that are known for their sexual deviance, or she frequents certain hotels, bars, and the like, where she has connections. Red-light districts localize sex for sale in various forms, such as X-rated movies and peep shows, bottomless dancers, massage parlors, adult book stores, and prostitutes. Cities of all sizes have such districts, although commercialized sex is never re-stricted solely to these districts. Since it can be argued that such ser-vices are necessary for some people and are beneficial to society be-cause others are not forced into providing the services that prostitutes perform for a price, it seems reasonable that such districts should be allowed to exist. Indeed, if efforts were made to restrict commer-cialized sex to these districts, the civil rights of others would not be violated by being exposed to sexual behaviors that they do not en-dorse and that they find offensive.

Using a prostitute's services takes a certain amount of courage be-cause the customer must disclose something of his sexuality to her as part of the transaction. Other people may prefer to keep their feelings about sex to themselves. These people are apt to visit the pornogra-pher rather than the prostitute.

Pornography

What is pornography? You may say that it is the obscene portrayal, in words or pictures, of explicit sexual acts. But what does "obscene" mean? It may be enough for you to say "I know it when I see it," but what is smut to one person may be art to another. Government agencies, interested in establishing general guidelines as a basis for lawmaking, have stumbled on this very problem of definition.

LEGAL REGULATION

Obscenity has been regulated by federal legislation for about a century and a half. In the 1957 Roth decision, the Supreme Court devised a constitutional test to define obscenity so that it could be excluded from the First Amendment's protection of freedom of speech. In the Roth decision the Supreme Court declared that material was obscene if it manifested all three of the following criteria: (1) the dominant theme taken as a whole must appeal to purient interest (undefined); (2) it must be offensive according to contemporary community standards (community undefined); and (3) it must lack any "redeeming social significance."[13]

During the 1960s, a series of test cases attempted to determine whether a particular piece of material could be legally called obscene. The net effect of the court decisions in these cases has been to expand the range of material that is offered protection by the First Amendment and to restrict the material to be defined as obscene. The Roth criteria have been vaguely defined and difficult to apply. When the Commission on Obscenity and Pornography undertook its study, therefore, it had to come to its own conclusions about what it should study. It decided to concentrate on those materials that were at least potentially sexually stimulating and which might be deemed offensive to some segments of the population. The most recent Supreme Court decision has turned the whole matter of definition of obscenity over to the local communities. Hence, Larry Flynt, publisher of *Hustler* magazine, was tried in Cincinnati, Ohio in 1976. He was fined and sentenced to thirteen months to twenty-five years in jail for participating in organized crime and distributing obscenity, but *Hustler,* remains on the newsstand in most parts of the country.

Community standards in most places are ill-defined, rapidly changing, and in need of attention. They cannot be relied on as dependable criteria for determining truth or beauty. At best they define what is acceptable, but what is acceptable to some is an offense to others in a pluralist culture such as ours. One person's sex is another person's smut. The First Amendment rightly protects the pornographer, the preacher, and the general in their freedom of speech, but it also implies some restraints on their part.

The pornography commission refused to define obscenity for the

[13]W. Cody Wilson, "The American Experience with Pornography," in *Social Change and Human Behavior,* George Coelho and Eli Rubenstein, eds. (Washington, D. C.: N.I.M.H., 1973), p. 120.

purposes of regulating the distribution to adults because it did not propose such legislation. It did attempt to define what is meant by "explicit sexual material" for the purpose of regulating the distribution of such material to "young persons" (deliberately left unspecified as to age).

> *Explicit sexual material means any pictorial or three-dimensional material including, but not limited to, books, magazines, films, photographs, and statuary, which is made up in whole or in dominant part of descriptions of human sexual intercourse, masturbation, sodomy (i.e., beastiality or oral or anal intercourse), direct physical stimulation of unclothed genitals, or flagellation or torture in the context of a sexual relationship, or which emphasizes the depiction of uncovered adult human genitals; provided however, that works of art or of anthropological significance shall not be deemed to be within the foregoing definition.*[14]

This seems like a pretty clear-cut definition. But the Commission's proviso that art and works of anthropological significance should be excluded still leaves a lot to the individual's judgment. How does one objectively differentiate art from pornography? Doesn't anything in the human experience have anthropological significance or does only material from other cultures have such significance? Thus, the question of what constitutes pornography is still unanswered.

Pornography is not simply an attack on convention. It historically is a rebellion against conventionally defined love. Chief targets of the pornographer have been the Church and the clergy. An example of a frontal attack on conventional Christianity occurred in 1931 when D. H. Lawrence wrote *The Man Who Died.* In this tale, Christ discovers the joys of the flesh. After He has risen, he meets a priestess of Isis who teaches him the importance of physical passion.

> *He untied the string on the linen tunic, and slipped the garment down, till he saw the white glow of her white-gold breasts. And he touched them, and he felt his life go molten. Father! he said, why did you hide this from me? And he touched her with the poignancy of wonder, and the marvellous piercing transcendency of desire. Lo! he said, This is beyond prayer. It was the deep, interfolded warmth, living and penetrable, the woman, the heart of the rose. My mansion is the intricate warm rose, my joy is this blossom!*[15]

In spite of its rather explicit sexuality, Lawrence's work is not commonly called pornography. Though his assertion that Christ found his kingdom in the dark rose beneath the navel of a priestess of Isis is

[14]*The Report of the Commission on Obscenity and Pornography* (New York: Bantam Books, 1970), p. 456.

[15]D. H. Lawrence, *St. Mawr & the Man Who Died* (New York: Random House, 1953), p. 207.

extreme profanity from one point of view, the style of the writing and the careful disclosure of human nature and motivation are not of the genre commonly called pornographic. It was not aimed at, nor did it reach, a wide audience. It is literate, insightful, and often eloquent in its prose, and deserves to be called erotic rather than pornographic. Such distinctions are important, though they are not widely agreed on nor often reflected in the terminology of the law.

Pornography can be generally defined as the production and distribution of sexually explicit material for sale to the general public.

THE BUSINESS

The ever-changing distinctions between gutter filth and respectable erotics are reflected in the financial statement of the more popular national magazines. The once triumphant *Playboy* is losing out to *Penthouse* and *Hustler.* Hugh Hefner has placed his fifty-four-room Chicago mansion on sale for 2.5 million dollars, and his clubs are closing. The new operating officer, Derick Daniels, insists that *Playboy* will not "join our competitors who are yapping along in the gutter. We won't become a journal devoted to gynecology." Vice President Mike Murphy says the "gutter filth" published in *Playboy's* thirty-seven rivals is so offensive that many companies will not advertise in such journals. As a result *Playboy's* advertising income is rising, while its circulation is declining. (It was still ahead of *Penthouse* by about 300,000 copies last year, but *Penthouse's* circulation was up to 600,000 last year and is still rising.) Says Murphy, *Playboy* "is the only men's magazine that if you take away the girls you still have a magazine." Bob Guccione, editor of *Penthouse,* replies, "Let em try it, I'd love it we've stolen their thunder. They're no longer the number one men's magazine—we are."[16]

The pornography commission tells us that "approximately 85 percent of adult men and 70 percent of adult women in the United States have been exposed at some time during their lives to depictions of explicit sexual materials in either visual or textural form. Most of these exposures have apparently been voluntary."[17] Between one-quarter and one-half of those people who have ever seen pornography have purchased it. About 18 percent of the women and 31 percent of the men reported that they knew of a shop that specialized in sexually related materials. The commission estimated the total traffic in the porn industry to be $650,000,000 to $700,000,000 in 1969. Some of the material covered by these figures would not be considered objectionable by any but the most stringent community standards. Perhaps

[16]Associated Press, September 23, 1977. Recorded in the *Wilmington News Journal,* p. 6.

[17]Report *of the Commission on Obscenity and Pornography,* p. 23 ff.

the most important finding of the commission was their conclusion that there was no evidence of organized crime or of a vast single porno industry. Rather, a large number of comparatively small entrepreneurs are engaged in the industry. Some of these do very well, but some lose their shirts (as well as their pants).

DOMINANT ELEMENTS IN PORNOGRAPHY

Pornography's selling power can be attributed to its distortion of the importance of sexuality in our lives. During the most repressive era of Victorian morality, when convention discredited the importance of sexuality, pornography extolled sexual intercourse as the only thing that really mattered in life. Experienced people take such exaggeration in stride. But as a model for young or relatively inexperienced individuals to follow, pornography presents a host of problems. This is particularly true in an age that, while recognizing the individual's rights to form his or her own standards, no longer provides rigid cultural guidelines. By looking at the dominant elements that characterize pornography, we may be able to isolate potential troubles.

Figure 15–6
If Snow White *were playing at this theater, the dwarfs would get more than just tucked into bed. (© Leif Skoogfors, Woodfin Camp & Associates)*

Trouble in this sense does not mean that pornography leads to sex crimes. It refers to the educational aspects of pornography—what it teaches us about sex and sexual relationships.

Disembodiment and Disassociation. Pornographers often claim that their descriptions of human lovemaking represent accurate portrayals of real-life behavior. In point of fact, pornography most commonly is highly selective and conventionalized in what it describes. It is as gross a distortion of the experience of human embodiment as the ascetic denial it sought to overcome. Some examples should help to clarify this. The point is most blatantly made in such works as *The Romance of Lust,* published in the 1870s. For example,

> *The Count had fucked the Egerton while we were engaged above the divine Frankland. Our first post was suggested by the Egerton, who had been yet less fucked than any. She had been also greatly taken with the glories of the Frankland's superb body, and especially struck with her extraordinary clitoris, and had taken curious lech of wishing to have it in her bottomhole while riding St. George on my big prick. We all laughed at her odd choice, but agreed at once, especially the Frankland, whose greatest lech was to fuck every fair young woman with her long and capable clitoris. A fairer*

Figure 15–7
The Commission on Obscenity and Pornography has found that, in spite of our fears, exposure to pornography does not seem to lead to sex crimes or sexual delinquency. (Joel Gordon)

*creature than the lovely Egerton could not be found. The Frankland ad-
mitted that in her inmost heart she had longed thus to have the Egerton
from the moment she had first seen her and her delight and surprise at
finding the dear Egerton had equally desired to possess her, fired her fierce
lust with increased desire. I lay down, the Egerton straddled over, and
feeling the delight of my huge prick when completedly imbedded, she spent
profusely with only two rebounds. Then sinking on my belly she presented
her lovely arse to the lascivious embraces of the salacious Frankland. . . .
The Count next took the Benson in cunt while I blocked the rear aperture,
and the Frankland once more enculed the Egerton, who dildoed herself in
cunt at the same time; all of us running two courses. We then rose, puri-
fied, and refreshed. When our pricks were ready it was the Egerton who
took me in front and the Count behind, and the Benson who had grown
lewd on the Frankland's clitoris, was sodomized by her and dildoed by herself. The Egerton still suffered a little in the double stretching, so that we
ran but one exquisite bout, enabling us, whose powers began to fail, to be
re-excited, and to finish with the double jouissance in the glorious body of
the Frankland.*[18]

Marcus comments that this passage manages "to combine extreme
fantasy with absolute cliche."[19] What is described is the various possible combinations for sexual coupling, but done in such a way as to
omit most of the feelings and even most of the people involved in
such "exquisite bouts." What is depicted is an autoerotic fantasy, not
a group of people engaging in sexual intercourse. What is asserted—
counter to convention of the time—is the enormous sexual desire of
women and the potency of the penis. These people are the multi-
millionaires in the Victorian sexual economy. They have endless
resources and spend them freely.

Modern pornography may go into a bit more detail, but the fantasy element remains dominant. Take, for example, the following ex-
cerpt from an article entitled "Plumbers Help" in *Club International*.
Our plumber has been engaged in sniffing the crotch of the panties of
the lady of the house—left carelessly in the bathroom—when she enters the room.

*'Make me fuck you.' She said huskily.
The scent of her pussy lingered in my nostrils. I reached for her arm, but
she dashed out and threw herself across the double bed in the next room.
While I fumbled with my pants she knelt forward and stuck her flawless
ass in my direction. Her slit glistened shamelessly. A fine, gossamer sheen
coated the purplish kiss where her labia met in their silken nest. Her cunt
was sopping.*

[18]Steven Marcus, *The Other Victorians: A Study of Sexuality and Pornography in Mid-Nineteenth-Century
England,* © 1964, 1965, 1966 by Steven Marcus, Basic Books, Inc., Publishers, New York, p. 275.

[19]Ibid., p. 275.

I sat down on the bed and cupped my hand atop her sultry muff. But before I could slide a finger inside, she rolled away, back onto the carpet.

'Bitch,' I cried, tired of her frantic teasing. My cock stood stone solid. 'You better hope I don't catch your ass unless you want the living shit fucked right out of you.'

I could tell this was her kind of talk. Her whole body quivered at the words. She stopped dead and spread her legs like a child squatting to piss, then slid her middle finger to the dripping hilt of her snatch.

'That's right plumber,' she gasped, 'Tell me what you are going to do if you grab me! Tell me how you're going to shove your giant cock-head in my mouth. . . . How you're going to make me suck your fat prick until you shoot your hot sperm down my throat!!'

'I don't have to tell you,' I growled, mauling her face with my jutting hard-on. 'Just open up and suck!'[20]

Again the passage reflects a male's fantasy about how he wishes a woman would tease him, not an actual occurrence. In this instance, the woman is pictured as the aggressive seductress who, nevertheless, wants to be used. Their dialogue is highly improbable. What are described in some detail are the genitals and their secretions. This selection seems a bit descriptive because the prick ejaculates and the cunt oozes. But the exaggeration needed to carry off the fantasy renders the description less credible: "giant-cock head". . . . hot (not warm) sperm . . . jutting hard-on . . . "mauling her face."

The fantastical origin of such a story is nowhere better suggested than in the plumber's rapid tiring of her "frantic teasing." The only thing she did that could be interpreted as frantic teasing was to put herself in an inviting position on the double bed and, when he reached out for her, to avoid him. Any teasing that had previously occurred was in his head, while he was sniffing her pants, which, he assumes, she must have deliberately left around for him to sniff. Such is the behavior in fantasy land. It presents us with no real problem unless we think that such behavior should exist outside of our heads.

A recent issue of *Hustler* (August, 1977) attempted a major breakthrough in realism. It featured a lovely lady with her legs apart and her inner lips exposed. A circle drawn around her genitals contained the words, "Scratch 'N' Sniff," inviting the several million readers of this magazine to scratch the picture and sniff the genuine odor of a "hot pussy." Needless to say, after many letters expressing disappointment in the results—"smelled like lilacs, a perfume atomizer, or industrial strength Janitor in a drum"—*Hustler* concluded that,

[20]Gerald Benson, "Plumbers Help," *Club International* (September 1977), p.56. Contrast these two pornographic descriptions with the examples of actual lovemaking provided by Reich and Dodson in Chapter 18.

"the natural aroma of a juicy cunt is too difficult to capture. But if any of our readers has any idea as to how it can be done, let us know. We're open to suggestions."[21] The distance between promise and fulfillment in pornography is similarly great.

Infinite Pleasure without Satisfaction. Sex acts occur over and over again in pornographic literature because no one is fulfilled or satisfied in the process. The perpetuation of sexual stimulation, not its resolution, is what is sought. There is no rest here at the job of sex, and little joy either.

Most pornography is written by men for the purposes of arousing men, not for the purpose of satisfying them. However, because of its repetitive patterns, its hollow clichés, and its limited descriptive interest, most people have had enough after fifteen hours of continued exposure. For a considerable time afterwards, people are more or less immune to it.

Pornography may have some social function as a means of arousal (and a number of recent books on human sexuality and sex therapy suggest its use in this regard), but it is totally inadequate as a guide to lovemaking. While pornography may enhance fantasy, and thus enable some people to enjoy their real-life lovemaking more, its role in this regard is—or ought to be—quite limited because of the inherent limitations of its expression and imagery. In the long run, the depiction of insatiable desire leads to frustration, not to infinite pleasure.

Common Humanity Versus Exploitation of Women and Children. Pornography claims that sex is the great leveler and the universal equalizer. The reality of pornography is something else. Women are objects. They are little more than carriers of cunts, as men are little more than the cocks they boast of. But every orifice of the female is expected to be open to the prodding of every protuberance of the male.

Hustler features a "Beaver Hunt" each month. Readers are invited to send in a "sharply focused color photograph—no black and whites, please—of your favorite nude model, along with a short personality profile. Coax her to be as candid and original as possible, and be sure to fill out the model release form."[22] The magazine declares that if they decide to use a woman's photograph, she will receive fifty dollars as a modeling fee. The October, 1977 issue featured fourteen photos—including one of a dog in a suggestive pose. The photos are displayed on the tile floor of a bathroom (as suggested by the bare toes, lowered

[21]*Hustler* (August, 1977).

[22]*Hustler* (August, 1977), p. 105.

pants, and belt of a seated man looking down at the photos). There are cigarette butts and burnt matches on the floor. This slice of life may be taken by some as humor or as an example of our own reading habits, but it is difficult to deny the meaning behind the place assigned to the woman at the man's feet.

These magazines also carry articles that strongly condemn the abuse of women and children, but the overall impact of the magazines and the heritage of pornography is the subjugation of women for the pleasure of men. In point of fact, neither men or women are portrayed as individuals. They are both appendages to their genitals. It's just that the man is almost always on top.

SMUT AND SELF-DISCLOSURE

Expanding the First Amendment rights of freedom of speech to cover obscenity and pornography implies that a human right is being infringed upon, and some aspect of humanity denied its place in the sun. Undoubtedly so. Pornography has provided some valuable information about sexual behavior and has sometimes been the only way by which sex education has been conducted in the past. It has its use as a means of arousal and for some people today is a source of sexual satisfaction. But, in spite of its usefulness, it distorts the nature of human self-disclosure even as it reveals the innermost secrets of sex.

Nakedness is the symbol of openness and self-disclosure. It is not the only means by which we disclose ourselves, though it may be a means. But two people naked in bed together need not be intimate or open to one another.

Many lovers engage in the activities portrayed in pornographic movies such as *Deep Throat* or *The Devil and Miss Jones,* but they are concerned that such erotic interest and desire might offend their partners. Pornography contends that such concern for others is mere conventionality and at worst prudery. However, without care and compassion, sex ceases to lead to mutual self-disclosure and becomes abuse. Pornography does not distinguish between the abuse and the self-disclosure. Indeed it makes much of the lack of need for such a distinction and, thereby, sets sex and intimacy further apart.

THE READERSHIP

The commission concluded that roughly three-quarters of all adult males in the United States had been exposed to explicitly sexual material before the age of twenty-one. Most of these men reported that they were very interested in pornography when they were adolescents and that there was a lot of it around. The typical patron of adult bookstores and movies, however, was "predominantly white, middle-aged, married males dressed in business suit or neat attire, shopping or attending the movie alone. Almost no one under 21 was observed in these places, even where it was legal for them to enter."[23] But, nevertheless, many people are concerned about the effect of pornography on young people.

For this reason, the commission studied the effects of exposure to such material. The commission's report concluded that there is no reliable evidence at present that exposure to erotic material leads to sex crimes or to sexual delinquency.[24] Exposure may temporarily change

[23]Report *of the Commission on Obscenity and Pornography,* p. 25.

[24]Ibid., p. 32.

Figure 15–8
(Woodfin Camp & Associates)

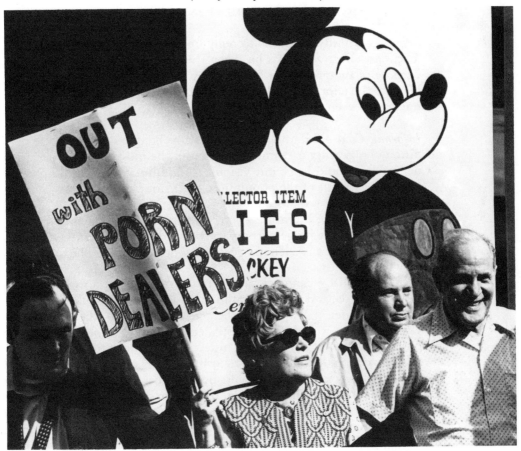

a person's pattern of sexual behavior, but, over the long-run, exposure to erotic material had little or no lasting effect on people's sexual attitudes. In research studies, some people responded positively to erotic stimuli that other people found to be offensive or unpleasant, just like in real life. In sum, the majority of the commission contended that there is little evidence that pornography has harmful social effects. As a result, the commission recommended the expansion of sex education programs rather than the imposition of legal restrictions on pornography. The commission's recommendations, which will be discussed in more detail shortly, go much beyond the scientific data available—as the commission's majority readily recognized—and rely on active citizen participation in sex education to deal with the problems posed by our current conflicts in sexual values.

THE SOCIAL REGULATION OF PORNOGRAPHY

Society currently attempts to regulate pornography in various ways. The least effective means has been the long arm of the law, not only because of the protection provided by the First Amendment but also because the effort to regulate pornography primarily or solely by legal means has been costly and ineffective.

Informal Control. Pornography cannot be contained by a single definition of obscenity or pornography. Even the most generally accepted definitions would leave out visions of the human that are important to large segments of the population. For example, James Joyce's *Ulysses,* Ovid's *Metamorphoses,* and D. H. Lawrence's *Lady Chatterly's Lover*—all great works of literature—were once labeled as pornographic. The standards used to judge pornography should be community standards and exposure to any such images should be voluntary. The question is how to ensure this.

In a pluralist society, we cannot rely on the universality of community standards, and the attempt to make the content of nationally distributed material subject to the variations found throughout the United States would mean costly editing that would prohibit the publication and distribution of much worthwhile material. The commission concluded that the majority of the people in the United States believe that adults should be able to read what they want to read. The focus of whatever legal regulation we might wish to impose should be on the distribution and display of such materials—not on their content. The content must be regulated by having to compete with richer more fully human images of sex in human loving. In a society just freeing itself from the burden of repression in matters of sex, a broad-scale sex education program is the only way to accomplish this.

The commission recommends the following as characteristics of its proposed sex education program.

1. Its purpose should be to contribute to healthy attitudes and orientations to sexual relationships so as to provide a sound foundation for our society's basic institutions of marriage and family.

2. It should be aimed at achieving an acceptance of sex as a normal and natural part of life and of oneself as a sexual being.

3. It should not aim for orthodoxy; rather it should be designed to allow for a pluralism of values.

4. It should be based on facts and encompass not only biological and physiological information but also social, psychological, and religious information.

5. It should be differentiated so that content can be shaped appropriately for the individual's age, sex, and circumstances.

6. It should be aimed as appropriate, to all segments of our society, adults as well as children and adolescents.

7. It should be a joint function of several institutions of our society: family, school, church etc.

8. Special attention should be given to the training of those who will have central places in the legitimate communication channels—parents, teachers, physicians, clergy, social service workers, etc.

9. It will require cooperation of private and public organizations at local, regional, and national levels with appropriate funding.

10. It will be aided by the imaginative utilization of new educational technologies, for example, educational television could be used to reach several members of a family in a family context.[25]

Sex information per se is necessary but not sufficient. What we need to know is what people make of the information in their daily lives. The pornographer contends that his version of loving is the most accurate, honest statement available, and there are few dissenting opinions. At present the teacher and the preacher feel forced to be silent about how they use the sexual information they have acquired in their own lives.

What we have hidden out of modesty can and should be discussed tastefully. What we know about human sexual behavior must be

[25]Ibid., pp. 54–55.

coupled with what we value in human loving and presented openly so that we may improve our language, our imagery, and our art of loving. This cannot be accomplished if, out of some misguided notions of the inherent baseness of explicit sexual material, we are unwilling to talk about our loving. Nor can it be effectively accomplished if we do not take into consideration the feelings and sentiments of others. Pornography, if it reflected people's true values and not unrealistic fantasies, might be a valuable way to enrich our personal experience of lovemaking.

Summary

Sex is commercialized in industrial societies in a number of ways. The most widespread and subtle way is the use of sexual themes and imagery in the sale of products on the consumer market. However, because every offense is a lost sale, advertising is generally quite restrained in its expression of sex. It suggests rather than explicitly portrays sexuality.

Social pressure also operates upon the prostitute who cannot simply peddle her wares anywhere. She must understand quickly what is involved in a transaction in order to prevent being blackmailed or sent to jail. Although the majority of men may visit a prostitute at least once in their lives, the prostitute's trade is mainly composed of regulars who use her services because they are satisfied customers. Learning the ropes from others in the trade involves little explicit training in techniques. The experienced woman will generally observe the new girl and offer advice later. However, the prostitute who cannot learn quickly what her customer wants and please him in the process of giving it, is not likely to stay in business. Call girls now operate in some cities with little reliance upon madams or pimps.

Pornography is the most explicit form of commercialized sex that is visible to the public. The explicitness of the prostitute's role is largely a private matter. Pornography has been regulated by law ineffectively because obscenity cannot be precisely defined. One person's smut is another's art. The report of the Commission on Pornography recommends that it be regulated by informal social means, primarily through increased sex education in families, churches, and schools. The distribution and sale of pornography should be the object of the law's effort in regulation, not the content. In order for the content to be regulated, it is necessary for more average examples of human lovemaking to enter the public discourse as erotic literature or art. By bringing real people into the lovemaking scenes, the obviously fantastical images of the pornographer can be corrected.

Sex and the Law

16

It is most embarrassing to any lawyer, who is proud
of being a member of the legal profession,
to write any analysis of the law as it pertains to sex.

Robert Veit Sherwin

If the laws governing sex offenses were to be universally accepted and voluntarily enforced in the United States, the vast majority of us would be labeled "sex offenders" and fined or imprisoned by a tiny minority who could do little else than operate the criminal justice system. This bizarre situation does not occur because most of us do not accept the law and do not voluntarily give ourselves up for our so-called "crimes." Many of the laws governing sexual behavior are unenforceable, because the "crime" occurs between consenting adults in private. These "victims" are not about to bring a complaint before the law because they do not feel that they have been harmed or that they have harmed others. Because they have conducted themselves in private, there are no witnesses.

Even those sex offenses that are regulated by laws are often poorly enforced because no one is generally convinced that they should be. There are times when public indignation is expressed against porn shops and prostitutes and police enforcement increases, but over the long run little is done to curb the traffic in such enterprises. Nowhere, save possibly in family law, can one find a body of law so out of step with public sentiment, so capriciously enforced, and so generally ineffective as in the case of those laws pertaining to sex offenses.

This chapter first examines some of the characteristics of the sex offender and how the label came about. Then it will consider the general characteristics of the various laws enacted to control such undesirable behavior. Finally, it will discuss the broader issues of the role of law in the regulation of sexual behavior and what seems to be its preferable role in a pluralistic society such as our own.

The Sex Offender

In America, legal sexual conduct is currently limited to heterosexual hugging, kissing, mouth-body (but not mouth-genital) contact, and hand-body contacts. Coital contacts are legally limited to marriage. All other sexual behavior is technically illegal and subject to punishment. The study of sex offenders is at least as much a study of the efficiency or inefficiency of the criminal justice system as it is a study of people who have certain characteristics in common. (See Figure 16–1.)

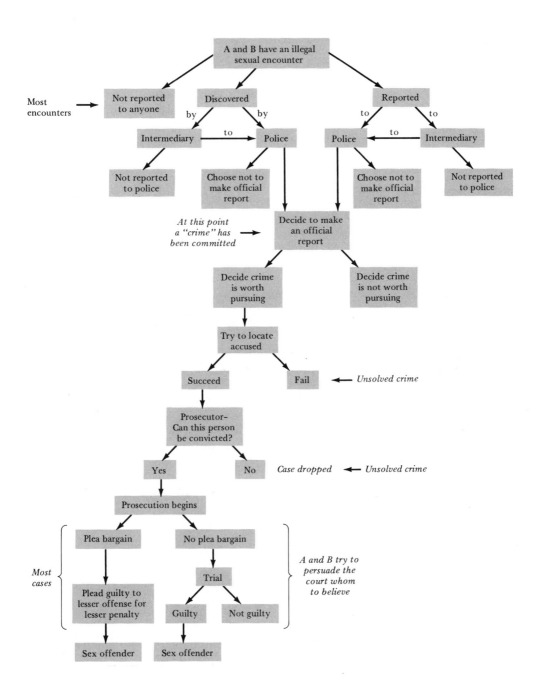

Figure 16–1
A study of the sex offender. (Adapted from John H. Gagnon, Human Sexualities, Glenview, Ill.: Scott, Foresman and Company, 1977. Copyright © 1977 by Scott, Foresman and Company. Reprinted by permission.)

STEREOTYPES AND REALITIES

Most of us have an image of the sex offender as a particular type of person. This stereotype is perpetuated by the legal terminology. "Crimes against nature," "lewd and lascivious acts," are legal terms used to define the sexual crimes. Before the Kinsey reports, the American public was so uninformed about normal sexual behavior that it accepted essentially ascetic norms as accurate descriptions of actual or natural behavior. People who seemed to go beyond these norms in any significant way were likely to be labeled sex offenders.

The sex offender depicted as a sexual beast reaffirmed the public view that the sexual impulse was both dangerous and explosive, that it needed to be repressed and controlled to prevent its destructive consequences. The typical reported case was the rape murder of a child by a sex offender with many previous sex convictions who had been released to prey upon the community by an incompetent parole board. Such newspaper reports could fascinate and thrill a population living in sexual ignorance and tension.[1]

This image of the sex offender is still held by some law enforcement officials as well as by the general public. The courts often adhere to the notion that the law should enforce a particular morality with a vengeance. The following is taken from the court record of a trial in the State of California on September 2, 1969. The judge is speaking to a minor accused of having committed incest with his sister.

The Court: There is some indication that you more or less didn't think that it was against the law or was improper. Haven't you had any moral training? Have you and your family gone to church?
The Minor: Yes, sir.
The Court: Don't you know that things like this are terribly wrong? This is one of the worst crimes that a person can commit. I just get so disgusted that I just figure what is the use? You are just an animal. You are lower than an animal. Even animals don't do that. You are pretty low.

I don't know why your parents haven't been able to teach you anything or train you. (You) people, after 13 years of age, its perfectly all right to go out and act like an animal (sic). It's not even right to do that to a stranger, let alone a member of your own family. I don't have much hope for you. You will probably end up in a State's prison before you are 25, and that's where you belong anyhow. There is nothing much you can do.

I think you haven't got any moral principles. You won't acquire anything. Your parents won't teach you what is right or wrong and won't watch out.

[1]John Gagnon, *Human Sexualities* (Glenview, Ill.: Scott, Foresman and Company, 1977), p. 295.

Apparently, your sister is pregnant, is that right?

The Minor's Father: Yes.

The Court: Well, probably she will have a half a dozen children and three or four marriages before she is 18.

The country will have to take care of you. You are no particular good to anybody. We ought to send you out of the country. . . . You belong in prison for the rest of your life for doing things of this kind. You ought to commit suicide. That's what I think of people of this kind. You are lower than animals and haven't the right to live in organized society—just miserable, lousy, rotten people.

There is nothing that we can do with you. You expect the country to take care of you. Maybe Hitler was right. The animals in our society probably ought to be destroyed because they have no right to live among human beings. If you refuse to act like a human being, then, you don't belong among the society of human beings.

Figure 16–2
Henry Giarretto, a specialist in the treatment of people who have been involved in incestuous relationships, feels that the best way to help such people is through therapy rather than the law. According to Giarretto, sexual feelings between family members are normal, but giving into them can have very damaging effects, particularly between fathers and daughters. (Mark Kauffman, People Weekly © Time, Inc.)

Defense Attorney: Your Honor, I don't think I can sit here and listen to that sort of thing.
The Court: You are going to have to listen to it because I consider this a very vulgar, rotten human being.[2]

The crime of incest has so angered this particular judge that he engaged in a level of defamation for which he was later censured. He generalized one boy's action into a reflection on an entire minority group and even asserted the value of genocide. The horrors of incest combined, in this judge's mind, with a quite negative stereotype of a minority group to produce a particularly abusive image of a sex offender. "Sex fiend," "sexual moron," "sexual psychopath," and other defaming legal labels derive from such mental images.

In fact, the sex offender is as likely to be suffering from a poorly expressed sexuality as he is from an uncontrollable sexual drive. Ralph Slovenko recounts the story of a young man he knew whose problems with sexual expression were acute, but who had not yet been labeled a sex offender. The young man appeared to be a perfectly normal person. An examination of his morals would have found him flawless, but inwardly he was in great turmoil.

> *This particular young man at the time was a virgin and worried about it. He masturbated a great deal, to relieve his loneliness or anxiety, from whatever source. A fair measure of his fear of sex may be illustrated by his remark that he wished it were "over with." At the time I chatted with him a trying situation presented itself. A girl rather well-known for her promiscuity showed an interest in him, and he decided to deflower himself. The preparation was mountainous: manuals on sexual technique, a new sweater, the traditional jug of wine, and much more. The day before the date, he expressed concern and finally doubt that the mechanics of the sexual act could be mastered by a beginner. He was afraid he might not attain an erection. His repetitive words were embarrassment! and humiliation. At the thought of buying a prophylactic, he realized that his arrangement would not work out. The enormity of the venture struck him. He canceled the date. The sex, even if he had engaged in it, would have left him as lonely and unrelated afterwards as before. And he is in perpetual rage, the pacing rage of a caged animal. It smolders far beneath and only seldom is the glow seen. But his stomach is in constant ferment and he takes pill after pill to rid himself of the pain.*[3]

This young person is obviously headed for difficulty. His problems

---

[2]Superior Court of the State of California in and for the County of Santa Clara, Juvenile Division. Court 1. San Jose, California, September 2, 1969. 10:24 a.m.

[3]Ralph Slovenko, "Sex Laws: Are They Necessary?" in *Sexuality: A Search for Perspective,* eds. Donald L. Grummon and Andrew M. Barclay (New York: Van Nostrand Reinhold Company, 1971), p. 143.

derived from his inability to adequately express his sexuality, not from the too-free expression of it. Although the young man is aware of the law, it seems unlikely that it will exercise any particular restraining effect on him. This young man's bondage is not to the law. His internal chains are more binding and are only incidentally forged in such a way that his behavior appears to conform to the very restrictive laws now on the books. Few people would argue that this person's sexuality is being regulated by the laws. A better case might be made for the argument that his internal time bomb has been set in operation by the same forces that constructed the repressive sexual codes and can only be defused by a quite different approach, a totally different understanding of sexuality communicated in warmth and acceptance, rather than in cold rejection. In this case, current sex legislation seems a particularly blunt instrument with which to regulate sexual behavior.

Legal Definition of Sex Offenses

In effect, the law defines all nonreproductive genital behavior between adults as illegal, regardless of marital status in most cases, and regardless of whether or not such behaviors occurred in private. The intent of such legislation is clearly to enforce a very narrow view of sexual morality rather than to regulate sexual behavior in a reasonable way. To understand this better, it is necessary to look at how the law defines certain sex crimes. There is little uniformity in the definition of these crimes, and so the following is only suggestive.

SODOMY LAWS

The typical sodomy law reads as follows:

> *Every person who shall carnally know, or shall have sexual intercourse in any manner with any animal or bird, or shall carnally know any male or female by the anus (rectum) or with the mouth or tongue; or shall attempt intercourse with a dead body is guilty of sodomy.*[4]

Some sensitive people overreact to such laws. Sherwin recounts his experience with a young married couple who resolved their sexual difficulties by using cunnilingus to help the wife to achieve orgasm. Some months after having made a satisfactory sexual adjustment, the young husband brought home the news that cunnilingus was illegal

[4]This composite picture is constructed by Robert Veit Sherwin, "The Law and Sexual Relations," in *Human Sexuality: Contemporary Perspectives,* Eleanor S. Morrison and Vera Borosage (eds). (National Press, 1973), p. 286.

in their state and was punishable by sixty years in prison or more. Both became hysterical and they reported themselves to the police. Their case did not go to court because family contacts averted the proceedings. This may seem incredible or foolish to some readers, but many still abide by the notion that the law is holy, just, and good (even in its attempts to regulate sexual morality).

Sodomy laws are most often used to prosecute homosexuals. Such laws have also been used in divorce proceedings. For example, an aggrieved husband who feels that his wife's sexual desire is excessive can accuse her of "nymphomania." The threat to expose such "infamous and degenerate needs" in a court of law may force the wife to settle for less than she might otherwise be entitled to. Since advising anyone to commit a felony is in itself a felony, marriage counselors and sex therapists in many states are subject to arrest if they advise their clients to include oral or anal contact in their lovemaking. Mutual masturbation, even in the case of married people, is also condemned in some states.

FORNICATION

Sexual intercourse between unmarried people, or fornication, is prohibited by law in thirty-one of the fifty states. Welfare recipients are the favored target of this particular law. *Playboy* found that of 266 fornication cases tried between 1968 and 1972, 260 involved racial minorities. Sometimes fornication is defined as "living in a state of open and notorious cohabitation." In Arizona, such behavior is a felony punishable by imprisonment for not more than three years. It makes no difference in most cases if both adults are consenting to live together.[5]

Legal proceedings have magnified the problems of unwed mothers. Designed ostensibly to protect the woman, paternity suits in fact are rigged against her. She must testify in court in very precise terms how, when, and where the defendant's penis entered her vagina. Sherwin concludes, "The entire procedure implicitedly indicates that the Court regards her as a whore, and that the only reason the Court listens to her at all is for the sake of the taxpayer, in that support for the child (not for her) should be obtained from the father rather than from welfare."[6] In one state, should the unwed mother desire to place her baby for adoption, she must obtain the permission of the alleged father or else concede that she has no idea who he might be, thus openly admitting on the record that she is promiscuous.

Abortion laws are still being changed according to state prefer-

[5]Herant Katchadourian and Donald T. Lunde, *Fundamentals of Human Sexuality*, 2nd ed. (New York: Holt, Rinehart and Winston, 1975), p. 510.

[6]Sherwin, "The Law and Sexual Relations," p. 288.

ences. Congress, however, has recently refused to allocate federal funds for women on welfare to receive abortions that might be determined to be legal in their respective states, thus perpetuating the priviledge of abortion on demand for the rich and a coat hanger to be used as an instrument of abortion for the poor.

RAPE

It is not possible to determine just how much coercion is involved in sexual behavior in the United States, but one study on a single university campus concluded that about a quarter of the women studied had been forced to do something sexually that they did not want to do at some point. Not all of these acts could be considered rape, and, in fact, most of them were not so considered by the women themselves. They do, however, suggest something about the extent to which males feel free to force themselves on females, even in the more ordinary situations in our society. Rape, forced sexual intercourse with a woman other than a spouse, is considered the most serious sexual offense covered by the criminal law. It remains one of the few crimes for which the Supreme Court considers execution to be a proper punishment. Rape laws reflect our sexist society in curious ways. Originally, they were written to protect the property rights of men (husbands and fathers). In the nineteenth century, virginity was highly valued. If a man discovered that his wife was not a virgin after he married her, he could divorce her. Such an attitude toward virginity greatly contributed toward the definition of rape as a terrible crime, punishable by death.

Only women can be raped. More conservatively, only those whose previous sexual behavior has conformed (in the opinion of the jury) with the social norms governing appropriate sexual behavior can be raped. A prostitute cannot be raped in common opinion. If the victim has had sexual relationships with the accused in the past, he is not likely to be convicted. If she is a "sexual libertine, a divorced woman, a common-law wife, or an adulterer," her sexual behavior is commonly deemed inappropriate, and she is not guaranteed protection under the law—though she may receive it in some instances.[7] Since the law almost everywhere recognizes the husband's right to his wife's body (with or without her consent), a wife cannot be raped by her husband. Women who are separated from their husbands have a difficult time proving rape. The woman's past sexual behavior was once admitted as evidence against the credibility of her testimony. Some states still permit such evidence, but others are disallowing it.

Even so, the testimony of the victim is ordinarily not enough to

[7]The Yale Law Review, quoted in Frank Scarpetti and Ellen Scarpetti "Victims of Rape," *Society* (July/August, 1977) pp. 29–32.

"I was raped and my father blamed me.
We were finally able to talk it out with
New York Women Against Rape."

Counseling is free and confidential.
(212) 877-8700

The School of Visual Arts Public Advertising System

Figure 16–3

convict a man of rape. If there is no corroborating evidence—no
sperm in the vagina, no bruises, no witnesses, no torn clothing, no
blood—prosecution is difficult, even though penetration without consent can occur without providing such evidence to the examiners.
There is also a tendency to blame the victim for the crime. A recent
California case made headlines when a young girl was declared to

have been "asking for it" because she was hitchhiking alone when she was raped. Her assailant was not charged. In another case, a Wisconsin judge acquitted a young man in a rape case because the woman in question had been wearing a shorter dress than the judge deemed appropriate.

As a result of these difficulties, most people accused of rape are acquitted or allowed to plead guilty to a lesser charge. In 1975, only 41 percent of those adults charged with rape were convicted. An additional 12 percent pleaded guilty to lesser charges.[8] This conviction rate is a substantial increase over previous years. Some analysts feel that there is a tendency not to convict because in the eyes of the jury, the punishment is too severe for the crime. In point of fact, in California the average time spent in prison for forcible rape—rape in which violence is proven—is 36 months, which is less than the average prison term of those who have committed so-called sex perversions (sodomy and indecent exposure). The number of people charged with forcible rape has declined since 1956—from 9.9 people per thousand population to 7.2 per thousand in 1972.[9] However, it is estimated that only 10 to 50 percent of all rapes are actually reported. Therefore, the number of people charged with the crime or the number convicted do not represent an accurate disclosure of the crime's prevalence. Some women's groups are contending that the actual incidence of rape is increasing.[10]

A study by the Institute for Sex Research at Indiana University indicates that the typical rapist tries to avoid detection, plans the crime in advance, and tends to rationalize the crime in terms of the woman's having given consent. Some apparently believe that the victim cooperated in the act: "She didn't struggle," "she voluntarily removed her clothes," "she enjoyed it," "she encouraged me." Forcible rape is more likely to be committed by males under the age of twenty-five. The incidence declines with increasing age. Their victims are typically not in the same age group, often being younger than the rapist.[11]

Women can defend themselves against rape by taking some precautions. Since most rapes occur in the victim's home, it is important that all windows on the ground floor be properly shielded, that doors have bolts that cannot be jammed, and that mailboxes or telephone

[8]Martin Haskell and Lewis Yablanski, *Criminology, Crime and Criminality* (Chicago: Rand McNally, 1974), p. 340.

[9]Ibid., p. 379.

[10]See data presented in Boston Women's Health Collective, *Our Bodies, Ourselves* (New York: Simon and Schuster), p. 156.

[11]Paul H. Gebhard, John H. Gagnon, Wardell B. Pomeroy, and Cornelia V. Christenson, *Sex Offenders, An Analysis of Types* (New York: Harper & Row, 1965), pp. 197–206.

Figure 16–4
A rape victim should not hesitate to seek help.
(Michael Heron)

listings do not give away the fact that a woman is living alone. It might be useful to add a ficticious roommate to the mailbox and to use initials, rather than one's full name, in the telephone directory. Self-defense courses can provide some assistance, but often a woman is reluctant to hurt someone, even when the person is hurting her. The first blow has to count, or otherwise the woman risks further enraging her attacker.

Rape victims should seek immediate help. A friend is helpful in providing support through the necessary examinations in the hospital and with the police. A rape crisis center may provide useful support and information on what to do immediately after a rape. A woman should not follow her inclination to go home and shower. She must record what happened to her to the best of her memory, appear before a police investigator immediately and undergo a medical examination not only for purposes of determining the extent of her injuries but also to establish evidence should she decide to prosecute the rapist. Even though she may not appear to be physically hurt, she may be suffering from internal injuries. It is also important that she be checked for pregnancy and venereal disease. Should she decide to take estrogen as a "morning after" preventative, she should be aware of the increased risk of cancer. If pregnancy is determined, an abortion should be considered and arranged for as soon as possible. A second check for venereal disease should be sought about six months after the incident.

None of these procedures are likely to be pleasant. Indeed, some women have reported feeling that the medical examination was the second rape because of the obvious indifference of the examining physician. But these procedures are being improved. Dealing with the psychological damage may take much longer. Talking it out is preferable to keeping it to yourself. A number of settings for such a discussion are possible, including the rap sessions at a rape crisis center. Sometimes husbands or boyfriends do not understand. They are enraged at the rapist and apparently insensitive to the victim, or they wonder what all the fuss is about if the female isn't obviously wounded. Finding an understanding listener is not always easy, but the effort should be made.

There have been notable changes in legal opinion and status since 1970.[12] The change is toward seeing rape as a crime of violence rather than as a crime of passion, and to remove its sexist connotations by making it a more sexually neutral offense such as sexual assault, sexual battery, or criminal sexual conduct, in which presumably, both sexes could participate. The trend is away from allowing the victim's past sexual behavior to be introduced as a means of casting doubt

[12]See Scarpetti and Scarpetti, "Victims of Rape."

upon her integrity. Women's groups also tend to seek less severe penalties, less plea bargaining, and more convictions. The criminal justice system is modifying its practices to include special units dealing with rape victims. Often these units have female members. Personnel are trained to respect the feelings of the victim and to hear her side of the story without prejudice.

A curious alliance has begun to develop between white women's groups and white conservatives seeking law and order. Both groups campaign for prosecution and conviction of the rapist. It so happens that the lower-class black male is most often charged with rape. While black rapists face the same prosecution as white rapists, they are more likely to be convicted and typically receive stiffer sentences. Of the 455 persons executed for rape between the years 1930–1964, 405 were black.

Having sex with a person who is under the legal age of consent can lead to a charge of statutory rape, even if no force was involved. Statutory rape laws are often biased against the male. It is unreasonable to assume an age of consent as high as sixteen or eighteen, for example, since many women of this age look quite a bit older and are, in fact, able to give or withhold their consent to sexual intercourse. An example of an abuse of these statutes occurred in New York State, where five fifteen-year-old boys were convicted as youthful offenders because they had intercourse with a seventeen-year-old girl known to be a prostitute to whom they had paid the proper fees. She was three weeks short of her eighteenth birthday (the age of consent in New York at the time) and was not convicted of prostitution.[13]

PROSTITUTION

Prostitution has been part of human sexual expression from time immemorial. It has not always been an offense. It was legal, for example, in ancient Greece. For a time it looked as though one of the chief effects of the sexual revolution was to allow a middle-class male to replace the prostitute with a sexual partner from his own class. However, call girls are still a part of the corporate structure. Their services come under the heading of "entertainment," and their fees can be paid for in tax deductions and charged under various credit systems.

The common streetwalker is the main target of laws against prostitution. Most laws are directed at her violation of the public sense of decency. For example, a Colorado code concludes:

> *Any prostitute or lewd woman who shall, by word, gesture or action, endeavor to ply her vocation upon the streets, or from the door or window of any house, or in any public place, or make a bold display of herself, shall be guilty of a misdemeanor, and shall be fined not more than $100, or im-*

[13]Sherwin, "The Law and Sexual Relations." p. 202.

Figure 16–5
In most states it is a crime to be a prostitute, but not a crime to make use of a prostitute's services.
(© Sepp Seitz, Woodfin Camp & Associates)

prisoned in a county jail for no less than ten days nor more than three months or both.[14]

This law is aimed primarily against soliciting. In Oregon, both the prostitute and her John (her male client) are prosecuted, but this is unusual. Most states outlaw advertising for the purpose of solicitation. Recent proposals for legal reform of laws governing prostitution declare that it should be considered a social nuisance and its public aspect regulated, but that it should not be considered a crime in itself.

The prostitute commonly serves the role of allowing middle-class males, and to a lesser extent females, to live out their sexual fantasies. Her clients may not be potent under any other conditions than those that their fantasy dictates. They are hardly to be considered sex fiends in spite of the often bizarre behavior their fantasies demand. While it is a crime to be a prostitute, it is not a crime to make use of the services of a prostitute in most states. This is another example of the discrimination in the formulation of the laws governing sexual offences.

NUISANCE BEHAVIOR

Voyeurism and exhibitionism are commonly considered nuisance behavior and are normally treated as misdemeanors. The voyeur, a person who likes to watch people do sexual or private things, is com-

[14]Colorado Statues Annotated (1935), Chapter 48, Sec. 214.

monly called a "peeping Tom." Looking into windows while walking down the street is a very common human tendency, but the peeping Tom goes further and walks up to the windows. This behavior, though offensive, is relatively harmless because the peeper generally does not want to enter the window. He just wants to watch. We know very little about voyeurism because most of it goes undetected, unreported and unrecorded.

The exhibitionist, commonly called a "flasher," displays his penis in public. Such an individual is rarely likely to do any harm, except for the shock he gives his victims; it is not in our common sexual script for a man to expose his penis to a woman in public. Women are not usually convicted of exhibitionism, though they may be charged with indecent exposure.

The Law in Theory and Practice

John Noonan points out that the law has three primary functions: the channeling function, the coercive function, and the teaching function. We most often think of the law in terms of its power to coerce, to force us to behave in certain ways. But the other functions are equally important. Noonan contends that the emphasis on the law as coercion is derived from a basically negative view of men and women. In fact, many people are not so much bad as confused. The other functions of the law can be used to clear up this confusion.

In its coercive function, the law aims at curbing or preventing behavior considered to be destructive to others. It is not universally effective in doing this. We must remember that relatively few criminals are caught. Even fewer are prosecuted, and fewer still are punished. These points are true in all areas of criminal law, not just in those pertaining to human sexuality. But, granted that this is so, we should not abandon the notion of the law. Nor should we abandon the attempt to regulate sexual behavior because of the ineffectiveness of rehabilitation programs and the instances in which imprisonment actually worsens the situation. These are not good aspects of the criminal law, but they should not be used to conclude that no attempt should be made to regulate sexual behavior by means of criminal law. The important question is how the criminal law should be used.

The obvious shortcomings of the criminal law in its coercive function are compensated for in part (in Noonan's view) by the other functions. It is clear, Noonan contends, that the institutions of marriage and the family are socially supported by the criminal laws against fornication and adultery. The Judeo-Christian notion of marriage as a life-long monogamous relationship involving the exclusive sexual rights of the spouse and the equality of the spouses before the law is an ideal that has taken a long time to evolve. It represents considerable progress in human rights over the views of Roman law and should be preserved.[15] It excludes polygamy and nonmarital sexuality, Noonan argues, because these are seen as less desirable ways of relating to others. The law is slow to reflect social change and this is a good thing. Alternative life styles need time to prove themselves.

The teaching function of the law is seen most clearly, Noonan contends, in the case of abortion, where much of the current opposition is given to laws declaring the fetus's right to life in the past, and this right must not be taken away by concerns for the rights of the mother in the present. Right-to-lifers contend that the fetus has been given a right to life over the mother's religious conviction. An example is the Jehovah's Witnesses who refused blood transfusions to save their babies as a matter of religious conviction. On at least two occasions, the courts have ruled that the transfusions should be given.[16] In such cases, the law is teaching us about the value of human life. "Life is the only ultimate civil right. Life is the only right of the child in the womb."[17]

At first, consideration of these latter functions of the law—teaching and channeling—seem more appropriate to a state in which one can assume broad general agreement on values. As described, the channeling function seems most restrictive in our society because it simply assumes that there is, in fact, one best way for the family to exist, or one best way to contract a marriage. Both of these points are in much dispute. The teaching function also assumes some general agreement. The right-to-lifers are a minority—but an effective one. The Model Penal Code permits much diversity to be legally expressed in sexual life styles. This is appropriate for a pluralist society.

THE MODEL PENAL CODE

The general guidelines that any sexual behavior between consenting adults in private is not the law's business is supported in the penal code. This focuses the concern of the law and law enforcement officials on the regulation of public behavior—not the enforcement of a particular set of moral principles. This shift in emphasis, however, presupposes that certain values are widely shared in the population. The most obvious of these are the assumptions that consent is neces-

[15]John I. Noonan, Jr., "Sexual Freedom and the Three Functions of the Law," in Grummon and Barkley, eds., *Sexuality,* p. 161.

[16]*Raleigh Filkin-Oaul Memorial Hospital* v. *Anderson,* 42 N.J., 428, 201, 1964. See Noonan, "Sexual Freedom," p. 169.

[17]Noonan, "Sexual Freedom," p. 170.

sary and protection from harm a prime concern. These values can be realized without prescribing what people do in private, so long as harm is restricted to the parties involved. If the concept of harm is extended to third parties (persons not involved in the private behavior who—by word of mouth, for example—might be offended or harmed), then the value of personal privacy is likely to be violated. There have been some examples of the enforcement of sodomy laws against married couples because their behavior was heard about through the means of innocent third parties such as their children who happened upon their lovemaking and told others about it. These persons became offended at what they heard. It seems reasonable to infer that in such cases the offense rendered by the hearing was less than the harm that might be done by the law's invasion of privacy in the attempted enforcement of sodomy laws.

What law should attempt in the case of the regulation of sexual behavior is the prevention of harm, exploitation, or abuse. Rape, therefore, is a crime primarily because it is forced upon another without consent. It can often be violent. Even if the sexual aspects of rape are ignored, the lack of consent and the physical and psychological abuse of the victim are sufficient grounds for expecting the intervention of the criminal justice system. Evidence of such events can normally be obtained without a great deal of disclosure of the specifics of sexual histories or elaborate documentation of the sexual behavior involved. Documentation of the lack of consent and the use of coercion seems at least as easy as the documentation of penile-vaginal penetration and is certainly less likely to invade the privacy of the victim. Indeed, the law is beginning to recognize rape as at least as much a crime of violence as a sex crime.

The public display of most sexual behavior is widely recognized as offensive in our society. In other societies this is much less true. Given our cultural predisposition to regard sexual behavior as private matters more appropriately expressed in the intimate community, it makes sense to regulate its public expression without concern about what occurs between consenting adults in private. The peeping Tom is offensive at the level of nuisance because it takes place in public. In both cases the behavior is forced on the victim in the sense that no attempt is made to obtain consent. Both forms of behavior can reasonably be regulated by legal means, without going into the pros and cons of indecent exposure. Furthermore, since the harm done to the victim in both of these cases is relatively little more than the experience of shock or offense, the crime should not be severely punished and, in fact, is not in most cases. It might be severely punished, however, if it becomes a morals case—if people allow themselves to become outraged at such behavior.

Seeing the function of law in the regulation of sexual behavior in this manner clearly limits its sphere of influence. Morality, particularly sexual morality, derives from an understanding of what it means to respect the rights of others at least at the level of seeking consent and causing no harm. Such an understanding is shaped by education and example in the intimate environment, not by the formulation of legislation intended to perpetuate a single understanding of what loving relationships should be.

In a pluralist culture in which there are in fact many modes of loving and many styles of living, the law can best function as a means of preventing harmful behavior in public. It would be greatly assisted, in this task if the society should in fact value the different modes of loving and encourage people to experiment in their development of compassionate life styles. The law can regulate such public behavior so long as it respects the behavior of consenting adults in private.

Summary

Our present criminal law attempts to enforce a behaviorally outdated conception of sexual morality on a pluralistic culture in which most people not only do not practice such a morality in their lives, but do not give ascent to it in their values. Under such conditions the law is abused by sporadic enforcement, inappropriate punishment, and widespread indifference. Laws enacted to govern sexual behavior often are used in divorce proceedings, and invite blackmail and corruption in the criminal justice system itself.

The legalization of all sexual behavior between consenting adults in private was proposed by the model penal code would go a long way toward improving the effectiveness of the criminal justice system. The system could regulate sexual behavior that is perpetuated on a victim and would free law enforcement officials from having to attend to a large number of victimless crimes that now demand their attention.

Sex and Health

17

In the beginning, God created the heavens,
the earth, and venereal disease. . . . The pox is a pitiless
creditor and grants grace to no one.

Philippe Ricord

VD
is no way
to treat
a
friend

In recent years gonorrhea has been the most prevalent reportable disease, with syphilis not far behind. Over a million cases of gonorrhea were reported in 1977, which represented a slight decrease from earlier years.[1] The incidence of primary and secondary syphilis has been around 20,000 cases a year since 1970. When most people talk about venereal disease (VD), they are talking about syphilis and gonorrhea.

Calling syphilis and gonorrhea "venereal diseases," after Venus the goddess of love, is a supremely ironic label. Venereal diseases have a great deal to do with moist mucus membranes, but virtually nothing to do with love. These diseases are transmitted through sexual contact. In fact, some people consider them to be the price paid for having sex. But the disease spreads much more from our lack of caring for one another and from our lack of loving than from our loving. The man who is aware that he is infected with one of these diseases and does not inform his partner gives evidence of not caring. The physician who condemns infected patients as promiscuous sinners or who is indifferent to their feelings is not caring for them. Through such noncaring the disease spreads.

Our current epidemic of syphilis and gonorrhea is directly related to the Vietnam War. Many American soldiers had sex with Vietnamese women who were forced into prostitution by the ravages of war. The indifferent treatment of the women and the ineffective treatment of the soldiers produced a resistant strain of gonorrhea, the so-called Vietnam Rose, which was introduced into the United States when the soldiers came home. It is making war, not love, that has contributed most to the spread of these diseases in the past. This is important to realize because the diseases now called venereal can be eradicated only if people having sex and those who may be called upon to treat them care for one another enough to work together in its prevention.

In this chapter, we first examine the historical development of the major venereal diseases, syphilis and gonorrhea. Then we describe other venereal infections, their diagnosis, and their treatment. The chapter closes with some observations of syphilis and gonorrhea.

[1]The Center for Disease Control, Atlanta, Georgia, May 23, 1977. Information on the year 1976 can be obtained from *VD Fact Sheet 1976* (Atlanta, Georgia: Center for Disease Control, 1978).

Historical Perspectives on Venereal Disease

Bacteria are thought to be among the world's oldest living things. The bacteria that cause gonorrhea and syphilis are so fragile that they cannot live for more than a few seconds outside of the human body. When these two diseases developed, where they came from, and how they spread remain a mystery. The dominant view among physicians is that in the fifteenth century syphilis was brought from the New World to Europe by the sailors returning with Christopher Columbus. However, a second, less well-accepted theory contends that there is evidence of syphilis going back into prehistory and that it probably began with the emergence of cities around 10,000 B.C. Some believe that the leprosy referred to in the Bible was, in fact, syphilis.

The case of gonorrhea is more complicated. The gonorrhea bacillus was not clearly isolated from the one that causes syphilis until 1879.[2] Prior to that time most physicians considered the symptoms of syphilis and gonorrhea to be those of a single disease.

Although there are some references in ancient writings to symptoms that may have been related to venereal disease, syphilis did not become a major concern in Europe until around the fifteenth century.

The Holy Roman Emperor, Maximilian, referred to it as an "evil pox" in his Edict of 1495 and said it had "never occurred before nor been heard of within the memory of men."[3] In fact, during the fifteenth and sixteenth centuries most European countries became aware of the existence of syphilis, and each was likely to blame the epidemic on its enemies. The English, for example, called it "the French disease" or "the Spanish pox," depending on the political situation at the time. In his book, *Contagion,* published in 1530, the poet/physician Fracastor contended that diseases were transmitted by "seeds" or "germs" and that syphilis was often transmitted in sexual intercourse.[4]

It is probable that the Columbus theory of the origin of syphilis is not true. There is no convincing evidence that the bones of pre-Columbian peoples in the New World were syphilitic. In Europe, bone records are more numerous. But a number of diseases leave lesions on bones that are similar to those caused by syphilis. In addition, people at that time had the tendency to pin the label leprosy or contagion on a host of diseases. If it was not brought to Europe by the

[2]Louis Lasagna, *The VD Epidemic* (Philadelphia, Temple University Press, 1975), p. 18.

[3]Hans Zinsser, *Rats, Lice and History* (New York: Bantam, 1935).

[4]Lasagna, *The VD Epidemic*, p. 25.

crew of Columbus's expedition, it is nevertheless evident that an epidemic of syphilis erupted at the turn of the sixteenth century. The disease spread quickly through Europe and was carried to India and China by Spanish and Portuguese explorers.

Although VD was common in western Europe after 1500, precise details are lacking because very few records were kept. It is not possible to determine the incidence of these diseases until military records of the eighteenth and nineteenth centuries begin to give us some partial insight. The major armies of the world experienced significant decreases in cases of syphilis over the period ranging from 1860 to 1910. The army of the United States was a notable exception. Its rates rose sharply after the Mexican, Civil, and Spanish American Wars.[5]

By 1910, it was possible to take blood tests as well as microscopic tests for syphilis. Scandinavian countries began active treatment of the disease and greatly reduced its prevalence. The program in the United States, however, did not become effective until about 1938. In 1938, one out of every ten Americans could expect to contract syphilis.[6] Rates varied by race, age, and region, as revealed through the analysis of the draft records of soldiers. The highest rates were found among blacks in the South.

THE NATIONAL VD PROBLEM SINCE 1950

An increase in syphilis due to World War II had been anticipated, and the expected epidemic was contained. It was not until the 1950s that the incidence of venereal disease again began to increase significantly. This rise resulted from the apparent success in containing the disease, the increased exposure of GIs to prostitutes in Korea and Vietnam, the use of the pill, and an increase in sexual permissiveness in the population at large. In 1949, both syphilis and gonorrhea were thought to have been contained in the United States.[7] By 1958, however, the optimism had waned.

Overconfidence is only a part of the explanation for the resurgence of VD. In 1956, the routine blood test was dropped as a requirement for hospital accreditation and many were questioning its value as a required test before a marriage license could be granted. Federal funding dropped from a high of $17 million to only $3 million in 1955.[8] Because people thought the problem had been solved, doctors were no longer trained to treat syphilis and gonorrhea and, consequently, misdiagnosed these diseases and mistreated them. Gon-

[5]Ibid., p. 19.

[6]Ibid.

[7]Ibid., p. 1.

[8]Ibid., p. 2.

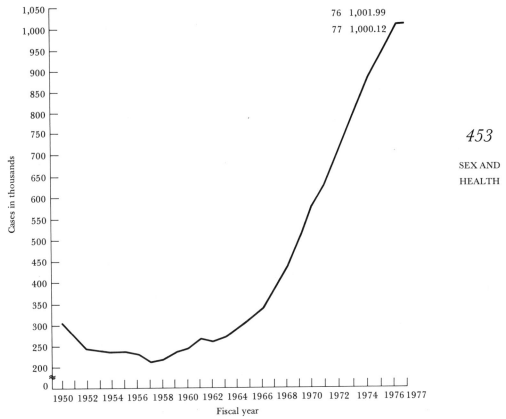

1,050 ┐
1,000 ┤   76 1,001.99
  950 ┤   77 1,000.12
  900 ┤
  850 ┤
  800 ┤   453
  750 ┤
  700 ┤   SEX AND
  650 ┤   HEALTH
  600 ┤
  550 ┤
  500 ┤
  450 ┤
  400 ┤
  350 ┤
  300 ┤
  250 ┤
  200 ┤
    0 ┴

Cases in thousands

1950 1952 1954 1956 1958 1960 1962 1964 1966 1968 1970 1972 1974 1976 1977
Fiscal year

Figure 17–1
Reported cases of gonorrhea in the United States, 1950–1977.
(U.S. Department of Health, Education, and Welfare)

orrhea rates increased rampantly. In 1957, there were slightly more than 200,000 reported cases of gonorrhea. By 1976, the number of reported cases had passed 1 million; it has just begun to fall off a bit (See Figure 17–1).[9] The number of reported cases of primary and secondary syphilis rose from a low of 6,500 cases in 1957 to rates remaining around 20,000 reported cases per year from 1961 on. In 1977, there were 20,362 cases reported.[10] It must be remembered that in both cases the reported figures are considerably lower than the actual number of cases. Perhaps only one in four infected people actually come in for treatment.[11]

Similar outbreaks in VD have occurred in other countries. In 1969,

[9]Center for Disease Control, private correspondence, May 23, 1978.

[10]Center for Disease Control, private communication.

[11]Boston's Women's Health Collective, *Our Bodies, Ourselves* (New York: Simon and Shuster, 1971), p. 98.

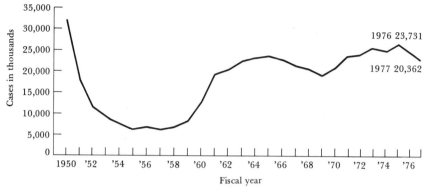

Figure 17–2
Reported cases of primary and secondary syphilis in the United States, 1950–1977.
(U.S. Department of Health, Education, and Welfare)

England and Wales recorded the highest level of gonorrhea ever, rising 14 percent over the previous year. Sweden reported 485 cases per 100,000 population in 1969.[12]

Around the world, the rates of gonorrhea increased between 1969 and 1970. There was a 14 percent increase in Denmark, Norway, and England. The Swedish rate increased 23 percent and the French, 20 percent. The Swedish rate began to level off in 1970, the first indication in the developed world that the gonorrhea outbreak that began in the mid-fifties was beginning to abate. Trends in reported cases of syphilis were more varied. In general, there were increases around the world during the early seventies, but less dramatic than those for gonorrhea. A notable exception was Belgium, whose rate increased 42.8 percent between 1969 and 1970. Among those people who are especially likely to develop venereal disease are young people, seafarers, tourists, and migrant workers. College students experienced higher than average increases in VD in the early 1970s.[13]

The Diseases and Their Treatment

Although all VD type diseases can cause considerable discomfort and pain, and some can cause serious complications, the major diseases are considered to be gonorrhea and syphilis. Most of the serious consequences of these major diseases derive from long-term effects in un-

[12]K. Kiraly, "The Venereal Disease Problem Around the World," *Epidemia: Venereal Disease, Proceedings of the 2nd International Venereal Disease Symposium*, St. Louis, 1972 (New York: Pfizer Laboratories, 1973), p. 124.

[13]Ibid., pp. 124–26.

treated cases. Both gonorrhea and syphilis respond readily to proper treatment in the vast majority of cases, but careless treatment or inaccurate diagnosis can create complications.

SYPHILIS

The word syphilis probably comes from the Greek words meaning "swine" and "love."[14] The hero of Fracastor's poem (in which the term was first used) was a young swineherd named Syphilis, who had the disease. The bacterial organism, or spirochete, that causes syphilis was discovered in 1905, and the Wasserman blood test for syphilis was developed shortly thereafter.

The spirochete that causes syphilis is an extremely elongated corkscrew-shaped organism that is difficult to grow in culture. It belongs to a genus of spirochetes called *Treponema,* which are common to the human species. Because these spirochetes are extremely fragile, they require intimate contact in order for them to be transmitted from one individual to another. It is extremely unlikely that syphilis can be spread in any other way.[15]

The symptoms of syphilis are generally described in terms of three separate states: an early period that includes the first two years after infection, a latent period during which there are no symptoms, and a late period in which the signs of syphilis can be observed about ten years after infection. Blood tests, however, will reveal the presence of spirochetes in the blood during latency. Syphilis is contagious only during the early stages.

Early Syphilis. The primary diagnostic sign of early syphilis is the *chancre,* or skin lesion, that develops at the point of contact with the infected person who transmits the disease. Most commonly, these lesions appear on the anus or genitals, but they can also occur on the lip, mouth, fingers, and breast. The chancre usually begins as a small module that erodes and becomes moist. There is frequently nothing particularly characteristic about it. It may, or may not, be hard. There may or may not be more than one of them. The only other sign is a firm, painless, movable lymph gland that has received the infection at the point of local lymph drainage. For example, if the chancre were on the penis, the swollen lymph gland would be in the groin.

In most cases, these chancres heal without treatment. Indeed, we know from a number of studies that among those persons who acquire

---

[14]Saul Blau, "The Venereal Diseases," in *The Encyclopedia of Sexual Behavior,* eds. Albert Ellis and Albert Averbanel (New York: Jason Aronson, Inc. 1973), p. 1023.

[15]Theodor Rosebury, *Microbes and Morals* (New York: The Viking Press, 1971), pp. 69–70.

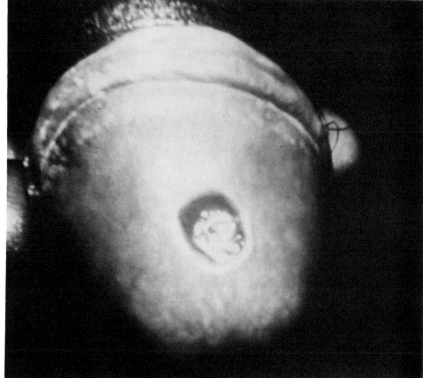

Figure 17–3
Primary syphilis: chancre of the glans.
(U.S. Department of Health, Education and Welfare)

syphilis and receive no treatment, 50 percent will not experience any disability or inconvenience, 25 percent will be left with residual effects of the disease, and some 25 percent will suffer serious disabilities and even death as a result of the untreated infection.[16]

Before the chancre disappears, however, it is most often the case that the lesions of secondary syphilis develop.[17] These lesions of secondary syphilis develop from two to six months after infection. They represent the initial reactions of various tissues exposed to the spirochetes. These lesions occur in such a variety of forms that they may well be confused with many nonsyphilitic skin conditions. They are ordinarily painless and do not itch. In the typical case, they disappear

[16]Blau, "The Venereal Diseases," p. 1024.

[17]R. R. Wilcox, "Perspectives in Venereology—1966," *Bulletin of Hygiene* 42, (1967), 1167–1200.

within a few weeks, but occasionally persist for as long as a year.

Other symptoms commonly associated with early syphilis include headaches, malaise, low-grade fever, sore throat, and occasional, faint pains. None of these are particularly distinctive of syphilis and can be caused by a number of other illnesses.

Latent Syphilis. There are no clinical signs for latent syphilis, which usually occurs about two years after infection in the untreated person. Recent improvements in blood tests for the spirochete, however, make it much more likely that syphilis can be detected even in its latent stage than was possible just a few years ago.

Late (or Tertiary) Syphilis. The symptoms of late syphilis are almost overwhelming in their multiplicity. They usually occur between the tenth and thirteenth year after infection. The skin lesions of late syphilis are noninfections and devoid of sphirochetes. These late lesions may occur in the mouth, tongue, throat, eyes, bones, and joints. Virtually every organ of the body can become involved.

The stages described here pertain to syphilis that has been caught from another individual, normally during sexual relations. This kind of syphilis is called *acquired syphilis. Congenital syphilis,* however, is not acquired through sexual contact, but is transmitted by the mother to the child during pregnancy. Fortunately, penicillin therapy is so effective in this particular situation, that even if given late in pregnancy, the baby may be born completely free of syphilis. If congenital syphilis is untreated, however, the earliest signs resemble the lesions of late syphilis except that these lesions are heavily infected with spirochetes and are infections. As with late untreated syphilis, untreated congenital syphilis can infect any organ of the body with devastating results.

Diagnosis. Syphilis is normally difficult to diagnose because its symptoms are so varied. Diagnosis depends on careful consideration of a patient's medical history, prevalence of the disease in sexual partners, and the results of laboratory tests. All people who develop a sore on a sexual organ should be checked for syphilis. The most general test for syphilis is a blood test. More than 200 different tests have been developed. A clinical examination normally includes a search of the entire body for signs of skin rash.

Treatment. Since 1942, syphilis has been characteristically treated with penicillin with virtually 100 percent effectiveness. If, for some reason, the person cannot take penicillin, Aureomycin and Terramycin are equally effective. It may be necessary to administer up to a

Figure 17–4
It is critical that anyone who suspects a venereal infection
have it checked out immediately.
(Michael Heron)

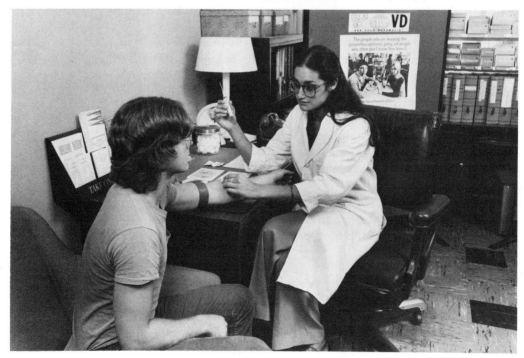

dozen doses of an antibiotic, depending upon the stage of the disease and the drug used. This presents something of a problem for clinicians because their patients sometime refuse to return for treatment or forget about it after the symptoms disappear. People with cases of early syphilis can be effectively treated with large doses of penicillin injected into each buttocks in a single visit. People who have had sexual contact with infected individuals should be contacted and encouraged to seek treatment.

GONORRHEA

Commonly known as "the clap" or "hot piss," the word gonorrhea derives from the Greek word meaning "a flow of seed." The celebrated Greek physician, Galen, first used the term in 140 B.C. to describe the characteristic discharge from the genitals of the infected person. The symptoms of gonorrhea are much more confined to the urinogenital tract than are those of syphilis. The most common sites of infection are the urethra in the male and the cervix in the female. The causative agent is the gonococcus, *Neisseria gonorrhoeae.*

Symptoms. The most common symptom in the male is the discharge of a creamy greenish-yellow pus from the penis. This occurs from two to seven days after infection. This discharge is rather watery at first, but usually thickens within forty-eight hours. It may be the only early symptom of the disease, but most often it is accompanied by a burning sensation on urination. The tip of the penis may become swollen and red. As the infection spreads up the urethra, urination usually becomes more painful, and erections are often painful also.

If left untreated, the disease may spread, causing local and general complications. Infection of the local lymph glands, prostate gland, and epidydimus, and restriction of the urethra are common complications. It sometimes happens that the organism enters the bloodstream and spreads, more generally producing inflammations of the joints, skin infections, and inflammations of the spine and heart. Such complications are associated with fever and marked weakness. Prior to the introduction to modern antibiotics, gonorrhea occasionally resulted in death.

In the female, vaginal discharge is the first common complaint. The vulva may be red and irritated. Some burning may be experienced upon urinating. In most cases, however, gonorrhea in the female will probably go unnoticed. This makes it extremely important that her sexual partner inform her of any infection he might have.

Two major complications result from a lack of early treatment in the female: infection of the Bartholin glands adjacent to the vagina and infection of the fallopian tubes. If the Bartholin glands become infected, a large, tender swelling usually appears on one or both sides of the vulva. This may rupture and discharge pus or may progress to form a firm cyst that must be surgically removed. Infection of the fallopian tubes may cause sterility if it is not treated.

Rectal infection is a fairly common form of gonorrhea in male homosexuals who practice anal intercourse. Infection of the mouth and throat in either sex is relatively rare, but normally involves the adenoids and tonsils when it does occur.

At one time, gonorrhea was responsible for one-third of all cases of blindness in children. A drop of 1 percent silver nitrate solution into the eyes of the newborn, however, effectively prevents such infections. The treatment also causes some pain to the infant. Such a procedure is being replaced by the use of penicillin in some locations. In spite of the excellent results of the treatment, however, there are still some cases reported in which babies already bear the irreversible scars of ulceration, and blindness may result.

Female children are more likely than male children to be subject to infection in childhood. This is most often explained as a nonvenereal infection, although sexual assault, mutual masturbation, or sexual experimentation may be responsible. The most common symptoms are an inflamation of the vulva and vagina with little or no complications in other organs. Most often the characteristic discharge is noticeable.

Diagnosis and Treatment. Gonorrhea is diagnosed by microscopic analysis. At present, there are no effective blood tests available. The preferred treatment is penicillin, given in large doses. Because the prostitutes in Vietnam were given low doses of penicillin in a half-hearted effort to clear up the disease among American GIs, a strain of

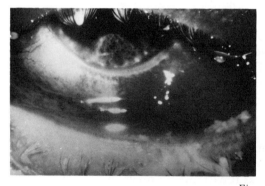

Figure 17–5
Left, gonoccal opthalmia; right, corneal clouding, a sequel of gonoccal opthalmia. At one time, gonorrhea was responsible for one-third of all cases of blindness in children, due to this infection. It has now been brought under control with the use of 1 percent silver nitrate solution. (U.S. Department of Health, Education, and Welfare)

gonorrhea developed that was extremely resistant to penicillin. The low dosage killed off a number of the gonococci, but allowed others to survive and reproduce resistant offspring. Nevertheless, most cases of gonorrhea can be cleared up by two large injections of penicillin in the buttocks given at the same time. Normally a follow up test is required five to seven days after the first treatment. Complications such as urethral strictures, infected fallopian tubes, and chronic arthritis may require special surgical or physical therapies.

The current high rate of gonorrhea has stimulated researchers to reduce some of the mystery surrounding the disease and its diagnosis. More effective treatment will soon be available. For example, researchers have discovered that differences in iron metabolism of laboratory animals affect their susceptibility to infection by gonococci. Virulent gonococci are in fact distinguished from nonvirulent forms of gonococci by their iron requirements and by pili—hairlike appendages on their surface. It has been demonstrated that some laboratory animals can be protected from infection by being injected with pili. Therefore, it seems reasonable that a vaccine against gonorrhea may soon be developed. A blood test may be forthcoming in the near future also. Infected people produce antigens to the gonococci and these antibodies could serve as the basis for a blood test. Indeed, it is now thought probable that gonorrhea represents several strains of gonococci and that an individual may develop a natural immunity to one strain through the buildup of the antigens in the body; unfortunately, such an individual may fall prey to another similar strain for which no antigens are present in the body.[18]

The most current theory about the way in which gonorrhea spreads is that a core of infected people maintains the epidemic. At least 20 percent of these sexually active people are infected at any given time. Because this core continues to reinfect its members, those who are treated will soon come down with the disease again and will spread it to others, unless they are cured again. Prevention now focuses upon locating this core population and continually treating it until the disease is stamped out. The Center for Disease Control in Atlanta, Georgia, put this notion into effect toward the end of 1975 and began retesting its previously treated population. It found that about 15 to 25 percent of these previously treated people had indeed been reinfected. These figures compare with only 4 percent reinfection for noncore individuals. The increased rates of reinfection suggest that the core model helps locate core members and may shortly serve to reduce the number of persons involved in the core by carefully screening them out.[19]

[18]"Gonorrhea: More of a Problem but Less of a Mystery," *Science* 192 (April 16, 1976), 244–46.

[19]Ibid., p. 245.

International gonorrhea rates are beginning to decrease, but Sweden is most remarkable in its decline. The number of reported cases in Sweden in 1975 was only half the number reported in 1969. The other Scandanavian countries—Norway and Denmark—do not show comparable declines. The most probable explanation for Sweden's decline is the government-promoted program for contraception, which promotes the condom. The condom is not 100 percent effective against gonorrhea, but with care can serve as an effective prophylaxis. It seems to be working in Sweden, as the rates of gonorrhea decreased and the sale of condoms increased.[20]

CHANCROID

Chancroid bears some resemblance to syphilis. It usually appears as a small, conical elevation of the skin that may soon rupture and cause a ragged sore. This typically occurs about twelve to thirty-six hours after infection. The causitive agent is the streptobacillus, *Hemophilus durceyi.* In contrast to the chancres caused by syphilis, chancroid sores are always painful and usually bleed readily when they are touched. Most often they are a few millimeters to two centimeters in diameter, but they can spread to cover large areas of the skin. Since chancroid sores can cause reinfection in the patient, they are likely to be found in formation surrounding the initial infection or on surfaces in apposition to the infected area. These sores are found almost always on the skin, and rarely on mucus membranes. In the male, the common site of the lesion is on the prepuce frenulum, or shaft of the penis. In the female the usual sites are on the labia majora, vestibule of the vagina, or the clitoris. In both sexes, they may also extend to the perineum, thighs, abdomen, and anus.

About a third of the cases of chancroid develop infections in the lymph glands. A painful swelling in the groin may result. This may progress to an open sore, which, if not treated, may drain for months.

Diagnosis and Treatment. Chancroid is diagnosed microscopically by examination of smears of material taken from the affected lymph gland. A vaccine (skin test)—the Ito-Reenstierna test—is often helpful, but is not always definitive. Complications of diagnosing chancroid result from the fact that it may have been contracted simultaneously with other venereal diseases. Such complications require extensive testing and expert diagnosis.

With proper treatment—usually by means of sulfa drugs—chancroid can be effectively cured. Treatment usually takes from three to eight days, with the pain subsiding within twenty-four hours. Within this time, the lesions begin to heal and pus no longer forms.

[20]Ibid., p. 245.

HERPES SIMPLEX TYPE II

Considerable difference of opinion exists over the incidence of this disease. Some contend that it accounts for less than 1 percent of all current cases of VD reported annually in the United States. Others place it after gonorrhea in prevelance.[21] It is caused by a virus, and the symptoms, though unpleasant, may not be thought serious enough to report. It is a serious mistake not to report it because of the complications of recurrent infections and because of the danger of infecting others.

Symptoms. In the case of males, tiny blisters usually form on the penis and scrotal skin. These blisters are usually painful when touched. They may rupture and form tiny sores on the skin. In the female, blisters commonly appear on the inside of the vagina, on the cervix, and less commonly on the vulva, thighs, and buttocks. There may be some fever associated with the blisters, some headache, and enlargement of the lymph glands. Within two to four weeks the symptoms disappear without treatment. No immunity develops, however, and the virus normally lives within the body for the life of the individual. Reinfection may occur during periods of stress. Women who have had this infection are more susceptible to cervical cancer. Infections of the newborn vary from mild symptoms that leave no after effects to severe brain damage and death. Pregnant women should consult their physician for possible damage to the fetus if an infection is discovered.

Diagnosis and Treatment. The disease is diagnosed by microscopic analysis or by direct examination of the blisters. There is no known cure for Herpes Simplex. Treatment is directed toward relieving the symptoms, which may disappear within several weeks even without treatment. At present the best protection against Herpes infection is to keep the body in good health by sufficient rest and nutrition.

LYMPHO-GRANULOMA VENEREUM

Lympho-granuloma Venereum (LGV) is probably caused by a virus, although this has not yet been definitely established. It is primarily contracted in vaginal, anal, and sometimes oral-genital intercourse, but can also be spread in other ways through close physical contact. The nonsexual spread of LGV is more common in tropical countries where less clothing is worn and where the skin is often moist with sweat.

LGV is a disease of the lymphatic system, the disease-fighting sys-

[21]See Boston Women's Health Club Collective, *Our Bodies, Ourselves,* and Bernard Goldstein, *Introduction to Human Sexuality* (New York: McGraw Hill Book Co., 1976), p. 221.

tem that in many ways parallels the circulatory system except that it transmits a fluid that has much fewer red corpuscles and many more white corpuscles in it. When the body is invaded by bacteria, the white cells attack and consume the bacteria. The bacteria are destroyed in the lymph glands, which may become inflamed in the process. Most persons have experienced swollen neck glands during a cold. These are the lymph glands fighting the cold virus. In LGV, the glands themselves are attacked.

Symptoms. From five to twenty-one days after infection, a very small, painless pimple resembling a sore appears on the sexual organs. In the male, it is usually on the glans of the penis or the urethra. In females, it can appear anywhere on the vaginal lips or in the vagina. Within a few days it disappears, often without being noticed.

From the site of early infection LGV spreads to the lymph glands. From ten to thirty days after infection, the lymph glands become swollen and fuse together in a sausage-shaped mass called a "bubo," if located in the groin. The lymph glands are destroyed and the bubo breaks open at the surface of the skin in a running abscess. In the minority of cases, the bubo disappears by itself even without treatment. In women, the infection often occurs in the deeper lymph nodes rather than on the surface, as in the case of males. Both men and women may experience fever, loss of appetite, and joint pains in the early stages.

If treatment is delayed or the bubo does not appear, and the disease continues, complications can arise anywhere from several months to twenty years later. The complications involve other parts of the body; the anus and rectum become infected in women in two days. The virus can spread from the vagina to the rectum via the lymphatic system or it can be deposited directly in the anus by means of anal intercourse. In homosexual men, the anus may become similarly infected. Pain and a bloody-pus discharge are the first symptoms of this complication. Eventually, the anus can be narrowed by scar tissue causing severe constipation and great pain. Late infections of the genital tract cause blockage of the normal lymph flow and what is called LGV elephantises (a great enlargement of the genital tissue) results. This is more common in women than in men. If left untreated, the excessive growths that occur in anal strictures and genital elephantises can cause cancer.

Diagnosis. LGV must be diagnosed by means of a skin test and a blood test, since its symptoms can readily be confused with syphilis, chanchroid, and granuloma inguinale. In the skin test, a small amount of "modified Frei antigen" is inserted under the skin. The presence of a small blister surrounded by a red border within two to three days signifies LGV. This is usually confirmed by means of a blood test called the LGV complement fixation test.

Treatment. Although LGV can be cured by antibiotics, it responds slowly to treatment. At least three weeks are necessary to exterminate the disease in most cases. The antibiotic that is preferred in the treatment is tetracycline, taken by mouth every six hours for a total daily dose of two grams. This drug should not be used by pregnant women. One of the sulfa drugs is a second choice. Dosage is four grams for a period of twenty-one days. Surgical treatment for the removal of the bubos is commonly employed. Since this is a difficult disease to eradicate, follow up examinations should be given every few months for the first year after infection and every year for several years thereafter.

GRANULOMA INGUINALE

This disease occurs rarely outside of the tropics. Most cases in the United States occur in the South. Because it is rare, it is not well understood. The assumption is that it is transmitted by sexual intercourse, but that is not very contagious since only one of a sexually active pair may have the disease.

Symptoms. From two days to six months after infection, a painless bump or blister appears on the sexual organs or near them. The blister soon becomes an open sore. It is raised, rounded, velvety, and bleeds easily. It does not heal on its own but grows larger and more painful without treatment. These symptoms occur more commonly in men than in women.

Diagnosis and Treatment. The bacteria causing this disease, *Donovania granulomatis,* must be observed under the microscope in order for a positive diagnosis to be made. Tetracycline is the preferred antibiotic used in the treatment of granuloma inguinale. A daily dose of two grams taken over a ten to twenty day period is normally sufficient to cure the disease. Streptomycin and Ampicillin, a synthetic form of penicillin, is also effective in treating granuloma inguinale. However, streptomycin may produce serious side affects if taken in such large doses, and its use should be avoided if possible.

VENEREAL WARTS

These warts are caused by a virus similar to those that cause common skin warts. It is presently believed that these viruses are sexually transmitted, but cases are known in which individuals who have had the warts have had a single sexual partner who does not have them.

Genital warts appear one to three months after infection. In men, they most commonly appear on the glans and foreskin of the penis with the urethral opening, shaft, and scrotum less likely sites. Anal intercourse will produce warts in or around the anus. In women, they most commonly appear on the lower part of the vagina, but the vaginal lips and cervix may be affected as well. The warts can be single or multiple and can grow together to form a large tissue mass. They tend to grow larger if kept moist by vaginal discharge from other diseases.

Diagnosis is based on simple observation. Treatment consists of removal of the warts by means of such chemicals as prodophyllin. Prodophyllin should be left on for six hours, then washed off with soap and water, or it will cause chemical burns that are slow to heal.

Two additional diseases deserve attention, even though they are not transmitted primarily by sexual intercourse. These diseases are relatively minor vaginal infections, but they produce symptoms that are sometimes confused with those of VD.

TRICHOMONIASIS

About a quarter of all gynecological patients in the United States are infected by the organism *Trichonomonas vaginalis*—a one-celled organism similar in appearance to a sperm. The result of the infection is a vaginal discharge and irritation. It is believed that about 4 percent of all males in the United States are also infected, but the fact that the parasite often resides in the urethra without producing symptoms makes diagnosis in males difficult.[22]

Sexual intercourse is the major means of transmitting this organism, but bath water, low-chlorine swimming pool water, towels, and douche nozzles have also been known to transmit the disease.

The symptoms in some ways resemble gonorrhea. A greenish-yellow discharge is usually the first sign of infection, followed by irritation, swelling, and reddening of the vaginal lips. A frothy or bubbly irritating substance is present in the vagina and may infect the urethra, bladder, and bartholins glands. In the male, there is normally little or no discomfort in housing the parasite.

Trichomonas vaginalis is diagnosed by microscopic analysis and is commonly treated by returning the vaginal fluids to normal acidity through the ingestion of metronidazole three times daily for about one week.

VAGINAL THRUSH

Another common vaginal infection is caused by a fungus, *Candida albicans*. It thrives in the presence of sugar and is common among dia-

[22]Goldstein, *Introduction to Human Sexuality*, p. 217.

betics. The common symptoms of vaginal thrush are white patches on the vulva and on the interior of the vagina, which when removed, leave bleeding sores. A white, cheesy discharge and severe itching usually draw attention to the fungus invasion. Since this fungus is present everywhere, it may be trasmitted by many means and can lie dormant in the vagina until the conditions are right for its growth. These conditions, characterised by high concentrations of sugar, are most likely to occur as a result of diabetes, pregnancy, or menstruation. Vaginal thrush is diagnosed by microscopic analysis and treated through insertion of antifungal suppositories twice daily for about two weeks.

Finally, we should not overlook the relatively common infection of pubic lice called crabs.

PUBIC LICE (CRABS)

The louse, *Phthirus pubis,* which infects the pubic area, looks very much like a crab when viewed under a microscope. It has three pairs of claws and four pairs of legs, but fortunately is no larger than a pinhead. The louse moves by swinging from hair to hair and can cling tenaciously to the pubic hairs with its tiny claws. Normally, however, it is content to remain fastened to a single hair, feeding from tiny blood vessels near the surface of the skin. If separated from its host, the crab louse dies within twenty-four hours.

This tiny louse is normally yellowish in color and is difficult to see on normal skin. When full of blood, however, it is a rusty red. These lice mate frequently during their thirty-day lifetime and the female lays about three whitish oval eggs a day which she fastens firmly to a pubic hair. These eggs mature in seven or eight days.

Pubic lice are normally transmitted during close sexual contact, but it is possible to become infected from sleeping in a bed that has been used by an infested person.

Symptoms include an intolerable itching in some people who apparently develop an allergy to the bite of the louse. Others experience nothing. Scratching will not bring relief and may spread the lice to other hairy parts of the body. Some people develop a mild rash composed of small blue spots as a result of crab infestation.

Pubic lice can be readily killed through the use of a drug called gamma benzene hexachloride, available in cream form under the name "Kwell." It can be obtained from a drugstore without a doctor's prescription. Treatment brings rapid relief from itching and should be repeated in four days. Since the lice die within twenty-four hours, wearing clothing that has not been worn during that length of time will not cause a reinfestation.

Prevention of Venereal Disease

In this section, we are concerned primarily with the prevention of syphilis and gonorrhea, although some of the measures suggested will also help to prevent other venereal infections. The most useful prevention against syphilis is soap and water. A shower or bath immediately after having sex will significantly reduce the likelihood of catching the disease. A condom offers considerable protection against gonorrhea. Neither of these two procedures will provide 100 percent protection, but they both will significantly reduce the risk of being infected.

Because up to 80 percent of women who are infected with gonorrhea do not know that they have the disease, it is imperative that their partners inform them of any infection they experience. The symptoms of gonorrhea are much more likely to occur and be noticed in the male. Women will find that an antiseptic douche and a soap-and-water washing of the genitals will help prevent VD. It has recently been discovered that certain contraceptive foams, jellies, suppositories, and creams are also effective in the prevention of VD. Cooper Cream, Ortho Creme, Certane Vaginal Jelly, Ortho-Gynol Jelly, Milex Crescent Jelly, Koromex—A Vaginal Jelly, and Preceptin Gel are among those known to have some preventative effects.[23] At present, there are no vaccines against VD, but there are indications that a vaccine against gonorrhea may soon be available.

From the point of view of public health, VD prevention must involve a number of coordinated efforts. The first level of prevention must be education. One recent study discovered that high-school students were woefully ignorant of many aspects of VD, even though over half of all people who have VD are under twenty-five years of age.[24] In 1972, there were 200,000 reported cases of gonorrhea among adolescents, representing an estimated one-quarter of the actual cases.[25] Most of these are in low income, city areas.[26] High-school and college programs aimed at informing students about VD are an important step in its prevention, but will not guarantee it.

Treatment is further complicated by the legal requirement in some

[23]Singh et al., "Studies on the Development of a Vaginal Preparation Providing Both Prophylaxis against Venereal Disease and Other Genital Infections and Contraception," *British Journal of Venereal Disease* 48 (1972),. 57.

[24]Jack Hayes and John H. Littlefield, "Venereal Disease Knowledge in High School Seniors," *The Journal of School Health* 9 (Nov., 1976), 546–47.

[25]Joan Haskin et al., "Project Teen Concern: An Educational Approach to the Prevention of Venereal Disease and Premature Parenthood," *Journal of School Health* 4 (April, 1976), 231.

[26]Blau, "The Venereal Diseases," p. 11.

states that adolescents must have the parents' consent before receiving treatment. This clearly seems counter-productive to the aim of prevention, but is in line with the notion that somehow VD is a punishment for sexual encounters. The basic step toward prevention in VD education is to recognize that VD is a disease like any other disease. It can be treated once it is diagnosed with little or no pain to the patient.

Most large cities have free VD clinics where tests can be procured and penicillin and other treatment provided. It is very important that anyone who has become infected with VD inform any sexual partners of this infection and encourage them to seek treatment. The clinics will attempt to acquire the names of all individuals with whom the infected person has had sex in order to prevent the spread of the disease. Normally, they treat such information as confidential. To not inform others of an infection is likely to have serious consequences for them and perpetuate the spread of the disease to others. Planned Parenthood or a local hospital can usually provide information about such free clinics.

Summary

There are a number of diseases that are contracted primarily through having sex, but the most common by far are syphilis and gonorrhea. Both are currently at epidemic proportions throughout the world, although we are beginning to see signs of a down turn in the number of cases reported.

The symptoms of these diseases can easily be confused by the layman with nonvenereal diseases of less serious consequences. Symptoms of syphilis, the great mimic, defy elaboration. Gonorrhea is commonly unrecognized in the female. It is, therefore, critical that anyone who suspects an infection have it checked out at a clinic. These are often free and can be located by calling a local hospital or Planned Parenthood clinic.

Fortunately, most venereal diseases respond quickly and effectively to treatment. Several simple precautions can also reduce the likelihood of catching the disease. A soap and water shower and the use of a condom are two readily available prophylaxes that will not totally prevent V.D., but will reduce the likelihood of its occurrence.

A great deal of care must be taken by responsible individuals who become infected with V.D. or who must treat infected persons. Care and consideration can increase the likelihood of cooperation between all parties, which is so necessary to the elimination of these destructive diseases.

Section Five

Values

A prominent element of our Western tradition has simply assumed that what people said they believed *should* determine what they did. This is a popularized implication of the doctrine of free will. Thus, if you profess to believe that sex is an evil passion, you should abstain from sex or in some other way bring its evil influence under control. The sacrament of Holy Matrimony was the dominant means by which the West has attempted to control the evil influences of sexual passion. If you as a westerner do not abstain or marry, it follows that you either do not believe that sex is evil or that your will is weak and you are unable to realize your good intentions. In the first instance you are likely to be branded a notorious evil person, in the second you are likely to be treated with pastoral concern. In the middle ages you might have been considered possessed by the devil and burned at the stake by those who were officially more concerned with the salvation of your soul than your body.

Today it is more likely, however, that if you retain some element of the belief that sex is evil, and still persist in experiencing it outside of marriage, you will simply do so clandestinely with an appropriate feeling of guilt. Beliefs do indeed affect how we behave, but they do so in various ways. As a result, it is not enough for anthropologists to simply study what people say should be done, they must observe what is actually done and how the culture—as well as the individuals in it—handle any discrepancies that might exist between what is professed and what is done.

These are very complex issues that have only been touched upon lightly in this book. They are important to bear in mind, however, when we approach the issue of sexual values. Sexual values are basic beliefs about sex, such as whether it is good or evil, important or unimportant, more characteristic of men than women, and so forth. This book has assumed that sex is good, that it is a very important part of our lives, and that the differences between the

sexes are not as important as their similarities in regard to sexual passion. This final section spells out some of the implications of these assumptions (which I personally believe) for sexual behavior.

I look first at the issues raised by cultural relativity. Sex is valued differently by different cultures and by different people within subgroups of the same culture. What does this have to say about the importance we might attribute to sex? Next some guidelines taken from the Humanist Manifesto are presented. The Humanist Manifesto states that certain rules make for better sex and assumes that the experience of love is a reality for most people. Finally, I look at two interfaces of sex and love. The first is the experience of love as an occasion for sex. In such sexual experiences, sex becomes a means by which love is given and the self is shared rather than being primarily a means through which we seek to validate ourselves through the notches on our bedposts. Sex thus becomes one of the many kinds of peak experiences that are common in life but sometimes not highly valued. The second way of looking at sex and love is sex as an occasion for love in which the sexual experience itself opens up a person to a life of love. This seems to be an often sought after, but rarely realized experience.

Not everyone will agree with the evaluations made in this section. We live in a pluralist society in which there are many ways of looking at sex. Some of these were suggested in chapter 1. I consider it part of the wonder of human sexuality that such diversity exists. To the extent that we can freely fashion a sexual life style, freely affirm a set of beliefs about sex, and live out some of these in our lives, we have intentionally shaped a significant segment of our lives. Fortunately, sex has never been merely a matter of beliefs, nor human life itself simply a matter of living up to a set of propositions. Beliefs are at best maps that can help us to live with a greater sense of direction and purpose, but "the man is not the territory." Whatever we can say about beliefs, they must be continuously open to the experiences of living that are beyond belief.

Sex and Love

18

In the past, sex was considered an expression of romantic love.
These days, however, emphasis on sexual techniques and variety of
sexual acts gives many people the impression that these are the key
to sexual pleasure. Is love extraneous to sexual pleasure?
We get into definitional problems of what love really is, but
essentially I think this is a new myth,
that techniques are all important . . . its
the relationship that is crucial; if you want to
call it love, fine, but its the quality of that interpersonal relationship
that is going to determine the quality of sex,
not the techniques.

Wardell Pomeroy

We come finally to the problem of the value of sex in our lives. Is it the most important thing or not important at all? Both of these positions have been well championed, as has virtually every position in between. In the past, the question of value has been mainly the concern of philosophers and theologians. But increasingly, social scientists are becoming more sensitive to the issue. There has been a great rebellion against our traditional understandings of what sex ought to be. This has been brought about, in part, by scientific research on sex. A number of people, therefore, feel that science will resolve our sexual problems and will do away with the question of sex's value by further improving our understanding of what sex is. For these people, a chapter on the value of sex is redundant. But no amount of accurate description of what human sexuality is will resolve the issue of what it ought to be.

In the past, church and state have struggled to impose their conceptions of what sex ought to be. Much of the struggle has been destructive and coercive. The criminal law, which describes sexual offenses as crimes against nature, continues this struggle today. However, at the same time, others are struggling to place the evaluation of sexual experience back into the hands of individuals.

In one sense, only you can write this chapter. Only you can say how important sex ought to be in your life, based on your experience of what sex has been and your desires about what sex could be for you. This chapter is meant to provide you with a framework to discover your own sexual values. Perhaps you will find yourself arguing with this chapter more than you have with the other chapters. Such resonance can be enriching rather than confusing, if we recognize that we do not have to fully agree about these matters.

Cultural Relativity and Sexual Ethics

In simple terms, cultural relativity urges us to appreciate the fact that, if we were Romans, we would do as the Romans do. Each culture has its own way of looking at sex, and we must not let our cultural values blind us to the validity of the values chosen by another culture. Thus, the Mangaians' free expression of sexuality is perfectly valid for them, and the repression of sex is also perfectly valid for the residents of Inis Baeg. Each culture makes choices out of a vast number of alternatives, and generally there are very good reasons for the choice finally made.

In simpler societies, one rule—one value system—is generally accepted by most of the people. In more complex societies, however, such mass agreement on values is difficult to achieve without totalitarian methods. Thus, in America today, we find many different points of view about sex. This has given rise to many different sexual life styles. Some people hold—for differing reasons—that many other things are more important than sexual intercourse. They dramatize this by abstaining from sex. In contrast, experiments such as Sandstone contend that the whole of life should be radically restructured through the freeing of sexual expression. In a complex pluralistic society such as our own, there are many sexual life styles from which to choose, and all of them have somewhat different answers to the question of how important sex should be.

As individuals, you and I face some problems as a result of this pluralism. One of the most obvious problems is that we can't participate in all of these different life styles. They are mutually contradictory on

Figure 18–1
(© George W. Gardner)

a number of dimensions. Even if they were not, the sheer numbers of different points of view make the act of choosing inevitable. It takes time to acquire new skills, new roles, and a feeling of being comfortable with a new life style. There is not enough time, even if we devoted the whole of our lives to an exploration of sexual life styles, to experience all of them. Although we might recognize in ourselves the potential to fulfill all conceivable sexual life styles, from the most violently sadomasochistic to the most objectively contemplative, we must choose from a relatively limited number of such styles in the shaping of our lives. We can choose with some awareness of the likely consequences, or we can simply let things happen to us. In both cases, we are going to express relatively few understandings of the importance of sex. The ones we do express in our lives may not seem consistent with one another. Thus, choice may simplify our problems, but it does not solve them.

If we choose with awareness from among those sexual life styles and behaviors that contribute toward a greater value called love, there will be a difference in the quality of our lives and in the quality of our society. Most people would probably say that love is more important than sex. All sex is not love nor is it capable of expressing love. Love has become disassociated from sex. In much of our tradition, love and sex have actually been set in opposition. As a result, many of us believe that sex, in any form, is preferable to the repression of sex for the sake of a higher love. It is apparent from studies of how we raise our children that many of them do not have much of an experience of love in their lives. Whatever the term might mean to them, it is not associated with caring for others. Many children grow up deprived of love in most of its forms. We may talk about love as a higher value, but many people will not really be able to understand what we mean.

One of the paradoxes of the sexual revolution is that many people do not find sex to be pleasurable, let alone loving, in spite of their increasing experience. According to Rollo May,

> . . . *many therapists today rarely see patients who exhibit repression of sex in the manner of Freud's pre-World War I hysterical patients. In fact, we find in the people who come for help just the opposite; a great deal of talk about sex, a great deal of sexual activity, practically no one complaining of cultural prohibitions over going to bed as often or with as many partners as one wishes. But what our patients do complain of is lack of feeling and passion.*[1]

It might be argued that this is to be expected. We live in a time when openness is valued. The Victorian age was repressive. It is natural

---

[1]Rollo May, *Love and Will* (New York: W. W. Norton & Company, Inc.). Copyright © 1969 by W. W. Norton & Company, Inc.

that people today would have different problems than people living in the Victorian era.

The use of the word "intimacy" instead of the word "love" in many books and articles devoted to sexual adventuring is precisely right. The modern view of sex distrusts love. "Love" is not a scientific term. It is hard to define precisely. It suggests obligation and working at a relationship as well as strong emotion and desire. Intimacy, on the other hand, suggests merely openness and familiarity. But intimacy can breed contempt as well as fostering love. Sexual intimacy can be an occasion out of which love arises, but it need not be so.

Basic Principles

The January, 1976 issue of *The Humanist* contains a statement of a new bill of sexual rights and responsibilities that has been endorsed by many leading humanists and sexologists.[2] It contains nine principles and some concluding commentary about the context in which the principles should be understood. The commentary concludes that the principles cannot be realized unless the individuals holding them possess certain attributes; for example, an adequate degree of autonomy and control over the sexual function, reasonable satisfaction in living, an enjoyment of the pleasures of the body, and a respect for the rights of others. "Only as these conditions are met will loving and guilt-free sexuality be possible."[3]

THE NATURE OF SEXUALITY

Sex is an expression of intimacy, a source of enjoyment and enrichment, and a way of releasing tensions as well as a means of reproduction. A number of religious groups have come to adopt this broader view of sexuality because people are moving away from our tradition of fundamentalist Christian asceticism that asserts that the nature of sexuality is purely its reproductive function. The acceptance of nonreproductive aspects of human sexuality is a major tenant of modern views about sex. This change in viewpoint, which has occurred relatively recently in the West, has far-reaching consequences for our

---

[2]Lester Kirkendahl, "A New Bill of Sexual Rights and Responsibilities," *The Humanist* (January/February 1976), pp. 4–6. Reprinted by permission.

[3]Ibid., p. 6. In the following discussion of this manifesto, I have condensed the articles into one or two sentences given at the beginning of each paragraph and then added my commentary. I trust that my condensation accurately reflects the intent of the manifesto, but my commentary is my own interpretation.

evaluation of sexual behavior. Indeed, the rest of the principles of the manifesto make little sense without this assertion.

THE EQUALITY OF INDIVIDUALS

All individuals are entitled to equal consideration. Clearly the feminist movement is the latest attempt to impress upon us how much our understanding of sexuality and our sexual behavior are shaped by men who have remained largely insensitive to the sexuality of women and have often considered feminine sexuality, not to mention the woman herself, to be inferior and undeserving of equal consideration. As our founding fathers learned, it is an easy thing to state that all individuals are equal, but it is difficult to realize in practice.

In terms of sexual behavior, this principle means that women are as entitled to sexual gratification and fulfillment as men—an assertion still unaccepted by a large number of men and women in the United States. Among other things, women should be as free as men are to express their sexuality, to initiate sexual encounters, and to manage the lovemaking to please themselves as well as their partner; in short, to fully reciprocate or to abstain as they see fit. Neither men nor women have the right to dominate each other, though in fact both may do so.

REPLACEMENT OF TABOOS

Among the most prominent of these taboos in the eyes of humanists are the absolute prohibitions on premarital sex, extramarital sex, abortion, distribution of contraceptive information, and, para-

Figure 18–2
(© Ellen Pines, Woodfin Camp & Associates)

doxically, the oversacramentalization of sex. Sex does not always need to be a solemn, sacred experience, nor does it need to be an expression of intense ecstasy or passion.

Our conception of what can be accepted and enjoyed in our sexual behavior has been far too restricted in the past by rule-makers who failed to see the virture in exceptions. There are ways of sexually relating outside of marriage that can be loving without violating the marriage contract. To call these immoral because they are non-marital is to take a narrow view of both morality and marriage. On the other hand, to assert that flaunting rules is always virtuous is equally rigid. The basis of evaluation of any relationship is the quality of caring and concern, not the extent to which it adheres to any particular set of rules. But, then, we must know what it means to love for this to be a fully useful guideline.

THE RIGHT TO INFORMATION ABOUT SEX

Every person has the right to receive sexual information and to consider accepting sexuality for pleasure as well as for reproduction. Some people want to restrict public access to information about sexuality because they feel that learning will lead to doing. They may also feel that the family, rather than professionals, however technically competent, ought to be the primary teachers in matters of sex and loving. While these points of view have their merit, it is obvious that more knowledge leads to more intelligent decision making. Clearly, children should be exposed to information about sex differently than adults who have had broader sexual experience, and the way in which information is disseminated is important. Material on sex should clearly be given as information rather than as advice, and some consideration should be given to the context within which the information is being disseminated. But, in spite of this, we must affirm people's right to know.

PLANNED PARENTHOOD

Potential parents have both the right and the responsibility to plan how many children they want and how far apart they want to have them, taking into account both social needs and their own desires. How this should be done, once a couple decides that it should be done, can be determined by considering the effective contraceptive techniques available and the ways that these techniques can be related to the couple's style of lovemaking.

SEXUAL MORALITY AND CARING AND RESPECT FOR OTHERS

In this sense, sexual morality is not a special kind of morality. The rules governing sexual behavior, therefore, do not need to be considered as a special set of moral principles, but can be seen as the same principles governing what would be considered to be moral behavior in other areas of life, such as in the management of a business or the operation of a household. In large measure, we have been prevented from seeing this moral unity because sexual behavior has been considered so different (usually in terms of its baseness, its powerful drive, or its potential for abuse) that it deserves a special consideration. There are some people who still feel that sex is qualitatively different and who would propose that sexual ethics are special.

THE MORAL VALUE OF PHYSICAL PLEASURE

The fear of hedonism and the concern for practical accomplishment has so infused our conception of loving as work and obligation that the pleasure we derive from it is either devalued or seen as a problem to be coped with. The basis of this fear lies in the traditional notion that it is sinful to be nice to our bodies. Admitting that they enjoy such sensual pleasures as good food, fine clothes, and orgasm makes many people feel guilty or embarrassed. It is certainly time that such physical pleasures be celebrated as a part of an abundant life.

SEX AND THE LIFE CYCLE

We are sexual throughout our life, not just during our reproductive years. This is a fairly new idea that comes out of the understanding that sex can be more than baby making. Even some of the more advanced thinkers, just a little less than a century ago, did not think of older people and children as having sexual feelings. Many of us have great difficulty putting this notion into practice today. Children have the right to their sexuality, which is often expressed in the exploration of their bodies and in a form of self-pleasuring that should not be confused with masturbation. Many people are still uncomfortable thinking that elderly people enjoy sex, though there are no physical reasons why they shouldn't. Most adults in the United States shy away from touching each other in public—and often resist being touched in private. This nongenital form of sexuality may best be called sensuality and is often confused with the sin of that name. We should be permitted to express our sexuality within much wider bounds of propriety. Masturbation has just begun to be liberated. Men have always practiced it with secret fascination; women, however, have been more reserved. Both are awakening to the possibilities of masturbation as the legitimate expression of pleasure.

VALUES AND SEXUAL BEHAVIOR

Among the most important of these values are the avoidance of hurting another or putting them at a disadvantage while sexually relating

Figure 18–3
(© Abigail Heyman,
Magnum Photos, Inc.)

to them; the seeking of free consent; the endeavor to establish open communication about what is expected both now and in the future in regard to this sexual relationship; and a striving to empathize with the sexual partner. The golden rule is a starting point for the development of sexual empathy.

Just as they are, these principles can serve as valuable guides for sexually relating. They become even more meaningful when they are related to the experience of love.

In our secular society, many people are cut off from an understanding of love as a peak experience, and their personal lives may be marked by bad experiences at the hands of those who have loved them. There may be little in their immediate experience that can signify warm, accepting love. Therefore, some general indicators of better sex are helpful. Better sex, in this context, tends toward love, but the focus of our concern is on sex, not love.

BETTER SEX

In her analysis of better sex, Sara Ruddick considers sexual pleasure as an immediate experience readily available to almost everyone.[4]

[4]Sara Ruddick, "Better Sex," in *Philosophy and Sex,* eds. Robert Baker and Frederich Elliston (Buffalo, New York: Prometheus Books, 1975).

However, when defining better sex, she focuses not on pleasure and our capacity to increase it, but rather upon what she calls "complete sex." A precondition for completeness, in her view, is *embodiment;* a conscious celebration of the body or, at minimun, a feeling of being at home with our bodies. Our society, however, teaches disembodiment.

Complete sex is reciprocal sex. It involves demands that one's feelings be recognized and a willingness to recognize the feelings of one's sexual partner. Complete sex requires active participation, not passive acceptance, on the part of both partners, though their behavior may alternate between the two. It is an active affirmation of one's own and one's partner's desire. "With passivity comes a kind of irresponsibility in which one can hide from one's desires, even from one's pleasure, playing seducer or victim, tease or savior."[5]

Not all sex acts should be complete. However, complete sex has moral significance because embodiment, activity, and mutual responsiveness are conducive to our psychological well-being and because they counterbalance our current tendencies to falsify the body and disassociate ourselves from it. Complete sexual acts help us to overcome the shame and disgust that reinforce disembodiment. The mutual responsiveness of complete sex acts is also beneficial because it satisfies our need to be recognized as real people with real desires. Complete sex acts seem to lead away from fear toward affection. "It is clear that we need not feel for someone any affection beyond that required (if any is) simply to participate with him in a complete sex act. However, it is equally clear that sexual pleasure, especially as experienced in complete sex acts, is conducive to many feelings—gratitude, tenderness, pride, appreciation, dependency . . . that when stable and habitual are conducive to love."[6]

The Experience of Love

The attempt to relate sex to love presupposes that they are not the same. This is not merely a semantic game. There are numerous occasions for confusion. In the past, we have talked about the subject of sex by using the word love out of a false sense of modesty or in the attempt to deceive. Men have tended to say, "I love you," when they really mean, "I want to go to bed with you." Women have tended to say "I love you," when they really mean "I enjoyed being in bed with you."

[5]Ibid., p. 97.

[6]Ibid., pp. 98–99.

Sex sometimes refers to the sensation of arousal, which may be equated with erotic love. It refers to a set of behaviors that are frequently—though not always—taken to be expressions of caring. Sex provides the occasion for open and intimate self-disclosure. In common usage, sex refers to gender and suggests to many people the longing of an incomplete person seeking completion with another complementary, and also incomplete, person. Sexual behavior clearly provides an occasion for love. It can even be said to create love under some circumstances. Both sex and love can provide pleasure as well as pain, though we more readily associate both with pleasure.

Sex is commonly thought of as pertaining to bodily sensations and behaviors, and love to relationships. Yet being sensitive to one's own body and its responses to another is a way of being sensitive to one's relationship with that person. Similarly, our sensitivity to the changing nuances of a love relationship can be enhanced by an awareness of our bodily responses.

Sex without love—without an awareness of a loving relationship—is not necessarily bad. It is just different. The situation in which we find ourselves helps define for us whether we are making love or having sex or both. It is important to be clear about what we are doing and to have some assurance of our partner's assent and understanding. Deception usually causes tension and thus makes enjoying either love or sex more difficult. You and your partner may each have an understanding of what is happening between you, but separate understandings generally result in separate experiences. A true merging of two people comes about through the merging of their separate understandings about the experience they are about to share in. This can lead to better sex. It can also lead to love.

LOVE AS AN OCCASION FOR SEX

The experience of love is fundamentally the awareness of being acceptable, valuable, and worthy at the level of self-awareness. It is the perception of being in touch with all other things in the universe at the level of relationships. The experience of being ultimately acceptable and presently in need of nothing changes the valence of sexual relationships from taking to giving. In such loving everyone wins. In much of our everyday experience of love, however, one individual wins at the cost of another's loss.

Abraham Maslow distinguished between *deprivation love* and *being love*.[7] He contended that deprivation love is basically a thirsting to fill a need. It is clearly not wrong to need. In some sense, we have all been deprived and we all need love. The need to be cared for, the

---

[7]Abraham Maslow, *Beyond the Farthest Reaches of Human Nature* (New York: The Viking Press, 1971), p. 42.

need to be accepted, the need to be loved must be adequately met, or pathology will result. Deprivation love can be, in Maslow's view, a difficiency disease. People who suffer from it are like great holes into which other people must pour more and more love until the deficiency is overcome. A relationship may break up long before this occurs, because the partner tires of giving and not receiving. For such people a sexual adventure may prove to be totally unsatisfying because it is impossible to receive enough in so short a time.

What Maslow calls being love arises not out of need, but out of experience itself after deprivation needs are met. The dynamics of these two types of love are obviously quite different. Those healthy people whose need-love has been adequately met do not need to constantly receive love and are much more able to give it. People who seek love out of their need for it experience frustration. They never seem to get enough. People who love out of being-love rather than deprivation love experience wholeness. As a result, they make different demands upon the economy of love. Indeed, they reverse the everyday economy of love, which is largely need-love oriented, creating conditions of abundance rather than scarcity. They become givers rather than takers.

In the dynamics of sex there does not seem to be anything comparable to being-love as a common experience. There is the image of it, however. This image has been called *pornotopia*. In the Victorian ages, sex was defined largely in terms of a scarcity economics based on the conservation of semen. Those who spent foolishly overdrew their account and suffered from *spermatorrea*, a gradual loss of vitality that could end in insanity and death if not corrected. Pornotopia was the fantasied world of abundance created by the pornographer. This other Victorian world promised that sexual energy could never run

Figure 18–4
(© Jim Anderson, Woodfin Camp
& Associates)

Figure 18–5
*(M. Hardy, © 1970, Woodfin
Camp & Associates)*

out and thus that men and women could spend themselves freely. However, although the pornographer depicted sexual excess in which pleasure was experienced, fulfillment was lacking. Thus the economy was still an economy of scarcity. The Victorians tried very hard to separate love from sex. Marriage was a private contract entered into reverently, discreetly, and in the fear of God for the social purpose of procreation. Children were a return on the investment of semen. Outside of marriage, men could experience sexual pleasure with women for whom they need not assume further responsibility, so long as they did not excessively squander their resources on them. If the economy of love is a closed, private system, then love spent on one person cannot be spent on another. Victorians could not accept the notion of either free sex or free love. Rollo May contrasts our experience with theirs by noting that "the Victorian person sought to have love without falling into sex, the modern person seeks to have sex without falling into love."[8]

The Victorian's closed economy model has dominated our study of loving and especially our study of human sexuality. Most of us experience love in terms of the constraints imposed by the scarce resources of time, energy, and material goods that must be spent on one person at the cost of not being spent on another. In those sexual encounters in which we are aware of love at all, we are most often oriented

[8]Rollo May, *Love and Will*, p. 45.

toward deprivation love. But being love is also a part of our experience, though it is not often highly valued. In everyday life, it occurs in brief episodes and afterward seems rather insignificant.

Two Eastern Paths to Enlightenment. In the West, we most often talk about love in terms of interpersonal relationships. In Eastern cultures, however, love is not as exclusively associated with other people. It is a characteristic of the universe itself and can be experienced directly by stilling the mind and allowing oneself to simply be. Consider the following accounts of the experience of enlightenment given by Japanese practitioners of Zen.

An American school teacher, female, age thirty-eight, recounts that

A life time has been compressed into one week. A thousand new sensations are bombarding my senses, a thousand new paths are opening before me. I live my life minute by minute, but only now does a warmth pervade my whole being, because I know that I am not just my little self but a great big miraculous self. My constant thought is to have everybody share this deep satisfaction.[9]

A Japanese executive, male, age forty-seven:

4 A.M. of the 29th/Ding, dong! the clock chimed. This alone is. This alone is! There's no reasoning here. Surely the world has changed. But in what way? The ancients said the enlightened mind is comparable to a fish swimming. That's exactly how it is—there's no stagnation. I feel no hindrance. Everything flows smoothly, freely. Everything goes naturally. This limitless freedom is beyond all expression. What a wonderful world! Dogen, the great teacher of Buddhism, said: Zen is the wide, all encompassing gate of compassion. I am so grateful, so grateful.[10]

The word "love" is not always used in the description of such enlightenment, but it is clear from the accounts of those who have experienced it that love would not be an inappropriate word to describe their experience of the ". . . wide all encompassing gate of compassion."

Enlightenment as a result of the practice of Zen may come in a flash or never. There is no guarantee that one will ever experience "it, but the determination to achieve it has been assumed by people of all social statuses and its achievement has been widely recognized. The promise of such an experience is now engaging thousands of people in the West. Interestingly enough, most of those who undertake the practice of Zen attempt to do so as they would any other endeavor. They attempt to achieve enlightenment through effort, usually of an

[9]Philip Kapleau, ed., *The Three Pillars of Zen* (Boston: Beacon Press, 1965), p. 245.

[10] Ibid., p. 208.

intellectual sort, as in the resolution of *koans* (Zen riddles) or through sheer physical exertion. This is often the least effective approach. The experience of enlightenment is the experience of having been taken over. The bliss of enlightenment opens up the economy of love in enlightened people's lives, and they love and live out of abundance rather than out of scarcity.

Eastern religions can be as puritanical as ours about sex, in spite of the fact that they often place great emphasis on the nature of our experience as physical beings. Ordinarily body consciousness should lead to guru consciousness (consciousness of the person or persons whose love has called one forth), and guru consciousness should lead to God consciousness. The healthy body is a means to healthy relationships and, through meditation, is the base from which one can achieve God consciousness. In the understanding of some practitioners, the achievement of God consciousness, by whatever means, encourages neglect of the body and a rejection of the physical world. Very frequently the notion of body consciousness excludes sexual arousal because, as in our tradition, it is perceived of as pulling the practitioner away from the ascent to God consciousness.

However, in some Tantric forms of yoga, sexual intercourse is practiced as a means of ascent to God consciousness. In the overcoming of the distinctions of gender that is a result of Tantric devotion, the worshipers are elevated, not deprived. The performance of the ritual of tantric sex, like all rituals, can take precedence over the experience of elevation and love. Like all rituals, it takes practice in order to be free within the techniques and procedures recommended. But, properly understood, the ritual is quite secondary to the experience and can be adhered to or not, depending on the inclination of the lovers.[11] In Tantra, the sexual force is harnessed as a means of transforming consciousness. Abstinence before the ritual assures a build-up of sexual energy. The transformation is variously understood.

> *The Tantra Asana (various positions for intercourse) unite the spirit and matter and enable a person to attain full self-realization—this effect is a transformation of consciousness. Tantric Yoga accepts this world as Purush (Man) and Prakriti (Woman) and makes self-realization possible; they pursue their union through deepening and making two into one (twoness transformed into oneness).*
>
> *From the Tantric viewpoint the perfect human form is the melting together of man and woman in the self—so that the individual con-*

[11]A short description of Tantric sex is provided in Swami Janakananda Soraswati, *Yoga, Tantra and Meditation* (New York: Ballentine Books, 1975). A more detailed understanding is given in Herbert V. Guenther, *The Trantric View of Life* (Boulder, Colorado: Shambhala Publications, Inc., 1976).

sciousnesses merge into a shared consciousness. This state is called Ananda, eternal bliss, the highest joy.[12]

The details of a well-executed ritual are far beyond what can be provided here. But the instructions given to the lovers regarding their entering into intercourse suggest the Tantric attitude toward sexuality.

Then proceed with the intercourse. This can be done in two ways, either a) an introductory way or b) the proper way:

a) Joyfully and unreserved, like gods, give yourselves directly to the act, as if gods and goddesses were invited into your bodies, letting the joy and the pleasure go on but also any doubt or blocks that may appear, let everything happen—accepted and released—everything is part of the universe, this is not my property, neither desire nor suffering—everything we do is devoted and in this devotion we live.

b) You assume a yogic position. You don't do this mechanically or by getting up and then lying down again. No. Do it without even for an instant losing contact with each other, without interrupting the play you unite pleasurably and sensually. . . . There are many variations but the back must be straight or held as in a yogic pose, and you must be able to remain motionless in this pose indefinitely, while experiencing each other physically and psychically, entering together into an unbroked sexual meditation. Remain motionless as long as possible; the experience of universal union can occur at any point and you can hold it as long as possible. The shortest time for a pose should certainly be a little over half an hour, for any change or experience to take place in your consciousness.[13]

Training increases the likelihood that the experience will occur, but the training is clearly secondary to the experience. It should never become an end in itself.[14] Those who are anxious about their sexual performance may find that the attempt to adhere to a ritualized procedure increases their frustration, rather than increasing their satisfaction. One should always be free within whatever structure or ritual one chooses.

Asceticism Redefined. This Eastern approach to the direct awareness of love is not as alien to the West as we might at first imagine. We do

[12]Soraswati, *Yoga, Tantra and Meditation,* p. 77.

[13]Ibid., pp. 79–80.

[14]Exposure to books like the *Karma Sutra,* for example, tend to mislead the Western mind in the same way as pornography entices through technique. The point of view that says "do these things in order to experience bliss" completely misses the point. The sexual techniques of Tantra or Karma Sutra come after some awareness of Ananda or bliss—out of some awareness of enlightenment. They are not, in themselves, means of achieving bliss.

Figure 18–6
(Dan Budnik, © 1971, Woodfin Camp & Associates)

not need extensive training in Zen or yoga in order to understand what is experienced here. We can and do experience it. It's just that we seldom value much of what we experience. We can reclaim some of this lost awareness by recognizing that we have in fact experienced moments of enlightenment, moments when we have become suddenly insightful. This experience is not a function of religious training, but a part of human experience upon which all religions are built because they value it more than most ways of looking at the world.

One of the reasons why you may be reluctant to admit to having such moments of enlightenment is that you may not consider your peak experiences to be very large ones. They may appear more as molehills than mountain tops. It does not matter, according to David Steindhl-Rast.[15] Regardless of the height of your peak experience, it is recognized as such by the fact that you were touched by something

---

[15]Brother David Steindhl-Rast is a member of the Benedictine order and director of a small contemplative community off the coast of Maine. This section is heavily indebted to his article, "The Monk in Us," in *Earth's Answer; Explorations of Planetary Culture at the Lindesfarne Conferences,* eds. Michael Katz, William P. Marsh, and Gail Gordon Thompson (New York: Lindesfarne/ Harper and Row, 1977), pp. 14–31. I am also indebted to the article by Mark Harris, "A New Monasticism: Thoughts on Some Old Patterns and on Some New," *Plumbline! A Journal of Ministry in Higher Education* (June 1977), pp. 10–13.

and, as a result, the world became more meaningful. Most of our attention these days is spent achieving some goal or producing some product, as we feel the need to take things in hand and make something of our world. But, in peak experiences, we find joy in the world as it is. We are temporarily freed from the pressure to do and feel free just to be. This moment of realization is no different from the more intense emotional insights apparently achieved by intensive effort in Zen. Perhaps it is because these moments come on us without our effort and seem to be common in our experience that we do not treasure them more.

Steindhl-Rast points to several paradoxes in these experiences. First, their content is often very elusive. They are very difficult to describe to other people. Commonly, if we talk further about these experiences, we recognize that somehow all that we can say is that we got lost in them.

> *Oh I just lost myself, I lost myself when I heard this passage of music, or I just lost myself looking at that little sandpiper running after the waves; as soon as the waves come the sandpiper runs back and then the sandpiper runs after the waves. You lose yourself in such an experience, and after you lose yourself for a little while, you are never quite sure whether the waves are chasing the sandpiper or whether the sandpiper is chasing the waves or whether anybody is chasing anybody. But something has happened there and you really lost yourself in it.* [16]

This is a childlike wonderment, not an adult asking philosophical questions about cause and effect. The noise inside one's head becomes stilled in such experiences. Paradoxically, in those moments in which we have lost ourselves, we can also say, "That was when I seemed most alive." If we are strung out over our past in a nostalgic search for significance or we are anxiously engaged in scanning the future for possibilities of fulfillment, there is nothing of us left in the present. "Then something comes along that's practically nothing, that little sandpiper or the rain on the roof, that sweeps me off my feet, and for one split second I am really present where I am." [17]

Another paradox of peak experiences is the experience of overcoming separateness. If you were alone during a peak experience, if a sunset caught your eye and you lost yourself in it, for example, you might have first thought, "Gee, I wish that I could share this." But, as the experience intensified, you weren't missing anyone because you were at one with the experience itself and thus with all the world.

Finally, it is characteristic of such experiences that in them, in a flash, everything makes sense. This sense is not a solution to a prob-

[16]Steindhl-Rast, "The Monk in Us," p. 19.

[17]Ibid., p. 20.

lem, but simply an unconditional "yes" to the world. You say inwardly, "yes," and the whole thing falls into a pattern. The world becomes meaningful, whole. You fit in and are acceptable.

A courageous trust that life can contain peak experiences is what is often called faith. Faith is not "reason on its knees." Faith is the opposite of fear. It is the feeling that it is safe to let go.

What is really essential to all religions is this kind of faith, this courageous trust in life. The difference between religions are interesting and important at a certain level, but when they are held onto rigidly—as when we assert that Christianity is essentially patriarchal—they are expressions of fear, rather than of faith.

Fear in its religious expressions takes all sorts of forms. Dogmatism is the most obvious one. Scientism is another one, but it's just a different kind of dogmatism. Fundamentalism is one. Moralism is one, because you hang on to something that you can do. . . . As long as you can do it you have it under your control.[18]

Enjoying sex in the context of this courageous trust in life is a peak experience indeed. Some people are able to find such peak experiences in sexual adventuring, without recognizing that they have such experiences in everyday life. But this is not often the case. For most people, orgasm itself is the goal of sexual encounter, and the conscious pursuit of such a goal prevents the encounter from becoming a peak experience. In sex with being-love, the pleasure derives not only from the orgasm, but also from the feeling of being freely spent in that orgasmic release. This freedom derives from the affirmation of the peak experiences found everywhere. It is not necessary—indeed it is destructive—to seek them solely in sex. Within such being-love, sex becomes not an end in itself, but a means by which the gift of self can be freely given and sexual activity fully enjoyed.

SEX AS THE OCCASION FOR LOVE

Sex with love can be approached from another perspective. The experience of sex can open one up to love. Not all sex will do this. The pursuit of sexual experience as an end in itself is particularly unlikely to do so, though, in some cases, sexual behavior has indeed become the occasion for a peak experience of love. One of the clearest examples of this kind of an experience is found in Charles Reich's *The Sorcerer of Bolinas Reef*.[19] Reich tells us that he had never experienced genital sex until he was in his forties. In the 1950s, as a young attorney, he had lived as a single person in Washington and had expe-

[18]Ibid.

[19]Charles Reich, *The Sorcerer of Bolinas Reef* (New York: Bantam Books, 1976).

rienced the loneliness of a very impersonal city to the utmost. His dating never produced much intimacy. The relationships that he developed with women were more in the nature of social necessities, escorts for public occasions, than beginnings of deepening friendship or love. They never lasted beyond a few dates. He matured at Yale, where he wrote *The Greening of America* while he was a member of the faculty of the Law School. At Yale, he also discovered that he had sexual desire for men. His students had to inform him of this fact because by this time in his life he had so repressed his erotic feelings that he could no longer identify them. He was surprised that he was thrilled by the touch of another man's hand.

Reich left Yale for San Francisco, where he was determined to embark more fully upon his own experience of sexual awakening. After establishing himself in his apartment, he invited a male model to visit him at his home.

When the bell rang, I held my breath, and opened the door. My senses were totally alert, my feelings absolutely frozen. There was a polite blond young man of about twenty. His hand felt soft and there was a surprising freshness to him as if he had just come from a shower. He apologized for being a bit late. His respectful manner made me feel a bit easier.

We sat down on the couch. 'There's something I've got to explain to you,' I said in my professional manner. 'This may be hard to believe, but I don't know what sex is like or what to do. It's something I want to try, however. It's important for me to try it, I've made up my mind. Whatever happens will be fine with me. I don't know if I will feel anything. Are you comfortable with this situation? If not, maybe we can just talk. Here, is it all right if I hold your hand?'

I let him feel my trembling hand. He held it softly and gently. No one had held me in that way since I was a child.

We talked a little. He liked the beach. He had an easy life, he said. Many interesting people, lots of free time. 'Do you feel less anxious now?' he said.

'Could we go into the bedroom and take our clothes off?' I bravely asked. 'I would like to know how that feels.' He shed his clothes easily, no underwear beneath his jeans. His body was beautiful. My feelings stirred. 'Let's lie down next to each other,' I suggested, still intrepid. 'Show me what people do.'

He touched me and rubbed me softly and gently. I relaxed into the feelings he gave me. He was detached but easy and reassuring, even sweet. I relaxed still more. He put his hand on my penis. I would have expected to flinch and shudder at this totally unheard of, forbidden, unthinkable action. But it was a most beautiful feeling.

I was filled with awe and wonder that one person could make another person feel so good. The pure floating beauty of how he was making me feel seemed truly spiritual. What a miracle that another person, a person I did not even know, a person I was paying, could make me feel like that, it was a gift from the Gods. From the Gods, and this young man.

He put his mouth around my penis, and I accepted that, and it made the sunlight flooding into me still brighter, the dark mysterious spaces opening up still more magically. And then, in what felt like the first purely instinctual, wholly natural act of my life, I turned and opened my mouth to his penis, and instead of the utter repulsion I would have expected, I felt unknown pleasures.

Finally, we lay side by side and he held me again and quite naturally and wonderfully, I had an orgasm. And with that, bells of relief and happiness rung in my head. I am all right! I can do it! I am a normal, natural, sexual being! I am not frightened and frozen, I have the power to feel. It is not so hard after all. If you relax nature does the work.

What a joke, what discovery—it is so easy! How long I have been frightened when there was nothing to fear, how long I have envied others for what was in me too. Yes, I have lost thirty years. That is a bitter thought. But in some way those thirty years were all repaid by this single glorious moment. What cosmic glee and laughter swept me—to have taken a crazy chance and be able to say I was right!

I gave Kent twenty-five dollars, then ten more. 'I want you to know you've changed someone's life today,' I said. 'I guess you have good times and bad times in your work, but today you did something good, today you did the rarest thing of all things and made a difference in another person's life.' He kissed me on the cheek and was gone.[20]

Reich experienced more sexual encounters with male models, all of them different. He continued to affirm his sexuality. After some weeks he became good friends with a young woman, and in time they became lovers. It is not possible to do justice to the insights of such a marvelous book in a few paragraphs. It is clear, however, that his sexual experience with Kent was a major turning point in his life. It opened him up to the reality of his own feelings and to the experience of love.

There are many who would agree that sex is an essential means of discovering love. In her book, *Liberating Masturbation*, Betty Dodson encourages women to learn how to masturbate as the primary means of discovering self-love.

Masturbation is a meditation on self-love. Since so many of us are afflicted with self-loathing, bad body images, shame about body functions, and confusion about sex and pleasure, I recommend an intense love affair with yourself. We can then move into positions of self-love, strength and plea-

---

[20]Ibid., pp. 158–60.

sure by discovering our own sexual response patterns, learning to turn our-selves on, and giving ourselves massive doses of love and support.[21]

In her experience, this liberation of self-love through masturbation has not been detrimental to her relationships. Indeed, it has freed her to be more completely present in them.

> *One of the most liberating sexual experiences I have ever had was the time I was able to masturbate to orgasm with my lover. Although he and I had decided masturbation should be a natural part of our sexual exchange, actually sharing it for the first time was extremely difficult for both of us. First I had to get up enough courage to watch myself in front of a mirror. When I saw I didn't look funny or awful—I simply looked sexual and intense—I was reassured and able to make the breakthrough with him. It was the beginning of my freedom from the romanticized image of sex—a Sexual Independence Day. I celebrated by showing my lover that I could have a first-rate orgasm by myself. This kind of exposure naturally made me feel very vulnerable.*
>
> *It meant I had to face the fear of losing him. He would see I wasn't dependent on him for orgasm, and I faced the possibility of devastating criticism backed by 2,000 years of moral indignation.*[22]

For Dodson, discovering guilt-free masturbation and being able to share that experience with others opened up her life. She was an erotic artist, but had not been able to think of her own genitals as beautiful. An experience with another lover helped her develop a more positive attitude toward herself.

> *One of my first lovers was a devoted appreciator of female genitals. We got into oral sex (I was determined to try everything) and once after I had a really good orgasm he said, 'You have a beautiful cunt. Let me look for a moment.' Oh groan . . . oh no, I felt a sinking feeling and I told him I would really rather he didn't. I thought to myself . . . 'What kind of sick perverted nut wants to LOOK at genitals?' He wanted to know what was the matter. Evidently, I had turned a bit green, and I said I had those funny inner lips that hung down like a chicken. Convinced my genitals were certainly not pretty, I didn't particularly want anyone looking at them. 'Wow!' he said. 'A lot of women are made like that. It's perfectly normal, actually, its one of my favorite styles of genitals.' Off he goes to a closet, coming back with a stack of magazines of crotch shots. Forty-Second Street porno shop Beaver Books. . . . I was shocked but interested. . . . By the time we had gone through several magazines together I had an idea of what a woman's genitals looked like. What a relief! In that one session,*

---

[21]Betty Dodson, *Liberating Masterbation* (New York: Betty Dodson, Box 1933, 1974), p. 43.

[22]Ibid., pp. 8–9.

I found out I wasn't deformed, funny looking or ugly. . . . I was normal, and as my lover said, actually beautiful.[23]

In discovering self-pleasure, Betty Dodson discovered self-love and became able to freely give of herself in a wide variety of sexual contexts. Like Charles Reich, a sexual experience made a profound difference in her life. Both experienced their sexual awakening in their middle years, and both describe it in spiritual terms.

In her firm conviction that even an exclusively masturbatory sex life can be a perfectly valid and abundant one, she affirms what appears to be a position diametrically opposite to that of Steindhl-Rast. Both she and Reich came to love through the experience of sex, while Steindhl-Rast comes to sex through the experience of love. It is a matter of belief to affirm that it is the same love in each case, for there is no way to open each person up and compare their love-sex experiences. In each case, however, there is much evidence of their capacity to love in their reaching out and touching the lives of others most tenderly.

In the past, we have been inclined to judge the quality of love by specifying its form. In the case of fundamentalist Christian asceticism, the denial of sex was thought of as an indicator of an affirmation of a greater love. We have seen some of the results of this type of self-denial. The burning of witches during the inquisition bears ample testimony to the cost of a celibate clergy's repression and denial. On the other hand, it is equally blind to believe that abstinence cannot arise out of a greater love. The issue is not whether one abstains or not, but rather the basis on which one abstains. There are many who bear witness to the fact that love can be directly experienced without sex in an abundant affirmation of life.

Similarly, we have been inclined to judge masturbation and homosexual behavior as intrinsically evil. The first has been seen as a major form of self-abuse, the second as a major perversion. But the issue is not whether one masturbates or not, whether one has had a homosexual experience or not, but rather the base out of which these experiences occur and the results they produce in one's life. In fact, most people have experienced both masturbation and have had some homosexual experience. But few have felt the effects of such experience as powerfully as Reich and Dodson. The most common affirmation of these behaviors in the experience of most people today is probably in whatever pornography they have read. This may be useful for some purposes, as it was for Betty Dodson's self-discovery, but we cannot rely on pornography to tell us much about the people who are performing these behaviors.

[23]Ibid., pp. 24–25.

In the everyday experience of sex-love, the only person with whom we have direct experience is ourself. Sexual passion may seem to be an overwhelming desire to us, or we may feel frozen and unfeeling like Reich. More and more people are willing to admit that sex is no big thing and is in fact quite often boring. Havelock Ellis declared that sex was the central problem of life. Two modern researchers, William Simon and John Gagnon, have declared that saying anything about sex is giving it more importance than it deserves. Thus, even the experts disagree. This is why you must rewrite this chapter for yourself. It is not because it doesn't matter what I say or what we do, or because anything goes. It is because only you can say what sex is for you. Only you can know how whatever you experience sexually contributes to, or detracts from, your living and your loving.

Index

508

INDEX